Villanava (810) 519 7490
7170

The J. Ranade
UNIX® Primer

Other McGraw-Hill Titles of Interest

The J. Ranade
UNIX® Primer

Jay Ranade

Saba Zamir

McGraw-Hill, Inc.

New York   San Francisco   Washington, D.C.   Auckland   Bogotá
Caracas   Lisbon   London   Madrid   Mexico City   Milan
Montreal   New Delhi   San Juan   Singapore
Sydney   Tokyo   Toronto

Library of Congress Cataloging-in-Publication Data

Ranade, Jay.
  The J. Ranade Unix primer / Jay Ranade, Saba Zamir.
      p.   cm.
  Includes index.
  ISBN 0-07-051141-1 (hard)   —ISBN 0-07-051249-3 (pbk)
  1. Operating systems (Computers)   2. UNIX System V (Computer file)
I. Zamir, Saba.   II. Title.
QA76.76.063R355   1993
005.4'—dc20   92-38243
                                                                  CIP

UNIX is a registered trademark of UNIX System Laboratories, Inc.
OSF/1 is a trademark of the Open Software Foundation

1 2 3 4 5 6 7 8 9 0   DOC/DOC   9 9 8 7 6 5 4 3

ISBN 0-07-051141-1 (HC)
ISBN 0-07-051249-3 (PBK)

The sponsoring editor for this book was Jerry Papke.

Printed and bound by R. R. Donnelley & Sons Company.

This book is dedicated to my sister,
Chander Ranade Kapoor
and my brother-in-law
Jeewan L. Kapoor

                Jay Ranade

To my adorable niece,
Saman Rehman,
and equally lovable nephews,
Omar Zamir and Gibran Rehman

                Saba Zamir

ABOUT THE AUTHORS

JAY RANADE is the author of numerous best-selling McGraw-Hill titles, including two VSAM books, two books on SNA, and others. He is a senior systems architect and assistant vice president with Merrill Lynch.

SABA ZAMIR is a project manager at Teleport Communications Group and is a co-author of *C Primer*, Third Edition, and the *C++ Primer for C Programmers*.

Contents

Part 2   Programming the Shell

Part 3   The UNIX Editors

Part 4   File/Text Manipulation Tools

Part 5 Document Formatting Utilities

Part 6   Software Tools/System Administration

Preface

UNIX has been in existence for a long time. It was on the computer scene before anybody knew about DOS or OS/2 or Microsoft Windows. It has drawn more controversy than probably any other operating system. There are people who love it too much, and then there are those who are indifferent to its existence. In its early days, for good or bad reasons, it was touted as the operating system for the scientific and engineering community. It was said that it was too complex to be considered at all by the business community. As everybody knows, some of us in the information technology business feel offended when somebody tells us a system is too complex to learn. Maybe that kind of challenge (besides the superior architecture) made UNIX a popular operating system.

Many years ago (make it five), we read a remark about UNIX: "It neither dies nor flies!" Well, many, many years ago, we also read somewhere, "Giants move slowly and steadily, and once they gather momentum, it is difficult to stop them." And UNIX, the giant of an operating system (we are not talking about memory but about its features), is gradually gaining more and more momentum.

UNIX has received such as eminence in the recent past that the term *workstation* is associated only with this operating system in the common parlance. If you run anything else, it is called a PC. Some of the better known workstations, such as SUN, Hewlett Packard's Apollo, IBM's RS/6000, and DECs DecStation, run UNIX or a version of UNIX. IBM provides it (called AIX) on its mainframes and workstations as well as PS/2s. Big Blue also talks about providing interoperability between its Systems Application Architecture (SAA) platform and the AIX platform. If there is a serious hardware vendor who wants to stay in business for some time, it will have a serious commitment to UNIX. This is probably the only non-vendor-specific operating system (unlike IBM's MVS, DEC's VMS, Microsoft's DOS and Windows, and so on) which is available on a multitude of hardware platforms. And maybe this is the primary reason for its industrywide acceptance!

Why This Book

UNIX books have been in existence for as long as UNIX has been in existence. And we are talking about a fairly long time. Any bookstore's computer bookshelf will probably have a well-stocked section exclusively on UNIX and related subjects. So why another book? As we already said, people have been associating UNIX with the scientific and engineering community. Although this is not an accurate statement as we see this market, authors have been writing UNIX books to match the complexity of their writing style to the perceived complexities of the scientific and engineering environment. They fail to see the latent beauty and simplicity of this marvel of creation. In this book, we have strived to capture those elements and present them in a manner which should be painless for the readers to comprehend. In essence, this is the soul of this book—simplicity in style and thoroughness of subject coverage.

Who This Book Is For?

This book is for anybody who would like to learn UNIX in a comfortable manner. Since different variations of UNIX are really not that different from one another, this book should apply to any environment. If you already know another operating system (say DOS, OS/2, MVS, VM, or VMS), this should be a breeze. However, if this is the first operating system you are trying to learn, it should be equally effective. If you already have access to a workstation, we urge you to try various examples as you read; however, absence of such access should not slow down your learning experience either.

A Word on the Style Used

In the last 10 years, information technology has been progressing by leaps and bounds. There is so much information and knowledge pouring out that it is difficult to comprehend it all. It is like trying to sip water from a fire hose. In the next 10 years, it will probably be like sipping water while standing under Niagara Falls. Good books ease the process of learning. We have worked hard to make the process of learning easy and pleasant. We understand that most of you are too busy to spend a lot of time learning new things. As we perceive from various letters received every day, you liked the easy style of our previous books (e.g., *C++ Primer for C Programmers*). This book should be equally effective or even better. As we are getting older, we are getting better. But we would love to hear from you if we have succeeded in our endeavors. Please drop us a line at the following address:

Jay Ranade Series
P.O. Box 338
Grand Central Station
New York, NY 10163

What Environment This Book Is For

This book is written for the workstation/PC environment. Since various flavors of UNIX are not that different from one another, it should be applicable to any environment, such as AIX, UNIX, ULTRIX, HP-UX, SunOS, OSF/1, etc.

Final Word

We firmly believe that this book will teach you UNIX in the most pleasant manner. Learning UNIX will be a painless experience. After finishing this book, you will be able to work in such an environment with a high degree of confidence and competence. Let us know if we are right.

Jay Ranade

Saba Zamir

Acknowledgments

Authors are not the only people involved in the process of writing and publishing. It's a well-coordinated effort involving reviewers, critics, editors, production supervisors, cover art designers, marketing people, and the patience of authors' family members and friends. So our thanks are owed to all such people who made this book possible.

First of all, we must thank our reviewers, Dr. Sidnie Feit and Tom Hagan, whose comments and critique helped us improve the quality of the book. Mr. Gerald Papke, senior editor at McGraw-Hill, as usual, was encouraging when the going became tough and understanding when delays became inevitable. We feel proud to work with him and feel that he is the best computer book editor in the industry, period. Our thanks to Eileen Kramer for the beautiful book cover.

Saba would like to thank Ron Sirvent, whose valuable advice helped shape the initial writing phase of this book. Thanks are also owed to Billy Boyd, for helping out as he did with WordPerfect-related questions, and for being so gracious and unassuming in his help! Many thanks go to Nevine Abdel-Wahab, for the thoroughness with which she reviewed the book, the time that she invested in it, the valuable advice, and the patience with which she has dealt with the authors through the whole process! Saba also gratefully acknowledges Chander Ranade, for reasons that she knows best and Imran Hashmi, for being such a good friend.

Finally, Jay would like to thank his wife Ranjna for her understanding, and his daughter Sheena, who is too little to understand.

Saba would like to thank her parents, Ammi and Abjani, and Khalida Azhar and Azhar Hussain for their love and support which is given so unconditionally. Thanks are due to her husband David, for his quiet support. And last but not least, Saba wants to thank her son Richad, because his innocent smile takes all the tiredness away.

Jay Ranade
Saba Zamir

The Foundation

1

An Introduction to UNIX

1.1 A Busy Day in the Life

Assume that you are an employee in a busy company who has a hundred and one things to do. Following is a list of tasks that you must get done by the end of the day, in addition to a bunch of other things:

1. Create and edit a document that forecasts the sales potential of product A. This document already exists, in the form of a rough draft.

2. Include information in this document from another that was typed by a colleague.

3. Save the document.

4. Format and typeset it, so that its appearance is acceptable.

5. Print it.

6. Inform your boss that the job has been completed.

7. Make a backup of the document.

OK. It doesn't seem like a whole lot of work needs to be done here. But wait. Being a hard-working and dedicated employee (as undoubtedly you are), you want to perform these tasks in as organized and efficient a manner as possible. Following is the additional list of capabilities that would make this possible.

- You would like to be able to place all of your documents in an area that is dedicated to you alone. Within this designated area, a *subarea* should be created which will contain documents that relate solely to product A.

- You would like all documents within this designated area to be accessible only by you. Privacy of data is important.

- According to your list, a document that was previously prepared by a colleague needs to be accessed. Luckily, this document was stored in an area that is accessible by all employees. However, its name is a mystery. All that you know is that it contains some information on product A. You would like to be able to search all documents that refer to product A.

- Once the required information has been obtained, you would like to save the work done in a file which has a descriptive name, perhaps `product_a.doc`.

- Next, this document would have to be formatted so that it appeared to be professionally typeset.

- Then this document would be printed to the printer. Multiple hard copies would be required for distribution. Since you have other things to do, you don't want to hang around and wait for the print job to finish before tackling the next item on the list. A second task would need to be initiated before the first one has been completed.

- Next, your boss would need to be informed about the successful completion of the job: he has been rather anxious as to its status. The problem here is that he is in and out of the office a lot. The message must be mailed to him electronically.

- Then, since anything that can go wrong may go wrong, you would like to make a backup of the document to tape.

- Finally, you don't wish to tie up anyone else's work while you are busy doing yours. The system should not be dedicated to you alone.

1.2 AN OPERATING SYSTEM

The set of tasks just listed can be performed efficiently by the set of utilities and programming tools that are supplied by an operating system. An operating system is the software that supervises and coordinates the functioning of different hardware and software resources of a computer; it ties everything together. Without an operating system, a computer would be useless to its users. It would serve no purpose.

1.3 THE UNIX OPERATING SYSTEM

UNIX is an operating system that provides its users with the tools required to perform a wide range of tasks. This system comes equipped with powerful tools for software development, resource management, text manipulation, document processing, and user interaction.

Please note that the set of tasks listed can just as well be performed by other operating systems. Later on in this chapter we will describe those features of UNIX which uniquely differentiate it from other systems. For now, we just want to introduce you to some of the basic functionality that can be derived from it. Let's continue our discussion.

The UNIX operating system is composed of three major parts:

■ The kernel

The *kernel* is the core of the UNIX system. It manages the hardware and software resources of whatever computer it exists on.

■ The file system

The *file system* allows the user to structure the layout of the data in the system.

■ The shell

The *shell* is a program that interprets commands that are typed at the terminal, and executes them into actions if they follow the specified command syntax. (Incidentally, the shell also responds, usually in meaningful ways, to requests that do not follow the specified command syntax!)

1.4 Basic File System Structure and the Shell

We return to the example to see how UNIX can be made to work for you. You will be introduced to some UNIX commands as you read through the remainder of this chapter. These will be referred to only briefly. Detailed explanations will follow in subsequent chapters. For now, we just want to get you comfortable with the system.

Here's a brief synopsis of your requirements, and how UNIX can be used to supply the necessary support to fulfill those requirements.

- You would like an area within the system that is dedicated to you alone, and to create and store a file in it.

UNIX gives you this capability by allowing you to create a directory. Consider a directory to be a location with an identifying name. Items (or files) can be stored in this location and accessed as necessary. Any number of sublevel directories can be created under this directory. This file layout scheme is referred to as the *UNIX file system*. Since this structure originates at the top level (think of this as the root) and subdivides into multiple branches (like an upside-down tree), the UNIX file system is considered to be tree-structured or hierarchical in nature.

A directory can be created as follows:

```
mkdir directory_1
```

The command above results in the creation of a directory called `directory_1`. The following command will place you into the directory specified:

```
cd directory_1
```

Typing the above will result in the current directory being set to `directory_1`. Within `directory_1`, a directory called `product_a` can be created as follows:

```
mkdir product_a
```

Within each directory, any number of files can be created. (Of course, limitations are placed by the physical size of the space allotted to that directory.) Consider a file to be a designated area within a directory with an identifying name. What files are placed in which directory is up to the owner or user of the directory. Hopefully, that person would have taken the time to organize their placement in the correct location.

We are interested in creating a file called `product_a.doc` in the directory `product_a`. Files can be created using any one of the standard UNIX editors, or via redirection. We will not dwell on the concept of redirection in this chapter (it will be explained in detail later on in the book). Instead, we introduce you to the `vi` command used to create a file.

Before a file can be created, we have to place ourselves in the directory that the file will be stored in. Let's do a `cd` (change working directory) to `product_a`:

cd product_a

And now create the file:

vi product_a.doc

Typing the above will open up a screen window in which text can be entered and edited. Text is entered via the `a` or `i` command. The file is saved as follows:

:wq

Existing files within a directory can be viewed as follows:

ls

Typing `ls` will result in files within the current working directory being displayed.

Thus, a directory contains files, and files contain chunks of data or information. Of course, a directory can be empty (contain no files), and a file may contain no information, it may simply have a name. Details such as these will be discussed later on in the book.

■ You would like to limit access to your directories and files.

UNIX allows commands to be typed at the terminal which designate permissions for directories and files. At the time that files or directories are created, a prespecified set of permissions that is designated by the system administrator or yourself, or the permissions simply default to those set by the vendor. The scope of the permissions varies for the person who created the directory or file, the group that the person belongs to, and the world at large (i.e., remaining users that exist within the system). The command `chmod` can be used to specify permissions on files and directories. This is the command you would use to disallow read, write, or execute access to everyone except yourself.

```
chmod 700 product_a.doc
```

The above command will give you read, write, and execute permission for the file product_a.doc, since you created it. All other users will be disallowed any kind of access to it.

■ You would like to search for another document. All that is known about the document to be searched for is that it contains a reference to product A.

UNIX allows text patterns to be searched for within files that exist in one or more directories via the grep command (there are other commands as well. Details will follow in later chapters). This is how the grep command is executed:

```
grep "product_a.doc" *.*
```

Typing this command will result in the text pattern product_a.doc being searched for within all files. (All files are specified via the symbols *.*; an asterisk is called a metacharacter in UNIX.) A subset of the files that exist within the directory in which the command is issued can also be specified. If the text pattern is found, the name of the file, followed by a colon, followed by the line of text that contains the pattern will be displayed. Nothing will be displayed if the pattern is not found.

Assuming that the required document is found, you can go back into editing product_a.doc, and merge either a part of the document that was produced by your colleague, or all of it. The resulting file will once again be saved using the :wq command within the vi editor.

■ Next, you would like to typeset product_a.doc.

UNIX provides several document formatting utilities, such as nroff, troff, and the ms macro package which is used in conjunction with nroff and troff. Each of these will be discussed later on in the book.

■ Next, you need to print multiple copies of the finished document. But you want to execute the next command without having to wait for the print job to finish.

UNIX allows files to be printed to the printer, usually via the command `lpr` followed by the file name:

```
lpr product_a.doc
```

UNIX also allows tasks to be scheduled in the background. This implies that it is a multitasking operating system: it can perform several tasks or processes at the same time. After `lpr product_a.doc` is typed at the system prompt, the system prompt will redisplay. UNIX is now ready to execute the next command. The print command is already executing (or has been scheduled) in the background.

- So far, things have progressed smoothly, and a letter can now be mailed to your boss via electronic mail.

UNIX has sophisticated utilities that allow user communication, such as `mail`, `write`, and `mesg`, the most popular being `mail`. You promptly make use of this utility, and mail a nice descriptive letter to your boss.

- After sending mail, you need to make a backup of your work.

UNIX provides several commands that allow partial or full backup of the complete system, or parts of it. The utilities `tar` and `dump` are some of the more popular ones.

- Finally, you hope that other people can access the system while you are working with it.

This is really no problem, because UNIX is a multiuser operating system. More than one person can use it at any one time, without considerably affecting one another's performance. Information, resources, and utilities are efficiently shared among users.

Now you have an idea of some of the things that UNIX can do for you. However, tasks such as these can easily be implemented by other operating systems as well. What is it about UNIX that makes it so popular? What is it that makes it so powerful? We continue with a discussion of features of UNIX that differentiate it from other operating systems. But first, you need to know something about the different versions of this system that are currently in existence.

1.5 DIFFERENT VERSIONS OF UNIX

There are several versions of the UNIX operating system. These versions do not deviate profoundly, but there are differences. UNIX System V (and close associates) is the most universally available. This book is centered mainly around this version.

At the primer level, it is not of much significance which version exists at your installation. The majority of commands described in this book will produce the same (or technically similar) results, regardless of which version of UNIX they are implemented from.

1.6 DIFFERENT VERSIONS OF THE SHELL

As mentioned previously in this chapter, the shell is an integral part of UNIX. It provides the interface necessary for the user to communicate with the operating system. Communication with the system is necessary if any work is to be done on it. As you type commands at the system prompt, the shell interprets them and executes them into actions.

If you have some experience working with UNIX on different systems, you may have noticed that certain commands work one way on one system and another way on another system, although the versions of UNIX on the systems may be the same. Sometimes, a command that worked one way one day appears to work another way on another day. In our experience, we have seen quite a few novice UNIX users become quite puzzled by these apparently erratic events.

These differences in output, however, are not because UNIX is an erratic system, but because there are several versions of the shell floating around! What this means is that different commands in UNIX may execute differently, based on what shell they are executed from. As a matter of fact, some commands may not execute at all on one shell, as they would on another.

You should not be alarmed by what we just told you. Most commands in UNIX will execute in exactly the same way, regardless of which shell they are executed from. However, the differences are sometimes subtle, and sometimes powerful enough to warrant the use of one shell over another.

In this book, we take into consideration the output of commands as they are run from the three shells which are predominantly available with UNIX operating systems. These are the C, Bourne, and Korn shells. The C shell is becoming available on most UNIX operating systems that are supplied by major vendors, and provides more functionality than the Bourne. The Bourne shell is universally available on all systems. The Korn shell is a superset of the Bourne, and is more powerful than the other two. The capabilities offered by each shell are described in detail in Part 2 of the book, which describes shell programming.

All examples are initially run from the C shell. Then, after the explanatory text, differences in the output for the Bourne and Korn shells, if any, are described. The headings "Bourne Shell Implementation" and "Korn Shell Implementation" identify any differences.

1.7 UNIQUE DIFFERENTIATING FEATURES OF UNIX

And now we describe those features of UNIX that make it the unique and powerful system that it is. We start with a brief discussion on interoperability.

UNIX is a highly portable operating system. What this means is that it can be ported to a wide variety of hardware platforms. It is the only system which has been ported across various hardware platforms of major vendors such as IBM, DEC, HP, and SUN. Most operating systems are written for one specific machine or platform only. UNIX is an exception to the rule.

In addition to this, UNIX provides extensive utilities. These utilities are described in considerable detail throughout this book. As you read through each chapter, you will notice that most of the utilities, and all of the system editors, provide a uniform syntax for their commands. In other words, if you understand the command syntax of one editor, say vi, then it will be a cinch for you to learn the remaining editors, because, in essence, all of the commands and their syntax are the same. UNIX provides a consistent syntax for the commands available in its utilities and editors.

But perhaps one of the most powerful and uniquely differentiating features of UNIX is the ease with which the utilities provided can be combined. What this means is that the output of one utility can be fed as input to another, and the output of this utility can be fed as input to another. This is called formulating a *pipeline*. The final output of the pipeline is limited only by the extent of your requirements. This is a very powerful tool which allows you to customize required output as necessary.

1.8 OSF/1 OPERATING SYSTEM

The Open Systems Foundation has laid out specifications for a new operating system that is derived from different versions of UNIX, and given it the name OSF/1. Specifically, OSF/1 has integrated software obtained from IBM, University of California, Carnegie Mellon University, Encore, SecureWare, Mentat, and others. It utilizes the "Mach" kernel. This kernel was designed to support parallel processing and distributed computing.

OSF/1 offers enhanced functionality and greater flexibility than the current UNIX system. At the same time, it provides upward compatibility with UNIX applications. That is, UNIX applications can be run on OSF/1 systems without any major changes.

One of the strengths of OSF/1 is that it conforms to the POSIX 1003.1-1988 standard and the X/Open Portability Guide Issue 3(XPG3). At this level, you need not worry about what these standards are. What is important is that you understand that OSF's conformance to established standards results in a consistent and uniform user interface, with no hidden vendor-specific "surprises."

Since its introduction in October 1990, OSF/1 has been the focus of attention of major UNIX vendors. Some of the vendors who have expressed an intention to deliver OSF/1-based products are IBM, Hewlett-Packard, Digital, Siemens, Nixdorf, and Hitachi.

We have already mentioned that UNIX is a highly portable system, and also that it exists in several versions. As mentioned previously, the OSF/1 system attempts to standardize the features of UNIX and provide a uniform interface to its users.

The Open Systems Foundation truly advocates "open systems." The primary goal for OSF/1 is the provision of features that will allow portability of applications on different platforms. The need for this has arisen from the constant expansion of networks that encompass different hardware platforms, and the need to have them communicate and work in unison with one another. Portability results in increased processing power for the user. Applications written for one platform would execute on another without the need to rewrite them!

Although (as of the date of the writing of this book) it is uncertain just how much acceptability will be achieved by OSF/1, we do want you to be aware of the existence of this operating system. Therfore, at the end of each chapter, we will compare features of UNIX with those that exist for OSF/1, and describe any additional functionality that may be offered by it. Make sure you read this important section, because it is possible that major UNIX installations may migrate to the new OSF/1, thereby making it an important development platform of the future. All examples in the section on OSF/1 have been run on a DEC OSF/1 operating system. The examples presented in this section will produce the same or similar results when run on any other OSF/1-based operating system as well.

1.9 REVIEW

You should now have a basic feel for what UNIX is and how it can work for you. In the next chapter we will describe how you can log into the system, interact with it, type commands, create directories and files, move around from one location to the next, and more.

Part 1 of this book will introduce you to the basics. The remaining parts are more specialized. They will describe specific tools and utilities that exist within the system. The book is structured in such a way that if you completely understand Part 1, you can read any other part of the book out of sequence, without loss of continuity.

UNIX Basics

2.1 INTRODUCTION

In this chapter you will be introduced to the fundamentals that will allow you to interact with the UNIX operating system. Sample output of some very easy commands will also be described.

2.2 LOGGING IN

Before you can do anything with UNIX, you have to sign in to the system and gain access to it. Once this is done, the system can be used to execute any further commands.

All users are assigned names by someone who is called the *superuser*. As the name implies, the superuser is one who has special privileges. One of these privileges is the assignment of users and their related passwords. In your work environment, the superuser is probably the system administrator.

The superuser assigns names that are used to log in to the system. Yours could be your name, or the name of a group that you have been assigned to, or anything else.

So here you are sitting at the terminal and wondering where to begin. Well, the first step is really easy. All you have to do is hit a key, any key at all, and something like this will display on your terminal:

```
login:
```

Type the name assigned to you and hit the Return key. Next, the following prompt will appear on the terminal:

```
Password:
```

A password is a string of characters which, in conjunction with your user name, allows you to gain access to the system. Generally speaking, a system requires a minimum of six characters for the password. What your password will be is your choice entirely. Once entered, it will be yours to know alone; not even the superuser can figure it out. (Unless, of course, you decide or are required to tell someone!)

If you do not have a password, ask the superuser to assign it, and log in accordingly. If you already have one, just type it in, and press the Enter key. You will notice that the string of characters typed after this prompt will not be displayed on the terminal. The reason for this should be obvious: what use is a password if other people can see it?

When you depress the Return key, the system checks to ensure that the password you typed corresponds to your user name. If there is no correspondence, a message such as this will be displayed:

```
Login incorrect
```

There could be several reasons for this message:

1. A user name has not been assigned to you. Therefore, you have no sign on.

2. A user name has been assigned to you, but you did not type it in correctly.

3. A password has been assigned to you, but you did not type it in correctly.

Let's stop for a moment and visualize the following: Your name is Ron, and you have been assigned the password Sirvent. You sit down at the terminal, and this is what you type:

```
login: RON
Password: SIRVENT
```

and the system displays the following:

```
Login incorrect
```

You look at the error message and swear to yourself that no typing errors were made, and that the user name and password were typed correctly. Well, we forgot to tell you, UNIX is terribly case-sensitive. If a user name is assigned as follows:

```
Ron
```

then typing it in as RON just won't do. The same goes for the password. Make sure that the user name and password are typed exactly as they were assigned.

And another thing. UNIX is biased towards lowercase. Therefore, remember to turn your Caps key off. UNIX will not understand commands typed in uppercase.

OK. So you log in correctly. You can expect to see something like this on the screen:

```
Welcome. Tue Aug 6 11:15:15
$
```

This message will vary, based on your installation, and it can be customized as necessary. We will get into those details later on in the book.

The next thing we want you to notice is the prompt that displays on the screen after the welcome message.

```
%
```

This prompt can also vary, based on user name, installation, and the shell that you are in (shells will be explained in detail later on in the book). For example, if you were the superuser, the following prompt would probably display:

```
%
```

Some installations customize this prompt further. For example, something like this may display:

```
Company X:
```

Now that you're in, commands can be typed, and they will be interpreted and executed accordingly. Each command must be terminated with the carriage return or Enter key in order to execute. Once the command is executed, the system prompt is once again displayed, indicating that UNIX is now ready and waiting for the next command.

2.3 CORRECTING TYPING MISTAKES

Since none of us are typing experts, don't fret if you make a typing error. There is a command in UNIX which outputs the current system date. This command is executed by typing date at the system prompt. If you make a typing mistake, like this:

$ **dafe**

and hit the Return key, then the following will display:

dafe: Command not found.

If you do not hit the Return key, the mistake can be corrected in one of several ways. The first, and most obvious, would be to simply backspace to the location of the error by pressing the Backspace or Delete key, and retyping the command. The above typing mistake would be fixed by pressing the Backspace key 2 times, and retyping as follows:

$ **date**

The following would display on the terminal:

Wed Jan 22 16:54:16 EST 1992

Pressing the Control key (<Cntrl>) in conjunction with the character U erases the line completely. This is called the <kill> character. Take a look at the following example:

$ **dafe**

As you can see, a typing mistake has been made. Now type <Cntrl> U at the end of the line, as follows:

$ **dafe <Cntrl> U**

Doing so results in the deletion of the complete line, and the system response redisplays:

$

What would happen if <Cntrl> U had been typed somewhere in the middle of the line? Let's use the arrow key to position the cursor just after the a character. Now if <Cntrl> U is pressed, then the portion of the line which is prior to the cursor erases:

```
$ fe
```

Hence <Cntrl> U is used to erase the line prior to the current cursor position.

Please keep in mind that most installations will have <Cntrl> U as the combination sequence that will erase a line. However, this combination can also vary with different installations.

2.4 MORE CONTROL CHARACTER SEQUENCES

Sometimes, output spans more than one screen (there are 24 lines on one screen). At times like these, we may wish to halt the screen temporarily. Pressing <Cntrl> S will achieve this end. Output display may be resumed by typing <Cntrl> Q.

At other times, you may wish to terminate the execution of the command last issued. Pressing <Cntrl> C usually implements this feature. This is called the *Interrupt* key.

There is one more control sequence that is used often, and that is <Cntrl> D. This combination will be described in the section titled "Logging Out."

2.5 CHANGING YOUR PASSWORD

Your password can be changed by typing as follows:

```
$ passwd
```

The system responds with this message:

```
Changing password for Ron
Old password:
```

Respond to this by typing in your old password. When the <Enter> key is pressed, the system will ask you to retype your password. This safety feature ensures that no extraneous characters have been entered by mistake. If the retyped password exactly matches the one typed before, then this string becomes the new password. Here's the complete sequence of commands and responses:

```
$ passwd
Changing password for Ron
Old password: xxxxxx
New password: yyyyyy
Retype new password: yyyyyy
Password entry changed for Ron
```

Notice how we display a bunch of x's and y's for the password. Don't take these characters literally. What is intended here is to illustrate that whatever is typed at the terminal will not be echoed back to you. After all, it is a password!

Once again, different systems will display different messages, but the sequence of commands will be inherently the same. Furthermore, different systems can have varying restrictions on the contents of the password. For example, certain systems may require that it be exactly 6 characters long. Ours does. Here is the sequence of messages that will display if a password shorter than 6 characters is entered:

```
$ passwd
Old password: xxxxxx
New password: yyyy
Please use a longer password.
New password: yyyyyy
Retype new password: yyyyyy
Password entry changed for Ron
```

If you make a mistake when retyping the new password, here's what displays:

```
$ passwd
Old password: xxxxxx
New password: yyyyyy
Retype new password: yyyyyx
Mismatch - password unchanged.
$
```

All systems insist that there be no spaces embedded within that string. Here's what displays on our system when we try to include a few spaces in the middle of our passwords:

```
$ passwd
Old password: xxxxxx
New password: yy  yy
Retype new password: yy  yy
Entry not changed (password probably is incorrect)
$
```

Once properly entered and accepted, passwords are coded or encrypted in a special file that is contained within the system. Because of this special feature, no one can figure out what your password is. What this implies is that if you are in the habit of forgetting things, then you may have a problem remembering what your password was. But that's OK too. Passwords can be reset by you or the superuser, as necessary.

Bourne Shell Implementation

The `passwd` command executes in the same way when it is executed from the Bourne shell. The wording of some of the messages that display on typing an invalid password can differ with different vendors.

Korn Shell Implementation

The `passwd` command implements in the same way when it is executed from the Korn shell. The wording of some of the messages that display on typing an invalid password can differ with different vendors.

2.6 FORMAT OF COMMANDS

A command is a sequence of characters which instructs the system what to do. There are no embedded spaces within the command itself. However, commands can be followed by arguments and options, each argument or option being separated from the others by one or more spaces. An argument works in conjunction with a command to produce a certain type of output. Here is an example of a command that is followed by 2 arguments:

```
$ grep Hello file1
```

In the example above, `grep` is a UNIX command which invokes one of the system utilities which searches for the string of characters in the target file. `Hello` is the first argument; this is the string that is searched for. `file1` is the second argument; this is the target file which is searched.

If this pattern is found, then the complete line which contains the specified string is displayed:

```
Hello there.
```

If this pattern is not found, then the system prompt is displayed:

```
$
```

Notice that each argument is separated from the others by a space. Let's increase the number of spaces between each argument and see if output is modified in any way:

$ **grep   Hello   file1**

Hitting the Return key results in the same output.

Let's take out the spaces and see what happens:

$ **grepHellofile1**

This time the system responds as follows:

```
grepHellofile1: Command not found.
```

We may safely conclude that commands and their arguments must be separated by spaces.

Commands can also be followed by options. Options serve to modify the output in some way. They are usually prefixed with a dash or hyphen (-). Here's a very simple command that lists the current system date and time.

$ **date**

The system responds as follows:

```
Wed Jan 22 16:55:16 EST 1992
```

Now let's add an option to the original command. Notice how the option is prefixed with a hyphen.

$ **date -u**

Now the system responds as follows:

```
Wed Jan 22 21:55:14 GMT 1992
```

The −u option displays the date in Greenwich Mean Time (GMT). As you can see, the option has worked in conjunction with the original command and modified its output. Now let's play around with the original syntax and see if the output is affected in any way. First, let's insert more spaces between the command and its option:

```
$ date        −u
```

The system responds as follows:

```
Wed Jan 22 21:56:14 GMT 1992
```

No problem here. Now let's take put some spaces between the hyphen and the option:

```
$ date   −   u
```

And here's the system response:

```
usage: date [−a sss.fff] [−u] [+format] [yymmddhmm[.ss]]
$
```

The reason for this output is that if a valid command is entered with an invalid option, then UNIX responds with a message that indicates the correct usage of the command.

There is a command in UNIX that lists the directory contents. This command is ls. We are going to use this command to illustrate the use of multiple options. Right now, it is not important for you to understand the contents of the output. What does matter is for you to see how the output varies with the use of each option. Here goes:

```
$ ls
$
```

Typing ls by itself results in nothing but the system prompt. This indicates that the current directory has no files. Now we will use this command with an option that requests the operating system to show all files, including the ones that are hidden. Here's the output:

```
$ ls −a
.  ..
$
```

This time, the system displays a dot (.) and a pair of dots (. .).

Now, we will use another option which instructs the system to display the contents of the directory in a long listing. The −l option is used to do this.

```
$ ls −a −l
total 4
drwxr−xr−x  2 Ron    512 Jan 20 17:18  .
drwxrwsr−x 16 Ron   3072 Jan 20 17:18  ..
$
```

This time we received a more detailed description of the contents of the directory. As indicated previously, it is not important right now to understand what is being displayed. Instead, you should be concentrating on how the output varies with the option entered.

Let's try to group the options together and see if there is any difference in output:

```
$ ls −al
total 4
drwxr−xr−x  2 Ron    512 Jan 20 17:18  .
drwxrwsr−x 16 Ron   3072 Jan 20 17:18  ..
$
```

As you can see, the output is the same. Suppose we took the spaces out:

```
$ ls−al
ls−al: Command not found.
```

As expected, spaces must be inserted between commands and their options. However, spaces are not required between the options themselves. They can be grouped together and preceded by a dash.

2.7 LOGGING OUT

When you are done working with UNIX, you should log out or sign off your session. Press <Cntrl> D. This is the *end of text* sequence, and is often used to end other activities as well (more on this later on in the book). As you log out, certain messages may be displayed.

Some systems allow exit from the system simply by typing logout or exit. Try it and see what happens.

2.8 ON-LINE HELP

The man command is used to describe the meaning and usage of UNIX commands. Its output is structured in exactly the same way as this command would be described in the UNIX Programmer's Reference Manual. This is on-line help that may or may not be loaded on your system. It is very rarely not loaded, since it is a very useful tool. If it is not loaded, then simply refer to the Programmer's Reference Manual for those commands that you wish to investigate further. The output for this command is usually divided up as follows:

NAME
Gives the name of the command, and briefly describes what it does.

SYNOPSIS
Presents a synopsis of how the command is to be used, including arguments and options, if any.

DESCRIPTION
Gives a detailed description of the command.

OPTIONS
Gives a detailed description of the options that can be used with the command.

EXAMPLES
Illustrates use of the command with examples and sample output.

FILES
Gives the names of the files which are required to execute the command.

SEE ALSO
Gives the names of related commands.

BUGS
Lists strange command behavior, or instances where the command produces unexpected results.

Page 27 contains a man page for the kill command, which is used to terminate an ongoing process. At this point in time it is not important for you to understand exactly how the kill command works, or even what a process is (they will be described later on in the book). What you should understand is that you have the capability to delve deeper into the functioning of a command (perhaps you are looking to see if one of the commands encountered in this book has other options, or what other commands within UNIX are related to it) either by referring to the UNIX Programmer's Reference Manual or the OSF/1 Commands Reference Manual, or simply by typing man followed by the command name.

2.9 OSF/1 CONSIDERATIONS

The procedures outlined for logging into and out of the system are the same in an OSF/1 operating system. The format of commands and the on-line help are also the same. OSF/1 requires that the password be no more than eight characters long. This requirement may also exist in some installations of UNIX System V. The actual number of characters required can vary with different installations and the specifications set down by your system administrator.

Man Page for the Kill Command

KILL(1)   USER COMMANDS   KILL(1)

NAME
    kill - send a signal to a process, or terminate a process

SYNOPSIS
    kill [-signal] pid ...
    kill -l

DESCRIPTION
    kill sends the TERM (terminate, 15) signal to the processes
    with the specified pids. If a signal name or number
    preceded by '-' is given as first argument, that signal is
    sent instead of terminate. The signal names are listed by
    using the -l option, and are as given in <signal.h>,
    stripped of the common SIG prefix.

    The terminate signal will kill processes that do not catch
    the signal, so 'kill -9 ...' is a sure kill, the signal
    cannot be caught. By convention, if process number 0 is
    specified, all members in the process group (that is,
    processes resulting from the current login) are signaled
    (but beware: this works only if you use sh(1); not if you
    have chs(1).) Negative process numbers also have special
    meanings; see kill (2V) for details. The killed processes
    must belong to the current user unless he is the super-user.

    To shut the sytem down and bring it up single user the
    super-user may send the initialization process a TERM
    (terminate) signal by 'kill 1'; see init(8). To force init
    to close and open terminals according to what is currently
    in /etc/ttytab use 'kill -HUP 1' (sending a hangup signal to
    process 1).

    The shell reports the process number of an asynchronous
    process started with '&' (run in the background). Process
    numbers can also be found by using ps(1).

    kill is built in to csh(1); it allows job specifiers, such
    as 'kill % ...', in place of kill arguments. See csh(1)
    for details.

OPTIONS
    -l   Display a list of signal names.

FILES
    /etc/ttytab

SEE ALSO
    csh(1), ps(1), kill(2V), sigven(2), init(8)

BUGS
    A replacement for 'kill 0' for csh(1) users should be
    provided.

2.10 REVIEW

In this chapter we helped familiarize you with some commonly used UNIX commands. You learned how to:

- Log in to the system.

- Correct typing mistakes using the Backspace or Delete key, or typing <Cntrl> U to delete the line.

- Change your password via the passwd command.

- Type commands with or without options at the shell prompt.

- Log out of the system.

- Get more help for a command using the available manuals, or by accessing the man command.

UNIX File Structure

3.1 Introduction

This chapter explains the concept of files and directories. Commands that access directories will be described in detail in this chapter. Commands used to manipulate files will be described in Chapter 4. You will gain an understanding of the UNIX system file structure by the time you conclude this chapter.

3.2 Files

Files are containers of information that have identifying names. For example, a file can be created that contains the following information:

```
This is a file
```

and is named `file1`. Henceforth, each time this file is to be accessed, it will be referred to by its name: `file1`.

Files can be manipulated in various ways. They can be changed, renamed, copied, and moved from one location to another. One file can be copied into another.

Files will be discussed in greater detail in the next chapter. For now, we just want you to understand what a file is, and how it relates to a directory. The next section will help you understand this.

3.3 DIRECTORIES

In order for a file to exist, it must be created and stored somewhere. Directories are locations within the system that are used to store files; they are collections of files. Like files, directories also have names; they can be changed, renamed, copied, and moved from one location to another. One directory can exist within another. We have already mentioned that a directory is a designated name of a location in the system. If you can think of your home as a directory, then your room would be a subdirectory within your home. If the contents of a directory are listed, then its subdirectories will also be listed. If the rooms in your home are listed, then your room would also be listed. Getting a little more technical, if `directory_2` is created within `directory_1`, then `directory_2` is a subdirectory of `directory_1`, or `directory_1` contains `directory_2`.

On the other hand, when it comes to directories, it would be perfectly valid to state that `directory_1` contains `directory_2`. `directory_2` is an individual entity within `directory_1`.

3.4 UNIX DIRECTORY STRUCTURE

As previously stated, you can have directories within directories. UNIX has a tree-structured directory system. Refer to Figure 3.1 for a sample directory structure. As you can see, `directory_1` contains 2 directories: `directory_2` and `directory_3`. `Directory_2` contains 3 directories: `directory_4`, `directory_5`, and `directory_6`. Notice that `directory_1` is at the root of it all.

This tree structure illustrated in this figure is analogous to the directory structure in UNIX. Within UNIX, `directory_1` is called the `root`; it is the root of the file system. It is designated by a slash (/). The root is the parent of all directories. Figure 3.2 illustrates this change in the original naming scheme.

3.5 HOME DIRECTORY

When you log into a UNIX system, you are automatically placed in a directory which is called your home directory. Each user is usually assigned his or her own home directory. Generally speaking, home directories are given the same name as your login name.

Figure 3.1 Sample Directory Structure

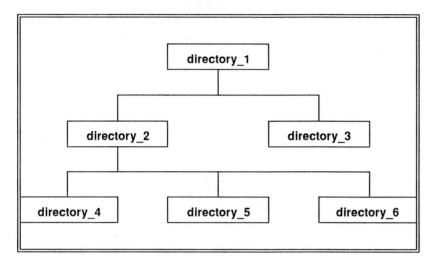

Figure 3.2 Root and Subsequent Directories

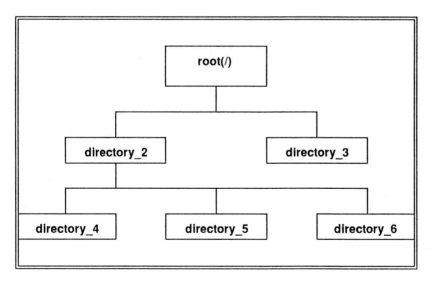

Since seeing is believing, consider the following example. Assume that there are three people assigned to a project in your department whose code name is REDHOT. (Yes, it's true. They're assigned to a REDHOT project.) Their names are Sally, Harry and Gary. Refer to Figure 3.3 for a picture of the directory structure that would be created for this scenario.

Figure 3.3 Creation of New Directories

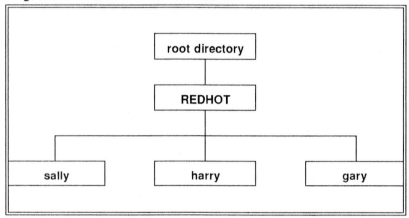

As you can see, a directory called REDHOT has been created under the root directory. REDHOT has three subdirectories: sally, harry, and gary. Now if Sally were to log into the system, she would be automatically placed in her home directory, which is called sally. But how will Sally know her location within the system? The answer is a very simple UNIX command which prints the current working directory: pwd. This is the response that Sally would get upon typing pwd at the system prompt:

```
$ pwd
/REDHOT/sally
```

Let's analyze the output. What displays on the terminal is a full path that indicates where the current user is positioned within the system. All directories and files within the UNIX system branch from a common origin. This is, as indicated previously, the root. The root is designated by the slash (/):

```
/
```

Under the root is a directory called REDHOT.

```
/REDHOT
```

This directory has been created for all users that will be working on the project called REDHOT.   Within REDHOT, three more subdirectories have been created for the individual users that have been assigned to the project.   One of them is sally:

/REDHOT/sally

If Harry were to type pwd (this command will be explained in due course), he would receive the following output:

/REDHOT/harry

and likewise for Gary:

/REDHOT/gary

Notice that each element is separated by a slash.

3.6 PATH NAMES, FULL AND RELATIVE

The output

/REDHOT/sally

specifies a path name.   There can be full path names and relative path names.   A full path name begins with the slash.   It is a complete specification of a location within the system starting from the root.   A relative path name, on the other hand, specifies a location not from the root, but from the location that you are currently in.   The following example should help clarify what is being said.

Suppose you have to go to a party, and have directions to get there from your house.   This would be analogous to a full path name.   Now suppose you get lost somewhere and you make a phone call to your friend, informing him of your current location, and he proceeds to give directions to his house from where you are currently located.   This would be a relative path name.

In terms of the example, if the location had to be specified as a full path name, it would be look like this:

/REDHOT/sally

But if the current location was REDHOT, then the path to the directory sally would be specified as follows:

```
sally
```

Notice that the leading slash is missing. Relative path names are not prefixed with a slash.

3.7 MAKING NEW DIRECTORIES

Sally would like to create a subdirectory within her home directory in which she will place the documentation for all of the applications that she will be developing for this project. First, she wants to know her current location in the system:

```
$ pwd
/REDHOT/sally
```

UNIX allows her to create a subdirectory with the command mkdir. Take a look at the following command:

```
$ mkdir document
$
```

This command creates a directory called document within the current working directory. Notice the absence of a slash before the name of the new directory. This indicates that the directory has been created using a relative path name; hence it exists relative to the current location, which is her home directory. The full path name for the new directory just created would be as follows:

```
/REDHOT/sally/document
```

Sally could also have created this directory using the full path name, as follows:

```
$ mkdir /REDHOT/sally/document
```

but this would only mean more typing for her. Specifying a full path name would make sense when a directory is to be created in a location whose path is different from the current working directory. For example, if Sally wanted to create the directory document for Harry and Gary, she would proceed as follows:

```
$ mkdir /REDHOT/harry/document
$ mkdir /REDHOT/gary/document
```

This time it was necessary for her to type the complete path name since the path for the target directories is different from her current location within the system.

Specification of the complete path is also necessary if the target directory is to reside *above* the current location. For example, if someone else called Robbie was assigned to the project, then Sally could create a personal directory for her as follows:

```
$ mkdir /REDHOT/robbie
```

Multiple directories can be created as follows:

```
$ mkdir /REDHOT/robbie  /REDHOT/bill
$
```

Do keep in mind, though, that unless Sally is the superuser, it is doubtful that she will be able to create subdirectories in directories owned by Harry or Gary.

Notice how one or more spaces act as the delimiter for the directory names. Multiple directories created in this way will exist at the same level in the tree directory structure. The result is illustrated in Figure 3.4.

Figure 3.4 Multiple Directories

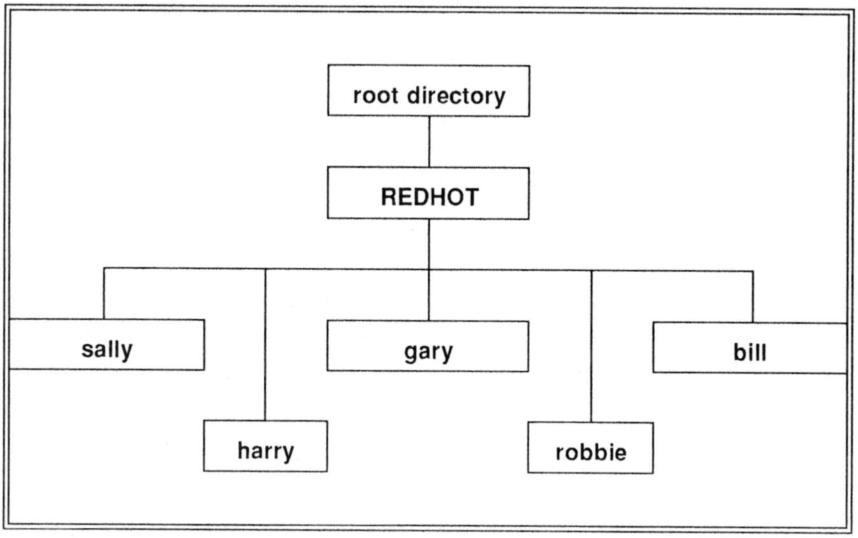

What would happen if we try to re-create a directory that already exists? Let's take a look:

```
$ pwd
/REDHOT/sally
$ mkdir /REDHOT/harry
File or directory already exists.
```

The system responds as expected. Within the same level, UNIX does not allow duplicate file or directory names. However, it would have allowed the creation of a directory called `harry` under `sally`, or even as a subdirectory under `harry`. If you take a look at their paths, then you will understand why the system allows this:

`/REDHOT/sally/harry`

and

`/REDHOT/harry/harry`

Bourne Shell Implementation

The `mkdir` command behaves in the same way when executed from within the Bourne shell. The content of the messages displayed is the same, but the wording can vary with different vendors.

Korn Shell Implementation

The `mkdir` command behaves in the same way when executed from within the Korn shell. The content of the messages displayed is the same, but the wording can vary with different vendors.

3.8 CHANGING DIRECTORIES

OK. A bunch of directories exist within the system. Refer to Figure 3.5 for the tree structure.

Figure 3.5 Tree Structure Directories

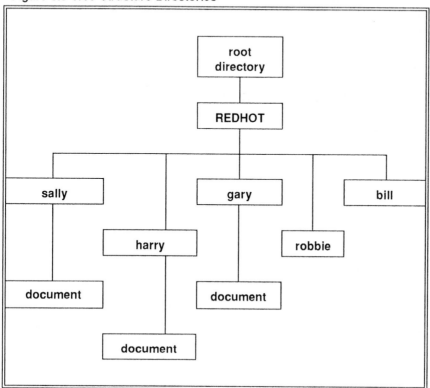

So how can we go from one directory to the next? UNIX allows us to do so with the command cd followed by the name of the target directory. As before, the name of the directory can consist of the full path or the relative path, depending on the current and target locations within the system.

Let's go back to Sally. Sally, once again a little confused as to where she is, types as follows:

```
$ pwd
/REDHOT/sally
```

OK. She's in her home directory. Sally would like to change her current working directory to document. This is what she would type at the terminal:

```
$ cd document
$
```

Notice the absence of the slash. This is a relative path; it indicates that Sally wants to transfer to somewhere from where she currently is. Now when she types

$ **pwd**

the system responds as follows:

`/REDHOT/sally/document`

Figure 3.6 indicates where Sally was, and where she is now.

Figure 3.6 Tree Structure Directories

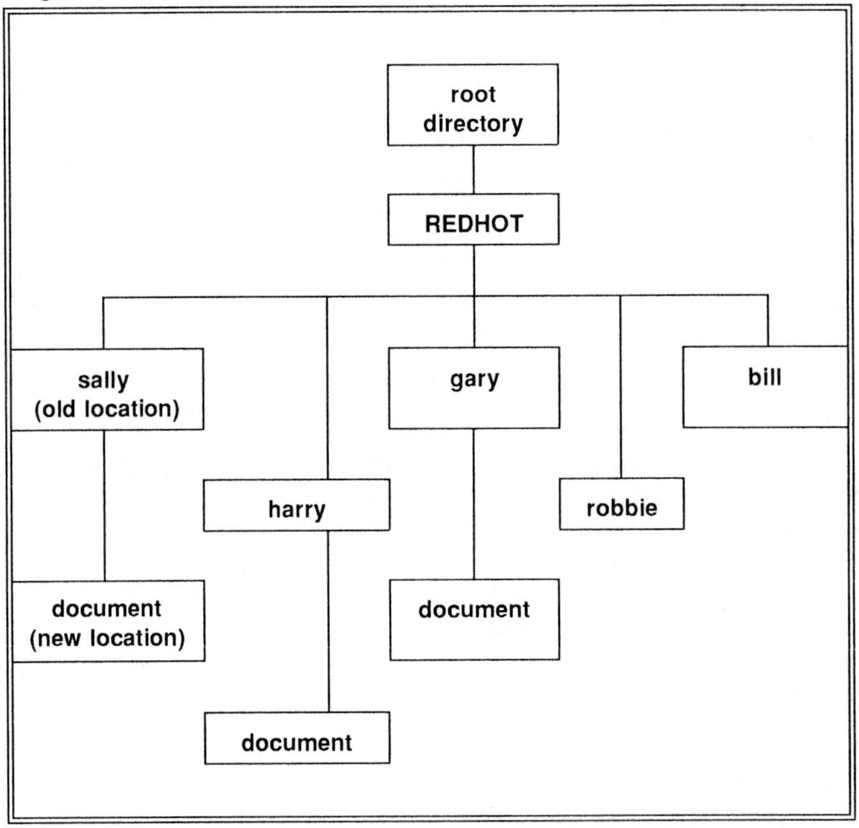

Let's have Sally try to go to Harry's `document` directory. She types as follows:

$ **cd harry/document**

and the system complains

```
harry/document not found.
$
```

This is because a mistake has been made in typing the path name of the target directory. When

$ **cd harry/document**

was typed at the terminal, the system thought the directory `harry` existed as a subdirectory in the current working location, which is `/REDHOT/sally/document`. If you look at Figure 3.7, you will see that the path specified is incorrect; and hence the error message.

Figure 3.7 Directory Paths

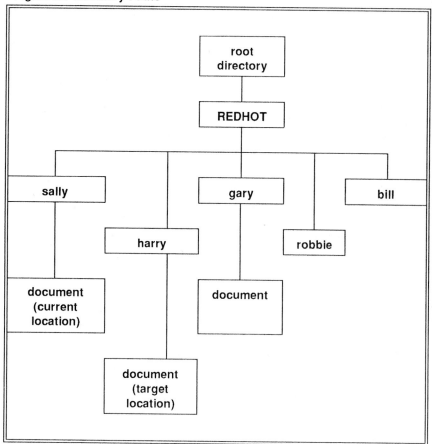

Sally needs to back up to the directory called `sally`, and then to REDHOT. Then, she has to proceed to `harry`, and then to `document`. She has to back up two, and then go down two.

UNIX allows its users to back up one directory by typing as follows:

```
$ cd ..
```

Thus, the `..` (dot dot) indicates the parent of the current working directory. (Incidentally, a dot by itself implies the current directory; more on this when we discuss how directories are removed at the end of the chapter.)

Let's go back to the example. Now, when `pwd` is entered, the system responds as follows:

```
/REDHOT/sally
```

OK. We need to back up one more:

```
$ cd ..
$ pwd
/REDHOT
```

Now, we have to go down two. We can type as follows:

```
$ cd harry
$ pwd
/REDHOT/harry
$ cd document
$ pwd
/REDHOT/harry/document
```

or, we could have taken a shortcut as follows:

```
$ pwd
/REDHOT
$ cd harry/document
$ pwd
/REDHOT/harry/document
```

The system allows this shortcut because the path name specified really does exist relative to the current location, which is REDHOT.

We will change directories again and go to Sally's `document` directory, to illustrate the shortcut taken in the next example.

```
$ pwd
/REDHOT/sally/document
```

The system would have allowed us to type all four commands on the same line, each separated by a semicolon, with or without separating spaces, as follows:

```
$ cd .. ; cd .. ; cd harry ; cd document ; pwd
/REDHOT/harry/document
```

Now if you were to take the time to count the number of commands we typed to get from where we were to where we wanted to go, you would come up with the number four. However, we could have gone to our target destination in one shot simply by utilizing one of the techniques that has already been described. That's right, you guessed it: by typing the full path name as follows:

```
$ pwd
/REDHOT/sally/document
$ cd /REDHOT/harry/document
$ pwd
/REDHOT/harry/document
```

Now that's a real shortcut!

Let's try a few more variations to see just what we can and can-not do with the cd command.

```
$ pwd
/REDHOT/sally/document
$ cd ../../harry/document
$ pwd
/REDHOT/harry/document
```

This worked. The command works from left to right. First, it changes the directory to the parent of the current directory.

```
$ cd ../
```

and is now in /REDHOT/sally. Next, it moves to the parent of the new working directory

```
$ cd ../../
```

and is now in /REDHOT. Then, it proceeds down to harry/document, and the new working directory becomes /REDHOT/harry/document.

Let's see what happens if we type cd with no parameters.

```
$ pwd
/REDHOT/sally/document
$ cd
$ pwd
/REDHOT/sally
```

Typing cd by itself places the user in his or her home directory, regardless of its location in the system. The home directory is set by the superuser. It could be the root directory, but more likely than not, it will be the directory named after your user name.

The same result would have been obtained by typing cd followed by the tilde character (~), as follows:

```
$ pwd
/REDHOT/sally/document
$ cd ~
$ pwd
/REDHOT/sally
```

Bourne Shell Implementation

The cd command using full and relative paths executes in the same way when implemented from the Bourne shell for all cases described, except the following. The Bourne shell does not understand the command

```
$ cd ~
```

and outputs the message

```
Command not found.
```

In addition to this, the wording of the messages displayed can vary with different implementations. However, the content will be the same.

Korn Shell Implementation

The cd command using full and relative paths executes like the Bourne shell for all cases described. Like the Bourne shell, the wording of the messages displayed can vary with different implementations. However, the content will be the same.

3.9 LISTING CONTENTS OF DIRECTORIES

Now that we know how to work our way from one directory to the next, it might be a good idea to be able to find out what's in these directories anyway. Recall that a directory can contain files in addition to subdirectories. The command ls lists the contents of directories in different ways. We will discuss this command next.

Take a look at the output for this command:

```
$ pwd
/REDHOT/sally
$ ls
document
```

The ls command lists the contents of the current working directory. The directory sally contains either a file or a directory called document. Although we know that document is a subdirectory, the output of the command does not indicate this.

Let's move down to the document subdirectory and list its contents:

```
$ cd document
$ pwd
/REDHOT/sally/document
$ ls
$
```

The result this time is the system prompt. This is because this directory does not have any files or subdirectories under it. Notice that we are listing the contents of the current working directory only. We can also list the contents of some other directory by using the full or relative path name. Here is an example which uses the full path name:

```
$ pwd
/REDHOT/sally/document
$ ls /REDHOT
bill   harry   robbie   sally
```

The output indicates that REDHOT contains four files or subdirectories: bill, harry, sally and robbie.

This ls command utilizes a relative path name. There will be no preceding slash:

```
$ pwd
/REDHOT/sally/document
$ cd ..
$ pwd
```

```
/REDHOT/sally
$ ls document
$
```

The directory document exists as a subdirectory under sally. Hence, a relative path name may be used. The output should require no further explanation.

Let's make the contents of our directories a little more interesting by throwing in a file in them. We will show you how to create a file with the echo command. There are many ways to create a file, but this is probably one of the easiest. Type the following at the system prompt:

```
$ echo "Hello.   This isn't too bad." > file1
$
```

The system will respond with its prompt. We don't want you to get too confused about what you just typed, so here's a brief explanation of what happened. The echo command "echoes" the string of characters that is enclosed in quotes. The quotes can be single or double. The second quote is followed by a space, and then the greater than sign (>). What the > sign does is redirect the output of the command from the standard output device (which is your terminal) to a file. In other words, if you had terminated the command right after the double quote, then Hello.   This isn't too bad. would have displayed on your terminal. Instead, this string gets written to a file whose name is designated by the string of characters that follow the > sign. You now have a file called file1 in the current working directory. Since seeing is believing, type ls and see what you get.

```
$ pwd
/REDHOT/sally
$ ls
document     file1
```

Now it displays two names: document and file1. Whether they are files or directories is still not obvious from the output. However, we would be able to find this out by using the command with the options that are available with it. Recall from the prior chapter that the output of UNIX commands can be modified by prefixing them with options, and that options are usually preceded with a dash or minus sign. The two options most commonly used with the ls command are −a and −1. The −a option results in all files and subdirectories being listed, even those which are hidden (more on this later on in the book). Yes, it's true. There are hidden files in directories. These files are prefixed with a dot (.). Here's sample usage of the −a option:

```
$ pwd
/REDHOT/sally
$ ls −a
.       ..      document        file1
```

As you can see, two new files, . and .., display. These are the hidden files.

The −l option requests a *long* listing of the output. Here is how the output is modified:

```
$ pwd
/REDHOT/sally
$ ls −l
total 2
drwxr-xr-x  2  sally  512 Jan 20 17:38 document
-rw-r--r--  1  sally  28  Jan 20 17:48 file1
$
```

Hence, the −l option results in more information than just the names of the files being displayed. What this information is will be discussed in detail at the end of this section.

The two options can be used in conjunction, as follows:

```
$ ls −al
total 4
drwxr-xr-x  3  sally  512 Jan 20 17:48 .
drwxr-xr-x  4  sally  512 Jan 20 17:38 ..
drwxr-xr-x  2  sally  512 Jan 20 17:38 document
-rw-r--r--  1  sally  28  Jan 20 17:48 file1
$
```

Please note that the ls command lists files and directories in alphabetical order. Based on your installation, these files may be listed either across the screen or in columnar format. However, the information displayed will be as described.

Now let's take a moment to understand the output being displayed. At the top of the output we see

```
total 4
```

This is the total number of files and directories found in the directory. Notice that the number corresponds to the number of entries displayed.

Next, we will analyze the following entry:

```
drwxr-xr-x  2  sally  512 Jan 20 17:38 document
```

The first field

```
drwxr-xr-x
```

can be divided up into four parts:

```
d   rwx   r-x   r-x
```

The first column of the first part is a d. This indicates that the corresponding entry is a directory. If it were a −, this would indicate that the entry was a file. (Refer to the entry for file1 for verification.)

The remaining three parts indicate the permissions that exist for the owner of the file, the group that the owner belongs to, and all other users within the system, in that order.

Hence, the first entry,

```
rwx
```

indicates the permissions for this entry for its owner.

The second entry,

```
r-x
```

indicates the permissions for the group that the owner belongs to.

And the third entry,

```
r-x
```

indicates the permissions for all other users of the system.

The columns within each part indicate the permission itself. There can be three types of permission, in this order:

```
r  read permission
w  write permission
x  execute permission
```

When a file appears with execute permission, it means that this file can be executed. (It may be a batch file containing system commands; more on this when we discuss shell scripts.) When a directory appears with execute permission, it indicates that this directory can be searched. A dash in a position indicates the absence of the permission. Hence, the entry

```
r-x
```

indicates that the user is allowed read and execute permission only. An entry such as

```
r--
```

would indicate read permission only.

The second field of

```
drwxr-xr-x  2  sally   512 Jan 20 17:38 document
```

is a 2. This is the number of links, or the number of identical copies of that entry that exist within the system. The number 2 indicates that the entry exists in the current directory and the subdirectory called document.

The next field of

```
drwxr-xr-x  2  sally   512 Jan 20 17:38 document
```

is "sally". This is the owner of the entity. The user sally owns the directory called document.

The next field, 512, shows the size of the file in bytes. Notice that document is displayed as a subdirectory and its size is indicated in bytes. UNIX treats a directory as nothing more than a file, whose contents are the names of the files and directories that it contains. The entry for file1 is as follows:

```
-rw-r--r-- 1   sally 28 Jan 20 17:48 file1
```

Notice that this file is only 28 bytes long.

The next field shows the date and time the file or directory was created.

Finally, the last field is the actual name of the file or directory.

Bourne Shell Implementation

The output for the ls command executed from within the Bourne shell will be the same for all examples illustrated in this chapter.

Korn Shell Implementation

The output for the ls command executed from within the Korn shell will be the same for all examples illustrated in this chapter.

3.10 REMOVING DIRECTORIES

Now that you know how to create directories, navigate between them, and list their contents, the next important thing that you should be aware of is how to remove them. The UNIX command rmdir followed by the directory name allows you to do so. Let's use it now to remove the document directory belonging to Sally.

```
$ pwd
/REDHOT/sally
$ ls -al
total 4
drwxr-xr-x  3 sally   512 Jan 20 17:48 .
drwxr-xr-x  4 sally   512 Jan 20 17:38 ..
drwxr-xr-x  2 sally   512 Jan 20 17:38 document
-rw-r--r--  1 sally   28  Jan 20 17:48 file1
$ rmdir document
$
```

Notice that the system responded with nothing in particular, only its prompt. This implies successful removal of the specified directory. Let's check:

```
$ pwd
/REDHOT/sally
$ ls -al
total 3
drwxr-xr-x  3 sally   512 Jan 20 18.10 .
drwxr-xr-x  4 sally   512 Jan 20 17:38 ..
-rw-r--r--  1 sally   28  Jan 20 17:48 file1
```

Sure enough, the directory is gone.

This directory was removed using the relative path name. Directories may be removed using the full path name as well. Here's an example that illustrates this:

```
$ pwd
/REDHOT/sally
$ ls -l /REDHOT/harry
total 1
drwxr-xr-x  2 sally   512 Jan 20 17:39 document
```

The output indicates the existence of a directory called document.

Now let's remove it using the full path name:

```
$ rmdir /REDHOT/harry/document
$ ls -l /REDHOT/harry
total 0
```

Keep in mind that it is unlikely that anyone except the superuser can remove a directory that is not owned by him or her.

There are no more files or directories left under the directory /REDHOT/harry. Hence the output total 0.

OK. Now let's try to remove the current working directory. Recall from earlier on in the chapter that a dot (.) references the current working directory. Here's sample usage of the command:

```
$ pwd
/REDHOT/sally
$ ls -al
total 3
drwxr-xr-x  3  sally  512  Jan 20 18:10 .
drwxr-xr-x  4  sally  512  Jan 20 17:38 ..
-rw-r--r--  1  sally  28   Jan 20 17:48 file1
$ rmdir .
rmdir: .: Invalid argument
```

The system could not understand the command typed. A dot "." implies the current working directory. The current working directory cannot be removed, since you are currently positioned in it. Look at the output if you type out the name of the current directory explicitly:

```
$ pwd
$ /REDHOT/sally
$ rmdir sally
rmdir: sally: No such file or directory
```

The directory to be removed is specified as such using a relative path name. What this indicates to the system is that a subdirectory called sally exists within the current directory, whose name is also sally. This points out two interesting things. First, it is legal to have subdirectories within directories with the same name; the system will be able to identify them correctly. Second, it appears that you have to be positioned in the parent directory of the directory to be removed, if only a relative path is specified.

OK. So let's move up one, and then try to remove sally from the system. Here is the sequence of commands and their output:

```
$ pwd
/REDHOT/sally
$ cd ..
$ pwd
/REDHOT
$ rmdir sally
rmdir: sally: Directory  not empty
```

The output message implies that directories cannot be removed if they contain files or subdirectories. If we are insistent on removing the directory `sally` from the system, all of its files and subdirectories must first be deleted. The command that deletes files is `rm` followed by the file name. This command will be discussed in detail in the next chapter. For now, let's just implement it, and then reissue the `rmdir` command.

```
$ cd sally
$ pwd
/REDHOT/sally
$ ls -al
total 3
drwxr-xr-x  3 sally    512 Jan 20 18:10 .
drwxr-xr-x  4 sally    512 Jan 20 17:38 ..
-rw-r--r--  1 sally    28  Jan 20 17:48 file1
$ rm file1
$
```

The system prompt displays, indicating successful execution of the `rm` command. Let's take a look:

```
$ ls -al
total 2
drwxr-xr-x  2 sally    512 Jan 20 18:10 .
drwxr-xr-x  6 sally    512 Jan 20 17:38 ..
```

So far, so good. Now, let's move up one level, and remove `sally` from the system. We will use the `ls` command without any options.

```
$ cd ..
$ pwd
/REDHOT
$ ls
bill   harry   robbie   sally
$ rmdir sally
$ ls
bill   harry   robbie
$
```

Looks good. Just what we wanted!

We want you to take a moment to realize something that we have been doing while explaining the `rmdir` command. Did you notice how we always did a `pwd` and `ls` before issuing the `rmdir` command? This is a good idea (highly recommended), since it informs you of your current working directory and its contents. Inadvertently removing files or subdirectories from a directory other than the one intended could result in quite a few sleepless nights for you, to say nothing of the guilt you would have to live with if they belonged to someone else! Always do a pwd and ls before executing rmdir.

Bourne Shell Implementation

The rmdir command executed from within the Bourne shell behaves the same way as it would from the C shell.

Korn Shell Implementation

The rmdir command executed from within the Korn shell behaves the same way as it would from the C shell.

3.11 OSF/1 Considerations

The directories within a typical OSF/1 file system are also arranged hierarchically, like an upside down tree, starting at the root. Full and relative path names are specified in the same way as described for the UNIX operating system. The mkdir, cd, ls, and rmdir commands also function in the same way. There is no difference in the permission set either.

3.12 Review

In this chapter we described the UNIX file structure in considerable detail. Here's a synopsis of some of the salient features within this chapter.

- Files are containers of information with identifying names.

- Directories are containers of information also, only their contents are files.

- UNIX has a hierarchical file structure.

- Path names can be *absolute*. This is a complete specification of the path within the system, starting from the root directory.

- Path names can be *relative*. This is the specification of a path starting from the current location within the system.

- Directories are created using the `mkdir` command:

  `mkdir new_directory`

  creates a directory called `new_directory` in the current location, if you have write permission on that directory.

- Directories can be created anywhere in the system by prefixing the name of the directory with its absolute path. Once again, it is necessary that the user creating the subdirectory have write permission for the directory that will contain it.

- The current working directory can be changed via the `cd` command:

  `cd new_directory`

  changes the current working directory to `new_directory`.

- Typing `cd` by itself places the user into his/her home directory. Typing `cd ~` works in the same way, unless you're executing it from the Bourne shell.

- Contents of directories are listed via the `ls` command:

  `ls new_directory`

  will list the contents of the directory called `new_directory`.

- Typing `ls -a` gives a listing of all files and subdirectories within a directory, including hidden files (these are prefixed with a dot, ".").

- Typing `ls -l` gives a long listing of the contents of the directory.

- A long listing allows us to review the permission sets of files and directories for the user who owns the file, the group that he/she belongs to, and the remaining users within the system, along with other pertinent information, such as size of file, date created, etc.

- Within a permission set, r indicates read permission, w indicates write permission, and x indicates execute permission. A dash symbol (−) indicates lack of that permission.

- Directories can be removed using the `rmdir` command:

  `rmdir new_directory`

  removes the directory called `new_directory`.

- A directory must be empty before it can be removed.

- The OSF/1 file system is structured in the same way. All commands described in this chapter behave the same way in an OSF/1 operating system.

4

Files

4.1 INTRODUCTION

Commands that are used to create and manipulate files will be discussed in this chapter. After you conclude this chapter, take some time out to explore the UNIX file system on your own. Browse through the directories, and list the contents of preexisting files. This exercise will help reinforce the concepts and commands explained in this and previous chapters. Later on in the book, we will take you for a guided tour ourselves.

4.2 NAMING FILES

Different installations have different maximum numbers of characters that can be used to name files. Check with your system administrator as to what this limit is at your installation. Generally speaking, the limit on most UNIX file names is very large (256 characters) Some systems truncate to a shorter name. If you feel the urge to create a file name longer than the required number (say it is 14 characters only), the system will conveniently truncate it to the proper length. For example, if you decide to call a file

```
details_and_examples
```

then the system wil rename it

```
details_and_ex
```

The file name `details_and_examples` is 20 characters long, and `details_and_ex` is 14.

Names can consist of a mixture of upper- and lowercase letters and other characters on the keyboard. Usually, meaningful names (which somehow imply the probable contents of the file) are created by combining upper- and lowercase letters and inserting an underscore where necessary. For example, in Chapter 1 you created a file called `product_a.doc`. Notice that we used only lowercase letters, but nothing is stopping you from calling it `Product_A.doc` (it looks much nicer, but is a little cumbersome to type!). Remember, UNIX is case-sensitive. A file called `product_a.doc` is not the same as `Product_A.doc`. Notice also that there is a period included in the file name.

Generally speaking, periods are used to separate the name of the file from its suffix. There are no limitations imposed by UNIX on the length of the prefix or suffix. The suffix usually implies the nature of the file. In the name

`product_a.doc`

the suffix is `doc`, which is short for document. This is not a hard and fast rule. You may choose to suffix document files with a `dct`, like so:

`product_a.dct`

or some other combination. The important thing is to be consistent in your naming style.

UNIX allows the use of other characters in file names as well. However, some combinations of special characters can be interpreted by the system to mean something other than a file name. For example, if you try to call a file by the name

`>file1`

the system will not create a file as such. Instead, it would execute a different sequence of events. It would be in your best interest to avoid special characters. Stick to letters of the alphabet, and numbers, if necessary; devise meaningful names; use underscores and periods; and be consistent in your naming style. Here are a few names that should present no problems:

`manhattan.map`   Indicates that the contents of the file have something to do with Manhattan, and a map. This file is probably a map of Manhattan.

`review.91`   Probably contains an employee's review for 1991.

`LogFile`   This could be a file which contains log details of a system.

`7_days_a_week` This file could contain anything that goes on 7 days a week.

Here are a few names that are acceptable to the system, but that we prefer to avoid:

`!@#$%`   Does not convey the probable contents of the file.

`.file`   Starts with a period. This is a file naming convention used by UNIX to name "hidden" files. Hidden files are those which do not display when directory contents are viewed with the `ls` command. The −a option has to be used in conjunction with `ls` to view hidden files. It would be best not to confuse personal files with hidden system files, unless you want the file that is being created to be hidden.

And here are a few names that are definitely a bad idea:

`$file`   Starts with a dollar sign ($). All groups of characters that are preceded by a dollar sign have a special meaning for the shell. Recall from Chapter 1 that the shell is what interprets and executes commands typed at the system prompt. Using this combination as a file name could lead to unexpected results when a command is issued with reference to this file.

`|there`   The | character also has a special meaning for the shell.

`>here`   The > character also has a special meaning.

The asterisk (*), the question mark (?), the square braces ([]) and the backslash (\) are some more characters that are interpreted in a special way by the shell. These will be explained in detail in the next chapter. For now, take our word, just stick to alphanumeric characters, underscores, and periods when naming files.

Bourne Shell Implementation

The rules for naming files created in a Bourne shell environment are the same.

Korn Shell Implementation

The rules for naming files created in a Korn shell environment are the same.

4.3 UNIX FILE NAMING CONVENTIONS

Now that you know what not to name files, let's take a look at some conventions that are adhered to by UNIX when it names its files. It is important that you know these, since UNIX expects you to adhere to its conventions.

C programs are suffixed with a .c. Header files used by C programs are suffixed with a .h. You should follow the same convention in naming C source code and header files.

Compilers produce object code, and these files are suffixed with a .o. You should not suffix any of your files with a .o.

UNIX has various utilities, such as SCCS (Source Code Control System), yacc, and lex. SCCS files all start with an s..

Various SCCS commands produce files that begin with a p., g., x. and z.. You should avoid prefixing non-SCCS files with any of these letters. yacc source code files are suffixed with a .y, and lex source files are suffixed with a .l. You should conform with these conventions as necessary. Most of these utilities will be explained in subsequent chapters.

4.4 CREATING FILES

Files can be created using standard UNIX editors. Editor commands which create and write to a file will be explained in detail in those chapters which are exclusively devoted to these editors. For now, we will use the echo command to create a few files. We will go back to Sally's home directory and create a few files there. Here is the sequence of commands:

```
$ pwd
/REDHOT/sally
$ echo file_1 > file1
```

```
$ echo file_2 > file2
$ man who > file3
```

The commands

```
echo file_1 > file1
```

and

```
echo file_2 > file2
```

simply create one-line files called file1 and file2. The next command may puzzle you. Recall from previous chapters that the man command is used to display the help text for a UNIX command. The who is a command that is used in UNIX to output the name of the current user or users of the system. But instead of the output displaying on the terminal, which is the standard output, we use the > symbol to redirect the output to a file called file3. Therefore, upon successful execution of this command, we will have a file called file3 which will contain the help text for the who command. This is a quick and easy way to create a file whose contents are greater than just the one-liners created for file1 and file2.

OK. So let's take a look at the contents of the directory.

```
$ pwd
/REDHOT/sally
$ ls
file1      file2      file3
```

That's fine. We will take a look at some commands which are used to list the contents of files next.

Bourne Shell Implementation

All examples illustrated in Section 4.4 will produce the same results when run from the Bourne shell.

Korn Shell Implementation

All examples illustrated in Section 4.4 will produce the same results when run from the Korn shell.

4.5 LISTING CONTENTS OF FILES USING CAT COMMAND

The cat command lists the contents of the file name that follows it. Let's try it now:

```
$ cat file1
file_1
$ cat file2
file_2
```

More than one file can be viewed via one command:

```
$ cat file1 file2
file_1
file_2
$
```

The order of the files can be changed:

```
$ cat file2 file1
file_2
file_1
```

which brings us to the reason why an obscure three-letter word called cat is used to list file contents! Cat is really an abbreviation for concatenate, which is precisely what this command does when more than one file name is specified. All files are concatenated and joined end to end, and either displayed to the standard output (this is the default) or copied someplace else. The prior example illustrated the display of the file contents to standard output. The next example concatenates the two files and writes them to another file, using, once again, the > operator:

```
$ cat file1 file2 > file4
$
```

Now the contents of file4 can be displayed using the cat command:

```
$ cat file4
file_1
file_2
$
```

If cat is used to display a nonexistent file, then the following message will display:

```
$ cat resume.doc
cat: resume.doc:  No such file or directory
```

Of course, the same message would display if the file name is misspelled or incorrectly typed:

```
$ cat file_4
cat: file_4:  No such file or directory
```

If the cat command is used to write to a preexisting file, for example file3, like so:

```
$ cat file1 file2 > file3
```

then the system would notify us of this:

```
file3:  File exists.
```

and file3 would not be overwritten.

Now let's do a cat on file3. Recall that file3 was created by redirecting the output for the help text for the who command to it. Try it now.

```
$ cat file3
```

As you can see, the file displayed and went off the screen pretty quickly, too fast for you to know what its contents were! Output can be suspended by hitting <Cntrl> S to suspend the screen, and <Cntrl> Q to resume screen display. Or, you can simplify your life by displaying contents using the more command.

Bourne Shell Implementation

Recall that in the C shell, the command

```
cat file1 file2 > file3
```

results in the message

```
file3: File exists.
```

being displayed. In the Bourne shell, this message would not be displayed, and file3 would be overwritten by the contents of file1 and file2. Aside from this, all examples will produce the same results; the wording of messages can vary.

Korn Shell Implementation

The Korn shell is similar to the Bourne shell with reference to the above command. Aside from this, all examples will produce the same result. The wording of the messages displayed can vary.

4.6 LISTING FILE CONTENTS USING MORE COMMAND

The command more can be used to list file contents. Take a look at the output:

$ **more file3**

```
WHO(1)     USER COMMANDS             WHO(1)


NAME
   who - who is logged in on the system

SYNOPSIS
   who [ who-file ] [ am i ]

DESCRIPTION
   Used without arguments, who lists the login name,
   terminal name, and login time for each current
   user.   who  gets  this  information  from  the
   /etc/utmp file.

   If a filename argument is given, the named file is
   examined  instead  of  /etc/utmp.   Typically the
   named file is /var/adm/wtmp, which contains a
   record of all logins since it was created.   In
   this case, who lists logins, logouts, and crashes.
   Each login is listed with user name, terminal name
   (with  /dev/  suppressed),  and  date  and  time.
   Logouts  produce  a  similar  line  without  a  user
   name.  Reboots produce a line with '~' in place of
   the device name, and a fossil time indicating when
   the system went down.   Finally, the adjacent pair
   of  entries  '|'  and  '}'  indicate  the  system-
   maintained  time  just  before  and  after  the  date
   command changed the system's idea of the time.

   With  two  arguments,  as  in  'who  am  i'  (and  also
   'who is who'), who tells who you are logged in as:
   It displays your hostname, login name, terminal
   name, and login time.
--More--(77%)
```

The `more` command displays the file that follows it one screen at a time. Notice the percentage figure in the bottom left-hand corner of the screen:

```
--More--(77%)
```

This number indicates the percentage of the file that has been displayed. Two options can now be taken. You may view the remaining file one line at a time. In this case, hit the Enter key for each line. Or, you may simply wish to view the next screen. For this, hit the space bar. Notice that the `more` command displays the last line of the previous screen as the first line of the next screen. This is necessary in order to maintain continuity.

Let's see what happens if more than one file name follows the `more` command:

```
$ more file1 file2
:::::::::::::::::
file1
:::::::::::::::::
file_1
:::::::::::::::::
--More--(Next file: file2)
file2
:::::::::::::::::
file_2
```

As you can see, the files are displayed in the sequence in which the file names appear. The name of each file is displayed before its contents. We just happened to `more` two files which are just one-liners. If any of these files exceeded one screen full, then the percentage figure would appear in the bottom left-hand corner of the screen. If you are done viewing the file, and wish to view the next, type q for quit at the time that the `--more--` message displays, and the next file will automatically be displayed.

If we try to `more` a file that does not exist:

```
$ more black_book
black_book:  No such file or directory
```

The response is the same as you would have received if you did a `cat` on a nonexistent file.

Bourne Shell Implementation

The `more` command works in the same way when implemented from the Bourne shell.

Korn Shell Implementation

The more command works in the same way when implemented from the Korn shell.

4.7 LISTING FILE CONTENTS USING TAIL COMMAND

The tail command can be used to display the last part of a file. The default is the last ten lines. This default can be overridden by using the – symbol, followed by a number. Here is its sample usage without any options:

```
$ tail file3
   gwen         ttym0   Apr 27 11:11
   ralph        ttyp1   Apr 27 11:25
   example%

FILES
   /etc/utmp
   /var/adm/wtmp

SEE ALSO
   login(1), w(1), whoami(1), utmp(5V), locale(5)
$
```

If only the last four lines are to be viewed, then type as follows:

```
$ tail -4 file3
```

Then system output follows from the fourth line from the bottom of the file:

```
   /var/adm/wtmp

SEE ALSO
   login(1), w(1), whoami(1), utmp(5V), locale(5)
```

Although tail is intended to view the last part of a file, it can be used to view any portion of the file by using the + sign, followed by a number. This instructs the shell to display the complete file starting from the line number indicated, and to count this line number from the beginning of the file. For example, if file3 is to be viewed from line 12 right through the end, then the following would be typed at the system prompt:

```
$ tail +12 file3
```

and output display would start at this line:

```
who [ who-file ] [am i ]
        .
        .
        .
```

Like cat and more, if the tail command is used to display a nonexistent file, then the system responds accordingly:

```
$ tail product_b.doc
tail: product_b.doc:  No such file or directory
```

Bourne Shell Implementation

All examples in Section 4.7 will produce the same result when implemented from the Bourne shell.

Korn Shell Implementation

All examples in Section 4.7 will produce the same result when implemented from the Korn shell.

4.8 FILES AND RELATIVE AND FULL PATH NAMES

In Chapter 3 we described how directories can be created using either the full or relative path names. Creation and manipulation of files is no different. Files can be created and viewed in directories below the current working directory using the relative path name:

```
$ pwd
/REDHOT/sally
$ echo letter > document/letter.doc
$
```

We use the echo command to create a file called letter.doc. But the name of this file is preceded with the relative path of the location in which this file is to reside. This file is not created in the current working directory, which is /REDHOT/sally. Instead, it is created in the /REDHOT/sally/document directory. It was unnecessary to type the full path name, since our current working directory is sally. Recall from Chapter 3 that relative path names are not preceded with a slash.

Let's take a look:

```
$ pwd
/REDHOT/sally
$ ls
document   file1   file2   file3   file4
$ cd document
$ pwd
/REDHOT/sally/document
$ ls
letter.doc
```

OK. Now let's pretend we are the superuser and create a file in Harry's home directory. This time we will have to use the full path name:

```
$ pwd
/REDHOT/sally/document
$ echo letter2 > /REDHOT/harry/document/letter2.doc
$
```

The display of the system prompt indicates successful execution. Let's take a look. But, instead of changing the working directory from /REDHOT/sally/document to /REDHOT/harry/document, let's see if we can take a shortcut and use the cat command with the full path name:

```
$ pwd
/REDHOT/sally/document
$ cat /REDHOT/harry/document/letter2.doc
letter2
$
```

Sure enough, the cat command can be used to display any existing file anywhere in the UNIX file system from the current location. It's not just the cat command; *All* shell commands can be executed in a like manner. Of course, error messages will be displayed if the full or relative path typed does not exist.

Bourne Shell Implementation

The text presented in Section 4.8 applies equally for commands implemented from a Bourne shell environment.

Korn Shell Implementation

The text presented in Section 4.8 applies equally for commands implemented from the Korn shell.

4.9 RENAMING FILES

Files can be moved from one location to the next using the mv command (short for move). Let's move Sally's file1 to Harry's home directory. We will move back to sally before proceeding:

```
$ cd ..
$ pwd
/REDHOT/sally
$ mv file1 /REDHOT/harry
$ ls /REDHOT/harry
document  file1
$ ls
file2   file3   file4
```

Notice that the name of the destination file is not specified in the first mv command:

```
$ mv file1 /REDHOT/harry
```

When the file name is not specified, then the new file is created with the same name. Also notice that file1 is missing from the current directory. The ls command is used with the full path name to display the contents of Harry's directory.

A file can be moved to another location, and renamed in the process:

```
$ pwd
/REDHOT/sally
$ mv file2 /REDHOT/harry/new_name_file
$
```

The mv command is used to move file2 from the current working directory to /REDHOT/harry. Within this directory, this file is renamed new_name_file. Let's take a look at its contents just to be sure:

```
$ cat /REDHOT/harry/new_name_file
file_2
$
```

A file can also be moved from one name to another; this, in effect, is simply a rename of the current file:

```
$ pwd
/REDHOT/sally
$ ls
document   file3   file4
$ ls document
letter.doc
$ mv document/letter.doc document/letter.sally
$ cat document/letter.sally
letter
$
```

Notice that the mv command is used with the relative path name to move the contents of letter.doc into letter.sally, in the same location. However, it was necessary to specify the path name, since the current working directory is different from the directory in which the command executes. If the path was not specified:

```
$ mv document/letter.sally letter.doc
```

then the file letter.sally would have been moved from the document directory and created in the current working directory under the name of letter.doc. Let's do an ls and find out.

```
$ pwd
/REDHOT/sally
$ ls
document     file3     file4     letter.doc
```

Bourne Shell Implementation

The mv command works in the same way when implemented from a Bourne shell environment.

Korne Shell Implementation

The mv command works in the same way when implemented from the Korn shell.

4.10 COPYING FILES

The cp command is used to copy files from one location to another. All of the features enumerated for the mv command also hold true for the cp command.

Let's assume Sally's directory is back to what it was before the mv commands were issued:

```
$ pwd
/REDHOT/sally
$ ls
document    file3    file4    letter.doc
```

The cp command can be used to copy a file from one location to another:

```
$ cp file3 /REDHOT/harry
$ ls /REDHOT/harry
document    file1    file3    new_name_file
$ ls
document    file3    file4    letter.doc
```

Notice that file3 now exists in Sally's directory as well as Harry's.

A file can be copied to another location, and renamed in the process:

```
$ pwd
/REDHOT/sally
$ cp file4 /REDHOT/harry/file5
$ ls /REDHOT/harry
document    file1    file3    file5    new_name_file
$ ls
document    file3    file4    letter.doc
$ cat file4
file_1    file_2
$ cat /REDHOT/harry/file5
file_1    file_2
```

Notice that the contents of file4 and file5 are exactly the same.

A file can also be copied into another file in the same location:

```
$ pwd
/REDHOT/sally
$ ls
document    file3    file4    letter.doc
$ cp file4 new_file
$ cat file4
file_1
file_2
$ cat new_file
file_1
file_2
```

But you cannot copy something into itself! That is, you cannot copy a file in the same location and call the new file the same name. We don't doubt that you are already aware of this one, but here's sample usage for the skeptics:

```
$ cp file4 file4
cp: file4 and file4 are identical (not copied).
```

If an attempt is made to copy or move a file that does not exist, then the system responds as you would expect it to:

```
$ cp file10 new_file
cp:  file10:  No such file or directory.
$ mv file11 next_file
mv:  file11:  No such file or directory.
```

Bourne Shell Implementation

The cp command works in the same way when implemented from the Bourne shell. The wording of the messages can vary.

Korn Shell Implementation

The cp command works in the same way when implemented from the Korn shell. The wording of the messages can vary.

4.11 PERMISSIONS ON FILES AND DIRECTORIES

In Chapter 3, under the section titled "Listing Contents of Directories," we described how to read the permissions on a file or directory obtained through an ls −l command, which gives a long listing. Let's review.

All files and directories created under UNIX have a set of permissions attached to them. Let's re-create file1 and do a long listing of it in Sally's directory.

```
$ echo Hello > file1
$ ls -l file1
-rw-r--r--  1  sally  6 Feb  11:32    file1
$
```

Breaking up the portion of the output on the left,

```
-rw-r--r--
```

the first entry,

```
-rw-
```

indicates that the owner of the file has read and write permission.
The first dash indicates that the name that follows belongs to a file.
If this first column was a d, then it would mean that the name that
follows is a directory. In subsequent columns, the presence of a
dash indicates the absence of the permission that the column would
contain. The first column always indicates read permission; the
second, write permission; and the third, execute permission. Hence,
the owner of this file, who is Sally, has read and write permission
on this file, but she does not have execute permission.

The owner is the user who initially created the file, regardless
of the way he or she created it. That is, the file could have been
created from scratch, or it could have been copied or moved from an
existing file.

The second entry,

```
r--
```

indicates that the group that the user belongs to has read
permission only for this file. Usually, a logical group of users is
assigned one group name. For example, all personnel assigned to
the project REDHOT may have been assigned to the group called
REDHOT.

The third entry,

```
r--
```

indicates that the remaining users of the system also have read
permission only for that file. The remaining users would consist of
those who use the operating system, but are probably assigned to
different projects, and hence belong to different groups.

In addition to read and write permission, you can also have
execute permission, which is designated by an x. Directories can
also have read, write and execute permission.

Now let's take a moment to understand what these permissions
mean. The interpretation of permissions for files and directories
varies slightly, so we will describe them for both.

Read Permission

Read permission for a file implies that the user can look at the contents of that file. Read permission for a directory indicates that the user can view the contents of that directory, that is, what files it contains. The `ls` command displays the contents. However, a long listing (`ls -l`) of a directory can be executed only if the user also has execute permission on that directory.

Write Permission

Write permission for a file indicates that the user can write to it, that is, edit, change, and/or modifiy its contents.

Write permission for a directory indicates that the user can create new files on it, and remove existing ones. Whether or not existing files within that directory can be written to would depend on the individual permissions for those files.

Execute Permission

Execute permission for a file indicates that the file can be used as a system command that will be interpreted by the shell, and executed in some way. That is, the contents of the file contain one or more system commands that can be executed.

Execute permission on a directory becomes applicable only if the user also has read permission on it. If so, then the user can issue the `cd` command (change directory) to change to it, and copy files that exist there to wherever.

4.12 Changing Permissions on Files and Directories

Permissions can be changed for files and directories, given that the commands are issued by the owner of that file or directory. We will illustrate how permissions can be changed for files only. However, all examples would apply equally if the name being operated on belonged to a directory.

The `chmod` command is used to change the permissions, or mode, of files and directories. Its syntax looks as follows:

```
chmod mode name
```

where `chmod` is the name of the command, `mode` is the specification of permissions, and `name` is one or more file or directory names, each separated by a space, on which the permissions are to apply.

chmod works by specifying permissions in two ways: through the use of numbers, which is called *absolute* mode, and through *symbolic* mode. We will describe absolute mode first.

4.12.1 Absolute Mode

Each permission has a number assigned to it.

Read permission is assigned the number 4
Write permission is assigned the number 2
Execute permission is assigned the number 1
A lack of a permission is designated by a 0.

One number can exist for the owner, one for the group and one for the public. A combined set of permissions is assigned by adding the permission numbers and specifying the relevant numbers in the appropriate order. The following examples will help clarify what has just been said.

Example 1:   A file called file1 is to be designated with read, write, and execute permission for the owner, read and execute permission for the group, and read permission only for the public.

Read permission is designated by a 4, write by a 2, and execute by a 1. Adding these numbers gives us a 7. Hence, read, write, and execute permission for the owner would be designated by a number 7 in the first position. The group is to have read and execute permission; their permissions would be designated by a 4+1, which is 5. The public is to have read permission only; this would be designated by a 4. Hence, the combination set of numbers would be 754. Let's try it now.

```
$ ls -l file1
-rw-r--r--  1   sally    7 Feb  11:32  file1
$ chmod 754 file1
$ ls -l file1
-rwxr-xr--  1   sally    7 Feb  11:32  file1
$
```

Example 2: file1 is now to be designated with read and write permission for the owner, group, and public.

Read permission is designated by a 4, and write by a 2. Hence, read and write permission would be designated by 4+2, which is a 6. The combination set of numbers would be a 666:

```
$ ls -l file1
-rwxr-xr--  1   sally     7 Feb  11:32  file1
$ chmod 666 file1
$ ls -l file1
-rw-rw-rw-  1   sally     7 Feb  11:32  file1
$
```

Example 3: file1 is now to be designated with read and write permission for the owner and no permissions for the group and the public.

Read and write permissions are designated by a 4+2, which is a 6, and lack of any permissions is designated by a zero. Hence, the combination set of numbers would be a 600:

```
$ ls -l file1
-rw-rw-rw-  1   sally     7 Feb  11:32  file1
$ chmod 600 file1
$ ls -l file1
-rw-------  1   sally     7 Feb  11:32  file1
$
```

Example 4: file1 is now to be designated with read, write, and execute permission for the owner, and execute permission only for the group and public.

Read, write, and execute permissions are designated by 4+2+1, which is equal to 7, and execute permission by a 1. Here's the command that implements this combination:

```
$ ls -l file1
-rw-------  1   sally     7 Feb  11:32  file1
$ chmod 711 file1
$ ls -l file1
-rwx--x--x  1   sally     7 Feb  11:32  file1
$
```

4.12.2 Symbolic Mode

Symbolic mode uses the following combinations to specify permissions:

- The letters u, g, o or a to specify who the permission is to apply to.

- The symbols +, − or = to add, remove, or assign permissions.

- The letters r, w, or x, to indicate the permissions themselves.

An explanation of the combinations listed above follows:

```
u  User's permissions
g  Group's permissions
o  Other's permissions
a  All, users, groups, and others
+  Add permission
−  Remove permission
=  Explicitly assign permission
```

We will illustrate the use of these permissions using the same examples as in the previous section.

Example 1:   file1 is to be designated with read, write, and execute permission for the owner, read and execute permission for the group, and read permission only for the public.

All groups are to have read permission. We can specify as such with the following combination:

```
a=r
```

The owner and the group are to have execute permission as well:

```
ug+x
```

The owner is to have write permission as well:

```
u+w
```

The public is to have read permission only, but this has already been specified by a=r (everyone got read permission). We will reset file1 to its original permission set:

```
$ chmod 644 file1
```

Now the combination will be specified:

```
$ ls -l file1
-rw-r--r--   1    sally    7 Feb   11:32   file1
$ chmod a=r,ug+x,u+w file1
$ ls -l file1
-rwxr-xr--   1    sally    7 Feb   11:32   file1
$
```

Notice how we assigned execute permissions to the owner and group with a +x, instead of =x. If we had assigned execute permission to the owner and group like this:

```
ug=x
```

then the read permission previously assigned to them would have been taken away. Here is what would have happened:

```
$ ls -l file1
-rw-r--r--   1    sally    7 Feb   11:32   file1
$ chmod a=r,ug=x,u+w file1
$ ls -l file1
--wx--xr--   1    sally    7 Feb   11:32   file1
```

Notice that the *others* group still has read permission. This makes sense, because their set of permissions is untouched after the first assignment.

Also note that each specification is separated from the next by a comma. Please note that the system would be unable to execute the command if there were spaces embedded between the commas. For example, if you were to use the chmod command like this:

```
$ chmod a=r, ug=x, u+w file1
```

then the system would respond as follows:

```
chmod: can't access u+w: No such file or directory
```

However, when we do a long listing of file1:

```
$ ls -l file1
-r--r--r--   1 sally      6 Feb 11 11:33 file1
```

As you can see, all groups have been assigned read permission. This is because the first part of the command was successfully implemented.

The above set of permissions could also have been achieved with the following combination:

```
$ ls -l file1
-rw-r--r--   1    sally    7 Feb  11:32   file1
$ chmod u+x,g+x file1
$ ls -l file1
-rwxr-xr--   1    sally    7 Feb  11:32   file1
$
```

This combination capitalizes on the current settings of the file, and simply adds permissions as necessary. The user and group are given execute permission in addition to the permissions that they already had: read and write for the user, and read for the group. The "others" segment already has the necessary permission (read), so there is no need to tamper with that setting. Let's continue with the next example.

Example 2:   file1 is now to be designated with read and write permission for the owner, group, and public.

The execute permission is to be taken away from the owner and the group. This would be designated with ug-x. Write permission is to be added to the group and "others" segment. This would be designated by go+w. Here's the complete sequence of commands:

```
$ ls -l file1
-rwxr-xr--   1    sally    7 Feb  11:32   file1
$ chmod ug-x,go+w file1
$ ls -l file1
-rw-rw-rw-   1    sally    7 Feb  11:32   file1
$
```

Example 3:   file1 is now to be designated with read and write permission for the owner, and no permissions for the group and the public.

The owner's permissions are the same; hence they need not be touched. Read and write permissions are to be taken away from the group and others; this would be achieved with go-rw. Here's sample usage:

```
$ ls -l file1
-rw-rw-rw-   1    sally    7 Feb  11:32   file1
$ chmod go-rw file1
$ ls -l file1
-rw-------   1    sally    7 Feb  11:32   file1
```

Example 4:   `file1` is now to be designated with read, write, and execute permission for the owner, and execute permission only for the group and public.

Execute permission is to be added to all. This can be designated by a+x, or simply by +x. You see, if the segment is not specified, then the permission is executed for the owner, the group, and the public; a is the default. We will use the default condition:

```
$ ls -l file1
-rw-------  1    sally    7 Feb  11:32   file1
$ chmod +x file1
$ ls -l file1
-rwx--x--x  1    sally    7 Feb  11:32   file1
$
```

4.12.3 Other Features of chmod

The command chmod can be used to change the permission of more than one file at the same time:

```
$ ls -l file1 file4
-rwx--x--x  1 sally   7 Feb 11:32 file1
-rw-r--r--  1 sally  14 Feb 11:34 file4
$ chmod +x file1 file4
$ ls -l file1 file4
-rwx--x--x  1 sally   7 Feb 11:35 file1
-rwxr-xr-x  1 sally  14 Feb 11:36 file4
$
```

Notice that file1, which already contained the permissions specified in the command, remained untouched.

If chmod is applied to a file that does not exist, then the system complains about it:

```
$ chmod +x file20
chmod: file20: No such file or directory
```

If chmod is applied to a file that you do not own, then the system complaint looks like this:

```
$ chmod +x /REDHOT/harry/document/harry_file
chmod: /REDHOT/harry/document/harry_file: Not owner
```

Notice that a full path name was used to change the permissions on a file that exists in Harry's document directory. But we were unsuccessful because the harry_file was not created under sally.

If chmod is used with a combination that is not valid,

```
$ chmod +k file1
```

or

```
$ chmod 999 file1
```

then the system outputs this error message:

```
chmod:  invalid mode
```

The message is the same if the permission set is not the first argument in the usage:

```
$ chmod file1 999
chmod:  invalid mode
```

Bourne Shell Implementation

All examples will produce the same output when run from the Bourne shell. The wording of the messages can vary.

Korn Shell Implementation

All examples will produce the same output when run from the Korn shell. The wording of the messages can vary.

4.13 REMOVING FILES

Files can be removed with the rm command, followed by one or more file names. Of course, you have to be the owner of the files, or the superuser, in order to remove them. If you are not, then the system will respond with a "Permission Denied" message. Let's remove file1 from Sally's home directory:

```
$ ls -l file1
-rwx--x--x  1   sally   7 Feb  11:32 file1
$ rm file1
$ ls -l file1
file1 not found
```

As you can see, file1 has been removed from the directory. What would happen if the file was write-protected?

```
$ ls -l file4
-r-xr-xr-x 1  sally     Feb 11  11:32 file4
$ rm file4
rm: override protection 555 for file4?
```

Responding with a y for Yes will result in removal of the file. Responding with any other key will result in the file not being removed from the system. The override protection message will always display the current permission set of the file that is being removed.

The system will respond in the same way if an attempt is made to remove a file that belongs to someone else and resides on a directory that you have write permission on. For example, assume that Sally belongs to the same group (REDHOT) as Harry. Suppose that the directory /REDHOT/harry has these permissions:

```
drwxrwxr-x  512  harry  28 Jan  11:00  harry
```

and within this directory exists a file called harry_file

```
-rw-rw-r--  7    harry  29 Jan  10:32  harry_file
```

As you can see, Sally has write permission on Harry's directory, because she belongs to the same group as Harry, and this group has rwx permission. Sally can attempt to remove harry_file as follows:

```
$ rm /REDHOT/harry/harry_file
```

but not before she answers a y to the question

```
rm: override protection 664 for /REDHOT/harry/harry_file?
```

The rm command can be used with the -i option. This will result in the system checking with you before the removal of the file or files:

```
$ ls
document   file3   letter.doc   new_file
$ rm -i file3 new_file
rm: remove file3: y
rm: remove new_file: n
file3: y
$ ls file3 new_file
file3 not found
new_file
$
```

Since the response to new_file was an n, it was not removed.

The −f option can also be used; the system will ask no questions before removing the files.

```
$ ls −l file1 file2 file3
drwxr-xr-x 2   sally 512 Feb 12 11:32 document
-r-xr--r-- 1   sally   7 Feb 12 11:32 letter.doc
-r-xr--r-- 1   sally   7 Feb 12 11:32 new_file
$ rm −f letter.doc new_file
$ ls
document
```

If an attempt is made to remove a directory with the rm command,

```
$ rm document
rm: document is a directory
```

the system informs you of this, and the directory is left untouched. Recall from Chapter 3 that the command used to remove directories is rmdir.

If a nonexistent file name follows the rm command,

```
$ rm black_book
black_book:  No such file or directory
```

then the system responds as above.

The rm command can be used with the −r option. This results in all files and subdirectories (and files in these subdirectories) in the current working directory being removed without any questions being asked by the system. For example, assume Bill is in his working directory:

```
$ pwd
/REDHOT/bill
$
```

Now Bill creates a few files and a subdirectory in his current location:

```
$ echo file1 > file1
$ echo file2 > file2
$ echo two > two
$ mkdir billydee
$ cd billydee


$ pwd
```

```
/REDHOT/bill/billydee
$ echo file3 > file3
$ echo three > three
$ cd ..
$ ls
billydee file1 file2 two
$
```

Issuing the ls command results in the contents of the directory /REDHOT/bill displaying. Now when Bill issues the following command:

```
$ rm -r *
```

the system simply removes all files and subdirectories from the current working directory. Let's issue the ls command to see what happened:

```
$ ls
$
```

As you can see, all files have been removed, along with the subdirectory billydee, and the files in billydee (file3 and three). If the rm command had been issued like this:

```
$ rm -r file*
$
```

then the ls command would display this output:

```
$ ls
billydee two
$
```

As you can see, only those files which matched the criterion specified were removed (files beginning with file and ending with zero or more characters). All files in billydee remain intact.

Bourne Shell Implementation

The rm command works in the same way when implemented from the Bourne shell. The wording of the messages can vary.

Korn Shell Implementation

The rm command works in the same way when implemented from the Korn shell. The wording of the messages can vary.

4.14 REVIEW

This chapter described all kinds of things that you can and cannot do with files. The following issues were discussed in particular:

- What to name files – most systems allow 14 characters as the maximum length.

- Avoid special characters while naming files: >, $, |, <, *, ?, [,], and \.

- Avoid using names that UNIX uses for its special files, e.g., files that begin with a dot (.), s., p., g., x., and z., and files that end with a .o and a .h.

- Conform to UNIX file naming conventions for program source code files, e.g., suffix with .c for C programs, .y for yacc programs, and .l for lex programs.

- How to create files with the echo command.

- How to list their contents with the cat, more, and tail commands.

- How to rename files with the mv command.

- How to copy files with the cp command.

- How to change permissions for files and directories using the chmod command. chmod can be used in absolute (number representation) or symbolic mode.

- How to remove files with the rm command, and the options that can be used with it.

You now know enough to navigate the UNIX file structure, and take a look at the files that come with it. We encourage you to explore a little on your own, before proceeding to the next chapter.

Redirection, Pipes, and Filters

5.1 INTRODUCTION

In this chapter we will describe a very powerful feature of UNIX which allows its users to redirect the input or output of commands which are executed by the shell. We will also describe another related and equally powerful feature which *filters* the output of one command and uses the filtered output as the input to another. In this way, one command is *piped* to the next.

5.2 DEFAULT INPUT AND OUTPUT

In all of the chapters that you have read so far, we have been illustrating the use of commands by displaying what you have to type at the system prompt, and then the output of what was typed. This output was either what the shell would display upon proper execution of the command, or an error message if the shell had reason not to execute the command. As far as the shell is concerned, it receives its input (that is, instructions as to what to do next) from what you type at the terminal. Then, either it executes the command and displays the output to the terminal or it outputs an error message.

In UNIX, the term *standard input* is given to where a program expects to read its input from. The default standard input is the terminal. The term *standard output* is given to where the program's output is to be written. Once again, the default output is the terminal. Error messages are sent to *diagnostic output*. The default for this is also the user terminal.

5.3 REDIRECTING INPUT AND OUTPUT

The UNIX operating system gives you the capability to change the default settings just described. And guess what! You have already implemented commands that changed these default settings.

Do you remember how we used the echo command to create file1 and file2? And also the way we created file3? We redisplay these commands now to refresh your memory:

```
$ echo file_1 > file1
$ echo file_2 > file2
$ man who > file3
$
```

Let's zero in on the first command.

```
$ echo file_1 > file1
$
```

This command created a file called file1. The contents of file1 were viewed using the cat command:

```
$ cat file1
file_1
$
```

OK. Now if you type the command without the > symbol, take a look at what happens:

```
$ echo file_1
file_1
$
```

As you can see, the letters file_1 displayed on your terminal. The echo command is used to display whatever characters follow it to standard output. Generally speaking, standard output is the terminal. In the previous instance, the output file_1 was written to the file name that followed the > sign. Thus, the > symbol was used to redirect the output to someplace other than the standard output. In the second instance, the > symbol was missing; hence the output went to the standard output, which is the terminal.

Now let's take a look at the output of this command:

```
$ man who > file3
$
```

The execution of this command resulted in the help text for the who command being written to `file3`. The `man` command displays the help text for the shell command that follows it. In this instance, the output of the `man` command was once again redirected to a file called `file3`, using the > symbol. Now let's execute this command without redirection:

```
$ man who
```

```
WHO(1)     USER COMMAND     WHO(1)

NAME
    who - who is logged in on the system

SYNOPSIS
    who [ who-file ] [ am i ]

DESCRIPTION
    Used without arguments, who lists the login name,
    terminal name, and login time for each current
    user.  who gets this information from the
    /etc/utmp file.

    If a filename argument is given, the named file is
    examined instead of /etc/utmp.  Typically the
    named file is /var/adm/wtmp, which contains a
    record of all logins since it was created.  In
    this case, who lists logins, logouts, and crashes.
    Each login is listed with user name, terminal name
    (with /dev/ suppressed), and date and time.
    Logouts produce a similar line without a user
    name.  Reboots produce a line with '~' in place of
    the device name, and a fossil time indicating when
    the system went down.  Finally, the adjacent pair
    of entries '|' and '}' indicate the system-
    maintained time just before and after the date
    command changed the system's idea of the time.

    With two arguments, as in 'who am i' (and also
    'who is who'), who tells who you are logged in as:
    It displays your hostname, login name, terminal
    name, and login time.

EXAMPLES
    example% who am i
    example!ralph ttyp0      Apr 27 11:24
--More--(79%)
```

Notice that the text for the who command now displays on the terminal. Also notice that --More-- displays in the left-hand corner. The reason for this is that man automatically *pipes* its output through more. It is not important for you to understand right now what a *pipe* is. What is important is that output was not redirected to a file; instead, it was displayed on the screen.

If you hit the space bar now, the remaining text will be displayed:

```
example%

example% who
mktg     ttym0      Apr 27 11:11
gwen     ttyp0      Apr 27 11:25
ralph    ttyp1      Apr 27 11:30
example%

FILES
   /etc/utmp
   /var/ad/wtmp

SEE ALSO
   login(1),  w(1),  whoami(1),  utmp(5V),  locale(5)

$
```

As you can see, the complete text for the who command displayed on the terminal.

As for the error messages, the diagnostic output, this too can be redirected to someplace other than the terminal. The reason for this could be that you do not want display of error messages interfering with what you are doing at the terminal. More on this (much more) later on in this chapter.

Bourne Shell Implementation

Standard input and output are redirected in the same way in the Bourne shell as in the C shell. All examples illustrated in this section will produce the same result.

Korn Shell Implementation

Standard input and output are redirected in the same way in the Korn shell as in the C and Bourne shells. All examples illustrated in this section will produce the same result.

5.4 REDIRECTING STANDARD OUTPUT

As you have already seen, the > symbol is used to redirect output
from the standard default to someplace else. Consider this symbol
as an arrow, which points to the direction in which output is to be
forwarded. We redisplay its sample usage because we will use this
example to illustrate how this command can and cannot be used.

```
$ echo file_1 > file1
$ cat file1
file_1
$
```

OK. Now let's put a few extra spaces around the > operator.

```
$ echo file_1      >      file1
$ cat file1
file_1
$
```

Extra spaces make no difference to the output. Now let's take
the spaces out.

```
$ echo file_1>file1
$ cat file1
file_1
$
```

Taking the spaces out did not make a difference either.
However, something like this would not work:

```
$ echofile_1>file1
echofile_1:  Command not found.
```

Obviously, the shell is as confused as anyone looking over your
shoulder watching you type would be! The interesting thing to note
is that the shell did not issue the message

```
echofile_1>file1:  Command not found.
```

The reason for this is that as soon as the shell sees the >
symbol, it creates a file whose name is the string of characters that
follows it. This file is created of zero length, that is, nothing is
written to it. All of this happens even before the command that is
to be applied to it is executed. Then, when the shell takes a look at
the incorrect syntax of the command, it outputs the error message.
Let's take a look at the directory to see if a file called file1 exists:

```
$ ls -l file1
-rw-r--r--   1  sally   0 Feb 18 12:54  file1
```

Sure enough, file1 is out there. Notice the zero byte length (to the left of the date). The file has been created, but nothing has been written to it.

Now let's see what happens if the file towards which output is being redirected already exists.

```
$ cat file1
file_1
$ echo This is file 1 > file1
file1: File exists
$
```

If the file already exists, then its contents will not be overwritten by the redirection, and an appropriate message is displayed. So how can we write to this file anyway? Well, some versions of UNIX allow us to use the >> symbol to append to a currently existing file. Keep in mind that most versions will result in the file being overwritten if it exists. Here is its sample usage:

```
$ cat file1
file_1
$ echo This is file1 >> file1
$ cat file1
file_1
This is file1
$
```

That's much better. What would happen if the file that is being appended to does not exist? Let's try it.

```
$ cat black_book
cat:  black_book:  No such file or directory
$ echo this is a black book >> black_book
black_book:  No such file or directory
```

The file is not created. This particular feature can vary with different installations; on some, a file will be created if it does not exist. Try it on yours, and see what happens.

The same features apply to the >> symbol (that is, more or fewer spaces around the symbol do not affect output) as to the > symbol.

Bourne Shell Implementation

All examples illustrated in this section will produce the same results, although the messages can vary with different installations.

Korn Shell Implementation

All examples illustrated in this section will produce the same results, although the messages can vary with different installations.

5.5 REDIRECTING STANDARD INPUT

The < symbol is used to specify that the input to the command that precedes it is to come from the file that follows it. Since what we have just said may seem nothing less than a riddle, here are a few examples that will help you understand what this is all about.

Recall that the cat command displays whatever follows it. So far you have seen the cat command used with an argument, which is the name of the file to be output. Now we will use the cat command with the input redirection symbol. But first, the echo command will be used to create a file called input:

```
$ echo This is an input file > input
$ cat input
This is an input file
$
```

OK. Now let's place the input redirection symbol in front of the cat command and see what happens:

```
$ cat < input
This is an input file
```

As you can see,

```
cat input
```

is exactly the same as

```
cat < input
```

The reason we display the two formats is so that you understand that the cat command concatenates the file names that follow to standard output, or whatever. Although we have been using the file names as arguments to cat, the use of the redirection symbol is a more explicit way of stating the nature of the command. Do keep in mind, though, that cat is never used this way. Subsequent examples will use the cat input syntax instead of cat < input. We now go one step further, and redirect the output of the cat command to another file. Here goes.

```
$ cat input > output
$
```

OK. So nothing displays on the terminal. Let's see what got written to the file that we called output.

```
$ cat output
This is an input file
$
```

Now you should be able to fully understand the sequence of events. The cat command was set to accept its input from a file called input. Then, its output was redirected to another file called output. Since output was written to a file, we once again used the cat command to display its contents.

Bourne Shell Implementation

Standard input can be redirected in the same way in the Bourne shell as in the C shell. All examples produce the same result.

Korn Shell Implementation

Standard input can be redirected in the same way in the Korn shell as in the C and Bourne shells. All examples produce the same result.

5.6 PIPING

Recall from Chapter 4 that we used the more command to view a file that was called file3. The reason for doing so was because this file's contents were longer than could be viewed in one screen. The more command displayed the file one screen at a time, and displayed a percentage figure in the left-hand corner, indicating the amount of file already displayed. In the beginning of the chapter we output the help text for the who command via the man pages. We also mentioned how the man page was automatically piped to the more command. Now we will explicitly *pipe* it to the more command. Type as follows:

$ man who | more

WHO(1)   USER COMMAND   WHO(1)

NAME
  who - who is logged in on the system

SYNOPSIS
  who [who-file] [am i]

DESCRIPTION
  Used without arguments, who lists the login name,
  terminal name, and login time for each current
  user.   who gets this information from the
  /etc/utmp file.

  If a filename argument is given, the named file is
  examined instead of /etc/utmp.   Typically the
  named file is /var/adm/wtmp, which contains a
  record of all logins since it was created.   In
  this case, who lists logins, logouts, and crashes.
  Each login is listed with user name, terminal name
  (with /dev/ suppressed), and date and time.
  Logouts produce a similar line without a user
  name. Reboots produce a line with '~' in place of
  the device name, and a fossil time indicating when
  the system went down. Finally, the adjacent pair
  of entries '|' and '}' indicate the system-
  maintained time just before and after the date
  command changed the system's idea of the time.

  With two arguments, as in 'who am i' (and also
  'who is who'), who tells who you are logged in as:
  It displays your hostname, login name, terminal
  name, and login time.
--More--

Take a moment to think about this. Apparently, the command
man who produced an output, which contained the help text for the
who command. Then, this output was used as the input to the
more command. The final result was the help text for who being
displayed via more. Take another look at the command:

$ man who | more

What you have here is a *pipe – the output for one command is
used as the input for another*. The output of man who is used as
the input to more. The | symbol is used to pipe the commands
together. The string of commands that hook up to each other in
this way are called a *pipeline*. We could have continued the
pipeline, maybe like this:

```
$ man who | more > file3
```

In this case, the help text for the who command is being piped to more, and the output of more is being redirected to a file called file3.

And now, here's an example that illustrates redirection of input and output and the use of a pipeline.

```
$ cat input | grep input
```

Before we proceed any further, let's break up the command and understand what is going on. The shell reads and executes a command from left to right. The first executable command is

```
$ cat input ...
```

The contents of the file input are fed in to the cat command, which simply outputs the characters it reads. Recall the contents of file1:

```
This is an input file
```

Then, this output is fed into the grep utility via the | symbol:

```
$ cat input | grep input
```

You were introduced briefly to grep in Chapter 1. (grep will be explained in detail later on in the book, when we discuss text manipulation.) This command searches for a text pattern in the specified files, and outputs the line containing the text pattern if it finds a match, along with the name of the file containing this line. It outputs nothing if there is no match.

Since grep finds a match on the text string input with the contents of the file, it outputs the line in the file that contains the match. (In our example, there is only one line, but you get the idea!) Here's the commmand displayed again, so you don't have to flip back a page, and the output:

```
$ cat input | grep input
This is an input file
```

Now we will expand this command further and redirect the output of the grep utility to a file called end_result instead of standard output:

```
$ cat input | grep input > end_result
```

Take another look at the last part of the command. Under normal circumstances, if grep were to find a match, it would have output the name of the file and the line with the match to standard output, which would be your terminal. However, we are redirecting output to yet another file called end_result via the > symbol.

Now the result of what grep found (or did not find) can be viewed at our leisure by doing a cat or a more on the file end_result. Let's take a look:

```
$ cat end_result
This is an input file
$
```

Sure enough, grep found a match and wrote its output to the specified file. If grep had not found a match, then a file called end_result would still have been created, but it would have been zero bytes long (that is, contained nothing). The reason for this is that as soon as the shell sees the > symbol, it creates an empty file to hold the results of the command. This feature was described earlier in the chapter. And now you can also understand why we warned you not to use this special character while naming files.

Let's try to pipe an output file that has been created by redirection into grep, and see what happens:

```
$ cat input > output | grep input > end_result
Ambiguous output redirect
```

The shell issues a complaint: this command did not work. The reason for this is that once the output is redirected to a file, it cannot be piped into another command. This is where it ends. You can either pipe standard output to another command, or redirect it to a file. You cannot redirect it to a file and then pipe this file into a utility in the same command. The above command would work if it were broken up as follows:

```
$ cat input > output
$ grep input output > end_result
$
```

Notice that this time the name of the file output is to the right of grep; it is now an argument to the grep utility. input, once again, is the text pattern that is to be matched, and the results written to end_result.

It should now be apparent to you that pipes offer quite a few possibilities within the UNIX system.

Bourne Shell Implementation

Pipes work in the same way in the Bourne shell as they do in the C shell. All examples will produce similar results, with one important exception. The redirection symbol > may overwrite an existing file of the same name, instead of issuing a message stating that the file already exists, as in the C shell. But this feature is a product not of the shell environment, but of the setting of an *environment variable* called `noclobber`. Please note that this variable can also be set in the C shell; it is not specific to the Bourne or Korn shells. We will not delve any further into this feature right now (this will be discussed in detail in Chapter 12, "The Shell Environment," later on in the book). If you are working in the Bourne shell, use the redirection symbol with caution. It is possible that it may overwrite an existing file of the same name. Check with your systems administrator for the particular setting at your installation.

Korn Shell Implementation

Pipes work in the same way in the Korn shell as they do in the C and Bourne shells. However, the setting of the environment variable `noclobber` will determine whether the > symbol can be used to overwrite existing files. Check with your systems administrator for further details with reference to the settings at your installation.

5.7 FILTERS

Our example above was specifically designed to be as elementary as possible, so that you could understand how redirection and pipes work, rather than getting bogged down in other kinds of details. In a real life situation, `grep` would in all likelihood be applied to large files, which could possibly contain thousands of lines of data. Since the output of the `grep` command is being saved to another file, its results are saved to be reviewed on an as-needed basis.

UNIX contains another useful utility called `sort`. (`sort` will be explained in detail in the chapters dealing with text manipulation.) As expected, this utility sorts and outputs its input as specified. We will now extend the pipeline and sort the output before it is written to `end_result`. But before we proceed to do so, we need at least a three-line file that can be sorted. This is how `file1` currently looks:

```
$ cat file1
file_1
This is file1
$
```

We will append one more line to this file. You will understand why in just a minute.

```
$ echo nothing >> file1
$ cat file1
file_1
This is file1
nothing
$
```

OK. Now we have a three-line file. And although it is only three lines long, it is still good enough for illustration purposes. We will feed file1 to the cat command:

```
$ cat file1 ...
```

and feed its output to the grep utility, which will find a match on the text pattern file:

```
$ cat file1 | grep file ...
```

Then, the output of the above command will be fed as input to the grep command. The output of grep will be piped to the sort utility, which will sort it in alphabetical order. This utility can be instructed to sort in reverse alphabetical order by using it with the −r option, and this is the option we will use:

```
$ cat file1 | grep file | sort -r ...
```

The final result will be written to the file called end_result:

```
$ cat file1 | grep file | sort -r > end_result
```

Now we will display the output of each command, before it is redirected or piped to the next. Perhaps we are belaboring the point, but we will take that chance, in the interest of your complete understanding of the subject matter. Trust us, the importance of the pipe and filtering features of UNIX cannot be overemphasized.

```
$ cat file1
file_1
This is file1
nothing
```

```
$ cat file1 | grep file
file_1
This is file1
```

Do you understand now why we appended `nothing` to `file1`? It was done to illustrate the filtering capability of the `grep` command. If you take a look at the output, you will see that `nothing` is missing from it. This line was not picked up because `grep` could not find a match for `file` in it. Let's continue.

```
$ cat file1 | grep file | sort -r
This is file1
file_1
```

Notice that the lines are now displayed in reverse alphabetical order, by virtue of the -r option. Here is the complete command:

```
$ cat file1 | grep file | sort -r > end_result
$
```

and if we were to do a `cat` to `end_result`:

```
$ cat end_result
This is file1
file_1
$
```

it contains the expected output.

The `grep` command acted as a *filter*, weeding out information that you did not need and picking up only relevant data. A filter is a program that reads input one line or character at a time, transforms it as necessary, and then writes the transformed data to standard output. The `sort` utility filters the information further, and uses the output of the `grep` command as its input. The output of the `sort` utility is written to `end_result`. The two filters are hooked up via pipes (|).

But the point that we want to get across is the difference between this command, which uses pipes:

```
$ cat file1 | grep file | sort -r > end_result
$
```

and this set, which achieves the same result without the use of filters:

```
$ cat file1 > temp_file1
$ grep file temp_file1 > temp_file2
$ sort -r temp_file2 > end_result
```

Notice the use of the temporary files called `temp_file1` and `temp_file2` created to hold the results. Therefore, one more command would have to be added to the set above, to remove the temporary files:

```
$ rm temp_file1 temp_file2
$
```

We can continue the pipe constructed in the original example; it need not end there. If the output was not being written to a file, it could have been piped to the printer via the `lpr` command. `lpr` is used to write its input to the printer (`lpr` will be explained in detail later on in the book). Here's how the command would have looked:

```
$ echo < input > output | grep this | sort | lpr
$
```

As you can see, the one-line command is performing quite a few operations which are transparent to its users! Also, piping is faster, since processing starts as soon as there are some data to work with. If there were no piping, then each command would have to be completed before the next one could be implemented. And for those of us who like to type with two fingers, there's much less typing involved; you could consider this the icing on the cake!

The redirection and piping features of UNIX are very powerful tools indeed. Complex operations can be performed via pipelines that filter information and ultimately produce the required result. We will continue to illustrate useful pipelines throughout the remainder of the book. For now, we just want you to understand how they work, and how powerful this feature is.

Bourne Shell Implementation

Filters work in the same way when implemented from the Bourne shell as they do in the C shell. All examples presented in this section will produce the same result when run from this environment.

Korn Shell Implementation

Filters work in the same way when implemented from the Korn shell as they do in the C and Bourne shells. All examples presented in this section will produce the same result.

5.8 REDIRECTION OF ERROR MESSAGES

Earlier on in the chapter we mentioned that the error messages that are displayed to the terminal can also be redirected to a file. The reason for this would be that you do not want to clutter up your screen with them, or you wish to store all messages encountered in a file that can be reviewed at a later date.

When errors are generated, they are normally written to a standard error file, which is by default directed to the terminal screen.

You can redirect error messages to a file by appending the symbol & to the redirection operator, followed by the name of the file that output is being redirected to. Here's sample usage:

```
$ cat black_book >& error_file
$
```

Doing a more to error_file will display its contents:

```
$ more error_file
cat: black_book:  No such file or directory
```

If an attempt is made to rewrite to this file:

```
$ cat resume.doc >& error_file
```

then the message displays to the screen:

```
error_file: File exists.
```

However, this problem can be resolved simply by using the append operator >> followed by the & sign:

```
$ cat resume.doc >>& error_file
$ more error_file
cat: black_book:  No such file or directory
cat: resume.doc:  No such file or directory
```

and we could continue along the same lines:

```
$ lslll >>& error_file
$ more error_file
cat: black_book:  No such file or directory
cat: resume.doc:  No such file or directory
lslll:  Command not found.
$
```

If you want the errors to disappear into infinity (that is, disappear forever), then the standard diagnostic file can be redirected to a file called `null`, which exists on one of the UNIX system directories called `dev`. Here's how this works:

```
$ cat black_book >& /dev/null
```

and no one will ever know all the mistakes you ever made! UNIX provides us with /dev/null. It is a device which is always empty, even when it is written to. And since seeing is believing, let's take a look at it:

```
$ cat /dev/null
$
```

As you can see, there's nothing in that file.

Bourne Shell Implementation

Error messages can be redirected to a file by appending the symbol 2> to the shell command being executed, followed by the name of the file that you would like the error messages written to. The symbol > by itself will not do the job. Here are a few examples that illustrate what has just been said.

```
$ cat black_book
cat:  black_book:  No such file or directory
```

We can redirect this message to a file as follows:

```
$ cat black_book 2> error_file
$
```

As you can see, no error message displays to the terminal. Now let's see if we have a file in the current directory called error_file:

```
$ ls error_file
error_file
$
```

Sure enough, the file is out there. Let's take a look:

```
$ cat error_file
cat:  black_book:  No such file or directory
$
```

You may wonder what significance the number 2 has in redirecting errors. This has to do with *file descriptors*. File descriptors are numbers that are associated with files. The number 2 is the file descriptor for the diagnostic output. The > symbol is the redirection operator. The number 2 instructs the shell that we are interested in redirecting the error messages. Incidentally, while we're on the subject, the number 1 is the file descriptor for standard output. Each time we redirected standard output, we could have preceded the > symbol with the number 1 and achieved exactly the same result. Therefore, the command

```
$ echo file_1 > file1
$
```

produces exactly the same output as the command

```
$ echo file_1 1> file1
$
```

The number 1 is the default case for standard output; hence it does not have to be specified explicitly. The number 0 is the default case for standard input. The command

```
$ cat 0< input
```

is exactly the same as

```
$ cat < input
```

Both commands feed input to the cat command from a file called input.

Korn Shell Implementation

The Korn shell redirects error messages to files similar to the Bourne shell. Please read the prior section for further details.

5.9 DISPLAYING AND SAVING OUTPUT

There may be times when you wish to see the output of a command on the screen, and also have it written to a file. The tee command is used to do this. Here is how it is used:

```
$ cat file1 | tee file_holder
file_1
```

The command above displays the contents of `file_1` to the terminal. It also writes the output to a file called `file_holder`. Let's take a look:

```
$ cat file_holder
file_1
```

Bourne Shell Implementation

The `tee` command works the same way when executed from the Bourne shell as in the C shell. The example illustrated will produce the same result.

Korn Shell Implementation

The `tee` command works the same way when executed from the Korn shell as in the C and Bourne shells.

5.10 REVIEW

In this chapter you got a taste of the power that can be derived from a UNIX operating system. We described some very interesting features, which were:

- UNIX defines three standard files: input, output, and diagnostic. The default settings for all three of these files are the user terminal.

- The default settings of these files can be changed, and input, output, and diagnostic output can be redirected, as necessary.

- Output is redirected via the > symbol:

```
cat file1 > file2
```

The command above redirected the output of the `cat` command, which is the display of `file1`, to `file2` instead of the terminal.

- Input is redirected via the < symbol:

`cat < file1`

The command above redirected the input to the `cat` command to come from a file called `file1`.

- Standard diagnostic output is redirected with the > symbol followed by the & sign in the C shell:

`cat black_book >& error_file`

or the symbol > preceded by the number 2 in the Bourne and Korn shells:

`cat black_book 2> error_file`

Assuming that there is no file called `black_book`, the above command would have written the error message that would normally have displayed on the terminal to the file called `error_file`.

- Pipes can be formed by feeding the output of one command as the input of another:

`man who | lpr`

The command above piped the help text for the `who` command to the line printer.

- A pipeline can be formed by hooking up one or more pipes, and the output of one command can be *filtered* before it is used as input to the next:

`man who | grep example | lpr`

The command above pipes the output of the help text for the `who` command to the `grep` utility. The `grep` utility takes this output as its input and tries to find a match on the text pattern `example`. All lines that contain the text `example` are *filtered* out and fed in as input to the printer.

Output can be redirected to a file, and displayed to the terminal at the same time, using the `tee` command:

`man file1 | tee temp_file`

UNIX Directories and Metacharacters

6.1 INTRODUCTION

In this chapter we will be describing a few more features of UNIX that make it the powerful operating system that it is. But before we go any further, as promised, it's time to take you on a guided tour of the UNIX file system. We think you now know enough about UNIX to understand the contents of the files that are in the directories that come with the system.

6.2 THE UNIX FILE STRUCTURE

The UNIX file structure comes with a set of directories that contain system files. We will start our tour at the *root* of the tree structure, which is a directory called `root` itself.

6.2.1 The root Directory

Starting at the `root` directory, let's do a long listing to see what it contains:

```
$ cd /
$ ls -l
drwxr-xr-x  1 root           7 Oct 15 17:32 bin
drwxr-xr-x  2 bin         6656 Jan 13 00:30 dev
drwxr-xr-x  8 bin         2048 Jan 13 00:30 etc
drwxr-xr-x  3 bin          512 Oct 18 09:52 home
```

```
drwxr-xr-x  1 root       20 Jan 13 00:30 production
drwxr-xr-x  2 root     1092 Jan 17 16:26 tmp
drwxr-xr-x 27 root     1024 Jan 13 00:30 usr
$
```

Now take a few moments to notice a few interesting aspects of what you see.

First, notice that all entries in root are directories. The first letter in the permission set is a d, which indicates this:

```
drwxr-xr-x   ...
```

These directories (except for home and production) are system directories. We will explain the contents of each later on in this chapter.

Second, notice that the owner of these directories is either root or bin. root and bin are two special users that exist in the UNIX system, and are used exclusively to maintain the UNIX file system. The owners of the directories listed can vary with different installations.

Next, notice the permission set for each directory:

```
drwxr-xr-x   ...
```

As you can see, each directory has read, write, and execute permission for the owner. These directories have only read and execute permission for the group and the public. This combination tells us the following:

- Only bin and root can remove the directories that exist under root. This is because only they have write permission for these directories.

- All users can read the files that exist on any of the directories contained therein. This is by virtue of the read permission in their permission set.

- All users can change to any of these directories via the cd command. This is because they have execute permission for these directories. Users can also copy files from these directories to wherever.

Since the directories under root are all system directories, (except for home and production, which were created by our superuser), it makes sense for these directories to have these permissions. Quite a few problems would ensue if an unassuming, inexperienced first-time user (or even an experienced user, for that matter) inadvertently removed one of the system directories or one of the system files that exist in these directories.

6.2.2 The bin Directory

Now let's take a look at the contents of each directory in the sequence in which they are listed under root. We will start with bin.

```
$ pwd
/
$ ls -l bin
-rwxr-xr-x  3 bin        4608 Nov  8  10:06  .
-rwxr-xr-x 27 bin        1024 Jan 13  00:30  ..
      .
-rwxr-xr-x  1 root      90112 Oct 11  1990   awk
-rwxr-xr-x  1 root       3496 Oct 11  1990   cal
      .
-rwxr-xr-x  1 root       8576 Oct 11  1990   cat
      .
-rwxr-xr-x  1 root       5368 Oct 11  1990   chmod
      .
-rwxr-xr-x  1 root       7136 Oct 11  1990   cp
      .
-rwxr-xr-x  1 root       7456 Oct 11  1990   date
      .
-rwxr-xr-x  1 root       3496 Oct 11  1990   cal
      .
-rwxr-xr-x  1 root       2416 Oct 11  1990   echo
      .
-rwxr-xr-x  1 root      65536 Oct 11  1990   lex
      .
-rwxr-xr-x  1 root       3552 Oct 11  1990   who
      .
$
```

Inside bin, make a note of the following:

■ All entries are files, as is indicated by a dash in the first column of the permission set:

    `-rwxr-xr-x`

■ All files are executables, as is indicated by the x, and they can be executed by all users of the system: the owner, the group, and the public.

- The file names should appear familiar to you. These are the names of the commands that you have been using in the previous chapters. The remaining files, represented by a dot, ".", (which we chose not to display, but you can view on your own) are also commands, some of which you will encounter in this book, all of which you will find explained in your UNIX programmer's manual.

bin is short for binary. The bin directory is where most (though not all) binary files or executables for the commands that come with the UNIX system are kept.

6.2.3 The dev Directory

Next, we will do a long listing of the dev directory:

```
$ ls -l dev
-rwxr-xr-x  3 bin         4608 Nov  8  10:06 .
-rwxr-xr-x 27 bin         1024 Jan 13  00:30 ..
   .
   .
-rwxr-xr-x  1 root       90112 Oct 11  1990  MAKEDEV
-rwxr-xr-x  1 root        3496 Oct 11  1990  audio
   .
-rwxr-xr-x  1 root        8576 Oct 11  1990  console
   .
-rwxr-xr-x  1 root        5368 Oct 11  1990  dna0
   .
-rwxr-xr-x  1 root        7136 Oct 11  1990  dni1
   .
-rwxr-xr-x  1 root        7456 Oct 11  1990  dni10
   .
$
```

The contents of this directory will not be familiar to you. This directory contains special files that are used by the input and output devices in your installation.

6.2.4 The etc Directory

A long listing of the etc directory reveals the following:

```
$ ls -l etc
drwxr-sr-x  8 bin         2048 Jan 13  00:30 .
drwxr-xr-x 21 root        1024 Jan 13  00:30 ..
   .
   .
```

```
lrwxr-xr-x   1 root            16 Oct 15 17:32 chown
    .
lrwxr-xr-x   1 root            15 Oct 15 17:32 cron
    .
drwxr-sr-x   2 root           512 Oct 14 16:55 install
    .
-rw-r--r-- 19 root           3131 Dec 19  1990 magic
    .
-rw-rw-rw- 19 root             66 Oct 16 12:12 motd
    .
-rw-r--r--  1 root            523 Nov 15 15:27 passwd
               .
$
```

All in all, this directory contains files and subdirectories that really don't fall into any special category. However, it does have important configuration files. These include the following:

- chown, which is a command that changes the ownership of files.
- passwd, the password file, which contains the encrypted passwords of all users of the system.
- cron, which is a special program that allows programs to be scheduled on any day of the week, and at any time of the day.
- motd, which is the message of the day file.

Other programs also exist. Some of these can be used only by the superuser. In addition to these, this directory contains files that are associated with the architecture of the machine that the UNIX system is running on.

6.2.5 The home Directory

This is a special directory that was created by our superuser for our particular installation. Within home are subdirectories named after each user of the system and owned by that user. Undoubtedly, your installation will have a similar setup. Explore a little, and see if you can find what it is called.

6.2.6 The production Directory

This is another special directory created especially for our installation. This directory contains subdirectories that contain the executables of the applications that are run in the production environment. See if you can locate where your production executables reside. It is possible that you may not be allowed to access this directory. If you do, we suggest that you limit yourself strictly to viewing the contents of this directory only. Don't play around with these files.

6.2.7 The tmp Directory

A long listing of tmp reveals the following:

```
$ ls -l tmp
-rw-------  1 sally    0 Jan 17 09:25 MTc001061
        .
-rw-------  1 sally   61 Jan 17 12:01 MTra01061
-rw-------  1 sally    0 Jan 17 09:25 Text1073.0
        .
-rw-------  1 sally    0 Jan 14 11:04 tty.txt.a00400
-rw-------  1 sally    0 Jan 14 17:04 tty.txt.a00461
        .
$
```

The tmp directory is used by programmers and the system to create temporary files. Notice that there are only files in this directory, and that each file has only 1 link. (The number indicating the number of links follows the permission set of each file.) This makes sense, since there is only one copy of each temporary file created. These scratch files are sometimes created automatically when the user of the system runs certain commands. They are usually cleared each time the system is rebooted, and periodically at other times. You should not store any files that you may need on a permanent basis over here.

6.2.8 The usr Directory

A long listing of the usr directory follows:

```
$ ls -l usr
drwxr-xr-x  3 bin      4608 Nov  8 10:06 bin
        .
drwxr-xr-x 43 bin      2560 Dec 13 1990  include
        .
$
```

The usr directory contains mostly subdirectories, which contain system files. Notice the directory called bin. We mentioned previously that the bin directory under root contains most of the system commands. /usr/bin usually contains the remaining system commands. The include directory contains the header files that can be used in C programs Here's a listing of a few that should ring a bell for those of you who program in C:

```
$ ls -l usr/include
-r--r--r--  1 root       1579 Oct 11 1990 malloc.h
-r--r--r--  1 root       9889 Oct 11 1990 math.h
                .
-r--r--r--  1 bin        1732 Oct 11 1990 stdio.h
                .
$
```

6.3 METACHARACTERS

Now that you have a fair idea of the contents of the system directories, we will describe a powerful feature of UNIX that allows you to work on groups of files and directories whose names match specified patterns. These search patterns can be applied to all commands for which such a search would be logical. For example, the search pattern would make sense if a group of files have to be edited, sorted, copied, moved, printed or listed.

Groups of names can be formed by specifying to the shell the exact pattern that must exist in order for them to be processed. For example, a group can be formed for all files that end with the suffix .doc, or start with the letter P, or contain digits 0 through 9 in them. A group can even be formed for all files, or for none at all. You will understand what we mean as you continue to read this chapter.

The shell finds matches with patterns through the use of the special characters (yes, those same special characters that we advised you not to use in file names). Once the specified pattern is found, it is substituted into the file name, and the command is executed on this file. These special characters are called *metacharacters.*

We will first present a list of these special characters and their meaning. Then numerous examples will be presented which will be illustrate their use.

Special Character	Pattern Matched
*	Match any character string. There is no limit to the length of the string; it can even be of zero length (null).
?	Match only 1 character, in the position in

	which this special character appears.
[range]	Match on any character contained inside the square brackets. A range can be specified by a hyphen in the middle.
[!range]	This particular search pattern is supported by the Bourne shell only, not by the C shell or the Korn shell. A match is found on all characters *except* those enclosed within the square brackets. A range can also be specified, in which case a match will be found on all characters *except* those contained within the range.

The patterns listed above can be combined to form a *combination* pattern, or used by themselves, in the location that you wish to find a match on. We will describe the use of the asterisk first. All commands will be issued to the /etc directory, simply because this directory contains a good combination of files and subdirectories.

6.3.1 Asterisks (*)

The asterisk is used to instruct the shell to match zero or more characters. We will do a search on all files or subdirectories that begin with an a. The searches will be issued from Sally's home directory.

```
$ pwd
/REDHOT/sally
$ ls /etc a*
No match
$
```

This probably isn't what you expected. Maybe you can guess the reason why the shell issued the message No match. We forgot the slash between the /etc directory and the pattern that is being matched:

```
$ ls /etc a*
```

The command issued results in the shell issuing a search on files or directories under root (/) that contain the letters etc, followed by a space, followed by an a, followed by anything. Since it does not find any files or directories that match these criteria, it issues the message. Learning from our mistake, let's reissue the command the way it was intended to be:

```
$ ls /etc/a*
/etc/aliases                    /etc/aliases.pag
/etc/aliases.dir               /etc/arp
/etc/adm:
acct           messages         messages.2        usracct
aculog         messages.0       messages.3
lpd-errs       messages.1       msgbuf
$
```

This time we receive an output. Please note that the files contained on the etc directory in your installation may not be the same as we find in ours. Try this command on your own and see what's out there.

Let's analyze the output. The system lists all files and directories which start with an a and are followed by zero or more characters (matching the wildcard character *), in alphabetical order. Take another look at the first two lines of output:

```
/etc/aliases                    /etc/aliases.pag
/etc/aliases.dir               /etc/arp
```

Notice that the entries are preceded with /etc/. This prefix displays only if a search is issued from a directory other than the one that is being searched. The output display would have been different if the current working directory was /etc. Here's sample output:

```
$ cd /etc
$ ls a*
aliases             aliases.pag
aliases.dir        arp
adm:
acct           messages         messages.2        usracct
aculog         messages.0       messages.3
lpd-errs       messages.1       msgbuf
$
```

Next, take a look at this portion of the output:

```
/etc/adm:
acct           messages         messages.2        usracct
aculog         messages.0       messages.3
lpd-errs       messages.1       msgbuf
```

The files displayed do not all start with an a. What the shell has done is display the contents of a directory whose name matched the pattern (this directory's name is adm). The contents of the directory have nothing to do with the match issued. Don't forget, the pattern was specified for the /etc directory, not /adm.

OK. Now let's find all files that start with anything, but end with an a.

```
$ ls /etc/*a
No match.
$
```

Notice the position of the asterisk.

Now we will find all files and directories that start or end with anything, but have an a somewhere in between:

```
$ ls /etc/*a*
/etc/aliases        /etc/format.dir      /etc/psdatabase
/etc/aliases.dir    /etc/fstab           /etc/pstat
/etc/aliases.pag    /etc/gettytab        /etc/rc.local
/etc/arp            /etc/halt            /etc/sa_msg
/etc/crash          /etc/ld.so/cache     /etc/sa_msg
/etc/defaultdom     /etc/magic           /etc/svdtab
/etc/dumpdates      /etc/mtab            /etc/termcap
/etc/fastboot       /etc/netmasks        /etc/ttytab
/etc/fasthalt       /etc/passwd          /etc/update
/etc/fbtab          /etc/printcap

/etc/adm:
acct       messages        messages.2       usracct
aculog     messages.0      messages.3
aculog     messages.1      msgbuf

/etc/install:
EXCLUDELIST      category.standalone     label.script
OWrelease        default_client_info

/etc/sm.bak:

$
```

This time we got a whole screen full of output. If you skim through the list, you will notice that the files and directories displayed either start with an a, (this would be a match on zero characters in front of the a); or have an a in between (as specified by *a*); and if we had some files that ended with an a, they would have displayed as well (match on zero or more characters after a).

Take a look at the last line of the output:

```
/etc/sm.bak:
$
```

Apparently, sm.bak is a directory, since its name is followed by a colon. Yet no files are displayed for it. Issuing a long listing on sm.bak should help clarify what's going on:

```
$ ls -l sm.bak
total 0
$
```

The message indicates that this directory contains zero files. That is why nothing was displayed for it.

6.3.2 Question Mark (?)

A question mark is used to match one character in the position in which it appears. Here's sample usage. This time all commands will be issued from within the /etc directory.

```
$ cd /etc
$ ls a?b
No match.
$
```

Apparently, there are no three-letter files or directories within /etc that start with an a, contain any character in between, and end with a b. OK. Let's try a different combination:

```
$ ls a?m
acct         messages      messages.2      usracct
aculog       messages.0    messages.3
lpd-errs     messages.1    msgbuf
$
```

Notice that the contents of the adm directory are displayed. This makes sense. The name adm is 3 characters long, starts with an a, and ends with an m, and the position of the d is the wildcard match in the position of the ?.

Since one question mark specifies a match on one wildcard, it follows that two question marks specify a match on two wildcard characters, like so:

```
$ ls a??
arp

adm:
acct         messages      messages.2      usracct
aculog       messages.0    messages.3
lpd-errs     messages.1    msgbuf
```

The system found a match on the file arp and the directory adm. Remember, the position of the question mark determines the position of the wildcard character.

6.3.3 Classes of Characters

Square brackets can be used to enclose a list of one or more characters that a match is to be found on. The characters enclosed within are called a *"character class."* The position of the square brackets indicates the position in which the match is to occur. Let's issue a search for all files that begin with a b or c, and end with anything.

```
$ ls [bc]*
bootparams      crash
$
```

Notice how the character class search pattern (the bc within the square brackets), is combined with the asterisk described earlier:

```
$ ls [bc]*
```

This command instructs the shell to search for any files or directories that start with a b or a c (as indicated by the position of the square brackets and the characters contained within) and end with zero or more characters (as specified by the asterisk). The output displayed meets the criteria specified. The way to read the pattern specified within the brackets is to insert an *or* between each two characters (unless it is a range, which will be described next). Hence, the following command,

```
$ ls [abcdxyz]*
```

would instruct the shell to search for all files that start with an a, b, c, d, x, y, or z; and end with anything else. Here's another example:

```
$ ls a[dr][mp]
arp

adm:
acct        messages      messages.2      usracct
aculog      messages.0    messages.3
lpd-errs    messages.1    msgbug
$
```

The command

```
$ ls a[dr][mp]
```

instructs the shell to find a match on all files or directories that begin with an a, are followed by either a d or an r in the second position, and end with either an m or a p.

As you can see, we are now combining different search patterns and narrowing the specifications as necessary. More on this later in this chapter.

6.3.4 Ranges of Characters

Square brackets are also used to specify ranges. A hyphen is inserted betwen the start and end of the range. We will change to the adm directory and issue a search on all files that start with the string messages and end with any number between 0 and 9:

```
$ cd adm
$ ls messages[0-9]
No match
$
```

Since you have already seen a list of the contents of the adm directory, this message may baffle you a bit. Well, the message that is being issued by the system is not invalid; there are no files that match the criterion specified. The reason the system could not find anything is because we are missing a dot in the search pattern. The command will be reissued accordingly:

```
$ ls messages.[0-9]
messages.0    messages.1    messages.2    messages.3
$
```

That's much better! Let's issue a range using letters of the alphabet:

```
$ ls [a-m]essages.[0-2]
messages.0  messages.1  messages.2
$
```

The search pattern here is to search for files that start with any character between a and m, contain the string essages. in between, and end with any number between 0 and 2.

Upper- or lowercase is significant:

```
$ ls [A-M]essages.[0-2]
No match.
$
```

The system was unable to find a match since the files begin with the small letter m, which does not fall into the range specified by uppercase A through M.

The truth of the matter is that ranges can be specified on any valid ASCII characters. The shell recognizes a range by the order in which the characters specified exist within the ASCII character set. We now present this table so that you get an idea of the kind of ranges that can be specified. Then we will advise you as to the kind of ranges that should be specified. Symbols and their octal equivalents only are presented.

TABLE 6.1 THE ASCII CODE

Octal	Symbol	Octal	Symbol	Octal	Symbol
000	^@	053	+	126	V
001	^A	054	,	127	W
002	^B	055	–	130	X
003	^C	056	.	131	Y
004	^D	057	/	132	Z
005	^E	060	0	133	[
006	^F	061	1	134	\
007	^G	062	2	135	]
010	^H	063	3	136	^
011	^I	064	4	137	
012	^J	065	5	140	`
013	^K	066	6	141	a
014	^L	067	7	142	b
015	^M	070	8	143	c
016	^N	071	9	144	d
017	^O	072	:	145	e
020	^P	073	;	146	f
021	^Q	074	<	147	g
022	^R	075	=	150	h
023	^S	076	>	151	i
024	^T	077	?	152	j
025	^U	100	@	153	k
026	^V	101	A	154	l
027	^W	102	B	155	m
030	^X	103	C	156	n
031	^Y	104	D	157	o
032	^Z	105	E	160	p
033	^[	106	F	161	q
034	^\	107	G	162	r
035	^]	110	H	163	s
036	^^	111	I	164	t

037	^–	112	J	165	u
040	[SP]	113	K	166	v
041	!	114	L	167	w
042	"	115	M	170	x
043	#	116	N	171	y
044	$	117	O	172	z
045	%	120	P	173	{
046	&	121	Q	174	|
047	'	122	R	175	}
050	(	123	S	176	~
051	)	124	T	177	DEL
052	*	125	U		

Read the table from top to bottom, and then continue with the next column. As indicated earlier, a range is recognized by the order in which the characters appear in the ASCII table. Thus, a range can be specified for numbers:

```
$ ls messages.[0-9]
```

or uppercase letters:

```
$ ls [A-Z]essages.0
```

or lowercase letters:

```
$ ls [a-z]essages.0
```

The following range is valid:

```
$ ls [A-z]essages.0
```

The above command would find a match on all files or directories which started with any letter between A and z, [, \,], ^, _, `, or a to z. If you refer to the table, you will see that the special characters in the match list fall within the range specified.

This range is also valid:

```
$ ls file[+-2]
```

A match will be found on all files that contain the string file, and end with a +, , (comma), –, ., /, 0, 1, or 2.

Recall from Chapter 3 that we advised you not to include any special characters in file names, since the shell interprets them to mean something else. Along the same lines, if we try to match a pattern explicitly on one of the special characters, the shell may not execute the command as expected. Consider the following example:

```
$ ls [<->]essages.0
```

Here we are instructing the shell to find a match on all files or directories that begin with any character in the < to > range (these are <, =, and >), and end with essages.0. The shell responds as follows:

```
-: No such file or directory.
```

There are ways around this, which we're not even going to tell you about because it is important that you adhere to the following two rules:

- Do not use special characters when naming files and directories.

- Specify logical ranges only, such as for numbers or lower- and uppercase letters.

If you do not, then you will probably end up receiving mysterious out-of-context messages from the shell, and specifying commands on groups of files that you did not expect would be matched on. The consequences could be quite disturbing if it's a command like rm (remove).

Bourne Shell Implementation

Additionally, the Bourne Shell allows you to specify a set of characters or ranges that the shell should *not* match on. These ranges are specified just as in Section 6.3.4; however, a ! is used to precede the characters. Hence, the following command:

```
$ ls [!f]*
```

would find a match on all files that do not begin with an f. This command:

```
$ ls file[!0-2]
```

would result in a match on all files that begin with the string file and end with any one character except 0, 1, and 2.

Korn Shell Implementation

The Korn shell allows the same range of metacharacters as the C shell. It also supports the ! character to specify a range that must not exist in the search pattern, like the Bourne shell.

6.4 COMBINING SEARCH PATTERNS

The search patterns specified above can be combined to customize the criteria as necessary. Remember, the location in which the pattern exists will be the location in which the search criterion will be applied. Here are some examples and explanations of their output.

Example 1: Find a match on all files that start with the string messages, followed by zero or more characters, followed by any number that falls within the range 0 through 9.

```
$ ls messages*[0-9]
messages.0    messages.1    messages.2    messages.3
$
```

The system matches a dot (.) in the position of the asterisk, and matches the numbers 0, 1, 2, and 3 for the range specified.

Example 2: Find a match on all files that start with any letter, followed by the string essage, followed by any two letters, and end with either the number 0 or the number 3.

```
$ ls ?essage??[03]
messages.0  messages.3
```

The files messages.1 and messages.2 are skipped.

Example 3: Find all hidden files.

```
$ ls .*
.:
acct          messages        messages.2      usracct
aculog        messages.0      messages.3
lpd-errs      messages.1      msgbug
```

```
. . :
adm            lost+found        preserve           yp
crash          net               spool
log            netnews           tmp
$
```

Recall that hidden files within UNIX begin with a dot (.). However, also recall that one dot implies the current directory, and two dots (..) indicate the parent directory. Trying to execute a search on all hidden files as indicated results in the contents of the current directory displaying – these are the files that follow

```
. :
```

and the contents of the parent of the current directory, which is the list that follows

```
. . :
```

Notice that one of the file names for the parent directory is adm, which is your current directory.

Example 4: Find all files.

```
$ ls *
. . . . . . . . . . . . . .
     .
     .
$
```

In the interest of saving space, we will not display the complete output here. It should suffice to state that all files are displayed, except the hidden files. The only way hidden files will display is if they are viewed with an –a option with the ls command, or explicitly, as in Example 3.

You should now have a clear understanding of how to match patterns within the UNIX system. We used the ls command to illustrate pattern searches. However, you may use the pattern-matching capability with any command (where it makes sense to do so). For example, you can copy a bunch of files that match a certain criterion from one directory to another; you can edit, move, and even remove groups of files in a similar fashion. We recommend that you refrain from using the rm command with wildcard characters until you are absolutely sure that you know what you are doing.

6.5 OSF/1 CONSIDERATIONS

OSF/1 adds *character classes* and *equivalence class characters* to its pattern-matching capabilities.

6.5.1 Character Classes

OSF/1 allows matches on *character classes*. Each character class contains a group of characters. A list of the classes supported by OSF/1, and the characters that are included in them, follows:

```
Classes    Characters Included

alpha      All characters in the alphabet
upper      All uppercase alphabets
lower      All lowercase alphabets
digit      All digits
alnum      All alphanumeric characters
space      Spaces
punct      All punctuation characters
graph      All graphical characters
cntrl      All control characters
```

The class to be matched is enclosed within colons and square brackets. Here's sample usage:

```
$ ls messages.[:digit:]
```

The command above finds a match on all files that begin with the string messages. and end with any character included in the digit character class.

6.5.2 Equivalence Character Classes

OSF/1 is an internationalized operating system. What this means is that users in different parts of the world can interact with the system as appropriate to their native language and locale. Locale refers to the geographical location that your system exists in. By changing the locale, the operating system can be made to respond in specific ways which are peculiar to the language and customs of that particular region.

As indicated in this chapter, the ASCII code set is used for pattern matching and range specification. This is the code set for the English language, and the one that is automatically defaulted to. If your locale is America, then you are automatically set up for this environment. However, other languages, such as French, German, and Japanese, have their own code sets, which include non-English characters. People in these countries may wish to match patterns for these characters. For example, a system in France may wish to find a match on all files that contain an a, á, â, or à.

OSF/1 offers this enhanced functionality by allowing you to specify patterns on *"equivalence class characters."* (a, á, â, or à would be considered equivalence class characters.) Pattern matching is specified by enclosing the character to be matched within two = signs, and the square bracket, as usual, encloses the whole thing. Here's sample usage, using the example just mentioned:

```
$ ls [=a=]*
```

The above command would find a match on all files that start with an a, á, â, or à and end with anything. Remember, however, that the specific character set that would be matched would depend on the setting of the locale for that system. Executing this command in a system whose locale is set to American English (the default), you would simply find a match on all files that begin with an a and end with anything.

6.6 REVIEW

In this chapter we took a tour of the UNIX directories, and then described the concept of metacharacters as they exist in the C, Bourne, and Korn shells. We also described the enhanced functionality offered by OSF/1 in pattern matching. Table 6.2 presents a synopsis of the system directories and their generalized contents; Table 6.3 summarizes the pattern specifications discussed.

Table 6.2 UNIX Directories

Directory	Contents
root	Contains remaining system directories. Owners of all directories contained therein are root and bin. Only root and bin can create, write, or remove files from this directory. All other users can view its files and copy them to their own directories.
bin	Contains executables or binary files only. Files are commands executed by the shell.
etc	Contains files and directories that do not fall into any special category. Contains important configuration files.
tmp	Contains temporary files created by system processes and the user. These files are removed periodically, and at boot-up time.
dev	Contains special files used by input and output devices at your installation.
usr	Contains mostly subdirectories which contain system files.

In this chapter we also learned how to issue commands on groups of files using pattern matching. Table 6.3 summarizes the features of the pattern-matching capabilities explained.

Table 6.3 Expressions for Pattern Matching

Pattern	Match Executed
*	Match on zero or more characters, in the position that the asterisk is found.
?	Match on one character only, in the position of the question mark.
[xyz]	Match on any of the characters found within the range specified on either side of hyphen.
[!x]	Bourne and Korn shells only; match on any character, as long as it is not specified in the brackets.
[!x-z]	Bourne and Korn shells only; match on any character, as long as it is not in the range specified in the brackets.

We also learned how to combine different pattern schemes, to come up with the exact match pattern required. Along the way, we advised you to specify logical ranges only!

Finally, we described how OSF/1 allows pattern matching on *character classes*, which are a collection of characters that belong to that class, and *equivalence character classes*.

Character classes are specified as follows:

```
ls messages.[:digit:]
```

where `digit` is a character class for all digits.

Equivalence class characters are significant for those countries whose alphabet includes letters not found in the English language and contains different pronunciations for the same letter, such as the letter a in French.   Equivalence class characters are specified as follows:

```
ls [=a=]*
```

where the shell will match the letters a,   á,   â,   or à.   The particular set of characters matched will depend on what the locale variable is set to, within the operating system.

Background Processing

7.1 Introduction

In Chapter 1 we mentioned that UNIX is a *multitasking* system. What this means is that UNIX can execute several jobs at the same time. We also said that UNIX is a *multiuser* system. What this means is that several users can issue commands at the same time. Combining these two features, we arrive at a *multiuser, multitasking* system. Hence, several users can execute several commands each at the same time. The number of commands that can be executed at the same time is usually limited only by the amount of memory and disk space available on your system. This chapter is devoted to describing the multiprocessing capabilities of UNIX.

7.2 What Is a Process?

When a command executes, or a program runs, or any other task is implemented by the shell, this is called a *process*. Every single command that we issued in the prior chapters, and will be issuing in this and subsequent chapters, is a process.

7.3 Foreground and Background Processes

There are two types of processes: foreground and background. When you type a command at the shell prompt, you have to wait for the shell to come back with a response before you can type another command. This is a *foreground* process. All of the commands that we have executed in the prior chapters were foreground processes. We did not have to wait for very long to obtain a response from the shell.

But what if the command that is to be implemented is expected to take a long time to execute, and you don't have the time (or the patience) to wait for it to finish before issuing the next command? These are the types of commands that it makes sense to run in the background. UNIX allows you to specify the execution of a command in such a way that you don't have to wait for it to finish before issuing the next one. This is called a *background* process.

7.4 EXECUTING A BACKGROUND PROCESS

A background process is executed by suffixing a command with the & sign. This kind of processing makes sense for those commands that take a while to execute. (Background processing also makes sense for those commands that are to be executed at a specific time, or periodically throughout the day. More on this later on in the book.) If a very large file (or several of them) is to be sorted, then the sort program is a good candidate for a command that should be executed in the background. We have a directory called document on our system which contains lots of text files. We will switch to this directory now and then issue the sort command on all files contained therein. Here goes.

```
$ cd /document
$
```

We will write the results to a file called sortedfile:

```
$ sort * > sortedfile &
[1] 2536
$
```

Let's understand the command.

```
sort *
```

sorts all files in the current directory. We use the wildcard character * to specify all cases. Output is redirected via the > symbol to a file called sortedfile:

```
sort * > sortedfile
```

and the shell is instructed to execute the command in the background, by appending an & sign at the end:

```
sort * > sortedfile &
```

The shell responds as follows:

```
[1] 2536
```

[1] is the job number. You need not be too concerned about this number. It displays only if you are working in the Korn or C shell. The next number is worth another look.

```
[1] 2536
```

2536 is the number which is assigned to this process by the shell. It is the *process identification number*, or PID. This number helps you track down this process, check its status, suspend it, restart it, terminate it, or whatever. But what displays after this number is even more important:

```
$
```

Yes, it's the shell prompt. The command is executing, but you don't have to wait for it to end before issuing the next command. The shell is ready and waiting, and it informs you of this by displaying the system prompt right away.

Bourne Shell Implementation

A background process is executed in the same way when run from the Bourne shell. However, this shell does not assign job numbers within brackets, like the C shell. The Bourne shell assigns PID numbers only. For example, scheduling a program in the background in a C or Korn shell results in the following output display:

```
$ sort * > sortedfile &
[1] 2536
$
```

Running the same command in the Bourne shell would result in the following output:

```
$ sort * > sortedfile &
2536
```

For this reason, the `jobs` command (which lists the status of background processes by job numbers) will not run in this shell.

Korn Shell Implementation

A background process is executed in the same way when run from the Korn shell as in the C shell. This shell also assigns job numbers like its C counterpart.

7.5 TRACKING DOWN A BACKGROUND PROCESS WITH PS

The command `ps` is used to list the processes that are currently executing in the system. `ps` stands for process status. It lists both foreground and background processes. Let's issue it now:

```
$ ps
  PID   TT STAT    TIME COMMAND
 2437  p3 IW      0:01 -bin/csh
 2536  p3 S       0:02 sort *.*
 2537  p3 R       0:00 ps
$
```

What displays on the terminal are the processes that have been activated by the current user. There are five components of the output:

`PID`

This is the process identification number.

`TT`

This is the terminal from which the process was started.

`STAT`

This is the current status of the process.

`TIME`

This is the amount of time that the computer has taken so far to execute the processes listed. Do not confuse this with the clock time.

COMMAND

This is the command typed to initiate the process.

And now, let's take another look at the output display:

```
PID  TT STAT    TIME COMMAND
2437 p3 IW      0:01 -bin/csh
2536 p3 S       0:02 sort *.*
2537 p3 R       0:00 ps
```

Notice the following:

- The ps command is a foreground process. We did not follow it with the & sign. sort was executed as a background process. The ps command lists both foreground and background processes.

- When the sort command was initially executed, the number 2536 displayed on the screen. Notice that this is the number which now displays next to the sort command in the list.

- The terminal listed for all three processes is p3. p3 is the designation of your terminal. It was specified as such by your superuser. If you see some other designations in this column, for example:

```
2437  p3 ...
2536  p2 ...
```

it indicates that you have logged on twice, once on terminal p3 and once on p2. The command which is listed next to p3 was issued from p3, and the one that is listed next to p2 was issued from terminal p2. The ps command lists all processes for the current user, regardless of the terminal from which the processes were initiated.

- Three symbols display under STAT. Several values can appear here, but the ones displayed are the more common ones. We will describe these now.

    IW   This indicates that the process is currently idle. (It has been sleeping for more than 20 seconds.) The W indicates that the process has been swapped out of memory, while other processes run.

S   This indicates that the process is sleeping (for less than 20 seconds) while the system is doing something else.

R   This indicates that the process is currently running.

In addition to these, there is another status worth a mention. This is status T. This status indicates that the process has been stopped. More on this later on in the chapter.

You should refer to your Programmer's Reference Manual (or type man ps | lpr to get a hard copy listing for the manual pages for this command) if you wish to find out what other kinds of status can display.

To go back to the example, notice that the ps command has an R for its status. This makes sense, because the ps command is the one that is running right now. The sort command displays with an S. This has to do with how CPU time is allotted to the processes running. It just so happens that at the time the ps command was issued, sort is in a "sleep" state; available resources are being diverted elsewhere. In order for the command to complete, the S would have to change to R.

7.5.1 Commonly Used Options with the ps Command

Some of the more commonly used options with the ps command are described next.

−l   The −l option gives more detailed output. It is a "long" listing. Here's sample usage:

```
$ ps -l
F UID PID PPID CP PRI NI SZ RSS WCHAN ST TT TIM CMND
1 201 246  245  0  15  0 88 188 kerna S  p0 0:01 csh
1 201 332  246 12  53  0 90 264       R  p0 0:09 sor
1 201 334  246 69  42  0 64 508       R  p0 0:00 ps
```

Most of the entries that you see in a long output should concern your system administrator more than you. They have to do with relevant statistics for processes that are running within the system. We will describe some which should interest you. If you require an explanation for all columns listed, refer to the Programmer's Reference Manual for further details.

UID
This is the user id of the owner of the process.

PID
As explained earlier, this is the identification number assigned to the process by the system.

PPID
This is the identification number assigned to the parent of the process. This is an interesting concept. Reference to the example will help you understand what this is. Take a look at the PID of the csh process. It is 246. Now take a look at the PPID of the sort command (it is abbreviated to sor in the example due to shortage of space). Notice that this number is 246. Now look at the PPID of the ps command. It is also 246. This makes sense. The shell is a process, and is assigned an identification number. Within the shell, the sort command is issued. Hence, the shell is the parent process of the sort command. The same is true of the ps command. These commands could not have been implemented unless they are within a shell environment. Now you should be able to understand the PID and PPID numbers.

PRI
This is the priority assigned to the process. The higher this number, the lower the priority assigned to the process within the system. This number cannot be changed by the user of the system. However, the process priority can be controlled somewhat by varying the number that appears in the column that follows it via the nice command. The column is titled NI for NICE. This command will be explained later on in the chapter.

We now describe another option which is commonly used with the ps command, and this is −a:

−a   The −a option provides the status of processes for all users, not just the current user. The −a option can be combined with the −l option to provide a long listing of all processes for all users within the system. Here's sample usage:

```
$ ps −al
F UID PID PPID CP PRI NI SZ RSS WCHAN ST TT TIM CMND
1 201 246  245  0  15  0 88 188 kerna S  p0 0:01 csh
1 201 332  246 12  53  0 90 264       R  p0 0:09 sor
1 201 334  246 69  42  0 64 508       R  p0 0:00 ps
1 203 338  243 70  13  0 45 180       S  p1 0:12 csh
1 203 339  338 60  42  0 90 264       R  p1 0:80 ls
```

Apparently, there is another user on the system who has been assigned the user ID 203, who is working off terminal p1, and who is currently running an ls command.

Bourne Shell Implementation

The ps command works in the same way when implemented from the Bourne shell as from the C shell. All examples will produce the same result.

Korn Shell Implementation

The ps command works in the same way when implemented from the Korn shell as from the Bourne and C shells. All examples will produce the same result.

7.6 THE JOBS COMMAND

Since job numbers are assigned at the time that processes are scheduled in the background, a special command called jobs can be used to display the status of background processes only by job numbers. Here's sample usage:

```
$ jobs
[1]     Running       sort *.* > sortedfile &
$
```

The jobs command can be used with the -l option to display the PID number as well:

```
$ jobs -l
[1]     +2536  Running       sort *.* > sortedfile &
```

Bourne Shell Implementation

The Bourne shell does not support the jobs command.

Korn Shell Implementation

The Korn shell also does not support the jobs command.

7.7 The NICE Command

The `nice` command is used to indicate to the system that the command that follows it is of low priority. The system takes this cue and assigns it a high priority number. Recall from the previous section that a high number in the priority column indicates a low priority for the associated process.

Please note that the `nice` command can be run in the background or foreground. We will run the `sort` command in the foreground to illustrate its sample usage.

While you are reading this section, also keep in mind that the system utilizes other criteria as well to assign numbers in the PRI column. If you run these examples on your system, don't be surprised if there is not too much variation in the PRI column, although you may be varying the NI column significantly.

Let's take another look at the output of a `ps` command used with the `-l` option and refresh our memory with reference to these two columns:

```
$ ps -l
F UID PID PPID CP PRI NI SZ RSS WCHAN ST TT TIM CMND
1 201 246  245  0  15  0 88 188 kerna S p0 0:01 csh
1 201 332  246 12  53  0 90 264       R p0 0:09 sor
1 201 334  246 69  42  0 64 508       R p0 0:00 ps
$
```

Notice the numbers in the PRI and NI columns. The `sort` command has number 53 next to it, and the `ps` command has a 42 next to it. Both of these commands have a zero in the NI (nice) column. Based on these numbers, the `ps` command has a slightly higher priority than the `sort` command (number 42 is less than 53). The highest priority is assigned to the shell (15). This makes sense and is necessary, because anything typed at the shell prompt is executed right away.

We will now use the `nice` command to assign an even lower priority to the `sort` command. Here's sample usage:

```
$ nice sort *.* > sortedfile &
$ ps -l
F UID PID PPID CP PRI NI SZ RSS WCHAN ST TT TIM CMND
1 201 246  245  0  15  0 88 188 kerna S p0 0:01 csh
1 201 332  246 12  82  4 90 264       R p0 0:09 sor
1 201 334  246 69  42  0 64 508       R p0 0:00 ps
$
```

Notice that the priority for the `sort` command is up to 82 (it is lower priority than before) and the value under the column titled NI is up to 4. This is the default value assigned to `nice` when it is not followed by a number.

The number assigned to the NI column can be controlled. The system accordingly varies the number in the PRI column. The command can be given lower priority still by following the `nice` command with a positive number:

```
$ nice +10 sort *.* > sortedfile &
$ ps -l
F UID PID PPID CP PRI NI SZ RSS WCHAN ST TT TIM CMND
1 201 246  245  0  15  0 88 188 kerna S  p0 0:01 csh
1 201 332  246 12  94 10 90 264       R  p0 0:09 sor
1 201 334  246 69  42  0 64 508       R  p0 0:00 ps
```

Notice that the NI column for the `sort` command goes up to 10, and the PRI number is still higher. There is an upper limit on the number that can be used with `nice`. In the C shell, it is the number 19. You can specify numbers higher than this, but `nice` will understand them to be no higher than 19, and display them as such in the NI column.

Conversely, commands can also be given a higher priority level by following the `nice` command with a negative number:

```
$ nice -5 sort *.* > sortedfile &
$ ps -l
F UID PID PPID CP PRI NI SZ RSS WCHAN ST TT TIM CMND
1 201 246  245  0  15  0 88 188 kerna S  p0 0:01 csh
1 201 332  246 12  80  5 90 264       R  p0 0:09 sor
1 201 334  246 69  42  0 64 508       R  p0 0:00 ps
$
```

Notice that the NI column went down to 5, and the PRI level also went down to 80, indicating a relatively higher priority than when this number was 94. For the C shell, the lowest number that can be specified with the `nice` command is −20. The capability to use the `nice` command with −20 usually exists only for the superuser.

Bourne Shell Implementation

The `nice` command works in the same way in the Bourne shell as the C shell. However, the default value assigned to the process which is implemented via the `nice` command in this shell is 10, as opposed to 4 in the C shell.

Korn Shell Implementation

The nice command works in the same way in the Korn as in the Bourne shell. However, the default value assigned to the process implemented via the nice command is the same as in the Bourne shell, the number 10.

7.8 CANCELLING FOREGROUND PROCESSES

Foreground processes can be cancelled by pressing <Cntrl> C. The system responds by redisplaying the system prompt and terminating display of output, if any.

7.9 CANCELLING BACKGROUND PROCESSES

Background processes are cancelled by typing kill followed by the process id number. Obviously, it is necessary for you to know the PID number of the process that you wish to cancel. We will run ps again to refresh our memory for the PID number, issue the kill command, and then take another look at what's going on.

```
$ ps
 PID  TT STAT    TIME COMMAND
2437  p3 IW      0:01 -bin/csh
2536  p3 S       0:20 sort *.*
2537  p3 R       0:00 ps
$ kill 2536
[1]     Terminated  sort *.* > sortedfile
$ ps
 PID  TT STAT    TIME COMMAND
2437  p3 IW      0:01 -bin/csh
2537  p3 R       0:00 ps
$
```

Notice, first, that the shell responds with a message

```
[1]     Terminated  sort *.* > sortedfile
```

and second, that the process number 2536 is missing from the output of the subsequent ps command issued.

Several processes can be killed at the same time simply by specifying the process numbers one after the other, each separated by a space. Here's sample usage:

```
$ ps
 PID   TT STAT    TIME COMMAND
2437   p3 IW      0:01 -bin/csh
2536   p3 S       0:20 sort *.*
2537   p3 R       0:00 ps
$ kill 2536 2537
```

The shell responds as follows:

```
[1]     Terminated    sort *.* > sortedfile
2537: No such process
$
```

Well, the reason why the shell issued the last message was because the ps command was issued in the foreground, and we had to wait for the prompt to reappear before issuing the next command. The ps process has already terminated by the time we issue the kill command. If we had terminated some other background process, then a message similar to the

```
[1]     Terminated    sort *.* > sortedfile
```

would have displayed.

If a parent process has children processes for it, and the parent process is killed, then its related children processes will also eventually be terminated.

It is possible that some processes do not get terminated, even though you have instructed the shell to do so. This has to do with the way the system sends signals to terminate processes. Signals are numbered from 1 through 15. The number 9 can be used to kill even those processes that were clever enough to avoid termination the first time around. For example, if a process with ID number 2300 refuses to die with this command:

```
$ kill 2300
$
```

then you can get rid of it for sure in this way:

```
$ kill -9 2300
[2]     Terminated    sort *.* > sortedfile
$
```

7.10 DISPLAY OF COMPLETION MESSAGE

The C shell responds with a message after the process scheduled is completed. Here's the message that displayed on our terminal:

```
[1]  Done            sort *.* > sortedfile
$
```

This message will display on standard output (unless standard output has been redirected elsewhere). It can display in the middle of the output of some other foreground command that may be implementing at the time. For example, suppose an `ls` command is being implemented at the time that the background process completes. The display could look something like this:

```
file1
file2
   .
   .
file9
[1]  Done            sort *.* > sortedfile
file10
   .
   .
```

Bourne Shell Implementation

Foreground and background processes are cancelled in the same way in the Bourne shell. However, a message is not displayed on the completion of a background process, as it is in the C shell.

Korn Shell Implementation

Background processes are cancelled in the same way in the Korn shell. However, a message is not displayed on the completion of a background process, as it is in the C shell.

7.11 SUSPENDING AND RESUMING PROCESSES

Sometimes, it may be necessary to suspend a foreground or background process which is executing (maybe it is eating up too much system resources at the time, or other tasks have to be given priority over it), and then resume its execution.

We will issue the `sort` command in the foreground, suspend it, reschedule it in the background, and then place it back in the foreground. Processes can be suspended by pressing <Cntrl> Z. Let's try it now:

```
$ sort *.* > sortedfile
<Cntrl> Z
Stopped
$
```

As you can see, the sort command is issued in the foreground (it is not followed by the & sign). After <Cntrl> Z is hit, a message is displayed indicating that the process has been Stopped. Let's do a ps to see what's going on:

```
$ ps
 PID   TT STAT   TIME COMMAND
 246   p0 S       0:01 -bin/csh
 246   p0 T       0:00 sort audit.doc auditjuly.doc
 349   p0 R       0:00 ps
$
```

Notice the T for STAT for the sort command. The T is the designation for a stopped or suspended process. The text that follows the sort command indicates the names of the files that were being sorted when the process was suspended.

The bg command can be used to force a suspended program to execute in the background:

```
$ bg
```

The system responds as follows:

```
[1]  sort *.* > sortedfile &
$
```

Let's do a ps just to be sure:

```
$ ps
 PID   TT STAT   TIME COMMAND
 246   p0 S       0:01 -bin/csh
 348   p0 R       0:00 sort audit.doc auditjuly.doc
 350   p0 R       0:00 ps
$
```

Notice how the status for the sort command has changed from T to R for Running. That's good. OK. Now if there were only some way we could put the sort command back in the foreground. UNIX allows us to do so with the fg command:

```
$ fg
sort *.* > sortedfile
$
```

Notice how the shell responds with the command that was executing in the background, and then displays the system prompt. However, it displays the system prompt only after successful (or unsuccessful) completion of the command. The background process is made to execute in the foreground.

If more than one process is placed in the background, via either the & symbol or the bg command, then fg will bring to the foreground the last command issued this way. (It executes on a last-in-first-out basis.)

Bourne Shell Implementation

Processes are resumed and suspended in the same way in the Bourne shell as in the C shell.

Korn Shell Implementation

Processes are resumed and suspended in the same way in the Korn shell as in the C shell.

7.12 OSF/1 CONSIDERATIONS

OSF/1 supports the C, Bourne, and Korn shells. All examples in this book have been run in a C shell environment. Therefore, everything that has been said will apply equally to commands that are executed in the C, Bourne, and Korn shells in an OSF/1 operating system. All examples will produce the same results.

7.12.1 The ps Command

OSF/1 allows the use of the −p option with the ps command, in addition to those described previously in this chapter. The status of a particular process can be obtained by following the ps command with −p and the process ID. Here's sample usage of the −p option with the sort command, assuming it has the process ID number 2536:

```
$ ps -p 2536
PID    TT STAT    TIME COMMAND
2536   p3 S       0:12 sort *.*
```

7.12.2 The kill Command

OSF/1 allows all processes within the current session to be killed immediately by following the kill command with the number 0, instead of the number -9. This is how the command would be issued:

```
$ kill 0
$
```

7.13 REVIEW

This chapter concentrated on describing one of the most powerful features of the UNIX operating system: background processing. Here's a synopsis of what we learned:

■ A process is a command or program that executes.

■ Processes can run in the foreground. You have to wait for these processes to end before you can issue another command.

■ Processes can be run in the background. You don't have to wait for these processes to end before issuing the next command.

■ Processes can be scheduled in the background by appending the & sign after the command. Here's sample usage:

```
$ sort *.* &
```

■ The ps command is used to keep track of foreground and background processes.

■ The ps command used with the -l option gives a long listing of the process status.

■ The ps command used with the -a option gives a listing of processes for all users in the system, not just the current user.

■ The jobs command can be used to display information for all background processes by job numbers.

■ The nice command is used to specify low-priority tasks. This priority can be subsequently increased or decreased as necessary.

■ Foreground processes can be cancelled by pressing <Cntrl> C.

■ Background processes can be cancelled by typing `kill` followed by the process identification number (PID):

```
$ kill 234
[1]  Terminated  sort *.* > sortedfile
```

■ Foreground processes can be forced into the background via the `bg` command.

■ Background processes can be forced into the foreground via the `fg` command.

■ OSF/1 supports all commands described in this chapter.

■ OSF/1 adds the −p option for the `ps` command, which allows only specific processes to be viewed.

■ OSF/1 allows all processes within the current session to be killed by using the `kill` command with the 0 option.

■ OSF/1 supports the Bourne and Korn shells, in addition to the C shell. The Bourne shell does not assign job numbers to its processes, does not understand the `jobs` command, and does not display a message on termination of a background process.

8

The vi Screen Editor

8.1 INTRODUCTION

You have now been introduced to some of the most commonly used commands within the UNIX system. We have made frequent reference to the *shell* throughout, informing you that the shell responds this way when it executes the commands typed at the terminal, and that way if it cannot execute a command, and so on. Now we are ready to teach you how to program the shell. What this means is that you can write scripts that are read by the shell, and have it execute commands in a certain order, based on criteria that you specify. Shell scripts allow you to customize the system as you wish and create your own tools and utilities. Shell scripts can even be used to create your very own commands within the UNIX system.

Sound exciting? Well, we're pretty excited about writing a few chapters on it! But before you can write a shell script, you have to know how to create a file, and write to it, using one of the editors available within the UNIX system. So, unfortunately, we have to hold off just a little bit more on the shell scripts, and write a chapter on *vi* instead.

vi is one of the most popular editors used within UNIX. Describing each command available in vi is beyond the scope of this book. However, we will describe just enough features of this editor so that you can comfortably create and edit files with it.

8.2 THE VI EDITOR

The `vi` editor is short for *visual*; it is also called the *screen* or *display* editor. When you call up `vi`, everything else on the screen blanks out, and a *window* opens up instead. This window will contain blank lines if the file being edited is new or contains no lines. If the file already has text, then the window will contain the beginning lines of this text. Inside this window, a new file can be created and written to, or an existing one edited. When you exit `vi`, the window closes, and you are placed back at the system prompt.

8.3 CREATING A NEW FILE

A new file is created by typing `vi` followed by the file name:

```
$ vi newfile
```

As you hit the carriage return key at the end of the line, the terminal screen is cleared, and a sequence of other events occurs. If there is an existing file called `newfile`, then it is read into the edit buffer, and displayed in the window. (More on this later on in the book.) If there is no file of this name, then the screen is cleared anyway, and the tilde character is displayed in the furthermost left-hand column. The name of the file displays in the bottom row, and next the message `[New File]`. Here's what the screen looks like:

```
~
~
~
~
~
~
~
~
~
~
"newfile" [New File]
```

If the file already exists, then statistics with reference to the number of lines and characters in the file will display. The message will look like this:

~

~

~

```
"newfile" 1 line, 6 characters
```

8.4 SIZE OF WINDOW

Notice that we have displayed 4 rows for the size of the window (there are 4 tilde characters in the left-hand column) on this page, and 10 on the previous page. This size can vary based on the baud rate (speed of your terminal) and the setting of the *window* option within the system. The `window` option can be set by typing as follows at the system prompt:

```
$ set window=20
```

Pressing the return key will result in the size of the window being set to 20 rows. Usually, the standard window is 24 lines, or the full size of your terminal screen. In a workstation environment, this settting usually reflects the size of the window within which `vi` is invoked. For the sake of simplicity, we are adopting a 10-line window screen.

The width of the window is always the full width of the screen. In our case, the width of the window is the width of the margins of the page.

8.5 EXITING VI

Before getting into details of how to enter text in `vi`, we think it wise to let you know how to exit gracefully out of the editor (that is, you won't need to go to your system administrator and ask him to kill the `vi` process, since you're stuck in "nowhere" land).

There are several ways to exit from `vi`. Two options are listed:

- Save document and exit. Press the Escape Key (ESC) (just to be on the safe side, more on this later), type :wq, and hit the carriage return key. Doing so results in the file being written to disk, the window is closed, and you are returned to the system prompt. By the way, typing :x or ZZ (no colon and no carriage return) achieves the same result.

- Exit without saving the document. Press the ESC key and type :q!. The file is not written to disk, but the window is closed, and you are returned to the system prompt.

8.6 TO ESCAPE OR NOT TO ESCAPE

In the vi editor, you can be in one of two modes: *input* mode or *edit* mode. At the beginning of the session, you are automatically placed in edit mode. What this means is that whatever you type is interpreted not as input to the file being edited, but as a command that is to be executed for that file. If you are in edit mode, then input mode can be invoked in several ways. These will be described in Section 8.7.

When you are in input mode, anything you type is considered as input for that file. Once in input mode, the only way to get to edit mode is to hit ESC (hence, the title of this section: *To Escape or Not to Escape).*

Beginners usually have a hard time understanding the importance of the ESC key when they are learning vi. They type commands in the window and keep hitting the carriage return key, and nothing happens. The reason for this is that they are still in input mode. They have to hit the ESC key to execute the commands. On the other hand, they try to enter text in the file, and the screen either beeps at them or flashes, or both. This is because they are in edit mode, and anything they type is being interpreted as a command. If it is not a valid command (as it probably isn't), then the system beeps or flashes back. If you should experience frustration as a result of either one of the scenarios listed, just press the ESC key or enter input mode.

On some terminals, there is no ESC key. If you happen to be working on one of these, press the ALT key instead, it works the same way. Pressing <Cntrl> – is another combination sequence that equates to the ESC key. On some terminals, the PF11 key (programmable function key 11) is the ESC key. Try this if nothing else works. And if all else fails, check with your system administrator.

8.7 HOW TO INPUT INFORMATION

Perhaps the best way to teach something new is to illustrate its use as it is being taught. We will open up a vi edit session and create a document called mylifestory. Then, we will edit the file created, and do other kinds of neat little things with it. Here goes.

First of all, type as follows at the system prompt:

$ **vi mylifestory**

The system responds as follows:

```
~
~
~
~
~
~
~
~
~
"mylifestory" [New File}
```

We indicate the current position of the cursor by the gray shaded box. Notice that the cursor is placed in the top left-hand corner of the screen. OK. So based on what we said in the prior section, right now we are in edit mode.

Since we have had a rather frustrating day, and this is just another day in our lives, and nobody is willing to listen to how difficult our lives have been in general, we have decided to write a document called mylifestory. The intent of this document is to bare our souls of all the pent-up hostility and frustrations experienced through the course of our everyday lives; consider it a diary, if you will.

Input mode can be entered in a variety of ways, all depending on where you want to start typing the document. If the document is empty, then type o (for open), and a line will be opened under the current cursor position. You can now start typing, and everything you type, until you hit the ESC key, will comprise the contents of the document. Let's try it now.

```
o
▨
~
.
.
```

Notice the o which now appears in the current cursor position. We display this character just so you know where you would be typing it. It will not display on the screen. Also notice that the line immediately below the o does not have a tilde. This implies that the line below the current cursor position is now available for input. As you type and fill up a line, the tilde characters will continue to move down and ultimately off the window. Please note that typing uppercase O will result in the line immediately above the cursor position being opened.

As you type and come to the end of the line, hit the carriage return key. vi is an editor, it is not a word processor; the carriage return key is not invoked automatically. If you do not hit the carriage return key explicitly, then the line will wrap around into the next line. However, this next line is not the second line, it is simply a rather long line which has wrapped around the width of the screen, and now displays in the second line. This does not look very neat, and creates problems when editing. As you read the document that follows, remember that there is an explicit carriage return at the end of each line.

```
Life is so hard.  Every day is the same old grime.
I wake up in the morning, and I'm always late.  It's
always cold and bitter in the winters.  It's alway
hot and disgusting in the summers.  My closthes are
never pressed.  My breakfast is alway s cold.  And
I never get enough sleep anyway.  Every day, its the
same old stuff. ▨
Life is so hard!▨

~
~
~
mylifestory [New file]
```

Reviewing the document reveals quite a few typing mistakes. It's time to go back into edit mode and correct the errors before continuing. We press the ESC key to get out of input mode into edit mode.

Notice that the cursor is currently positioned at the end of the last line. In order to correct the typing mistakes, we need to move the cursor from the current position to different locations within the document. There are several way to move the cursor. We describe these now.

8.8 MOVING THE CURSOR

The cursor can be moved in either one of these ways:

- If your keyboard has the arrow keys (up, down, left, and right), press the arrow that moves the cursor in the required direction. Each time an arrow key is pressed, the cursor will move one character in that direction. Pressing it multiple times (for example, three times) will result in the cursor moving in the specified direction that many times (three times).

  Please note that the arrow keys may not result in the cursor moving as indicated on some UNIX systems. Consult your system administrator if you should have this problem.

- For those who know how to type (and we don't mean the two-finger typists), the h, j, k, and l keys are used to move the cursor. Many vi users consider this to be the easiest way to move around the window, since the movement of the cursor is at the tips of their fingers, literally.

  Pressing the h key moves the cursor one character to the left. This makes sense, because when we type, the index finger of the right hand is positioned on the j key. One key to the left of the j key is the h key. Hence, the h key moves the cursor one character to the left.

  Similarly, pressing the l key moves the cursor one position to the right. This also comes naturally to typists, since the third finger of the right hand is positioned on the l key; it is the rightmost position of the hand on the keyboard.

  Pressing the j key moves the cursor down one line. Pressing the k key moves the cursor up one line.

Please note that the cursor movements listed for the h, j, k, and l keys work as indicated for small letters. Pressing capital J results in the implementation of a completely different command!

Entering uppercase J while in edit mode will result in the end of the current line being joined with the start of the next line. The carriage return between the two lines is deleted, and this can result in jumbled lines that are hard to untangle. Make sure you are aware of the case as you type in vi commands; otherwise some very unexpected events can take place.

OK. It's time to play around with the cursor before proceeding. Here's where we left off in the document:

```
Life is so hard.  Every day is the same old grime.
I wake up in the morning, and I'm always late.  It's
always cold and bitter in the winters.  It's alway
hot and disgusting in the summers.  My closthes are
never pressed.  My breakfast is alway s cold.  And
I never get enough sleep anyway.  Every day, its the
same old stuff.
Life is so hard!

~

~

~

mylifestory [New file]
```

The following mistakes have to be corrected:

closthes is misspelled in the fourth line. The word alway right above it should read always. On the next line, alway s has an extra space in it. On the next line, its should have been entered it's. The cursor is currently positioned right after the end of the last line.

We will illustrate movement of the cursors using the arrow keys. Pressing the ESC key results in the cursor being positioned over the exclamation mark. Pressing the up arrow key four times results in the current cursor being positioned over the i in disgusting. Next, the right arrow key will be pressed 27 times to move the cursor to the right and position it over the s in closthes.

Now if you were to take the time to go the specified number of column positions we indicate, in the text as it appears in the book, you would end up as we specify. This is because the cursor movement in a vi edit session is relative to the word that you are currently positioned at. Your best bet is to sit at the terminal, type the text as we did, and then position the cursor as specified.

Furthermore, in a real life situation, you rarely count the number of times that a key has to be pressed to get to where you're

going; you just press it in the direction of your choice, and continue
to press it until you are at your destination. The next two screens
illustrate the movement of the cursor as indicated.

```
Life is so hard.  Every day is the same old grime.
I wake up in the morning, and I'm always late.  It's
always cold and bitter in the winters.  It's alway
hot and disgusting in the summers.  My closthes are
never pressed.  My breakfast is alway s cold.  And
I never get enough sleep anyway.  Every day, its the
same old stuff.
Life is so hard!
~
~
~
~
mylifestory [New file]
```

```
Life is so hard.  Every day is the same old grime.
I wake up in the morning, and I'm always late.  It's
always cold and bitter in the winters.  It's alway
hot and disgusting in the summers.  My clothes are
never pressed.  My breakfast is alway s cold.  And
I never get enough sleep anyway.  Every day, its the
same old stuff.
Life is so hard!

~
~
~
mylifestory [New file]
```

Before proceeding any further, please make a note of the
following:

- The cursor key movement commands can be preceded by a count
  for the number of times the cursor has to be moved. Hence, the
  same results would have been obtained by typing 4 before the up
  arrow key and 27 before the right arrow key.

- Your screen may be unable to keep up with the speed with which the cursor keys are pressed. It is easy to go up, down, left, or right more than expected if these keys are hit in rapid succession.

- Pressing the left or right cursor key will take you only as far as the length of the line. For example, if the carriage return had not been hit explicitly at the end of each line, then hitting the h key repeatedly would have resulted in the cursor moving right up to the first character of the begining of the document. Conversely, hitting the l key would have placed the cursor at the end of the document. However, since the Return key was pressed, once the end or beginning of a new line is reached, the up or down cursor key has to be pressed to move to the line above or below the current cursor position.

- When the up or down cursor key is pressed, then the relative position of the cursor remains unchanged as much as possible. For example, if the cursor is currently positioned at the end of the line, and the up arrow or k key is pressed, then the cursor will position itself at the end of the line just above. This line may be shorter or longer than the current line. The cursor does not maintain its absolute position within the document. Instead, it maintains its relative position. Take a look at the following three lines and the position of the cursor:

```
I wake up in the morning, and I'm always late. It's
always cold and bitter in the winters.  It's alway
hot and disgusting in the summers.  My clothes are
```

Notice that the cursor is at the end of the line. Now if you press the k or up arrow key, the cursor will be positioned at the end of that line, as follows:

```
I wake up in the morning, and I'm always late. It's
always cold and bitter in the winters.  It's alway
hot and disgusting in the summers.  My clothes are
```

- Pressing the down cursor key repeatedly for a file that spans more than one screen will result in the file scrolling up as many lines as the number of times the cursor key is pressed at the bottom of the original window. For example, if the size of the window is 10 lines, and the down cursor key is pressed three times at the bottom of the window, then the file scrolls up three lines, and the third line of the original window becomes the first line of the new window. The system will beep or flash if you try to position the cursor beyond the last line of the file.

- Pressing the up cursor key for files that span more than one screen has the same result as that listed for the down cursor key, given that there is a portion of the file above the first line of the current window. The system will beep or flash if you try to position the cursor above the first line within the file.

- As you move down the window, the name of the file that was displayed in the bottom left-hand corner of the screen will disappear.

- You can move directly to a specified line by typing : followed by the line number that you wish to go to. For example, typing : 8 will position the cursor at the eighth line of the document being edited.

- You can position the cursor on the first character of the last line in the file by typing : $.

- Typing a dot implies the current line. Elaborating further, if a command is to be executed for a certain range of lines, then typing . followed by a line number (which should be a number less than the current line) followed by the command will result in that command being implemented for that group of lines.

- You can move from one word to the next on the current line by typing w.

8.9 DELETING SINGLE CHARACTERS

OK. Let's get back to mylifestory and edit it. We are already positioned on the word that requires modification. Let's take another look at the file:

```
Life is so hard.  Every day is the same old grime.
I wake up in the morning, and I'm always late.  It's
always cold and bitter in the winters.  It's alway
hot and disgusting in the summers.  My clothes are
never pressed.  My breakfast is alway s cold.  And
I never get enough sleep anyway.  Every day, its the
same old stuff.
Life is so hard!
```

```
~
~
~
mylifestory [New file]
```

A single character can be deleted at the current cursor position by typing the letter x. This results in the remainder of the line to the right of the current cursor moving left by one character. Remember, this is the small x, not uppercase X. Also keep in mind that the x you type at the current cursor position will not display; it will simply perform the specified deletion. We will delete the extraneous s from closthes and then use the j and h keys to position the cursor on the blank space in alway s. Here's how the screen looks now:

```
Life is so hard.  Every day is the same old grime.
I wake up in the morning, and I'm always late.  It's
always cold and bitter in the winters.  It's alway
hot and disgusting in the summers.  My clothes are
never pressed.  My breakfast is always cold.  And
I never get enough sleep anyway.  Every day, its the
same old stuff.
Life is so hard!
~
~
~
~
mylifestory [New file]
```

Typing another x at this position deletes the extra space, and the cursor positions at the s. Before continuing, make a note of the following:

- Prefixing the x with a number, for example 5x, will result in that many characters to the right of the current cursor position (in this case 4) being deleted, along with the character under the cursor.

- Typing x repeatedly results in the line to the right of the cursor position shrinking, until there are no more charcters left to delete for that portion of the line. Thus, an entire line can be deleted by typing x repeatedly. However, you don't have to count the number of characters for that line (and hence, the number of times that x has to be typed), because the system will beep and/or flash when the complete line has been erased.

■ Characters to the left of the current cursor position can be deleted by typing uppercase X. The character under the cursor remains unchanged. Hence, typing X at the first character on a line will result in the system beeping or flashing. Uppercase X can be prefixed with a number (just like the small x), to indicate the number of characters to the left of the current cursor (including the current position) that have to be deleted.

8.10 REINSERTING TEXT

Let's preview the document and see what has to be done next.

```
Life is so hard.  Every day is the same old grime.
I wake up in the morning, and I'm always late.  It's
always cold and bitter in the winters.  It's alway
hot and disgusting in the summers.  My clothes are
never pressed.  My breakfast is alway cold. And
I never get enough sleep anyway.  Every day, its the
same old stuff.
Life is so hard!
~
~
~
~
mylifestory [New file]
```

As you can see, the cursor is now positioned over the s in always. We have to add or append an s after the alway in the line It's alway hot . . .. We have to insert an apostrophe (') in its in the line . . . Every day its the . . ..

Text can be appended to the right of the current cursor position by typing a for append. Text can be inserted to the left of the current cursor position by typing i for insert. We will type k two times (or press the up arrow key twice) to move to the line above, type l (or press the right arrow key twice) to position the cursor over the y in alway, and then type a to append the letter s to the word. Let's do it now.

```
Life is so hard.  Every day is the same old grime.
I wake up in the morning, and I'm always late.  It's
always cold and bitter in the winters.  It's always
hot and disgusting in the summers.  My clothes are
never pressed.  My breakfast is always cold.  And
I never get enough sleep anyway.  Every day, its the
same old stuff.
Life is so hard!
~

~

~

~

mylifestory [New file]
```

Now, the cursor has to be positioned over the s in its so that an apostrophe can be inserted there. But first, we have to get out of input mode. The ESC key is pressed to do so, the j key is pressed thrice to go down three lines, and the h key is pressed repeatedly until the cursor rests on the s in its.

Next, an i is entered to insert text to the left of the current position, the apostrophe is typed, and once again the ESC key is pressed, so that we are now back in edit mode. Here is how the file looks now, and the position of the cursor after the insert:

```
Life is so hard.  Every day is the same old grime.
I wake up in the morning, and I'm always late.  It's
always cold and bitter in the winters.  It's always
hot and disgusting in the summers.  My clothes are
never pressed.  My breakfast is always cold.  And
I never get enough sleep anyway. Every day, it s the
same old stuff.
Life is so hard!

~

~

~

mylifestory [New file]
```

Before proceeding any further, make a note of the following:

- Text can be appended at the end of the line, regardless of the position of the cursor in that line, by typing `A`. For example, if the cursor is positioned like this:

```
Life is so hard!
```

then typing `A` will result in the cursor being positioned as follows:

```
Life is so hard!
```

and you are ready to append to the line:

```
Life is so hard!  And things just don't get better!
```

Don't forget to press the `ESC` key.

- Text can be inserted at the beginning of the line, regardless of the position of the cursor in that line, by typing `I`. In the prior example, the cursor was left positioned at the end of the line:

```
Life is so hard!  And things just don't get better!
```

Entering an `I` will result in the cursor being positioned as follows:

```
ife is so hard!  And things just don't get better!
```

and you are ready to insert My before life:

```
My ife is so hard!  And things just don't get better!
```

8.11 SAVING CURRENT AND OTHER FILES

Let's continue to insert text in `mylifestory`. We have increased the number of lines in the window so that it can contain more text.

```
Life is so hard.  Every day is the same old grime.
I wake up in the morning, and I'm always late.  It's
always cold and bitter in the winters.  It's always
hot and disgusting in the summers.  My clothes are
never pressed.  My breakfast is always cold.  And
I never get enough sleep anyway. Every day, it's the
same old stuff.
Life is so hard!  And things just don't get better.

   Work is boring.  My boss doesn't know what's going
on.  He's too busy manipulating people.  I didn't
get the promotion I was promised two years ago.  I'm
not learning any skills.  My colleagues think I'm
stuck up and over-paid.  I think they're all
over-paid.
mylifestory [New file]
```

OK. If we continue to type, the window will scroll up the number of lines over the size of the window, and the message "mylifestory [New file]" will disappear from the bottom of the screen. Let's continue.

```
Life is so hard!  And things just don't get better.

   Work is boring.  My boss doesn't know what's going
on.  He's too busy manipulating people.  I didn't
get the promotion I was promised two years ago.  I'm
not learning any skills.  My colleagues think I'm
stuck up and over-paid.  I think they're all
over-paid.
   Sometimes I wonder why I'm doing this.  And you
know what?
```

Notice how the file scrolled up. Let's wrap up mylifestory.

Life is so hard! And things just don't get better.

   Work is boring. My boss doesn't know what's going
on. He's too busy manipulating people.   I didn't
get the promotion I was promised two years ago.   I'm
not learning any skills. My colleagues think I'm
stuck up and over-paid.   I think they're all
over-paid.
   Sometimes I wonder why I'm doing this. And you
know what?
I'm still wondering!! It's not worth it. Where did
I go wrong???
Will it get ever get better?

The current file can be saved and written to disk by first
pressing the ESC key and then typing :w. The system responds as
follows:

```
"mylifestory" [Newfile] 20 lines 798 characters
```

   Notice that the system responds with the name of the file that
is being written to and statistics for the total number of lines and
characters written to that file.
   On reviewing the document, the whole piece reads more like a
mysobstory than mylifestory.   A duplicate file called
mysobstory can be created and written while editing the current
one with the command :w followed by the name of the other file.
In our example, we would type :w mysobstory. The system will
respond with file statistics for the file called mysobstory, just as
it did for the current file.   The edit session for mylifestory
continues to be open. Before proceeding any further, the following
related features should be noted:

- If the other file that is being written to already exists, then it
  will not be overwritten unless you type :w! mysobstory. An
  exclamation mark after the :w specifies to overwrite any
  existing file of the same name, if it exists.

- Portions of files (as opposed to the whole file) can also be saved
  to disk. Simply position the cursor on the line which is to be the
  first line of the new file, and type :#. This will give you the
  current line number for that file.   Assume that this is line
  number 13. Then, position the cursor on the line in the current
  file which is to be the last line of the new file, and type :#

again. This will display the line number again. Assume that this is line number 58. Now type as follows:

`:13, 58 w! newfile`

and hit carriage return. Lines 13 through 58 of the current file will be written to another file called `newfile`.

8.12 DELETING LINES

One line can be deleted by positioning the cursor anywhere on the line to be deleted, and typing dd. A group of lines can be deleted by following d with a number, specifying the number of lines to be deleted minus 1. And the carriage return key has to be hit as well. For example, typing d5 will result in six lines being deleted, including the one that the cursor is currently positioned on. Similarly, you can type dd prefixed with a number, to delete that number of lines. For example, 6 lines can be deleted from the current cursor position by typing 6dd.

In the interest of diplomacy, it would be best to delete the lines in mylifestory that deal with the boss. Let's position the cursor somewhere on the first line to be deleted, as indicated:

```
Life is so hard!  And things just don't get  better.

    Work is boring.  My boss doesn't know what's going
on.  He's too busy manipulating people.  I didn't
get the promotion I was promised two years ago.  I'm
not learning any skills.  My colleagues think I'm
stuck up and over-paid.  I think they're all
over-paid.
    Sometimes I wonder why I'm doing this?  And you
know what?
I'm still wondering!!  It's not worth it.  Where did
I go wrong???
Will it get ever get any better?
```

Type d6 and hit the <Return> key. Here's the result:

```
Life is so hard!  And things just don't get better.

know what?
I'm still wondering!!  It's not worth it.  Where did
I go wrong???
Will it get ever get any better?
7 lines deleted.
```

Notice how the system responds at the bottom of the screen.

8.13 Undoing Commands

If you take another look at the last window, you will realize that one line too many was deleted because we forgot to subtract one. Only six lines should have been deleted, instead of seven. At times like these, the vi editor offers the very useful (occasionally a life saver, we may add!) command which undoes the command last executed. This command is implemented by typing u. Doing so will result in the system responding with the message.

```
7 more lines
```

and the last command issued is undone – in this case, the lines deleted are reinserted into their old location.

8.14 Replacing Text

Existing text can be replaced (that is, typed over) by pressing the R key in the position from which the replacement is to take place. Pressing the ESC key gets you out of replace mode. Please note that you can replace the contents of the current line only. If you get to the end of the line, then you may press the Return key and continue to type. This will result in a new line being inserted between the current line and the next line. If the next line is to be replaced, then the ESC key will have to be pressed at the current line, the cursor positioned on the next line, and the R key hit again.

One character can be replaced at the current cursor position by typing r followed by the substitute character.

8.15 SEARCHING FOR PATTERNS

String patterns can be searched for from the current cursor position to the end of the file by typing a slash followed by the search pattern. For example, if all occurrences of the string My have to be searched for, then type /My. As usual, make sure you hit the ESC key first. The string will be matched exactly as it is typed.

The cursor will position itself on the M for the first occurrence of this string, if it exists. If there is no match, then vi will display a message indicating this.

```
Pattern not found
```

8.16 SUBSTITUTING PATTERNS

You can use vi to make changes to the complete file, or just a portion of it, by specifying the lines within the current file that are to be searched, the pattern to be substituted, and the substitute string. An example will clarify this. Suppose all references to My are to be changed to Our within the current file. The substitution would be implemented by typing as follows:

```
1,$ s/My/Our/g
```

1,$ specifies that the substitution pattern is to be implemented from the first line of the file right to the last line (recall that the dollar sign is used to indicate the last line of the file). s instructs vi to substitute. A slash follows the s. This slash must precede the pattern to be matched. My is the pattern. This pattern will be matched exactly as it is typed. Another slash follows the pattern, and the substitution string follows this slash. Another slash wraps things up. The g indicates that the change is global. If there is more than one match on one line, than the substitution will be made for all occurrences on that line. If the g did not follow, then the substitution would have taken place only for the first match within the line.

8.17 COPYING TEXT

In order to copy text from one location to another, the line numbers of the range of text to be copied and the line number of the location that it has to be copied to have to be ascertained. You can do so simply by typing # at any position within the required line numbers. Suppose lines 2 through 4 are to be copied after line 8. Here's how the `copy` command would be typed:

```
:2,4 co 8
```

Lines 2 and 4 will be included in the `copy` command.

8.18 MOVING TEXT

The `move` command is similar in syntax to the `copy` command. The difference is that the lines are deleted in the original location, and reinserted in the new location. Here's how the `move` command would be specified for the example illustrated in Section 8.17:

```
:2,4 mo 8
```

8.19 MERGING OTHER FILES

Often there is a need to merge an existing file into the current file. You can do so by positioning the cursor in the location in the file where the file is to be merged, and typing `:r` followed by the name of the file.

8.20 EXECUTING SYSTEM COMMANDS FROM WITHIN VI

UNIX commands can be executed from within a `vi` edit session by typing `:!` followed by the command exactly as you would type it at the system prompt. For example, you may wish to get a hard copy of the document you are editing without getting out of the edit session. The UNIX command `lpr` followed by the name of the file results in that file being printed to the printer. We can get a hard copy of `mylifestory` by typing as follows:

```
!lpr mylifestory
```

Bourne Shell Implementation

vi works in the same way if invoked from within the Bourne shell.

Korn Shell Implementation

vi works in the same way if invoked from within the Korn shell.

8.21 OSF/1 CONSIDERATIONS

vi works in the same way when it is invoked from within the OSF/1 operating system.

8.22 REVIEW

You now know enough about vi to create and write files. Table 8.1 briefly describes the notation and function of vi commands.

Table 8.1 vi Commands

Command	Syntax	Description
Create file	vi file1	Create file1.
Exit vi	:wq	Write file and quit.
	:q! :x ZZ	Exit without saving.
Input information	o	Open line for input below current cursor position.
	a	Append text to the right of the current cursor position.
	i	Insert text to the left of the current cursor position.
	O	Open line above current cursor position.
	A	Append text at end of line.
	I	Append text at beginning of line.
Position on lines	Left, right, up, down arrow keys.	Move cursor one position to the left, right, above, or below current position.
	Press h, j, k, or l keys.	Move cursor one position to the left, below, above, or to the right of current position.
		Either of the above commands can be preceded by a number to move the cursor that number of times.
	:n	Move to line n, where n is a number.
	:$	Move to last line in file.
	.	Implies current line.
	w	Move to next word in current line.

Table 8.1 vi Commands (Contd)

Command	Syntax	Description
Save current file to another	:w anotherfile	Write current file to anotherfile, given that anotherfile does not exist.
	:w! newfile2	Overwrite current file to newfile2.
	:m,n w newfile3	Write lines m through n of current file to newfile3.
Deleting characters	x	Delete character to right of cursor position.
	nx	Delete n - 1 characters.
	X	Delete character to left of cursor position.
Deleting lines	dd	Delete line at current cursor position.
	dn	Delete n - 1 lines at current cursor position (including current line).
Undoing commands	u	Undo the last command issued.
Replacing text	R<new text>ESC	Replace text starting from R and continuing until ESC is hit.
	rc	Replace only one character at current cursor position (c is character replaced).
Searching for patterns	/pattern	Position cursor at the next occurrence of pattern.
Substituting patterns	s/old/new	Substitute new pattern for old at current line.
	m,n s/old/new	Substitute all occurrences of new pattern for old from line m to n.

Table 8.1 vi Commands (Contd)

Command	Syntax	Description
Copy text	:m,n co y	Copy lines m through n to after line number y.
Move text	:m,n mo y	Move lines m through n to after line number y.
Implement system command from within vi	:!command	Implement UNIX or user-specified command from within the vi session.

Programming the Shell

An Overview of the Shell

9.1 INTRODUCTION

This chapter presents an overview of the all too familiar program that we have been making reference to throughout Part 1 of the book: *the shell*. As you read through the chapters, you must have noticed how we pointed out the differences in the output of commands (if any) when run from the *C* shell, *Bourne* shell and *Korn* shell. The next four chapters will describe in detail the features of each of these three shells, but this chapter will describe those features which are common to all of them. As you read through these chapters, keep in mind that all examples are initially run from the C shell. Then, Bourne and Korn shell variations are presented.

9.2 WHAT IS THE SHELL?

The *shell* is a program that interprets whatever you type at the terminal, and responds accordingly. A response to a valid command would be the execution of that command. A response to an invalid command would be an error message. The shell is the user interface to the operating system.

9.3 What Is the Kernel?

Before we go into details of how the shell works, it is important for you to understand how the UNIX operating system is configured. A detailed description is beyond the scope of this book; we will present only the fundamentals.

The heart of the UNIX operating system is the *kernel*. As you are already aware, there are many different versions of UNIX available. What you perhaps did not know was that these versions exist because of differences in the way the kernel is configured. As a matter of fact, it is the efficiency of the configuration of the kernel that determines the overall efficiency of that particular version of the operating system.

Libraries, utilities, and programs are not stored in the kernel, they are stored on disk. This implies that the shell also resides on disk, since, after all, it is only another program. The kernel, however, contains the operating system itself. You type a command at the terminal, a program called the shell interprets what you typed, and the kernel executes it. Let's elaborate on this further.

When you log into the system, a file is executed which sets your default shell. That is, you are automatically placed into a shell which your system administrator has designated as the one which will be your interface to the UNIX system. Thus, after you log in successfully, the shell starts up and is loaded into memory, and a prompt is displayed at the terminal. As indicated in Chapter 2, this could be the dollar sign prompt ($), the percent (%), or anything else that your system administrator (or the vendor of the operating system running at your installation) may have chosen to display.

After the prompt is displayed, the shell waits for you to type something at the terminal. As you hit the carriage return key, the shell reads whatever was typed, and then instructs the kernel to execute it. It searches for the program (that is, the command typed) on disk. If this command is found, it is loaded into memory, and executed. At this point in time, this program becomes a process. As the process executes, the shell goes to sleep (unless the program was instructed to execute in the background by using the & sign). Once the program is done, the shell wakes up again and waits for the next command to be typed.

9.4 Determining Your Shell

You can determine your current shell (call it the working shell, if you will) by typing as follows:

```
$ echo $SHELL
```

Although there are many types of shells available, our book narrows in on the three which are being made available in OSF/1 operating systems. The responses for each shell follow.

If you are running a C shell, the system will respond like this:

```
/bin/csh
```

If you are running a Bourne shell, the system responds:

```
/bin/sh
```

and it outputs

```
/bin/ksh
```

if you are running a Korn shell.

The C shell and the Bourne shell are standard and universally available with all UNIX operating systems (we haven't found one which does not have these two). A special license has to be obtained from AT&T in order to obtain the Korn shell.

In addition to this, a restricted version of the Bourne shell called the *restricted Bourne shell* can also be run on the OSF/1 operating system. Please refer to the section titled "OSF/1 Considerations" for further details.

9.5 CHANGING YOUR SHELL

Depending on the security features of your current installation, you may or may not be able to change to the shell of your choice. Check with your system administrator if you have any problems. If you do have access, then all that has to be done to change the working shell is to type as follows:

```
$/bin/csh
```

The command above switches you to the C shell. The following commands are used to switch to the other three shells:

```
$/bin/sh
$/bin/rsh
$/bin/ksh
```

As you switch between shells, you may notice that the system prompt changes. On our installation, the C shell prompt is customized to reflect the current working directory. The Bourne shell prompt is the dollar sign ($), and the Korn shell prompt is the number sign (#). The rsh is called the restricted shell; it is a specialized version of the Bourne shell. At your installation these prompts may be different. After you change the shell, and then issue the command

```
$ echo $SHELL
```

the system will still respond with the old setting. This has to do with the value stored in the variable SHELL. This concept will be explained in the next section.

Although you can switch shells as indicated, the switch will be temporary. If you log off the system and then log back in, you will be placed back into the default shell. The default shell can be changed permanently using the chsh command. Here's sample usage:

```
$ chsh
Changing login shell for Sally.
Old shell: /bin/csh
New shell: /bin/ksh
#
```

The above sequence of commands changes the default C shell to the Korn shell. Notice the number sign system prompt on the next line after the chsh command is executed.

If your default shell is the restricted Bourne shell, then you cannot change it to anything else.

9.6 FEATURES COMMON TO ALL SHELLS

All shells have the capability to:

- Store values in variables.

- Execute command files.

- Accept arguments to command files.

- Understand multiple commands typed in sequence.

- Formulate pipes and filters.

■ Assign literal meaning to special characters using single and double quotes and the backslash character.

■ Provide control structures for decision making, like other programming languages.

We now elaborate on all of these features except the last. Control structures will be described in detail in the next chapter.

9.7 STORE VALUES IN VARIABLES

Recall from the beginning of the chapter how the current working shell is displayed:

```
$ echo $SHELL
/bin/csh
$
```

We now delve deeper into the syntax $SHELL. The characters SHELL identify the name which is given to an environment variable that is specified for all users of the UNIX system. Environment variables are, as the name implies, variables that set up the environment in which you will be working. These variables are preset by the vendor that the system has been purchased from, and they can be reset by you, or by your system administrator. Environment (and shell) variables will be described in detail in the next chapter. For now, it is enough for you to understand that variables can be created, assigned values, and then used in shell scripts.

To go back to the command typed above, the five characters SHELL are assigned the path of the shell in which you will be working. Variables are not limited to those which specify the environment; they can be anything. Variables in the shell environment are assigned as they would be for any programming language, via the assignment operator =. Here's how the SHELL variable was assigned:

```
$ set SHELL=/bin/csh
$
```

Please note that spaces on either side of the assignment operator are not allowed. Here's what happens if you use them:

```
$ SHELL = /bin/csh
SHELL: not found
```

You can assign a value to a variable called maximum as follows:

```
$ set maximum=20
$
```

Variables that have been set can be referenced in subsequent commands by prefixing the variable name with a dollar sign and echoing them:

```
$ echo $maximum
20
$
```

Now you should be able to understand why typing $SHELL resulted in your current working shell being displayed.

Variables' names assigned within the shell must start with an alphabetic character or an underscore. The maximum length that can be assigned to a variable name has the same constraints as those for naming a regular file or directory.

Before we proceed any further, it is important that you understand that the shell cannot differentiate between data types. That is, although you type 20 at the terminal and assign this number to a variable called maximum, the shell stores the characters 2 and 0 in it, not the number 20.

Bourne Shell Implementation

In the Bourne shell, variables are set like this:

```
$ SHELL=/bin/csh
$
```

Notice that the keyword set is missing in the assignment. However, variables are referenced in the same way, that is, by prefixing them with a dollar sign:

```
$ echo $SHELL
/bin/sh
$
```

Korn Shell Implementation

Variables are set in the same way as they are in the Bourne shell. Variables are referenced in the same way as well.

9.7.1 Referencing Unassigned Variables

The C shell responds as follows if reference is made to an unassigned variable:

```
$ echo $non_existent
non_existent: Undefined variable
$
```

Null values can be explicitly assigned to variables in this way:

```
$ novalue=
$
```

Then, when `novalue` is referenced

```
$ echo $novalue

$
```

you get a null output, instead of the message that displayed previously.

Bourne Shell Implementation

The Bourne shell does not display a message stating that the variable referenced is undefined. Instead, it displays a blank line:

```
$ echo $non_existent

$
```

Null values are assigned to variables in the same way as in the C shell.

Korn Shell Implementation

The Korn shell displays the same responses as the Bourne shell.

9.8 EXECUTING COMMAND FILES

Shell commands can be typed directly at the terminal, like so:

```
$ date
Wed Jan 22 16:54:16 EST 1992
$
```

or you can create a file using the vi editor (or one of the other editors that will be described later on in the book):

```
$ vi command_file
```

Inside the window, simply enter i to insert text, type date, hit the ESC key, and then type :wq to write the file to disk. The system prompt will redisplay. Now take a look at the file:

```
$ cat command_file
date
$
```

OK. So far, so good. Now you can execute the command contained inside the file called command_file (it could have been called anything) as follows.

First, give the file execute permission for yourself, and anyone else that you expect will be using this file:

```
$ chmod +x command_file
$
```

Check out the permissions, to satisfy your curiosity:

```
$ ls -l command_file
-rwxr-xr-x   1  sally    6 Jan 20 17:38 command_file
$
```

and then simply type the name of the file:

```
$ command_file
Wed Jan 22 17:12:16 EST 1992
$
```

Doing so results in the command contained in the file being executed.

Summarizing, a command file is an ASCII text file with executable permission. It contains shell commands. Command files are usually called scripts or script files in UNIX.

9.8.1 Nonexecutable Executable Files

Suppose `command_file` was just another text file, and contained the greeting `Hello` in it:

```
$ cat command_file
Hello
$
```

Let's execute this version of the file, and see what happens:

```
$ command_file
command_file: Hello not found.
$
```

The shell complains that it cannot execute the command contained in this file, which is `Hello`. This is a valid message; there is no command called `Hello` within the UNIX system. However, along the same lines, remember that there was no command called `command_file` either, until you created it. You could just as well have created another file called `Hello`, written a valid command to it, and then executed `Hello`. `command_file` and `Hello` are executed just as if they were regular commands. The shell behaves in exactly the same way as it would for UNIX system commands, as explained earlier in the chapter. It reads what is typed at the terminal. It searches for a command of that name. If the command is found, it is loaded into memory and executed, just like any other program. If it is not found, then an error message is displayed. Now you should be able to understand what was meant when we said that you can even create your own commands within the UNIX file system.

9.8.2 Multiple Commands in Executable Files

More than one command can be placed in one executable file.

```
$ cat command_file
date
$
```

We will use the `vi` editor to add another line to this file. This is how the file now looks:

```
$ cat command_file
echo The date is:
```

```
date
$
```

Now let's execute it:

```
$ command_file
The date is:
Wed Jan 22 17:12:16 EST 1992
$
```

Notice how the echo command is used to write text to the terminal. The output is now more informative. Also notice how each command executes in the sequence in which it appears within the text file.

Bourne Shell Implementation

There is no difference in the response for any of the examples presented in Sections 9.8.1 and 9.8.2 when they are run from the Bourne shell.

Korn Shell Implementation

There is no difference in the response for any of the examples presented in Sections 9.8.1 and 9.8.2 when they are run from the Korn shell.

9.9 PASSING ARGUMENTS TO COMMAND FILES

Arguments can be passed to command files, thereby making these command files much more versatile and useful. For example, assume that there is a command file called list that gives a long listing of the file name that follows it. Here's how it looks:

```
$ cat list
ls -l
$
```

Each time the file list is invoked, a long listing of all files in the current working directory will be displayed. However, it is possible that there may be times when a long listing is required for only one file, not each one. The name of the file for which a long listing is desired can be sent as an argument to the command file by modifying list like so:

```
$ cat list
ls -l $1
$
```

and then invoking `list` followed by an argument, which is the
name of the file for which a long listing is required:

```
$ list file1
-rwxr-xr-x  1 sally 4  Jan 20 17:38 file1
$
```

Thus, each time you invoke `list`, whatever word follows it will
be substituted into the command file at the location of the symbol
$1, and the command executed accordingly.

9.9.1 Multiple Arguments

Let's see what happens if multiple arguments are sent to the file
above.

```
$ list file1 file2
-rwxr-xr-x  1 sally 4  Jan 20 17:38 file1
$
```

The shell simply ignores the second argument, because it has no
place to put it.

The problem can be fixed by adding placeholders for as many
arguments as needed within `list`. Here's the new listing:

```
$ cat list
ls -l $1 $2 $3 $4
$
```

Now up to four arguments can be supplied to `list`. What
happens if fewer than four arguments are sent anyway? Let's take
a look:

```
$ list file1 file2
-rwxr-xr-x  1 sally 4  Jan 20 17:38  file1
-rwxr-xr-x  1 sally 34 Jan 20 18:24  file2
$
```

It does not matter; unassigned arguments are assigned the null
value. How do we know that? Let's continue the discussion with
the next section.

9.9.2 Printing Arguments

As indicated, the arguments sent to command files can be printed by prefixing them with a dollar sign ($). Let's modify the list file and print the values of the arguments passed to it:

```
$ cat list
echo "Arguments passed are (1) $1 (2) $2 (3) $3 (4) $4"
ls -l $1 $2 $3 $4
$
```

Now list will be executed with a variable number of arguments.

```
$ list file1
Arguments passed are (1) file1 (2)  (3)  (4)
-rwxr-xr-x 1 sally 4   Jan 20 17:38 file1
$
```

Notice that null arguments are assigned to the second, third, and fourth arguments.

```
$ list file1 file2 file3 file4
Arguments passed are (1) file1 (2) file2 (3) file3 (4) file4
file3: not found
file4: not found
-rwxr-xr-x 1 sally 4   Jan 20 17:38 file1
-rwxr-xr-x 1 sally 34 Jan 20 18:24 file2
$
```

Notice the messages that display for file3 and file4.

```
$ list file1 file2 file3 file4 file5
Arguments passed are (1) file1 (2) file2 (3) file3 (4) file4
file3: not found
file4: not found
-rwxr-xr-x 1 sally 4   Jan 20 17:38 file1
-rwxr-xr-x 1 sally 34 Jan 20 18:24 file2
$
```

Notice that the fifth argument is simply ignored.

9.9.3 Counting Arguments

The $# is a special shell variable which contains a count of the total number of arguments sent to it. list will be modified to print the total number of arguments passed to it. Here's how it looks:

```
$ cat list
echo "Total arguments passed are: $#"
echo "Arguments passed are: (1) $1 (2) $2 (3) $3 (4)
$4"
ls -l $1 $2 $3 $4
$
```

Executing list with two arguments gives this result:

```
$ list file1 file2
Total arguments passed are: 2
Arguments passed are (1) file1 (2) file2 (3) (4)
-rwxr-xr-x 1 sally 4  Jan 20 17:38 file1
-rwxr-xr-x 1 sally 34 Jan 20 18:24 file2
$
```

Executing list with five arguments would give this result:

```
$ list file1 file2 file3 file4 file5
Total arguments passed are: 5
Arguments passed are (1) file1 (2) file2 (3) file3
(4) file4
file3: not found
file4: not found
-rwxr-xr-x 1 sally 4  Jan 20 17:38 file1
-rwxr-xr-x 1 sally 34 Jan 20 18:24 file2
$
```

Notice that the correct number of arguments sent to list is displayed. However, the fifth argument is still ignored in the long listing, because the shell has no place to substitute it into.

9.9.4 Referencing All Arguments

The $* variable is used to display all arguments sent to a command file. The list file will once again be modified to display this variable:

```
$ cat list
echo "Total arguments passed are: $#"
echo "Arguments passed are: $*
ls -l $1 $2 $3 $4
```

And here's sample usage:

```
$ list file1 file2 file3 file4
Total arguments passed are: 4
Arguments passed are: file1 file2 file3 file4
file3: not found
file4: not found
-rwxr-xr-x 1 sally 4  Jan 20 17:38 file1
-rwxr-xr-x 1 sally 34 Jan 20 18:24 file2
$
```

Bourne Shell Implementation

All examples in Section 9.9 (and its subsections) produce the same output when run from the Bourne shell. The only difference could be in the wording of the messages.

Korn Shell Implementation

All examples in Section 9.9 (and its subsections) produce the same output when run from the Korn shell. The only difference could be in the wording of the messages.

9.10 EXECUTING MULTIPLE COMMANDS IN SINGLE COMMAND LINE

Multiple commands can be executed from a single command line. The following operators are used to execute multiple commands:

```
semicolon (;)
```

Use of the semicolon causes commands to be executed in the sequence in which they occur.

```
&&
```

Use of the && symbols results in the next command executing only if the command that preceded it ran successfully.

```
||
```

Use of the || symbols results in the next command executing only if the command that preceded it did not run successfully.

```
|
```

Use of the | symbol results in the creation of a pipeline of commands. The pipeline will be discussed as a common feature of all shells in the next section. We include it in our list here because it is the execution of multiple commands in a single command line.

We now explain the use of each symbol listed.

9.10.1 The Semicolon (;)

Multiple commands can be issued from the same command line simply by delimiting each command with a semicolon. (You encountered the use of the semicolon when we were discussing directories, earlier on in the book.) Here's sample usage:

```
$ echo Hello > file1; ls file1; cat file1; rm file1; ls file1
file1
Hello
file1 not found
$
```

Notice that although five commands were typed, there is output for only three. This is because the shell would have responded with the system prompt on successful creation of file1 with the echo command and successful removal of this file with the rm command. However, since it found a semicolon, it simply went ahead and executed the next command in the sequence. Notice the absence of a semicolon at the end of the last command. It would not have made any difference if there was one. The system would have responded the same way.

9.10.2 The && Sign

Use of the && sign between two valid commands results in the next command being implemented only if the first command executed successfully. Take a look at this sequence of commands:

```
$ cat temp_file > backup_file && echo temp_file && rm temp_file
```

The first command instructs the shell to create a new file called backup_file and write the contents of temp_file to it:

```
$ cat temp_file > backup_file
```

The next command instructs the shell to echo temp_file:

```
...&& echo temp_file
```

and the final command instructs the shell to remove `temp_file`:

```
...&& rm temp_file
```

The three commands are joined via the `&&` symbol. This implies that the second command will execute only if the first command executes successfully, and the third will execute only if the second is successful.

Now suppose there was no file called `temp_file`. Let's see what happens when this command is executed.

```
$ cat temp_file > backup_file && echo temp_file && rm temp_file
cat: temp_file: No such file or directory
$
```

The output indicates that the first command failed. Hence, the second command, which was simply an `echo` command, did not execute, and the third command was never reached.

Here's another example:

```
$ cat file1 && cat file2 && cat file3 && cat file4
```

Assume that `file1`, `file3`, and `file4` exist, but `file2` does not. The shell will display `file1` and then stop execution of all subsequent commands. This is because it could not find `file2`; hence command 2 fails; hence command 3 is not executed, and command 4 is not even interpreted (the shell doesn't get to it). Command execution stops at the first hit of the condition being tested, and all subsequent commands, if they exist, are ignored.

9.10.3 The || Sign

Use of the || sign between two valid commands results in the next command being implemented only if the first command fails.

Assume that there is no file called `temp_file`. Take a look at the following sequence of commands:

```
$ cat temp_file > backup_file || ls -1 > temp_file
cat: temp_file: No such file or directory
```

The first command instructs the shell to create a new file called `backup_file` and write the contents of `temp_file` to it:

```
$ cat temp_file > backup_file
```

However, if temp_file does not exist, then the first command will fail. In this case, temp_file is created via the redirection symbol (>)

```
...  ls -l > temp_file
```

and a long listing of the contents of the current working directory is written to temp_file. The file will not be created if it already exists.

Command execution for multiple || stops at the first hit of a successful execution of a command. In this case, all subsequent commands, if they exist, are ignored. Take a look at this example:

```
$ cat file1 || cat file2 || cat file3 || cat file4
```

This time, assume that all files exist. A cat to file1 will succeed; hence all subsequent cat commands will be ignored and not implemented.

The || can be combined with the && to come up with an interesting sequence of commands:

```
$ cat temp > backup || ls -l > temp && echo "temp created."
```

There are three commands involved:

Command 1: cat temp > backup
Command 2: ls -l > temp
Command 3: echo "temp created"

Assume that there is no temp file. Here's the output:

```
cat: temp: No such file or directory.
temp created.
$
```

The first command fails, since there is no temp file; hence the message is issued. Since the first command is separated from the next by the ||, the second command executes (because the first command failed). The file temp is created by redirecting a long listing of the current working directory to it. The second command executes successfully. Since the second and third commands are separated by the && sign, and the second command executed successfully, the third command also executes, and temp created is echoed. OK. So now we have a file called temp. Let's reissue this command again:

```
$ cat temp > backup || ls -l > temp && echo "temp created."
$
```

This time, there is no output, and the system prompt displays. The first command is successful; temp is written to backup because temp now exists. The || sign prohibits the shell from proceeding any further, and all subsequent commands are ignored.

Bourne Shell Implementation

All examples in this section produce the same output if they are run from the Bourne shell. Only the wording of the messages may vary.

Korn Shell Implementation

All examples in this section produce the same output if they are run from the Korn shell. However, the wording of the messages may vary.

9.11 FORMULATING THE PIPELINE (|)

You have encountered pipelines earlier in the book. Recall that this is the situation in which the output of one command is fed into the input of another. This way, output is filtered, as necessary, one command after the next. Here are a few pipeline examples.

Example 1:   Get a printout of all files in the current working directory that are owned by the user sally.

```
$ ls -l | grep "sally" | lpr
```

The above command outputs a long listing of the current working directory. Then the grep utility is invoked, and this does a search on the output of the previous command for all lines that contain the pattern sally. All lines selected by grep are piped to lpr, which results in a hard copy printout.

Example 2:   Sort the files in the current working directory that are owned by the user sally. Get a printout of these files.

```
$ ls -l | grep "sally" | sort | lpr
```

The pipeline is extended by including the sort command in it. The sort will be implemented on the output of the grep command. The output of the sort command is further piped to lpr, which produces the hard copy of the results.

Example 3:   Find all files in the current working directory which contain reference to product_A.   For all files found, pick up only those that also contain reference to product_B.   Write the results to a file called Product_file.

```
$ grep "product_A" * | grep "product_B" * > Product_file
```

The pipeline above does a search on all files (the wildcard metacharacter * is used to pick up all files except the hidden ones) that contain the pattern product_A in them. The output is further filtered by picking up only those that contain the pattern product_B. The resulting output is written to Product_file via the redirection operator (>).

Bourne Shell Implementation

Pipelines and filters are created in the same way from the Bourne shell.

Korn Shell Implementation

Pipelines and filters are created in the same way from the Korn shell.

9.12 USING THE BACKSLASH AND QUOTES

We have illustrated the use of symbols which have special meaning for the shell, such as $, <, >, &, |, *, ?, [,], and others. If for some reason these characters are to be used literally within a command (that is, without the special meaning attached to them), then the backslash or quotes are used to precede the character, and the shell interprets it literally.

9.12.1 The Backslash

The backslash is used to instruct the shell to take the meaning of the single character that follows it literally. For example, assume that a file was erroneously created with the name >. An ls is to be done to this file, to make sure it's in the current working directory, and then it is to be removed. Here's how the shell would respond without using the backslash:

```
$ ls >
Missing name for redirect.
$
```

The shell thinks that a listing of the current directory is being redirected to a file. However, since no file name is specified, it issues the message. Now let's precede the > with a backslash:

```
$ ls \>
>
$ rm \>
$ ls \>
> not found.
$
```

As you can see, the backslash removed the special meaning assigned to the > symbol, and it was interpreted literally.

The backslash is also used as a continuation character; it instructs the shell to ignore the carriage return that follows it. For example, the backslash would come in handy for very long pipes or multiple commands. Suppose a cat is to be done to 12 files, call them file1 through file12. Since not all files will fit on one line, we decide to enter a carriage return after file8 and continue the command on the next line. However, when the carriage return is pressed at this location

```
$ cat file1 file2 file3 file4 file5 file6 file7 file8 <Return>
```

the shell proceeds to output all files if they exist! It perceives the carriage return as the delimiter for the command.

On the other hand, if the carriage return is immediately preceded by the backslash:

```
$ cat file1 file2 file3 file4 file5 file6 file7 file8 \<Return>
file9 file10 file11 file12
```

the shell responds by concatenating and displaying all files together if they exist, or issuing error messages for the files that do not.

Bourne Shell Implementation

The Bourne shell displays a > on the next line, if a carriage return is hit immediately after the backslash. The command is executed when the carriage return is hit without the backslash preceding it. Here's how it would respond to the command just illustrated:

```
$ cat file1 file2 file3 file4 file5 file6 file7 file8 \<Return>
> file9 file10 file11 file12 <Return>
<All files, if they exist, are displayed>
$
```

Korn Shell Implementation

The Korn shell response is similar to that of the Bourne shell.

9.12.2 The Single Quotes (' ')

The single quotes have a dual purpose. First, they can be used to instruct the shell to take the meaning of all special characters which are enclosed within literally. Second, they instruct the shell to take the enclosed characters, which may be separated by white space, as a group. We will describe the former usage first.

Suppose a file was erroneously created with the name >file>. Now this file is to be viewed, and if it contains garbage, it must be deleted. The following sequence of commands would be used to do so.

```
$ ls '>file>'
>file>
$ rm '>file>'
$
```

If the single quotes had not been used, then the output would have looked like this:

```
$ ls >file>
Missing redirect
$
```

Single quotes can also be used to keep characters which may separated by white space together as one group. For example, suppose the string `Product_B has no sales potential` is to be matched for all files in the current working directory. If the `grep` command is issued without enclosing the string in quotes, this is what happens:

```
$ grep Product_b has no sales potential *
grep: has: No such file or directory
grep: no: No such file or directory
grep: sales: No such file or directory
grep: potential: No such file or directory
file2:  As you can see, Product_b has no sales potential. This
$
```

Let's understand what happened. Since the string `Product_b has no sales potential` is not enclosed in quotes, the `grep` utility considers `Product_b` the match pattern, and `has`, `no`, `sales`, and `potential` as file names. Hence, it issues the messages `grep: No such file or directory` for each word. Since the last argument in the command is `*`, it issues a wildcard search on all files anyway, searching for a match on the string `Product_b`. It finds one such file, and displays its name along with the line which contains the pattern.

Now, let's enclose the string in quotes:

```
$ grep 'Product_b has no sales potential' *
file2: As you can see, Product_b has no sales potential. This
$
```

The output should require no further explanation.

9.12.3 The Double Quotes (" ")

Double quotes have the same twofold purpose as the single quotes, but with one important exception. They instruct the shell to take all special characters enclosed within literally, except the dollar sign ($), the back quote (`), and the backslash (\). Like the single quotes, they are also used to specify that the characters enclosed, which may be separated by white space, are to be treated as a single group. We will illustrate the use of the double quotes with each of the special characters listed.

■ The Dollar Sign ($)

At the beginning of this chapter we described how to determine which shell you are in. This is what is typed:

```
$ echo $SHELL
```

Typing this results in your current shell displaying on the terminal:

```
/bin/csh
$
```

Now let's enclose the variable in single quotes:

```
$ echo '$SHELL'
$SHELL
$
```

Notice how the $ sign followed by SHELL is displayed as is, and that the special meaning of the dollar sign is not given to it. Now let's enclose the variable in double quotes:

```
$ echo "$SHELL"
/bin/csh
$
```

This time, the current shell displayed, indicating that the shell interpreted the $ as if it were not enclosed in quotes. Now let's include some more special characters within the double quotes:

```
$ echo "||The shell is>> $SHELL"
||The shell is>> /bin/csh
$
```

The example above illustrates the dual purpose of the double quotes. The special characters || and >> were interpreted literally, and displayed as is. However, the $ sign maintained its special meaning, and the current shell displayed after the message.

■ The Back Quote (')

The back quote character is used to enclose executable commands. When the shell encounters the back quote, it tries to execute the characters enclosed as a command, just as it was typed at the system prompt. For example, take a look at this command:

```
$ echo "My name is `whoami`"
My name is sally
$
```

The command whoami is executed, its output is inserted in the location where it is encountered, and then the echo command displays the complete output.

You can enclose multiple commands inside the back quotes, each separated from the next by a semicolon, and create pipes and filters. There is no restriction on the number of commands that can be enclosed within, as long as they follow the correct syntax.

■ The Backslash (\)

The backslash is similar to the single quotes; it removes the special meaning (if any) of the character that follows it. Now take a look at the usage of the backslash inside double quotes:

```
$ echo "\$SHELL"
$SHELL
$
```

The output indicates that the special meaning of the dollar sign, (which is not ignored when found within double quotes) is ignored, because the $ sign is preceded by a backslash, which instructs the shell to take the next character literally! Hence, $SHELL displays, instead of your current shell.

Bourne Shell Implementation

All examples presented in Section 9.12 (and its subsections) give the same output when implemented from the Bourne shell.

Korn Shell Implementation

All examples presented in Section 9.12 (and its subsections) give the same output when implemented from the Korn shell.

9.13 OSF/1 CONSIDERATIONS

As you are already aware, OSF/1 supports the C, Bourne, and Korn shells. In addition to this, it also supports a restricted version of the Bourne shell called the restricted Bourne shell. The system prompt for this shell is:

```
/bin/rsh
```

This shell provides a more controlled environment within the shell and restricts the users from certain commands, thereby limiting their privileges and providing enhanced security for the overall system. It is similar in all other respects to the Bourne shell. Users in this shell are restricted from using the `cd` command (they cannot change directories), from using absolute path names (that is, execute commands in locations other than their current working directory), from redirecting output, or from resetting the environment variables `SHELL` and `PATH`. You have already encountered usage of the variable `SHELL`. The `PATH` variable will be described in detail in the next chapter, when we discuss control structures and global and environment variables in the shell.

Aside from this, the C, Bourne, and Korn shells respond in the same way in an OSF/1 operating system as they do in UNIX.

9.14 REVIEW

In this chapter we described the shell, how it interacts with the kernel, and those features which are common to the C, Bourne, and Korn shells. Specifically, we found out that

- The *shell* is a program that acts as a command interpreter.

- The *kernel* is the heart of the operating system. Libraries, utilities, and programs are stored on disk; they are not in the kernel.

- The shell interprets what you type at the terminal, and then instructs the kernel to execute it (if it can be executed).

Table 9.1 describes the usage of the commands explained in this chapter for the three shells under discussion.

Table 9.1 Overview of Common Shell Commands

Command	C Shell	Bourne Shell	Korn Shell
Determine your shell	echo $SHELL	echo $SHELL	echo $SHELL
Change shell	/bin/csh	bin/sh	/bin/ksh
Store values in variables	set variable=10	variable=10	variable=10
Send arguments	Use $1, $2, etc., in shell script	Use $1, $2, etc., in shell script	Use $1, $2 in shell script
Count total arguments	echo $#	echo $#	echo $#
Reference arguments	echo $*	echo $*	echo $*
Execute multiple commands	Use semicolon(;), logical and (&&), logical or (||)	Use semicolon(;), logical and (&&), logical or (||)	Use semicolon(;), logical and (&&), logical or (||)
Create pipes and filters	Use | to join commands to create pipes and filters	Use | to join commands to create pipes and filters	Use | to join commands to create pipes and filters
Take away meaning of one special character	Use backslash followed by character	Use backslash followed by character	Use backslash followed by character

Table 9.1 Overview of Common Shell Commands (Contd.)

Command	C Shell	Bourne Shell	Korn Shell
Take away meaning of all special characters	Enclose group of characters in single quotes	Enclose group of characters in single quotes	Enclose group of characters in single quotes
Take away meaning of all special characters except $, \, and '	Enclose group of characters in double quotes	Enclose group of characters in double quotes	Enclose group of characters in double quotes

The if Statement and the test Command

10.1 INTRODUCTION

A *shell* is, after all, a programming language, and therefore it provides the control structures that allow decision making. This chapter describes only one of these control structures, the `if` statement. The remainder of the chapter is devoted to an explanation of the `test` command, which is frequently utilized by control structures within shell scripts to test the successful or unsuccessful execution of commands contained therein.

10.2 CONTROL STRUCTURES

Control structures allow us to specify the conditions under which blocks of code are to be executed. The shell provides the following statements that allow for conditional execution:

- The `if` construct

- The `else` construct

- The `elif` construct

- The `case` construct

■ The `for` loop

■ The `while` loop

■ The `until` command

A discussion of the `if` construct follows.   The remaining constructs will be described in the next chapter.

10.3 THE IF CONSTRUCT

The flow of the `if` construct can be expressed as follows:

```
if command executes successfully
then
        execute this command
        and this command
        and this command
fi
```

To elaborate further, the command following `if` is executed. If this command is successful, then all commands between `then` and `fi` are executed in the sequence in which they appear. If the command following `if` is unsuccessful, then all commands between `then` and `fi` are skipped.

10.3.1 Command Execution and Exit Status

The successful execution of a command is assessed by its *exit* status. Whenever a command executes in UNIX, it returns a status in the form of a number which indicates whether it ran successfully or unsuccessfully. A status of zero indicates success, and a status of nonzero indicates that the command failed. To say this a little bit more technically, a successful command returns a *true* value, which is a zero, and an unsuccessful command returns a *nontrue* or *false* value, which can be any number except zero.

And so you may wonder exactly what constitutes the successful execution of a command. Here are a few examples that will help clarify this.

```
$ lpr file100
file100 not found
$
```

The `lpr` command did not execute successfully because it did not find the file that it was asked to list. This command returns a non-zero value to the system. The `ls` command would have executed successfully if it had found `file100`. In that case, it would have returned a zero status.

Here's another example:

```
$ grep "product_a" file1
$
```

The above command produces no output because it does not find the string `product_a` in `file1`. It does not produce an error message either. However, this command returns a nonzero value to the system because it did not find the pattern that it was asked to find, and therefore, as far as exit status is concerned, did not execute successfully.

```
$ ls -l | grep "anastasia" | lpr
lpr: standard input: empty input file
$
```

The above command outputs this message because `grep` is unable to match `anastasia` in the long listing that is produced for the current directory. Although the `ls -l` command executes successfully, and the `lpr` command would have executed successfully if it had something to print, the pipeline does not complete, and a nonzero status is returned to the statement. From this we can conclude that the *last* command that executes in a pipeline must be successful, *if that pipeline is to return a zero status to the system.*

Bourne Shell Implementation

The control structures listed apply equally to shell scripts that are written for the Bourne shell. In addition to this, commands return an exit status of zero if they execute successfully and nonzero if they are unsuccessful. All examples in Section 10.3.1 produce similar output. (The wording of some of the messages can be different.)

Korn Shell Implementation

All features described in the prior two sections hold true for the Korn shell. The examples produce similar output.

10.3.2 Displaying Exit Status

The C shell stores the exit status of the last command executed in a variable called status. After command execution, the value stored in this variable can be displayed by preceding it with a dollar sign and then *echoing* it. Here are the return values of the commands executed in Section 10.3.1:

```
$ lpr file100
file100 not found
$ echo $status
1
$ grep "product_a" file1
$ echo $status
1
$ ls -l | grep "anastasia" | lpr
$ echo $status
1
$
```

And here's a command that returns an exit status of zero:

```
$ date
Wed Jan 22 16:54:16 EST 1992
$ echo $status
0
$
```

Bourne Shell Implementation

The Bourne shell stores the exit status of the last command executed in the ? variable. Hence, the value stored in this variable can be displayed by preceding ? with the dollar sign ($). Here is how the return status would be tested in the Bourne shell:

```
$ ls -l | grep "anastasia" | lpr
$ echo $?
1
$ date
Wed Jan 22 16:54:16 EST 1992
$ echo $?
0
$
```

Korn Shell Implementation

The exit status of commands run from the Korn shell is also stored in the ? variable. Thus, the Korn shell is similar to the Bourne shell.

10.3.3 Some Examples

And now, here are a few examples that use the if statement. All examples are written to a script file called if_script. This script file is given execute permission via the chmod +x command, and executed simply by typing if_script at the command prompt.

Example 1:   If report_file exists in your current working directory, then print it and output a message.

```
$ cat if_script
if lpr report_file
then
   echo "Report_file sent to the printer."
fi
$ ls report_file
report_file
$ if_script
Report_file sent to the printer.
$
```

An ls of report_file in the current working directory indicates that it exists. When if_script is executed, report_file is output to the printer via the lpr command, the command returns a zero status to the operating system, and so the echo command within the then and fi keywords outputs the message.

Example 2:   If today is Friday, display a happy message.

```
$ cat if_script
if date | grep "Fri"
then
   echo "It's FRIDAY!  FRIDAY!   FRIDAY!"
   echo "Yes! TGI FRIDAY!!!"
fi
$
$ date
Wed Jan 22 16:54:16 EST 1992
```

```
$ if_script
Wed Jan 22 16:54:24 EST 1992
$
```

This example illustrates the use of a pipe in the `if` clause. The output for `date` is piped to `grep`, which tries to find a match on the string `Fri`. In the above example, executing `if_script` resulted in the output for the `date` command being displayed. However, the joyous greeting for Friday was not echoed, because `grep` was unable to find a match on `Fri`. If the current date was Friday, here's what would happen:

```
$ date
Fri Jan 24 12:34:20 EST 1992
$ if_script
Fri Jan 24 12:34:20 EST 1992
It's FRIDAY!   FRIDAY!   FRIDAY!
Yes! TGI FRIDAY!!!
$
```

Example 3:   If today is Friday, move `backup_file` to `temp` and echo a message. If there is no `backup_file` on the current working directory, issue a warning message.

```
$ cat if_script
if date | grep "Fri" && mv backup_file temp || echo "mv failed"
then
    echo "ALERT!!   ALERT!!"
    echo "There is no backup_file!!!"
fi
$
```

Two things can happen. Your current working directory may contain `backup_file`, or it may not. Let's consider the latter condition first. Here's the output if there is no `backup_file`:

```
$ script_file
Fri Jan 24 12:44:32 EST 1992
mv: backup_file: cannot access: No such file or
directory
Move failed
ALERT!!   ALERT!!
There is no backup_file!!!
$
```

Let's step through the output. The current date displays because the `date` command is run; there are no mysteries here.

The output for date is piped to grep, which attempts to find a match on Fri. grep succeeds in finding a match, and therefore the mv command is implemented. (Only successful execution of the grep command will result in the mv command being implemented, because the two are joined by an &&.) However, the mv command fails, because there is no backup_file. Since this command fails, the next command executes (they are joined by an ||), and the message Move failed is echoed. Now, since the last command in the pipeline executed successfully, the commands between the then and fi are executed, and the alert message is output.

OK. Suppose there is a backup_file. Let's see what happens in this case.

```
$ ls backup_file
backup_file
$ script_file
Fri Jan 24 12:44:32 EST 1992
ALERT!!    ALERT!!
There is no backup_file!!!
$
```

As you can see, the alert message displayed in this case as well! So why did this happen? Well, let's take another look at the pipeline:

```
if date | grep "Fri" && mv backup_file temp || echo "mv failed"
```

date executed, which is fine. grep was successful, and so the mv command was implemented. That makes sense too. However, in this case, the mv command executed successfully, and so the next command, which is the echo, never got executed, because the two commands are joined by the || symbols! However, since the mv command was the last one that implemented in the pipeline, and it was successful, a return status of zero is returned to the system, and so the commands between the then and fi are executed. Seems like we didn't program this shell script quite right! We leave it as an exercise to the reader to figure out how this shell script should have been written.

Bourne Shell Implementation

All examples in the prior section will produce the same output when run from the Bourne shell.

Korn Shell Implementation

All examples in the prior section will produce the same output when run from the Korn shell.

10.4 THE TEST COMMAND

Before continuing with the remaining constructs found in the shell language, we are going to describe the `test` command, which is frequently used within shell scripts to test conditions. The format of the `test` command can be expressed as follows:

```
test expression
```

If the expression evaluates as true, `test` returns a zero exit status. If the expression evaluates as false, a nonzero exit status is returned. The `test` command can be used to test

- Character strings

- Numerical values

- File types

We will illustrate the use of each type of test via the `if` construct.

10.4.1 Testing Character Strings

The `test` command looks like this:

```
test expression
```

The expression for testing character strings can follow any of these formats:

- `string1 = string2`

   `test` returns a zero exit status if `string1` is identical to `string2`.

- `string1 != string2`

   `test` returns a zero exit status if `string1` is not identical to `string2`.

- `string`

  `test` returns a zero exit status if `string` is not null.

- `-n string`

  `test` returns a zero exit status if `string` is not null.

- `-z string`

  `test` returns a zero exit status if `string` is null.

OK. Now that you know the facts, here are some examples that illustrate usage of the `test` command with character strings.

We will use the assignment operator to set two variables to character strings:

```
$ set today="Monday"
$ set tomorrow="Tuesday"
```

Bourne and Korn Shell Implementation

The `test` command works in the same way when executed from the Bourne and Korn shells. Remember, however, that the `set` keyword is omitted when setting variables.

10.4.1.1 Some Examples

And now the use of the `test` command, as it applies to the first condition:

- `string1 = string2`

  `test` returns a zero exit status if `string1` is identical to `string2`.

```
$ cat test_script
if test   "$1"   = "Monday"
then
    echo "The argument sent matches the string Monday."
fi
$
```

$1 inside the script file will be replaced by the argument sent to it at the time that test_script is invoked. Then, the argument sent will be compared to Monday, and if the two strings are identical, a value of zero will be returned by test to the operating system, and so the commands between the then and fi will be executed.

Although the double quotes are not required around "$1" or the string that the argument will be compared to (Monday), we recommend that you use them anyway. test_script will run without any problems if it is run with an argument. However, if test_script is executed without an argument and there are no quotes around the $1 and the comparison string, then the following message is displayed:

```
test_script: test: argument expected
```

This is because test is unable to differentiate the null argument sent to it. Let's take a look at the return status:

```
$ echo $status
1
$
```

If you do place quotes, executing test_script without any arguments results in no error message. The return status is zero:

```
$ test_script
$ echo $status
0
$
```

Let's execute test_script with the variable $today. (Recall that we stored Monday in today and Tuesday in tomorrow).

```
$ test_script $today
The argument sent matches the string Monday.
$
```

test_script will be modified to accept two arguments:

```
$ cat test_script
if test "$1" = "$2"
then
   echo "The two arguments are identical."
fi
$
```

Let's execute it now:

```
$ test_script $today $tomorrow
```

Since Monday is not equal to Tuesday, nothing is output.

```
$ test_script $today "Monday"
The two arguments are identical.
$
```

Monday is identical to Monday.

```
$ test_script $today
$
```

Monday is compared to a null string (the second argument is a null), they are not equal, and so nothing is output.

```
$ test_script
The two arguments are identical.
$
```

This output deserves a second look. Notice that no arguments are sent to test_script, and yet it says that the two arguments are equal. Well, null values are substituted inside $1 and $2, and since null is equal to null, the message is output. If $1 and $2 were not enclosed in quotes, test_script would not have executed, and this error message would have displayed instead:

```
test_script: test:  argument expected.
```

Now you should understand why we advised you to enclose the arguments in quotes in the script_file.

And now test_script will be modified to test for the next condition.

■ string1 != string2

test returns a zero exit status if string1 is not identical to string2. Let's modify test_script to test this condition next.

```
$ cat test_script
if test "$1" != "$2"
then
   echo "The two arguments are not identical."
fi
```

`test_script` will be run with different arguments. The output is self-explanatory:

```
$ test_script $today $tomorrow
The two arguments are not identical.
$ test_script $today
The two arguments are not identical.
$ test_script $today "Monday"
$ test_script
$
```

Notice that the last two commands produced no output, because the arguments were identical.

We continue with the next condition.

■ string

test returns a zero exit status if string is not null.

```
$ cat test_script
if test "$1"
then
   echo "The argument sent is not null."
fi
$ test_script "Hello"
The argument sent is not null.
$ test_script
$
```

The output should be self-explanatory. We continue with the next condition.

■ −n string

test returns a zero exit status if string is not null.

This condition is the same as the one just described; it simply has a different syntax:

```
$ cat test_script
if test −n "$1"
then
   echo "The argument sent is not null."
fi
$ test_script $tomorrow
The argument sent is not null.
$
```

And now finally, the last condition for strings:

■ −z string

> test returns a zero exit status if string is null.

> Here's the modified test_script file:

```
$ cat test_script
if test −z "$1"
then
   echo "The argument sent is null."
fi
$ test_script $non_existent
The argument sent is null.
$
```

The −z option is useful for testing variables that you think may have been preset, but aren't sure of.

Bourne Shell Implementation

All examples in this section will produce the same result when executed from the Bourne shell.

Korn Shell Implementation

All examples in this section will produce the same result when executed from the Korn shell.

10.4.2 Testing Numerical Values

As indicated earlier, the test command can also be used to test for numerical values. The format of the test command remains the same:

```
test expression
```

The expression for testing numerical values can follow any of these formats:

- `int1 -eq int2`

  `test` returns a zero exit status if `int1` is equal to `int2`.

- `int1 -lt int2`

  `test` returns a zero exit status if `int1` is less than `int2`.

- `int1 -gt int2`

  `test` returns a zero exit status if `int1` is greater than `int2`.

- `int1 -ne int2`

  `test` returns a zero exit status if `int1` is not equal to `int2`.

- `int1 -le int2`

  `test` returns a zero exit status if `int1` is less than or equal to `int2`.

- `int1 -ge int2`

  `test` returns a zero exit status if `int1` is greater than or equal to `int2`.

Before we proceed to illustrate the usage of the `test` command with numerical values, keep in mind that the shell reads the values stored in variables, or whatever is typed at the terminal, as characters. It is the expression syntax that makes it determine whether a test is being performed on character strings or integers. For example, if two variables are tested using the = operator,

```
$ more test_script
if test "$1" = "20"
   echo "Arguments are identical."
fi
$ test_script "10"
$
```

then the shell tests whether the string "10" is identical to the string "20". Let's output the value of `status` to see the value returned by `test`:

```
$ echo $status
1
$
```

test returns a 1 because the string 10 is not equal to 20. On the other hand, the numerical values of 10 and 20 could be tested using the −eq operator, like this:

```
$ more test_script
if test $1 −eq 20
    echo "Arguments are identical."
fi
$ test_script 10
$
$ echo $status
1
$
```

Once again, test returns a 1 because 10 is not equal to 20. Now take a look at this example:

```
$ more test_script
if test $1 = 10
    echo "Arguments are identical"
fi
$ test_script 010
$
$ echo $status
1
$
```

test outputs a 1 because it compares the string 010 to the string 10, and the two are not equal. Changing the format of test like this:

```
$ more test_script
if test $1 −eq 10
    echo "Arguments are identical"
fi
$ test_script 010
Arguments are identical
$ echo $status
0
$
```

results in test returning a zero, because the −eq implies an integer comparison, and 10 is equal to 10.

Bourne Shell Implementation

The Bourne shell supports the same syntax for numerical comparisons of integers as the C shell. Remember, however, that the variable $? is used to display the return status of the test command, instead of the variable $status.

Korn Shell Implementation

The Korn shell behavior is similar to that of the Bourne shell, and the variable $? is used to display the return status of the test command.

10.4.2.1 Some Examples

And now we will use the test command, as it applies to testing of numerical conditions listed above. Most of the output is self-explanatory, and will not be elaborated on any further.

- int1 -eq int2

  test returns a zero exit status if int1 is equal to int2.

```
$ cat test_script
if test "$1" -eq "$2"
then
   echo  "The   two   arguments   are   numerically
equivalent."
fi
$ test_script 5 005
The two arguments are numerically equivalent.
$ test_script .24 0.28
The two arguments are numerically equivalent.
$
```

The above output merits further explanation. Two decimal values are sent as arguments to test_script, and the shell perceives them to be numerially equivalent, although they are not. The -eq command works only with integer values, and the results will be ambiguous if fractional values are sent to it.

Bourne Shell Implementation

The above `test_script` will produce the same result if executed from the Bourne shell. The −eq command is meant to be used with integers only.

Korn Shell Implementation

The Korn shell is smart enough to discern that a noninteger value is being sent to it as an argument, and that the −eq works only with integers. The Korn shell outputs the following message:

```
test_script[3]: syntax error
#
```

10.4.2.2 Examples, Contd.

We return to the use of the `test` command as it applies to testing of numerical conditions using the C shell.

- int1 −lt int2

    `test` returns a zero exit status if int1 is less than int2.

```
$ cat test_script
if test "$1" −lt "$2"
then
    echo "The first argument is less than the second."
fi
$ test_script 5 005
$ test_script
$ test_script 4 5
The first argument is less than the second.
$ test_script "$today" "$tomorrow"
$
```

Notice the output for the last command. Two strings are compared using the integer comparison syntax. The output indicates that the first string is not less than the second. However, there is really no way to compare two strings using the −lt syntax; the results will be ambiguous.

Bourne Shell Implementation

All examples will produce the same result when implemented from the Bourne shell.

Korn Shell Implementation

All examples will produce the same result when implemented from the Korn shell, except the last. The Korn shell is smart enough to understand the type of argument sent to it, and issues an appropriate message. Here's the test run, and the message displayed:

```
# test_script "today" "tomorrow"
test_script[3]: Monday: bad number
#
```

10.4.2.3 Examples, Contd.

We continue to present examples using the C shell.

- int1 -gt int2

    test returns a zero exit status if int1 is greater than int2.

```
$ cat test_script
if test "$1" -gt "$2"
then
    echo "The first argument is greater than the second."
fi
$ test_script 5 005
$ test_script 4 5
$ test_script 5 4
The first argument is greater than the second.
$
```

- int1 -ne int2

    test returns a zero exit status if int1 is not equal to int2.

```
$ cat test_script
if test "$1" -ne "$2"
then
    echo "The first argument is not equal to the second."
fi
```

```
$ test_script 1 2
The first argument is not equal to the second.
$
```

test_script will be modified to ensure that a specific number of arguments are typed at the command line:

```
$ cat test_script
if test "$#" -ne 2
then
    echo "You must enter at least and no more than 2 arguments."
fi
$ test_script 1
You must enter at least and no more than 2 arguments.
$ test_script 1 2 3
You must enter at least and no more than 2 arguments.
$ test_script 1 2
$
```

■ int1 -le int2

test returns a zero exit status if int1 is less than or equal to int2.

```
$ cat test_script
if test "$1" -le "$2"
then
    echo "The 1st argument is less than or equal to the 2nd."
fi
$
$ test_script 1 2
The 1st argument is less than or equal to the 2nd.
$ test_script 2 2
The 1st argument is less than or equal to the 2nd.
$ test_script 2 3
$ test_script
The 1st argument is less than or equal to the 2nd.
```

Notice in the last command that two nulls are equivalent.

■ int1 -ge int2

test returns a zero exit status if int1 is greater than or equal to int2.

```
$ cat test_script
if test "$1" -ge "$2"
then
    echo "The 1st argument is greater than or equal to the 2nd."
```

```
fi
$ test_script 1 2

$ test_script 2 2
The 1st argument is greater than or equal to the 2nd.
```

Bourne Shell Implementation

All examples in this section will produce the same result when run from the Bourne shell.

Korn Shell Implementation

All examples in this section will produce the same result when run from the Korn shell, except where noted.

10.4.3 Testing Files

The `test` command also allows tests on the existence and properties of files. Remember that a directory is also considered a file in the UNIX file system, only the contents of a directory comprise the names of the files in it. Files can be tested for the following:

- `-d file`

  `test` returns a zero exit status if the file being tested is a directory.

- `-f file`

  `test` returns a zero exit status if the file being tested is not a directory.

- `-s file`

  `test` returns a zero exit status if the file has nonzero length.

- `-r file`

  `test` returns a zero exit status if the file is readable.

■ —w file

test returns a zero exit status if the file is writable.

■ —x file

test returns a zero exit status if the file is executable.

OK. Now to set up some variables:

```
$ set file1="/REDHOT/sally"
$ set file2="/REDHOT/sally/file1"
```

And now the test command as it applies to file tests:

■ —d file

test returns a zero exit status if the file being tested is a directory.

```
$ cat test_script
if test -d "$1"
then
   cd "$1"; pwd;
fi
$ test_script $file1
/REDHOT/sally
$ test_script $file2
$
```

$file1 is a directory; hence the test returns a zero exit status to the system, and the commands between the then and fi are executed.

■ —f file

test returns a zero exit status if the file being tested is not a directory.

```
$ cat test_script
if test -f "$1"
then
   cat "$1";
fi
$ test_script $file1
$ test_script $file2
```

```
file_2
$
```

$file2 is a file, and the cat command is executed in the second case.

■ -s file

test returns a zero exit status if the file has nonzero length.

```
$ cat test_script
if test -s "$1"
then
    echo "File is not empty.";
fi
$ test_script $file1
File is not empty
$ test_script $file2
File is not empty
$ echo > file100
$ ls -l file100
-rw-r--r--   1 zamir   0 Apr 1 13:37 file100
$ test_script "file100"
$
```

The last command did not result in the File is not empty message being displayed, because file100 is of zero length.

Notice that this command will always execute for directories, even if they contain no files. This is because all directories have an entry for themselves (the "." that displays when you do a long listing of it) and one for their parent directory (the "..", unless it's the root directory).

■ -r file

test returns a zero exit status if the file is readable.

```
$ cat test_script
if test -f "$1" && test -r "$1"
then
    cat "$1"
fi
```

We will send two arguments to test_script. The first one is a file, and the second one is a directory.

```
$ test_script "file1"
file_1
```

```
$ test_script "directory_1"
$
```

In the second example, nothing is output because the first command fails, since `directory_1` is not a file, and the second command is not executed.

■ -w file

test returns a zero exit status if the file is writable.

test_script can be modified to write to a file as follows:

```
$ cat test_script
if test -f "$1" && test -w "$1"
then
   echo "Appending to file" >> $1; cat $1
fi
$
```

We will send a file to test_script as an argument. The contents of this file are as follows:

```
$ cat file1
A new file
$
```

And here's the result:

```
$ test_script "file1"
A new file
Appending to file
$
```

The >> operator is used to append to an existing file. This command would have failed if the user implementing it did not have write permission for that file.

■ -x file

test returns a zero exit status if the file is executable.

We will create an executable file called log_file:

```
$ cat log_file
echo "`whoami` is logged in on `date`" >> logger
echo "Event logged."
$
```

This file executes the `whoami` command, concatenates its output to some text, and appends the output to a file called `logger`. `log_file` has execute permission, as you can see:

```
$ ls -l log_file
-rwxr-xr-x  1 zamir   70 Apr 1 14:28 log_file
$
```

And here's the `test_script`:

```
$ cat test_script
if test -f "$1" && test -x "$1"
then
   $1
fi
$
```

We send `log_file` as an argument to `test_script`:

```
$ test_script "log_file"
Event logged
```

Let's take a look at the file `logger`:

```
$ cat logger
zamir is logged in on Wed Apr 1 14:30:18 EST 1992
$
```

Bourne Shell Implementation

All examples illustrated in Section 10.4.3 will produce the same result when run from the Bourne shell.

Korn Shell Implementation

All examples illustrated in Section 10.4.3 will also produce the same result when run from the Korn shell, except where noted.

10.5 OSF/1 CONSIDERATIONS

All examples illustrated in this chapter will produce the same results when run from the C, Bourne, and Korn shells in an OSF/1 operating system. However, OSF/1 also offers the *restricted Bourne shell*. In this shell, those commands which include a `cd` to any directory other than the current one will not run.

10.6 REVIEW

This chapter listed the control structures that are available in the shell, and then presented a detailed description of the `if` construct. The general format of the `if` statement is like this:

```
if command executes successfully
then
     execute this command
     and this one
fi
```

All commands return a *status* to the system indicating whether they executed successfully or unsuccessfully. The `test` command is frequently used in shell scripts to test this return status. A value of zero is returned by `test` on successful execution of a command, and non-zero in case of failure.

You should now have a good idea of the power that is placed in your hands via the `test` command. Table 10.1 presents a synopsis of the major features.

Table 10.1 The test Command

Syntax	Explanation
test *expression* returns zero for *strings,* where *expression* is:	
string1 = string2	If string1 is identical to string2
string1 != string2	If string1 is not identical to string2
string	If string is not null
-n string	If string is not null
-z string	If string is null
test *expression* returns zero for *integers,* where *expression* is:	
int1 -eq int2	If int1 is equal to int2
int1 -lt int2	If int1 is less than int2
int1 -gt int2	If int1 is greater than int2
int1 -ne int2	If int1 is not equal to int2
int1 -le int2	If int1 is less than or equal to int2
int1 -ge int2	If int1 is greater than or equal to int2
test *expression* returns zero for *files,* where *expression* is:	
-d file	If file is a directory
-f file	If file is not a directory
-s file	If file has nonzero length
-r file	If file is readable
-w file	If file is writable
-x file	If file is executable

The Remaining Control Structures

11.1 INTRODUCTION

This chapter describes the remaining control structures that exist in the shell language. The following statements will be described and illustrated through shell scripts:

- The `else` construct

- The `elif` construct

- The `case` construct

- The `for` loop

- The `while` loop

- The `until` loop

11.2 THE ELSE CONSTRUCT

For each `if`, it's a good idea to have an `else`! The `else` statement is a good safety measure for those cases when the `if` command does not execute quite as you expected it to. The flow of the `else` construct can be expressed as follows:

```
if command executes successfully
then
        execute this command
        and this command
else
        execute this command
        and this command
fi
```

The command following if is executed. If this command is successful, then all commands between then and else are executed. If this command is unsuccessful, then all commands between the else and fi are executed.

11.2.1 Some Examples

The examples will be written to a file called else_script. The else_script will be given execute permission via the chmod command in order to have it execute.

Example 1:   If today is Friday, move backup_file to temp. If today is not Friday, do a long listing of the current working directory, and append the output to backup_file.

```
$ cat else_script
if date | grep "Fri"
then
  mv backup_file temp
else
  ls -l >> backup_file
fi
$ date
Fri Jan 24 19:45:10 EST 1992
$ else_script
Fri Jan 24 19:46:15 EST 1992
$
```

Notice that the output for the date command is the only output that displays. Example 2 builds on Example 1:

Example 2:   If today is Friday, move backup_file to temp, and echo a message stating this. If today is not Friday, do a long listing of the current working directory, and append the output to backup_file. Display a message after successful execution of this command as well.

This example asks us to perform inherently the same tasks as Example 1, plus display a few messages stating what happened, and somehow redirect the output for the date command. Here's the modified else script:

```
$ cat else_script
if date > scratch && grep "Fri" scratch
then
   mv backup_file temp
   echo "backup_file moved to temp."
   rm scratch
else
   ls -l >> backup_file
   echo "backup_file appended."
   rm scratch
fi
$ date
Fri Jan 24 19:45:10 EST 1992
$ else_script
Fri Jan 24 19:45:10 EST 1992
backup_file moved to temp.
$
```

Notice that the output for date is redirected to a temporary file called scratch, and that grep tries to find a match on Fri in this file. Whether or not a match is found, scratch is created and then removed via the rm command. If the current date was, say, Monday, then the output for else_script would be

```
backup_file appended.
$
```

11.3 THE ELIF CONSTRUCT

The elif construct provides a means of simplifying the structure of multiple if-else statements. If there are too many if-else statements, it becomes difficult to follow the flow of control of the statements, and it is easy to get confused as to which block of statements belongs to which level.

The flow of the elif construct can be expressed as follows:

```
if this command executes successfully
then
   do this
   and this
elif this command executes successfully
then
```

```
    do this
    and this
elif this command executes successfully
then
    do this
    and this
else
    do this
    and this
fi
```

The command following the if is executed. If this command is successful, then the commands contained within the then and elif keywords in the following block are executed. If this command is unsuccessful, then the shell tries to execute the command found for the next elif statement, and so on. Once the condition is hit where a command is successful, all subsequent commands for the remaining elifs are disregarded. The else block is the default condition, and is executed when none of the commands are successful.

11.3.1 An Example

This time the example will be written to a file called elif_script.

Example 1:   If the argument sent to elif_script is a directory, then do a long listing of its contents to a file called script. If the argument sent is a file, then write that file to script. If the argument sent is neither a file nor a directory, then echo a message. Output a message requesting an argument if none is provided. Output messages indicating the condition implemented.

```
$ cat elif_script
if test "$#" -ne 1
then
    echo "You must send 1 argument to elif_script."
elif test -d "$1"
then
    ls -l "$1" > script
    echo "Contents of directory written to script."
elif test -f "$1"
then
    cat "$1" > script
    echo "Contents of file written to script."
else
    echo "Argument sent is neither directory nor file!"
```

```
        echo "Please reenter argument."
fi
$
```

OK. Now we will execute this shell script for each of the conditions being tested. The output for the following sequence of commands is self-explanatory; hence it will not be elaborated on any further.

```
$ elif_script
You must send 1 argument to elif_script.
$ elif_script "file1"
Contents of file written to script.
$ elif_script "/REDHOT/sally"
Contents of directory written to script.
$ elif_script 10
Argument sent is neither directory nor file!
Please reenter argument.
$
```

11.4 THE EXIT STATEMENT

Before continuing with the remaining constructs, we introduce you to the exit statement. This statement is used to immediately get you out of the shell procedure. The format of the exit statement looks like this:

```
exit number
```

where number is the number that you wish to assign to the exit status that is returned to the system. If a number is not assigned explicitly, then the exit status of the last command executed in the shell script will be assigned. Here's sample usage:

```
$ cat exit_script
if test "$#" -eq 0
then
     echo "You must enter at least one argument!"
     echo "Processing cannot continue!"
     exit 1
fi
echo "Arguments sent are $*"
$ exit_script
You must enter at least one argument!
Processing cannot continue!
```

```
$ exit_script 1 2 3 4 "string_1"
Arguments sent are 1 2 3 4 string_1
$
```

The above script insists on one or more arguments. If none are sent, then it performs an immediate exit from the shell script. If arguments are sent, then it simply echoes them back to the terminal. The value of the above program is enhanced if you replace the simple echo statement with multiple commands that manipulate and test the arguments entered. We restricted the processing to just one command, to keep the example short and sweet. The exit statement bypasses complex if-else and if-elif-else constructs by providing an immediate exit from the shell procedure file.

We now continue with an explanation of the case construct in the next section.

11.5 THE CASE CONSTRUCT

The case construct allows the comparison of a single value against one or more alternatives. If a match is found, then the block of commands that follow the match are executed, up until the double semicolon. The format of the case construct will help clarify what has just been said:

```
case argument in
pattern 1)   execute this command
             and this
             and this;;

pattern 2)   execute this command
             and this
             and this;;

pattern 3)   execute this command
             and this
             and this;;
esac
```

argument can be an integer value or a string. The pattern to be matched on must be delimited by a closing brace. The double semicolons delimit the group of one or more commands that is to be executed if the pattern is matched, for each case. The esac (case spelled backwards!) delimits the case construct.

11.5.1 Some Examples

The script file will be called `case_script`. Once again, the output is self-explanatory, and hence will not be elaborated on further.

Example 1:   Make sure only one argument is sent to `case_script`, and that it is between the numbers 1 and 3.

```
$ cat case_script
if test "$#" -eq 0
then
   echo "Please enter one argument."
   exit 1
elif test "$#" -ge 2
then
   echo "Please enter only one argument."
   exit 1
else
   case "$1" in
     1) exit 0;;
     2) exit 0;;
     3) exit 0;;
   esac
   echo "Argument entered is not between numbers 1
and 3."
fi
$ case_script
Please enter one argument.
$ case_script 1 2
Please enter only one argument
$ case_script "one"
Argument entered is not between numbers 1 and 3.
$ case_script 1
$ case_script 4
Argument entered is not between numbers 1 and 3.
$
```

Notice that the `case` statement is nested within the `if-elif-else` construct. Also, the invocation of the `case_script` with the argument 1 resulted in no output. This makes sense, since we simply perform an exit if the number 1, 2, or 3 is sent as arguments. This shell script is intended to display output only if the wrong argument is entered.

The `case` statement can be used with string arguments as well. As a matter of fact, you can use the metacharacter pattern matching capabilities that are available with the UNIX system for your tests. We now refresh your memory for some of these metacharacters:

```
*        Match zero or more characters.
?        Match on a single character.
[...]    Match on the range specified.
```

You may use any of the pattern matching features available (explained in Chapter 6). We have listed the three main ones. Let's continue with another example.

Example 2:   Make sure the name of a file is sent as an argument to case_script. If so, and the file exists in the current directory, proceed as follows: (a) If the file is suffixed with a .doc, move it to the document directory. (b) If the file is suffixed with a .bck, move it to the backup directory. (c) If the file is suffixed with a .tmp, remove it from the system. Do nothing for all other files. Display a message indicating the action performed.

And here's the script file:

```
$ cat case_script
if test "$#" -eq 0
then
   echo "Please enter one argument."
   exit 1
elif test "$#" -ge 2
then
   echo "Please enter only one argument."
   exit 1
elif test -f "$1"
then
   case "$1" in
      *".doc") ls "$1" && mv "$1" document && echo \
           "$1 moved to document directory.";;
      *".bck") ls "$1" && mv "$1" backup && echo \
           "$1 moved to backup directory.";;
      *".tmp") ls "$1" && rm "$1" && echo \
           "$1 removed.";;
   esac
else
   echo "Argument entered is not a file."
fi
$ case_script
Please enter one argument.
$ case_script 1 2
Please enter only one argument.
```

```
$ case_script file1.doc
file1.doc moved to document directory.
$ case_script file2.doc
file2.doc moved to document directory.
$ case_script file1.bck
file1.bck moved to backup directory.
$ case_script file1.tmp
file1.tmp removed.
$ case_script 1
Argument entered is not a file.
$ case_script file1
$
```

First of all, notice that the asterisk is outside the double quotes. This is necessary, since the asterisk is interpreted literally inside the double quotes (the $, \, and ' are the only characters that retain their special meaning inside double quotes). Also notice the backslash, which is used to continue the command on the next line. The && sign is used to ensure the successful implementation of the last command before the next command is executed. When case_script is invoked with the argument file1, there is no output. This is because file1 is the name of a file, but it has no suffix, and therefore there is no match on any of the patterns specified in the case statement.

11.6 THE FOR LOOP

The for loop is used to execute commands contained within a block a specified number of times. Here's the syntax of the for loop:

```
for variable in value_1, value_2, ... value_n
do
      this command
      and this command
      and this command
done
```

The for loop is executed n times, or the number of times that value is listed. The first time around, value1 is substituted into variable, and then the block of commands between do and done are executed in sequence. Once this is done, value2 is substituted into variable, and the group of commands is executed again. The substitution continues until the complete list of values has been exhausted.

11.6.1 An Example

Here's an example that illustrates the `for` loop:

Example 1:   For each argument entered at the command prompt, display whether it is a file, a directory, or neither.

```
$ cat for_loop
for i in "$1" "$2" "$3" "$4"
do
   if test -d "$i"
   then
     echo "$i is a directory."
   elif test -f "$i"
   then
     echo "$i is a file."
   else
     echo "$i is neither a file nor a directory."
   fi
done
$
```

Sample usage of the `for_loop` script file follows:

```
$ for_loop file1 document 1 2 3
file1 is a file.
document is a directory.
1 is neither a file nor a directory.
2 is neither a file nor a directory.
$
```

This time we nest an `if-elif-else` construct within the `for` loop. Notice that only four place holders are provided, but five arguments are sent to the `for_loop`. The fifth argument is simply ignored.

11.7 THE EXPR COMMAND

Before continuing with the `while` loop, we will describe the `expr` command. (This command helps in the implementation of the `while` loop.) The `expr` command is used to evaluate arithmetic expressions. Recall that the shell recognizes no data types. If we type

```
$ set value 10+1
$
```

then echoing `value` will give this output:

```
$ echo $value
10+1
$
```

However, the `expr` command can be used to evaluate an expression and perform arithmetic on it. All you have to do is follow the keyword `expr` with the expression. The following arithmetic operators can be used within `expr`:

```
+    Add
-    Subtract
*    Multiply
/    Divide
%    Output remainder of division
```

The output for `expr` is the result of the specified operation. Here's sample usage:

```
$ expr 1 + 1
2
$ expr 1 - 1
0
$ expr 4 % 3
1
$
```

Please note that each element of the expression must be separated by spaces. Here's the result if you don't adhere to this rule:

```
$ expr 1-1
1-1
$
```

Furthermore, `expr` expects integers as its arguments. Trying to run expr with noninteger values results in this error message:

```
$ expr str + str
expr: syntax error at argument # 1
$ expr 1.2 + 1.3
expr: syntax error at argument # 1
$
```

And one more thing. You know that the * has a special meaning for the shell; it is used to match zero or more characters. Hence, if a multiplication is being performed via `expr`, the * must be preceded by the backslash (\), so that it may be interpreted literally. Here's how the expression would look:

```
$ expr 2 * 2
expr: syntax error at argument # 2
$ expr 2 \* 2
4
$
```

OK. Now let's describe the while loop.

11.8 THE WHILE LOOP

The while loop is also used to execute commands contained within a block a number of times. Here's the syntax of the while loop:

```
while this command executes successfully
do
        this command
        and this command
        and this command
done
```

The group of commands enclosed between the do and done is executed for as long as the command following the while keyword executes successfully (that is, returns a zero status). From this, it would be valid to say that the group of commands between the do and done will execute forever, if the command following while always executes successfully. (That's where we're going to bring expr into the picture.) On the other hand, it is possible that this group of commands may never execute – this would happen if the command following while fails. Section 11.8.1 presents some examples that illustrate its usage.

11.8.1 Some Examples

Example 1:   Print as many copies of a file as requested. The user should enter two arguments. The first argument should specify the file name, and the second the number of hard copies required.

Here's the shell script for the job:

```
$ cat while_script
if test "$#" -eq 2
then
   i=$2
   while test "$i" -gt 0
   do
      lpr "$1"
      echo "$1 sent to printer."
      i=`expr $i - 1`
   done
else
   echo "Please enter 2 arguments where"
   echo " Argument 1 is: file name"
   echo " Argument 2 is: Number of hard copies
required."
fi
$
```

This shell script requires a little bit more explanation than the others. We will step through each line. First, the test command is used with the $# variable to ensure that 2 arguments are entered. If so, then the group of commands between the then and else is executed. Here, an arbitrary variable called i is set to the second argument. This is the number of hard copies requested. Next, a while loop is implemented for as long as the second argument entered is greater than 0. Between the do and the done of the while, the lpr command is used to output the file to the printer, and the expr command is used to decrement the value of i. Notice that the expr command is enclosed within back quotes. This is necessary in order to implement the command and set the result of the expr to i. OK. Now let's implement while_script with various arguments.

```
$ while_script
Please enter 2 arguments where
   Argument 1 is: file name
   Argument 2 is: Number of hard copies required.
$ while_script "file1" 3
file1 sent to printer.
file1 sent to printer.
file1 sent to printer.
$ while_script "file1" "file2"
```

Notice the output of the last instance of while_script. There is no output. This is because the command while test "$i" -gt 0 fails for file2, because it is not an integer number.

11.9 THE UNTIL COMMAND

The until command is the flip side of the coin of the while loop. It is also used to execute commands contained within a block for a number of times, but only if the command following the until fails, or returns a nonzero status. Here's the syntax of the until loop:

```
until this command executes unsuccessfully
do
     this command
     and this command
     and this command
done
```

The until command is a good safety feature to be used to execute commands for as long as there is some kind of failure in the normal execution of everyday operations. The example in Section 11.9.1 presents a worst-case scenario.

11.9.1 An Example

Example 1:   If file1 is not found, do not proceed with regular processing. Continue to issue an alarm until someone terminates the execution of this shell script!

Although this example could be considered overkill, but the truth of the matter is that there are times when the absence of a critical file can be lethal to further processing. This example takes this situation into account. Here's until_script:

```
$ cat until_script
until ls file1
do
   echo "ALERT!! file100 MISSING!!!"
   echo "DO SOMETHING!@#"
done
$ until_script
file100: No such file or directory
ALERT!! file100 MISSING!!!
DO SOMETHING!@#
file100: No such file or directory
ALERT!! file100 MISSING!!!
DO SOMETHING!@#
file100: No such file <Cntrl> C
$
```

We were obliged to do something since this message would not stop displaying, so we hit <Cntrl> C to terminate execution of this script!

11.10 COMMENTS

Now that you are up to the level of writing fairly complex shell scripts, take the time to add comments to them. Add comments at the beginning of the script to state its purpose. Date it. Make sure your comments are valid statements of what is going on. Don't state how something is being implemented. Instead, state what is going on. Don't skimp on comments where they are needed. Don't overkill either.

Let's take a breather from all this good advice. Insert comments in shell scripts by inserting a number sign at the beginning of the line. We redisplay the `while_script` program with appropriate comments:

```
$ cat while_script
# This shell script prints a specified number of
# copies of a file to the printer. It expects
# two arguments; the first is the file name, and
# the second is the number of hard copies.

if test "$#" -eq 2
then
   i=$2
   while test "$i" -gt 0
   do
# print the file
# keep count in i
     lpr "$1"
     echo "$1 sent to printer."
     i=`expr $i - 1`
   done
else
   echo "Please enter 2 arguments where"
   echo " Argument 1 is: file name"
   echo " Argument 2 is: Number of hard copies
required."
fi
$
```

Bourne Shell Implementation

All control structures in the C shell are also supported by the Bourne shell. All examples will produce the same output.

Korn Shell Implementation

All control structures in the C shell are also supported by the Korn shell. All examples in this chapter will produce the same output.

11.11 OSF/1 CONSIDERATIONS

OSF/1 supports all of the control structures used to program the shell in the UNIX environment. All examples will produce the same output when run in an OSF/1 environment.

11.12 REVIEW

This chapter described the remaining control structures that can be used to program the shell. Table 11.1 summarizes the syntax of each.

In this chapter we also learned about:

■ The `exit` statement.

This statement allows immediate exit from a shell procedure. If a number is not explicitly assigned to it, the statement will contain the exit status of the last command executed.

■ The `expr` command.

This command is used to evaluate arithmetic expressions, and perform arithmetic using the standard arithmetic operators: + (add), − (subtract), * (multiply), / (divide), and % (remainder).

Table 11.1 Shell Control Structures

Construct	Description/Features
The *if - else* construct:	

if this command executes
then
    execute this command
else
    execute this command
fi
	If command following if is successful, then commands between then and else are executed.
	
	Otherwise, commands between else and fi are executed.

The *elif* construct:	

if this command executes
then
    execute this command
elif this command executes
then
    execute this command
else
    execute this command
fi
	If command following if is successful, then commands between then and elif are executed.
	
	If not, then command following elif is executed.
	
	If this is successful, then commands between then and else are executed.
	
	Otherwise, commands between else and fi are executed.

The *case* construct	
case argument in pattern 1) execute this;; pattern 2) execute this;; esac	Argument is a single value or integer or string. Match patterns are specified in pattern. They must be delimited by a brace. If pattern matches argument, then one or more commands following the match pattern are executed, up to the next double semicolon.

Table 11.1 Shell Control Structures (Contd.)

Construct	Description/Features
The *for* loop	
for var in value1, value2 do this command done	for loop executes for number of times that value is listed. value1 is substituted into var the first time. value2 is substituted into var the second time. Block of commands between do and done is executed for value1, value2, and so on.
The *while* command	

while this command executes
do
   this command
   and this command
done
	Command following while is executed.
	
	Block of commands between do and done is executed for as long as command following while executes successfully.

The *until* command	

until this command fails
do
   this command
   and this command
done
	Command following until is executed.
	
	Block of commands between do and done is executed for as long as command following until does *not* execute successfully.

12

The Shell Environment

12.1 INTRODUCTION

When you log into a UNIX system, you are automatically placed into a unique working environment that is defined by *environment* variables. Environment variables are those which set the values of parameters such as your home directory, the type of terminal that you will be working from, available paths for directory searches, and more.

Once inside the shell, you can set variables to values that may or may not have anything to do with your environment; they can reference values that are utilized by tasks that you have to perform in the current session. These variables are called *shell* variables; they are *local* to the particular session of the shell that you are working in. Once you exit the shell, these values are lost. This chapter describes environment and shell variables in detail.

In addition to this, when a command file is executed, a *subshell* is created which executes it. This subshell can be considered a child of the shell that you are working in. The environment variables maintain their values inside a subshell, but local variables do not. This chapter describes how values of local variables can be made visible to subshells as well.

This chapter also describes the *login* and *logout* scripts that are automatically invoked as you log into and out of the system. The commands contained inside these script files determine the environment that is automatically set up for you.

If you should decide to edit and customize any of your login files, we recommend that you store the original in a backup file, and then name it accordingly. Always keep a copy of the original login file; you never know what could go wrong!

12.2 LOGIN SCRIPT FILES

When you log into a system, a program called `login` is run. This program (among other things) verifies user name and password, and then looks for special *login* script files. Login script files set up your working environment.

There can be two kinds of script files, *system* and *local*. The next two subsections describe each.

12.2.1 System Login Scripts

System login scripts contain commands which set up a default environment for all users. This script file usually comes predefined from the vendor of your operating system. It is customized as necessary by your system administrator.

In a C shell environment, there is usually no system login script. Instead, two script files called `.cshrc` and `.login` are executed. These are considered local script files, and will be described in the next section.

Bourne Shell Implementation

The system login script for the Bourne shell environment is stored in `/etc/profile`. Here's a sample script file from our installation:

```
$ cat /etc/profile
# System Profile

trap 'echo `whoami` logged out on `date`' 0

if [! "$USER" ]
then
   USER=`whoami`
   export USER
fi
LOGNAME=$USER
export LOGNAME

LOGTTY=`tty`
HOST=`hostname`
export LOGTTY HOST
$
```

Although it is too early in the chapter to describe in detail the contents of this file, we ask you to take a second look at it and observe a few things. First of all, you will notice that the script file is nothing more than a shell script. This particular shell script will run only in the Bourne shell and Korn shell environments. (It contains syntax which the C shell will be unable to understand.) The first line of this shell script is an explanatory comment. Next, you see the word `trap`. `trap` is a command in the UNIX operating system which will be described in detail later on in the chapter. Next, you see an `if` construct. Notice the use of uppercase for some variable names, the execution of the `whoami` command (it is enclosed in back quotes, which results in the execution of whatever is enclosed within), and the keyword `export`. All of these will be explained in due course.

Korn Shell Implementation

System login scripts for the Korn shell environment also reside in `/etc/profile`. It is not necessary for the Korn shell to have a separate file because it is a superset of the Bourne shell, and provides upward compatibility for all Bourne shell scripts. That is, all Bourne shell scripts will run in a Korn shell.

12.2.2 Local Login Scripts

Local login scripts reside in your default login directory. These script files are executed after the system login script. They can be used to customize the values of environment variables to conform to your special needs.

In the C shell you can have two local scripts: `.cshrc` and `.login`. The `.cshrc` script is executed first. This is usually used to set up shell variables. However, it can be used to set environment variables as well. The difference between these two types of variables will be described in due course. The `.login` file is used to set up environment variables. Following are sample `.cshrc` and `.login` scripts:

```
$ cat .cshrc
#
# .cshrc file
# Initial setup file for C shells.
#
setenv username `whoami`
setenv PROMPT="{`hostname`:`echo $cwd`} "
```

```
set noclobber
set history=100
cd $HOME
alias bye     logout
alias ciao    logout
alias adios     logout
clear
$
```

Notice the `setenv` command. This is used to set environment variables. Also notice the `set` commands. These are used to set shell variables. At the end of the file is a group of `alias` commands. All of these terms will be explained in due course. Now take a look at the `.login` file.

```
$ cat .login
# .login file
# Initial setup file for C shells, executed after
# .cshrc.
#
umask 022
setenv PATH=.:/bin:/usr/bin:/usr/local/bin;
setenv EDITOR vi
date
$
```

Here we once again see the `setenv` command, and the `date` command.

■ The .cshrc Script File

The `.cshrc` file needs to be explained in greater detail because it provides additional functionality over the other login files.

Recall that in the beginning of the chapter we said that when a shell executes a process, it creates a subshell to do so. This subshell could be considered a child of the current shell. The subshell does not recognize the variables set in its parent shell. However, the `.cshrc` file is set up so that it executes each time a subshell is created. Consequently, the values of shell variables are consistent between a shell and its child process.

Bourne Shell Implementation

In the Bourne shell you have only one local login script, called `.profile`. This sets up both environment and shell variables. Here is a sample `.profile`:

```
$ cat .profile
# .profile -
# Local login script read after /etc/profile.
#
PATH=.:/bin:/usr/bin:/usr/local/bin:
export PATH
PS1='>>'
$
```

Korn Shell Implementation

The Korn shell uses the same .profile for its start-up file as the Bourne shell. However, since the Korn shell does provide features which are not present in the Bourne shell, it allows you to specify another startup file in the ENV variable. This is a shell variable which will be described in detail later on in the chapter. It is set equal to the name of the file which will contain the script which is to be executed in addition to .profile at login.

12.3 ENVIRONMENT VARIABLES

In this section we describe environment variables in further detail. In the C shell, environment variables are set with the setenv command:

```
setenv variable=value
```

We redisplay one of the setenv commands from the .cshrc file presented earlier.

```
$ setenv PROMPT="{ `hostname`:`echo $cwd`} "
```

The above command sets the PROMPT environment variable of the current user to the result obtained from the execution of the command

```
"{ `hostname`:`echo $cwd`}"
```

Elaborating further, inside the double quotes, the { will display literally. hostname is a program that outputs the name of the machine that you are working on. Since it is enclosed in single quotes, the program is executed and its output placed in the location indicated. This prompt will be individualized via the display of the hostname for each user. (It is unlikely that two machines in your installation have the same name.) Next, the :

displays literally. Then, the current working directory, which is stored inside a variable called cwd, is displayed via the echo command. Assume that the hostname is amity. This is how the value is ultimately stored in the environment variable PROMPT:

```
{amity: /home/whales/zamir}
```

By convention, environment variables are usually designated by all uppercase letters.

Bourne Shell Implementation

Environment variables are set in the Bourne shell via the assignment operator only. Then they have to be exported. Here's the syntax:

```
variable=value
export variable
```

Here are some of the settings from /etc/profile:

```
$ LOGTTY=`tty`
$ HOST=`hostname`
$ export LOGTTY HOST
```

The variable LOGTTY is set to the output produced by the execution of the command tty. tty is a program that displays the name of the terminal that you are working on. HOST is set to the output of the program hostname, which displays the designated name for the machine that you are working on.

The last line shows the use of the keyword export. We defer a detailed explanation of the export command to the next section, where local variables are described.

If the environment variables are set at the command line prompt, then their setttings will be local to the current session. If you would like these settings to be more permanent, simply insert an entry for them in the .profile file.

As in the C shell, by convention, environment variables are designated by all uppercase letters.

Korn Shell Implementation

Environment variables are set in the Korn shell in the same way as in the Bourne shell.

Furthermore, the settings are local, as in the Bourne shell. The settings can be made permanent by adding an entry for them in the `.profile` file or the file name specified for the ENV variable within `.profile`.

12.4 SHELL OR LOCAL VARIABLES

Shell variables will be described in this section. Shell variables are set via the `set` command:

```
$ set variable=10
$ echo $variable
10
$
```

Keep in mind that variables set at the command line prompt will be local to the session in which they are set. A shell variable can be made permanent by inserting an entry for it in `.cshrc` and re-executing the script file.

Bourne Shell Implementation

Shell variables are set in the Bourne shell via the assignment operator:

```
$ variable=10
```

Their values can be obtained by echoing them:

```
$ echo $variable
10
$
```

Unlike the C shell, the Bourne shell does not have a `.cshrc` kind of file that is run each time a subshell is created within the current working session. Here's a little shell script that illustrates what has just been said:

```
$ cat test_script
echo $variable
$ chmod +x test_script
```

Recall that `chmod +x` gives execute permission to the file or file names that follow it. Executing the script gives this result:

```
$ test_script
```

$

    As you can see, the shell displays a null value for $variable. However, there is a way in which values can be made available to subshells. This is via the export command. Typing as follows:

```
$ export variable
```
$

will make the value stored inside variable available to all subshells created from the parent shell in which the variable is exported. Now when test_script is executed,

```
$ test_script
```
10
$

the correct value is displayed. If you would like to make the assignment permanent, insert an entry for it in .profile, and make sure you export it on the next line.

    Once a variable has been exported, there is no need to reexport it if its value is changed. For example, if variable is reset, test_script is reexecuted:

```
$ variable=34
$ test_script
```
34
$

The correct value of variable is output.

Korn Shell Implementation

The Korn shell behaves the same way as the Bourne shell. Variables are set as follows:

```
$ variable=value
```

and values can be made visible to subshells via the export command:

```
$ export variable
```

12.5 MODIFYING EXPORTED VARIABLES

Variables can be set in the parent shell, automatically exported to the child shell via .cshrc, and then reset within the child shell. However, the reset value applies only to the child process; the parent shell will retain the value that was set in it. The text for the Bourne shell implementation for this section goes into further detail of what has just been said.

Bourne Shell Implementation

In the Bourne shell, variables have to be exported explicitly to all child subprocesses via the export command. However, the logic for variables that are reset in the child shells is the same as that in the C shell. Here's a sequence of commands that illustrates what has just been said.

```
$ variable=10
$ export variable
$ cat test_script
echo "variable in subshell is $variable"
variable=20
echo "variable reset in subshell is $variable"
$ test_script
variable in subshell is 10
variable reset in subshell is 20
$ echo $variable
10
$
```

The output should be self-explanatory.

Korn Shell Implementation

The Korn shell also exports variables via the export command. Its behavior is similar to that of the Bourne shell in all respects. The example presented for the Bourne shell will produce the same results when run from the Korn shell.

12.6 SOME COMMON BUILT-IN ENVIRONMENT VARIABLES

Following are the descriptions of some variables that are preset and builtin for you, and are common to almost all shells.

HOME

This specifies what your current working directory will be when you log into the system.

HOST

This is the name of the computer that you are working on.

LOGNAME

This specifies your login name.

PATH

This specifies the paths that are to be searched when commands are executed. The order in which the paths are encountered will indicate the order in which the directories will be searched.

SHELL

This specifies the shell that you will be placed in on login.

TERM

This specifies the type of terminal that you are working from.

A more detailed description of some of these variables follows.

12.6.1 The HOME Variable

This variable contains the path of the directory that you will be placed in as you log into the system. Reference it like this:

```
$ echo "$HOME"
/home/whales/zamir
$ cd $HOME
$ pwd
/home/whales/zamir
$
```

12.6.2 The PATH Variable

This variable contains a list of directories with their full path names. Each entry is separated from the next by a *colon* (:). The order in which these paths are listed is the order in which the shell searches for commands that are typed at the command line. Take a look at this entry for PATH:

```
$ echo $PATH
PATH=.:/home/whales/zamir/bin:/usr/local/sybase/bin
$
```

The entry above can be divided into three parts:

```
Entry 1:  .
```
This is the current working directory.

```
Entry 2:  /home/whales/zamir/bin
```

```
Entry 3:  /usr/local/sybase/bin
```

When you type a command at the system prompt, like so:

```
$ test_script
```

the shell first searches your current working directory for a command file of that name. If it does not find test_script in the current working directory, then /home/whales/zamir/bin is searched. If this search is also fruitless, then /usr/local/sybase/bin is searched. If the command is still not found, then a message indicating this is displayed:

```
test_script:  command not found.
$
```

Otherwise, the command is executed.

We encourage you to do a cat on the login script files and understand the values stored in the variables set for your particular environment.

12.6.3 The TERM Variable

The TERM variable is used to set the terminal type. This variable is used by screen-based programs, such as the vi editor, to set up the environment necessary for their proper functioning. For example, if TERM is set up to an incompatible terminal type for vi, then vi will not execute. You should leave the setting of this variable to your system administrator. The entries vary with different types of hardware.

12.7 SOME COMMON COMMANDS AND SETTINGS

Although each shell script is customized for the installation in which it runs, the following commands and settings are commonly found in most login script files.

12.7.1 The clear Command

This command simply clears the screen. Its syntax is as follows:

```
$ clear
```

12.7.2 The trap Command

This command cannot be run in the C shell environment.

Bourne Shell Implementation

The trap command is used to run one or more specified commands based on certain signals that are received from the terminal. The need for this arises from the default condition that occurs when there is no trap command. Suppose you hit <Cntrl> C in the middle of a process. As you do so, a signal is sent to the executing program, and the process terminates immediately. This may not be desirable for various reasons: the directories may not have been cleaned up properly, temporary files may not have been removed, and more. The trap command allows the specification of the commands that are to be implemented when certain signals that indicate an interruption in the normal execution of a program are received.

The syntax of the trap command is as follows:

```
trap command signal
```

command represents one or more commands that are implemented on receiving a signal.

Some of the more common signals that are transmitted are:

0   Indicates logout from the shell.

2   Indicates that an interrupt key, such as the Delete key, has been pressed.

15   Indicates that the process is being killed via a software process, such as the `kill` command.

Here's the `trap` command that you encountered in /etc/profile earlier in the chapter:

```
$ trap 'echo `whoami` logged out on `date`' 0
```

The above command displays the login name and date and time of logout when someone exits from the shell.

The `trap` command can be used to ignore signals as follows:

```
$ trap ""  2
```

The interrupt signal would be ignored.

You can review the current `trap` settings by typing `trap` with no arguments:

```
$ trap
0: 'echo `whoami` logged out on `date`'
$
```

Korn Shell Implementation

The `trap` command works in the same way when executed from the Korn shell as it does in the Bourne shell.

12.7.3 The set history Command

All commands that you enter at the command prompt can be stored inside what is known as the *command history*. These commands can be displayed at any time, and reexecuted simply by typing an exclamation mark followed by the number of the command.

The `set history` command is used to create a history buffer for a specified number of commands:

```
$ set history=100
$
```

The above command sets the history buffer to 100 commands. This implies that up to 100 commands that you type will be stored in this buffer. You can review what you have done so far by typing as follows:

```
$ history
1 set history=100
2 ls
3 pwd
4 vi product_a.doc
[5] $ _
$
```

You can reexecute a command from the history buffer as follows:

```
$ !!
```

This executes the last command. In our example, it will execute the command listed next to 4 (vi product_a.doc).

```
$ !2
```

This executes command number 2 in the history buffer (ls).

```
$ !-2
```

This executes the command that has the number of the current command, minus the number indicated. In our example, command number 3 is executed (pwd).

```
$ !set
```

This executes the last command that matches the character contained in the string following !. In our example, command number 1 will be executed, since the string set matches the command set history=100. If there was some other command between the current command and set history (commands 1 and 5), then that would have been executed instead.

And finally, you can save the commands used in the current login session and use them in the next with the following command:

```
$ set savehist=20
```

The above command saves the last 20 commands of the current session in the history buffer for the next session.

Bourne Shell Implementation

The Bourne shell does not support the `history` command.

Korn Shell Implementation

The Korn shell supports the `history` command like the C shell. However, the syntax is different.

The `HISTSIZE` variable is used to specify the size of the history buffer. This is how it is set:

```
$ HISTSIZE=100
$
```

The above command sets the history buffer to 100 commands. The commands stored inside the history buffer can be reviewed the same way as in the C shell:

```
$ history
1 set history=100
2 ls
3 pwd
4 vi product_a.doc
[5] $ _
$
```

Commands inside the history buffer are reexecuted like this:

```
$ r
```

This executes the last command. In our example, it will execute the command listed next to 4 (`vi product_a.doc`).

```
$ r 2
```

This executes command number 2 in the history buffer (`ls`).

```
$ r -2
```

This executes the command that has the number of the current command, minus the number indicated. In our example, command number 3 is executed (`pwd`).

```
$ r set
```

This executes the last command that matches the character contained in the string following `r`. In our example, command number 1 will be executed, since the string `set` matches the command `set history=100`. If there was some other command between the current command and `set history` (commands 1 and 5), then that would have been executed instead.

The Korn shell has no corresponding `savehist` variable like the C shell, which is used to save the last few commands of the current session in the history buffer for the next session.

12.7.4 The umask Command

This command is used to set the default permission set for every file or directory that will be created in your session. Like the `chmod` command, the `umask` assigns numbers to specify the permission set. However, unlike `chmod`, it does not specify the permissions that you will have, it specifies the permissions that are not to be granted. A few examples will help clarify what has just been said. But first, here's a list of the numbers and their correponding permission sets:

```
Octal Number   Permission Set

     0         Read/Write/Execute
     1         Read/Write
     2         Read/Execute
     3         Read
     4         Write/Execute
     5         Write
     6         Execute
     7         No permissions
```

Thus, specifying a user mask of 0 for a group indicates that the group has all permissions. Meanwhile, recall that the `chmod` command would use the number 7 to specify all permission sets. Hence, `umask` is, in effect, the inverse of `chmod`. And now for a few examples.

```
$ umask 011
$
```

The above command specifies that all files or directories that are created by the current user will have read, write, and execute permission for the owner, and read and write permission only for the group and all other users.

```
$ umask 022
$
```

The above user mask specifies that all files or directories created will have all permissions for the owner, and read and execute permission for everyone else. This is the setting in the .login file for the C shell presented earlier on in this chapter.

12.8 ALIASES

An alias is exactly what its name implies: a name for something. Aliases can be used as a shortcut to typing long commands that you frequently use; for example, an alias can be set for a long path name. Here's the syntax:

```
alias name command
```

where name is the alias name, and command is command. Here's sample usage:

```
$ alias facility 'cd /home/whales/zamir/dvlp/project/facility'
```

Henceforth, each time you type facility at the command prompt,

```
$ facility
$
```

the command specified in the alias will be implemented. Let's take a look:

```
$ pwd
/home/whales/zamir/dvlp/project/facility
$
```

You can use the unalias command to unset a previously set alias:

```
$ unalias facility
$ facility
facility:   Command not found.
$
```

The message indiates that the shell is unable to find a UNIX command, command file, or alias for that name.

An alias is the preferred way to rename UNIX commands.

Bourne Shell Implementation

The Bourne shell does not support the `alias` and `unalias` commands.

Korn Shell Implementation

The `alias` and `unalias` commands work in the same way when implemented from the Korn shell as they do in the C shell.

12.9 APPLYING CHANGES TO CURRENT LOGIN SESSION

As you know, the `.cshrc` or `.profile` files are read only on login. If you would like to have any of the settings that you make in these files made permanent for the current session (that is, without having to log out and log back in), type as follows:

```
$ source script_file
```

where `script_file` is the name of the login script modified.

Bourne Shell Implementation

The `source` command is specific to the C shell only, and cannot be run from the Bourne shell.

Korn Shell Implementation

The `source` command is specific to the C shell only, and cannot be run from the Korn shell.

12.10 DISPLAYING GLOBAL ENVIRONMENT VARIABLES

The global environment variables that exist for your session can be displayed by typing `setenv` at the command prompt. Here's what displays at our installation:

```
$ setenv
HOME=/home/amity/zamir
LOGNAME=zamir
```

```
LOGTTY=/dev/console
PATH=.:/home/amity/zamir/bin;/usr1/local/sybase/bin
SHELL=/bin/csh
TERM=sun-cmd
USER=zamir
PWD=/home/amity/zamir/document
DEFAULT_FONT=/usr/lib/fonts/fixedwidth/gallant.r.10
```

Most of the environment variables have already been explained. The remaining variables are self-explanatory.

We encourage you to type setenv at the command prompt at your installation, and try to understand the contents of the variables that display. The contents of these variables will be described in detail when we describe features specific to each shell in the next chapter.

12.11 DISPLAYING LOCAL VARIABLES

Local variables for your current session can be displayed by typing set at the system prompt. Here's what displays at our installation:

```
$ set
cwd      /home/amity/zamir/document
history  40
noclobber
notify
$
```

cwd displays the current working directory. history displays the value 40. The history variable is set to the number of commands that are to be stored in the history buffer. noclobber indicates that preexisting files will not be overwritten if output is redirected to them. notify notifies the user when processes run in the background are completed.

Now it's your turn to type set at the command prompt. Try to understand the contents of what displays at your installation.

Bourne Shell Implementation

Although global and local variables are both set inside the .profile file in the Bourne shell, global variables can be displayed by typing env at the command prompt, and local variables are displayed by typing set.

Korn Shell Implementation

Global and local variables are displayed in the same way in the Korn shell as they are in the Bourne shell.

12.12 RESETTING VARIABLES

Environment variables are reset via the unsetenv command. Take a look at the following sequence of commands:

```
$ echo "$HOME"
/home/whales/zamir
$ unsetenv HOME
$ echo "$HOME"
HOME:   Undefined variable
$
```

Shell variables are reset via the unset command. Here's sample usage:

```
$ echo "$variable"
10
$ unset variable
$ echo "$variable"
variable:   Undefined variable
$
```

Please note that you cannot unset the PATH environment variable once it has been set.

Bourne Shell Implementation

In the Bourne shell both environment and shell variables can be reset via the reset command. Here's how it looks:

```
$ echo "$variable"
10
$ unset PATH
$ echo $PATH

$ unset variable
$ echo $variable

$
```

As in the C shell, the `unset` command cannot be used to unset the value stored in `PATH`. In addition to this, the following variables cannot be reset once they have been set:

```
PS1
PS2
MAILCHECK
```

`PS1` is a variable that specifies the Bourne shell prompt. Its default value is $. `PS2` is the secondary prompt which displays when you continue a command on the next line via the backslash character. `MAILCHECK` is a variable that specifies in seconds the frequency with which the mail will be checked.

Korn Shell Implementation

The Korn shell uses the same syntax as the Bourne shell to reset environment and shell variables: the `unset` keyword is followed by the variable being `reset`.

In addition to this, like the Bourne shell, the Korn shell is unable to reset the `PATH`, `PS1`, `PS2`, and `MAILCHECK` variables once they have been set.

12.13 LOGOUT SCRIPTS

Logout scripts can be stored inside a file called `.logout`. This file will be automatically run each time you log out of your current session. This file must reside in your home directory in order to be executed as expected, and it must be given execute permission. Here's a sample logout file:

```
$ cat .logout
clear
echo ''`whoami` logging out on `date`''
rm *.tmp
$
```

The above script automatically clears the screen, displays the user ID and date and time of logout, and then removes all files suffixed with a `.tmp` on logout. Take a moment now to think of some of the tasks you would like implemented as you log out of the system. You may be surprised at just how useful this script file can be.

Bourne Shell Implementation

In order for a .logout file to be executed automatically on logout from the Bourne shell, you must set up a trap command in .profile to execute it. This is how you would set it up:

```
trap "$HOME/.logout" 0
```

The above command signals the execution of the .logout command when a zero signal is received. Recall that a zero signal is sent on exit from the shell.

Korn Shell Implementation

The Korn shell .logout file is executed in the same way as in the Bourne shell.

12.14 OSF/1 CONSIDERATIONS

OSF/1 provides enhanced functionality for the C, Bourne, and Korn shells in the following ways.

12.14.1 System Login Script, C Shell

The OSF/1 operating system provides a startup system login script for the C shell called csh.login. This script resides in the /etc directory. This shell script is executed first, followed by the .cshrc and .login scripts.

12.14.2 Local Login Script, Korn Shell

The OSF/1 operating system allows you to specify a local login script for the Korn shell called .kshrc. This script is similar to .cshrc, in that it is executed each time a child subshell is created from a Korn shell. However, before this file can be executed, the ENV variable in .profile must be set equal to the file name. This is how the entry would look:

```
ENV=.kshrc
```

12.14.3 Environment Variables

In addition to the built-in variables that are common to almost all shells, OSF/1 provides the following variables, most of which are a result of the special internationalization features that this operating system provides. As you read through this section, keep in mind that several UNIX systems which conform to specified standards set by various UNIX committees may also support these features.

LANG

This specifies the locale of your system. The setting for LANG results in corresponding settings for language, territory, and the character codeset. The default for this variable is C. The corresponding settings for this locale are English, the U.S., and the ASCII character codeset. Changing the LANG variable will result in the above three settings being changed for a particular country or area.

LC_COLLATE

This specifies the collating sequence that is to be applied to commands within the system which specify ranges or perform sorts. Sorts and ranges can vary with different languages. The default for this variable is the ASCII collating sequence.

LC_CTYPE

This specifies the classification rules for specific character sets. The default is the ASCII character set.

LC_MESSAGES

This specifies the language in which system messages will display. The default setting is the English language.

LC_MONETARY

This specifies the monetary format of the system. The default is the American format, which is dollars and cents.

LC_NUMERIC

This specifies the numeric format for the system. The default is the American format for these quantities.

`LC_TIME`

This specifies the date and time format of the system. The default is the American format of date specification.

12.14.4 The trap Command

In the OSF/1 operating system, the `trap` command can be used for all three shells: C, Bourne, and Korn.

Aside from these differences, all other features remain the same. All examples will produce similar output when run from the C, Bourne, or Korn shells in an OSF/1 operating system.

12.15 REVIEW

This chapter described in detail the working environment that is automatically set up for you when you log in to the system.

Table 12.1 summarizes the major features of each shell's environment.

Table 12.1 The Shell Environment

C Shell Implementation	Bourne Shell Implementation	Korn Shell Implementation
Execute system login scripts (path names follow)		
Not applicable	/etc/profile	/etc/profile
Execute local login scripts (file names follow)		
.cshrc; .login	.profile	.profile
Set environment variables (syntax follows)		
setenv var=value	var=value export var	var=value export var
Set shell or local variables (syntax follows)		
set var=value	var=value export var	var=value export var

Table 12.1 The Shell Environment (Contd.)

C Shell Implementation	Bourne Shell Implementation	Korn Shell Implementation
Make variables set in session permanent (method follows)		
Insert in .cshrc $ source .cshrc	Insert in .profile Cannot run source	Insert in .profile Cannot run source
Display global environment settings (syntax follows)		
setenv	env	env
Display local environment settings (syntax follows)		
set	set	set
Reset environment variables (syntax follows)		
unsetenv	unset	unset
Reset local variables (syntax follows)		
unsetenv	unset	unset
Specify aliases (syntax follows)		
alias name cmd	Not applicable	alias name cmd
Execute logout script (method and file names follow)		
Insert $HOME/.logout	Insert in .profile Use trap command	Insert in .profile Use trap command

This chapter also described some common built-in variables that exist in most UNIX systems.   Table 12.2 presents a synopsis of these.

Table 12.2 Shell Built-In Variables

Variable Name	Description	Applicable Shell
HOME	Default login directory	C, Bourne, Korn
HOST	Name of computer	C, Bourne, Korn
LOGNAME	Login name	C, Bourne, Korn
PATH	Collection of search paths	C, Bourne, Korn
SHELL	Default shell	C, Bourne, Korn
TERM	Terminal type	C, Bourne, Korn
PROMPT	System prompt	C, Bourne, Korn
EDITOR	Default editor	C, Bourne, Korn
PS1	Command line prompt	Bourne, Korn
PS2	Command continuation prompt	Bourne, Korn
HISTSIZE	Specify size of history buffer	Korn
MAILCHECK	Frequency of mail check	Bourne, Korn

We also described some commands and settings that are frequently utilized by shell scripts. Table 12.3 presents a synopsis of these.

Table 12.3 Some Common Shell Commands and Settings

Command	Description	Syntax
clear; all shells	Clear the screen.	clear
trap; Bourne, Korn	Execute commands based on signals received.	trap command signal; signal can be 0 (logout), 2 (interrupt), 15 (software termination), or others
history; C, Korn	Create history buffer for specified number of commands.	set history=n, where n is number of commands in buffer
savehist; C, Korn	Save commands in buffer for next session.	set savehist=n, where n is number of commands in buffer
noclobber; all shells	Do not overwrite pre-existing files via redirection.	set noclobber
notify; all shells	Notify user on completion of process.	set notify
umask; all shells	Specify permission set of all new files and directories.	umask nnn, where nnn is an octal number
alias; C, Korn	An alternative name for a command.	alias name command where name is the alias.

Finally, we described the enhanced functionality that OSF/1 offers over UNIX in the shell environments. It offers a system login script called /etc/csh.login for the C shell. It offers a .kshrc file that functions similar to .cshrc (it executes for each subshell) for the Korn shell. And it offers built-in environment variables that reflect the internationalization features that are incorporated in this operating system. These features may also be present in various UNIX installations that conform to the standards set by specified committees. Table 12.4 presents a list of these enhanced features.

Table 12.4 Additional Built-in Variables in OSF/1

Variable	Description
LANG	Defines system locale, comprising language, territory, and character codeset.
LC_COLLATE	Defines collating sequence.
LC_TYPE	Defines classification rules for character sets.
LC_MESSAGES	Defines language of system messages.
LC_MONETARY	Defines monetary format.
LC_NUMERIC	Defines numeric format.
LC_TIME	Defines date and time format.

Specific Features of the C, Bourne, and Korn Shells

13.1 INTRODUCTION

This chapter summarizes specific features of each shell. Most of these features you have encountered in previous chapters, and they will not be elaborated on any further. However, the review at the end of the chapter will list the commands that implement these features, and should serve as a refresher. The remaining features that you have not encountered will be described in detail. You will be able to understand the differences between the shells as you conclude this chapter.

13.2 THE C SHELL

The C shell supports the following features:

- Programming constructs, such as the `if`, `elif`, `else`, `case`, `for`, `while`, and `until` loops

- The `alias` command, which allows you to abbreviate or rename long commands

- Command history, which allows commands to be stored in a history buffer, and then reexecuted simply by typing the number of the command (preceded by an exclamation mark)

- Automatic file name completion

The C shell does not support the following features:

- Provision of a shell with restricted capabilities

- Ability to edit and reexecute a previously entered command (unless you reexecute a command by typing !! after issuing a history command – more on this later on in the chapter).

- Signal trapping, via the trap command.

We now describe its automatic file name completion capability. The remaining features have been explained in prior chapters.

13.2.1 Automatic File Name Completion

In order for this capability to work, you have to set one of the C shell's built-in variables called filec. Type as follows at the command prompt:

```
$ set filec
```

If you would like this entry to be permanent, insert an entry for it in .cshrc.

Once filec has been enabled, the C shell has the capability to complete a partially entered file name. However, keep in mind that the filec command works as illustrated only if there is one file that matches the string entered at the command line prompt. Let's continue with the example, and you will understand what we mean.

Here's how this works. Suppose you need a listing of a file that starts with the characters product. Simply type ls product at the command line prompt, and then hit the ESC key. The system will automatically append the remaining characters of the file name, if it exists and if there is only one file that matches the string entered. The command can now be executed simply by pressing the Return key. Here's sample usage:

```
$ ls product<ESC>
$ ls product_a <Return>
product_a
$
```

The example above illustrates the difference between using this automatic file name completion capability and entering one of the metacharacters to do a wildcard search. If you had entered one of the wildcard characters in this location, like so:

```
$ ls product*
```

then the sytem would have produced a listing of all files that start with the letters `product` and end with zero or more characters. When a metacharacter is used, the file name is completed and the command is executed all in one shot. On the other hand, pressing the `ESC` key results in the completion of the file name only; you have the option of executing the command by hitting the Return key.

We have already mentioned that this capability works only if you have one match in the current working directory. If there is more than one match, then the system will beep and/or the screen will flash. You can inhibit this behavior by setting the `nobeep` option, like this:

```
$ set nobeep
$
```

If you do decide to set this variable, and the system finds more than one match, it will simply do nothing. It will not append the first match it finds, beep, or anything else. A much better solution is to enter <Cntrl> D instead of <ESC>. Let's see what happens in this case.

Type the incomplete name of the file, as usual, at the command line prompt, and enter <Cntrl> D in the location where you would like file name completion to be performed. Doing so results in the complete list of all files that start with the characters entered being displayed. After the display, the incomplete command typed at the command line will redisplay, and now you have the option to type the file name of your choice (from the list that displays) and execute the command. Here's sample usage:

```
$ ls product<Cntrl> D
product_a   product_b    product_c
product_d   product_e    product_f
$ ls product
```

Notice that the incomplete command is once again displayed, and you now have the option to complete at the cursor position.

13.3 THE BOURNE SHELL

The Bourne shell supports the following features:

- Programming constructs, such as the `if`, `elif`, `else`, `case`, `for`, `while`, and `until` loops

- Provision of a shell with restricted capabilities

- Signal trapping, via the `trap` command

The Bourne shell does not support the following features:

- Ability to edit and reexecute a previously entered command

- The `alias` command, which allows you to abbreviate or rename long commands

- Command history, which allows commands to be stored in a history buffer, and then reexecuted simply by typing the number of the command (preceded by an exclamation mark)

- Automatic file name completion

Features of the Bourne shell will not be elaborated on any further, since they have been explained in prior chapters. We continue with the Korn shell.

13.4 THE KORN SHELL

The Korn shell supports the following features:

- Programming constructs, such as the `if`, `elif`, `else`, `case`, `for`, `while`, and `until` loops

- Aliases, which allow you to abbreviate or rename long commands

- Command history, which allows commands to be stored in a history buffer, and then reexecuted simply by typing the number of the command (preceded by an `r`.)

- Automatic file name completion

- Signal trapping, via the `trap` command

- Ability to edit and reexecute a previously entered command

The Korn shell does not support the following feature:

■ Provision of a shell with restricted capabilities

Incidentally, the Korn shell also provides the fastest execution time. If you review the capabilities of each shell, you will realize that the Korn is perhaps the most powerful of the lot.

We now proceed to describe the Korn shell's automatic file name completion capability, since it works slightly differently from the C shell's. Then we will describe how previously typed commands can be edited and then executed.

13.4.1 Automatic File Name Completion

In order for this feature to work, you have to set the predefined variable EDITOR to one of the editors available in UNIX. We will set EDITOR to vi:

$ **EDITOR=vi**

If you would like to make this setting permananet, insert an entry for it in .profile.

Once this variable has been set, the Korn shell has the capability to complete partially entered file names as follows.

Once again, suppose you need a long listing of a file that starts with the characters product. Type as follows at the command line prompt:

```
$ ls -l product<ESC>=
1)  product_a
2)  product_b
3)  product_c
4)  product_d
5)  product_e
6)  product_f
$ ls -l product
```

Now type a (for append), complete the name of the required file, and hit the Return key to execute the command.

The Korn shell does not understand a <Cntrl> D. If a <Cntrl> D is typed at the end of a line, then it responds as follows:

```
$ ls -l product<Cntrl> D
file not found
$
```

13.4.2 Editing of Command Lines

Previously entered command lines can be retrieved, edited, and then executed. In order for this feature to work, you use the built-in command called `fc` (fix command). This command has two formats. Here's the syntax of the first:

```
fc [-e editor] [-nlr] [range1] [range2]
```

We will now describe each entry.

`fc`

This is the name of the command.

`-e editor`

The -e option is used to specify the editor that will be used to edit the command line. If you do not specify this flag, the list of commands in the history buffer will be displayed, but you will not be able to edit them.

`-n`

The -n flag is used to specify that the commands in the history buffer be listed without numbers.

`-l`

The -l flag is used to specify that the commands in the history buffer be listed with numbers. Obviously, the -n and -l options are mutually exclusive.

`-r`

The -r flag is used to specify that the commands in the history buffer be listed in reverse order. Recall that the last command is the last one listed. Using the -r flag would result in the last command typed being the first one listed.

`range1 and range2`

These flags are used to specify the range of commands from the command history buffer that are to be listed. `range1` can be a number specifying the upper limit of the range. `range1` can also be a string containing the command which will form the upper limit of the range.   range2   will be the corresponding number or command at the lower limit.

And now, here are some examples that illustrate the usage of this format of the fc command.

Example 1:   List numbered commands 15 through 18 in the history buffer.

```
$ fc -l 15 18
15 EDITOR=vi
16 ls -l file3
17 ls -l file1
18 pwd
$
```

Example 2:   List commands 18 through 15 in the history buffer.

```
$ fc -l 18 15
18 pwd
17 ls -l file1
16 ls -l file3
15 EDITOR=vi
$
```

Example 3:   List all commands between the last ls and ps issued.

```
$ fc -l ls ps
23 ls
22 history=5
21 echo $history
20 set
19 ps
$
```

Example 4:   List all commands between the last ps and ls issued.

```
$ fc -l ps ls
19 ps
20 set
21 echo $history
22 history=5
23 ls
$
```

Example 5:   Edit commands 15 through 18 in the history buffer. Change all references to file3 and file to file40 and file60.

```
$ fc -e vi 15 18
```

```
EDITOR=vi
ls -l file3
ls -l file
pwd
~
~
~
~
~
~
"/tmp/sh1243.11" 4 lines, 36 characters
```

Typing the above commands results in the commands specified being placed in the vi edit buffer. Notice the name of the file that displays at the bottom of the screen. This is a temporary file name that is assigned to the group of commands in the buffer. You can now use vi to edit these commands as you wish. Here's what the screen looks like after we make the edits:

```
EDITOR=vi
ls -l file40
ls -l file60
pwd
~
~
~
~
~
~
"/tmp/sh1243.11" 4 lines, 36 characters
```

Now type :wq! to save the changes. The new set of commands will be executed in the sequence in which they were encountered. Here's the output:

```
file40 not found
```

```
file60 not found
/temp
$
```

As you can see, this particular feature of the Korn shell is a powerful tool that can be used to save time in retyping a lot of repetitive commands that are to be performed on a group of files.

We now continue with the second format of the `fc` command. Here's the syntax:

```
fc -e - [old string=new string] [match string]
```

A description of each option follows.

`fc`

`fc` is the name of the command.

`-e -`

This syntax is required to utilize this format of the `fc` command.

`[old string=new string]`

This option allows the string which matches `old string` in the command being edited to be replaced by `new string`.

`match string`

This specifies that the edit should be made to the most recent command in the history buffer which contains the match string.

And now, an example that illustrates the usage of this format of the `fc` command.

Example 1:   Change the last instance of the pwd command to an
             ls.

Typing `history` will give us an idea of the sequence of commands issued in the current session:

```
$ history
.
53 pwd
54 history
$
```

We do not list the complete history buffer because it is not necessary to do so to illustrate this example. That is, commands 1 through 52 do something else. The 53rd command is pwd. This command will be changed to ls via the fc command. Here's the syntax:

```
$ fc -e - pwd=l pwd
ls
f1    f2    file1    file2    file3    ts
```

13.5 OSF/1 CONSIDERATIONS

The C, Bourne, and Korn shell features enumerated in this chapter apply equally to these shells within an OSF/1 operating system. One difference is that the C shell in OSF/1 supports signal trapping using the trap command. (The trap command was explained in Chapter 12.) Aside from this, all examples will produce the same output when run from the various shells in this environment.

13.6 REVIEW

This chapter summarized features of the C, Bourne, and Korn shells, and then described some features of the C and Korn shells that are specific to these shells only. The tables that follow present a synopsis of the features of each shell. These tables summarize the major concepts presented in the past five chapters.

Table 13.1 presents the syntax of the programming constructs that are supported by each shell in pseudo-code.

Table 13.1 Programming Constructs for Each Shell

C Shell	Bourne Shell	Korn Shell

if command
then
    command
fi
	if command
	then
	    command
	fi
		if command
		then
		    command
		fi

if command
then
    command
else
    command
fi
	if command
	then
	    command
	else
	    command
	fi
		if command
		then
		    command
		else
		    command
		fi

if command
then
    command
elif command
then
    command
else
    command
fi
	if command
	then
	    command
	elif command
	then
	    command
	else
	    command
	fi
		if command
		then
		    command
		elif command
		then
		    command
		else
		    command
		fi

case argument in
pattern 1)
    command;;
pattern 2)
    command;;
esac
	case argument in
	pattern 1)
	    command;;
	pattern 2)
	    command;;
	esac
		case argument in
		pattern 1)
		    command;;
		pattern 2)
		    command;;
		esac

for
var in val_1, val_2
do
    command
done
	for
	var in val_1, val_2
	do
	    command
	done
		for
		var in val_1, val_2
		do
		    command
		done

while command
successful
do
    command
done
	while command
	successful
	do
	    command
	done
		while command
		successful
		do
		    command
		done

until command
unsuccessful
do
    command
done
	until command
	unsuccessful
	do
	    command
	done
		until command
		unsuccessful
		do
		    command
		done

Table 13.2 summarizes other features of each shell that you have encountered in previous chapters. The syntax of commands is presented.

Table 13.2 Other Features of the Shell

C Shell	Bourne Shell	Korn Shell
Feature: Aliases		
Description: Abbreviates or renames long commands.		
alias name cmnd	Not supported	alias name cmnd
unalias alias	Not supported	unalias alias
Feature: Command history		
Description: Stores commands in history buffer, and reexecutes.		
set history=n	Not supported	history=n
set savehist=n	Not supported	savehist=n
Feature: Automatic file name completion		
Description: System automatically completes partial file name entered at the command line.		
set filec ls name<ESC> ls name<Cntrl> D	Not supported	EDITOR=vi ls name<ESC>= Append name
Feature: Restricted shell		
Description: Shell that provides restricted capabilities.		
Not supported	/bin/rsh	Not supported
Feature: Edit commands in history buffer		
Description: Edits and reexecutes commands in history buffer.		
Not supported	Not supported	fc [-e editor] [-nlr] [range1] [range2] fc -e - [old=new] [match string]
Feature: Signal trapping via trap command		
trap cmnd signal	trap cmnd signal	trap cmnd signal

Part

3

The UNIX Editors

14

The ed Line Editor

14.1 INTRODUCTION

The basic UNIX *line editor* is called ed. It is available with every UNIX system. Unlike vi, which is a screen editor and works with a screenfull (or a window) of lines, ed works with specified lines only. In other words, only the current line can be edited. Although ed is rarely used, it is important that you understand that it is available in all UNIX installations. The vi editor is a screen editor. In order for it to work as such (i.e., as a screen editor), an environment variable called TERM has to be set up to conform to your specific terminal type. If you don't know what TERM should be set to, then you have a problem – ed, however, comes to the rescue, and allows files to be edited without resorting to vi. This chapter describes some basic ed commands.

14.2 CREATING A NEW FILE

A new file is created by typing ed followed by the file name:

$ ed newfile

As you hit the carriage return key, the system responds with a question mark. This indicates that the file that you are writing to does not exist in the current working directory. Here's what you will see:

```
$ ed newfile
?
```

If you were editing a preexisting file, then ed would display a number instead of a question mark. This number would indicate the total number of characters in that file.

14.3 EXITING ED

Before getting into details on how to enter text and save it, we consider it prudent to let you know how to exit ed. You have two options:

- Save file and exit. Type w (for write) and hit the Return key. The system will respond with the number of characters contained in the file. It will display 0 for a file which you have saved without inputting any information in it. Then type q (for quit), and you will be placed back at the command prompt.

- Exit without saving the document. Type q, and you will be placed back at the command prompt without any further messages being displayed.

14.4 INPUTTING INFORMATION

Information can be input for a file in two ways. A description of each method follows.

- Information can be entered into a file by typing a (for append). Everything that you type after that will be considered input for the file that is being edited. You exit out of append mode by typing a dot.

As you type text, make sure the Return key is hit in the location where you wish to break the line. Like vi, ed is an editor, it is not a word processor. If you don't hit the Return key, ed thinks that it there is one long line; it just wraps around and continues that same line.

Once you're ready to finish input to the file, type a dot on a line by itself. The dot should be the only character in that line. It should not be preceded by a space or anything else. Moreover, the carriage return should immediately follow the dot. If you do not follow these rules, the editor will not be able to understand that you are not in input mode anymore, and you may very well end up in nowhere land! (That is, you won't know if you're in input mode or any mode, for that matter.)

At this point in time, either you can save (or not save) the file and exit, or you can issue other commands to edit the file.

So anyway, here's a sample session that illustrates what we have explained so far. The position of the cursor will be indicated by the gray shaded box. Remember, there is an invisible explicit carriage return at the end of each line.

```
$ ed diary
?
a
Today was Saaturday.  I woke up at 7:00 am, although
I would have preferred to qake up much later.  But
my kid woke up, and I had to feeed him, because my
husband wouldn't budge. So I fed him, and then let
him play by himself, and I think I dozed off again.
```

Notice that input to the file starts right after the a, and input ends after the dot.

- Information can also be input via the i (for insert) command. Enter a dot (.) to exit out of insert mode.

Comparing the a with the i indicates that a inserts text after the current position and i inserts text before the current position. We now describe how you can position yourself on specified lines that require editing.

Previewing the document indicates that quite a few typing mistakes have been made. Saturday has been misspelled Saaturday. qake should read wake. feeed should be spelled feed. Which brings us to the next topic, how to edit lines. But before you can edit a line, you have to make that line the current line. The next section describes how to make a specific line the current line, in order to edit it.

14.5 POSITIONING ON SPECIFIC LINES

Remember, ed is a line editor. This means that you do not have a window as in vi, in which the cursor can be moved to position it at specific characters within a line and then modify them. Within ed, you can edit the current line only. In order to edit a line, you have to change your position in the edit buffer and make that the current line. The following commands are used to find the current position, and display and change the current line. We will illustrate their usage with reference to the document just typed.

■ Type p to display the current line that you are positioned at.

Before issuing a p to print the current line, the entire buffer will be displayed using the commmand 1,$p. This command will be explained in detail later on in the chapter; we utilize it now to help you understand your current position relative to the buffer.

```
1,$p
Today was Saaturday.  I woke up at 7:00 am, although
I would have preferred to qake up much later.  But
my kid woke up, and I had to feeed him, because my
husband wouldn't budge.  So I fed him, and then let
him play by himself, and I think I dozed off again.


p
him play by himself, and I think I dozed off again.
```

Typing p results in the current line being displayed on the next line.

■ Type .= to display the current line number:

```
Today was Saaturday.  I woke up at 7:00 am, although
I would have preferred to qake up much later.  But
my kid woke up, and I had to feeed him, because my
husband wouldn't budge.  So I fed him, and then let
him play by himself, and I think I dozed off again.
.=
5
```

The output indicates that the current line number is 5.

■ Type $= to display the number of the last line in the buffer:

```
Today was Saaturday.  I woke up at 7:00 am, although
I would have preferred to qake up much later.  But
my kid woke up, and I had to feeed him, because my
husband wouldn't budge.  So I fed him, and then let
him play by himself, and I think I dozed off again.
$=
5
```

■ Type n to position at a specific line number. n is the required
   line number.

```
Today was Saaturday.  I woke up at 7:00 am, although
I would have preferred to qake up much later.  But
my kid woke up, and I had to feeed him, because my
husband wouldn't budge.  So I fed him, and then let
him play by himself, and I think I dozed off again.
1
Today was Saaturday.  I woke up at 7:00 am, although
```

The relevant line displays, and this line becomes the new
current line. Type a dot (the dot represents the current line), and
the same line will redisplay.

If you try to position on a line that does not exist, ed displays a
question mark:

```
Today was Saaturday.  I woke up at 7:00 am, although
24
?
```

■ Press <Return> or + to go the next line from the current line:

```
Today was Saaturday.  I woke up at 7:00 am, although
<Return>
I would have preferred to qake up much later.  But
```

If you press <Return> beyond the end of the buffer, ed displays
a question mark:

```
him play by himself, and I think I dozed off again.
<Return>
?
```

■ Type a dash (–) to move back to the previous line:

```
–
husband wouldn't budge.  So I fed him, and then let
```

If you try to position beyond the start of the buffer, ed displays
a question mark:

```
Today was Saaturday.  I woke up at 7:00 am, although
-
?
```

- Type `.+n` to move forward *n* lines:

```
Today was Saaturday.  I woke up at 7:00 am, although
.+3
husband wouldn't budge.  So I fed him, and then let
```

- Type `.−n` to move back *n* lines:

```
.-3
Today was Saaturday.  I woke up at 7:00 am, although
```

14.6 VIEWING THE EDIT BUFFER

OK. So now we know how to move from one line to the next. Now let's take another look at the edit buffer. There are several ways to display the contents of the edit buffer.

- Type `1,$` to display the entire contents of the buffer. The `1` indicates the start range, and the `$` indicates the last line:

```
1,$p
Today was Saaturday.  I woke up at 7:00 am, although
I would have preferred to qake up much later.  But
my kid woke up, and I had to feeed him, because my
husband wouldn't budge.  So I fed him, and then let
him play by himself, and I think I dozed off again.
```

- Type `range1,range2p` to display the range of lines from `range1` through `range2`. The following command will display lines 2 through 4.

```
2,4p
I would have preferred to qake up much later.  But
my kid woke up, and I had to feeed him, because my
husband wouldn't budge.  So I fed him, and then let
```

- Type `np` to display one line only, where n is the line number. The following command displays line 3:

3p
my kid woke up, and I had to feeed him, because my

14.7 EDITING LINES

And now that you know how to view the current buffer, let's get down to business and correct the mistakes made while typing the original document. Let's take another look at the edit buffer:

1,$p
Today was Saaturday. I woke up at 7:00 am, although
I would have preferred to qake up much later. But
my kid woke up, and I had to feeed him, because my
husband wouldn't budge. So I fed him, and then let
him play by himself, and I think I dozed off again.

The s command is used to substitute one or more characters for another string. The s command can work with one or more lines. We now describe each option.

- Type s/old/new/ to substitute new string for the first occurrence of old string on the current line. Let's position ourselves at the first line, and make a few substitutions.

1
Today was Saaturday. I woke up at 7:00 am, although
s/Saaturday/Saturday/<Return>
p<Return>
Today was Saturday. I woke up at 7:00 am, although

In this example we display <Return> literally, so that you understand what is going on. In subsequent examples we will omit the Return key.

Continuing with the above example, notice the p after the s command. The p results in the changed line being displayed. The p could have been placed on the same line as the s command, like so:

s/Saaturday/Saturday/p<Return>

All subsequent commands will use this shortcut method of line display. In addition to this, please note that the substitute pattern must be delimited by a slash; otherwise ed will display another question mark.

- Type `ns/old/new` to substitute the first occurrence of the old string with new string on line number n. We will change `qake` to `wake` on line 2:

```
Today was Saaturday.   I woke up at 7:00 am, although
2s/qake/wake/p
I would have preferred to wake up much later.   But
```

A couple of points before we proceed. First, make sure that there are no embedded spaces in the substitute command. If you do decide to embed a space between, say, the line number and the s, ed will display its all too familiar question mark. Second, regardless of whether or not you append a command after the substitute, don't forget that slashes must be placed on both sides of the original pattern and the substitute pattern.

Let's continue with the discussion.

- Type `line1,line2s/old/new/` to substitute for the first occurrence of old string with new string for lines within `range1` and `range2`. Although our example does not present the opportunity to make a consistent change on a range of lines, but we will make something up anyway. Here goes.

```
1,$s/I/we/p
him play by himself, and we think I dozed off again.
```

As you take another look at the changes implemented, only the last line of the buffer displays. In this line, only the first occurrence of I has been replaced by we. We are interested in having all instances changed in one go, and displaying the complete buffer. Seems like we should undo the last command issued.

14.8 UNDOING THE LAST COMMAND ISSUED

The last command issued can be undone simply by typing u. The u will undo the immediately preceding command.

14.9 CHANGING ALL OCCURRENCES OF A STRING

All occurrences, as opposed to just the first occurrence, of a string on a line can be changed by appending g (for global) to the command string. We will first change all occurrences of the required string, and then print the complete file to see how the file looks. Here's sample usage:

```
1,$s/I/we/g
1,$p
Today was Saturday.  we woke up at 7:00 am, although
we would have preferred to wake up much later.  But
my kid woke up, and we had to feeed him, because my
husband wouldn't budge.  So we fed him, and then let
him play by himself,and we think we dozed off again.
```

That's much better! Now this paragraph conveys a feeling of togetherness between husband and wife (they both wake up at seven, they both feed the baby, and they both doze off again). However, this new aspect of togetherness makes the phrase my husband wouldn't budge appear a little bit out of context. And my kid in the third line has to be changed to our kid. Let's make the substitution for the third line first, and then find a way to delete the offending out-of-context phrase.

```
3s/my/our/p
our kid woke up, and we had to feeed him, because my
```

OK. Now let's find out how strings can be deleted.

14.10 DELETING CHARACTERS

The s command is used to delete one or more characters from the edit buffer. Simply position yourself at the line to be edited, or type the number of the line that contains the string, and delete like this:

```
4p
husband wouldn't budge.  So we fed him, and then let
s/husband wouldn't budge.//p
  So we fed him, and then let
```

Notice that the syntax for deletion now becomes

```
s/old//
```

that is, the place holder for new is null.

While we're at it, `feeed` has to be changed to `feed` in the prior line:

```
-
our kid woke up, and we had to feeed him, because my
s/feeed/feed/p
our kid woke up, and we had to feed him, because my
```

14.11 LOADING FILES INTO CURRENT EDIT BUFFER

Existing files can be loaded into the current edit buffer, and thereby appended or included in the current file. This feature can be implemented in two ways.

- A file can be appended to the existing edit buffer by typing `r filename`. We have a file called `sunday` in the current directory, and this will now be appended to the current file:

```
r Sunday
```

But first, let's review the contents of the current buffer:

```
1,$p
Today was Saturday.  we woke up at 7:00 am, although
we would have preferred to wake up much later.  But
our kid woke up, and we had to feed him, because my
  So we fed him, and then let
him play by himself,and we think we dozed off again.
```

Before merging in sunday, a few more edits are required:

```
3s/,because my /./p
our kid woke up, and we had to feed him.
```

OK. Now let's print the whole file, and merge in sunday:

```
1,$p
Today was Saturday.  we woke up at 7:00 am, although
we would have preferred to wake up much later.  But
our kid woke up, and we had to feed him.
  So we fed him, and then let
him play by himself,and we think we dozed off again.

r sunday
```

241

The system responds with the number of characters that are contained in the file sunday, which are now merged into the current file. Let's take a look at the final result:

```
1,$p
Today was Saturday.  we woke up at 7:00 am, although
we would have preferred to wake up much later.  But
our kid woke up, and we had to feed him.
   So we fed him, and then let
him play by himself,and we think we dozed off again.
   Now it's Sunday.  Although it's Sunday, the funny
thing is, it's just like Saturday.  Exactly!!  The
kid woke up at 7:00 am.  My husband did not budge.
I fed the baby at 7:15.  And then I let him play
in his crib, while I dozed off again.
```

- The current contents of the edit buffer can be replaced completely by another file by typing e filename. But if you have just merged two files together, make sure you write the new contents to the current buffer before attempting to overwrite it with this command.

For example, if we were to issue this command now:

```
e Sunday
241
```

ed would respond with the all too familiar question mark (?). Here's the solution:

```
w
471
```

The w command writes the file to disk, and ed responds with the total number of characters in the new expanded file. First, take a look at the buffer, and then issue the e command:

```
1,$p
Today was Saturday.  we woke up at 7:00 am, although
we would have preferred to wake up much later.  But
our kid woke up, and we had to feed him.
   So we fed him, and then let
him play by himself,and we think we dozed off again.
   Now it's Sunday.  Although it's Sunday, the funny
```

```
thing is, it's just like Saturday.  Exactly!!  The
kid woke up at 7:00 am.  My husband did not budge.
I fed the baby at 7:15.  And then I let him play
in his crib, while I dozed off again.
```
e sunday
```
241
```

The system once again responds with the new size of the file that is written to the current file. Here's what we have now:

1,$p
```
   Now it's Sunday.  Although it's Sunday, the funny
thing is, it's just like Saturday.  Exactly!!  The
kid woke up at 7:00 am.  My husband did not budge.
I fed the baby at 7:15.  And then I let him play
in his crib, while I dozed off again.
```

Since the current contents of the buffer are lost, and we're not quite done with this chapter yet, we revert to the original contents of the buffer.

u
1,$p
```
Today was Saturday.  we woke up at 7:00 am, although
we would have preferred to wake up much later.  But
my kid woke up, and we had to feed him.
   So we fed him, and then let
him play by himself,and we think we dozed off again.
   Now it's Sunday.  Although it's Sunday, the funny
thing is, it's just like Saturday.  Exactly!!  The
kid woke up at 7:00 am.  My husband did not budge.
I fed the baby at 7:15.  And then I let him play
in his crib, while I dozed off again.
```

The next section describes how to delete lines.

14.12 DELETING LINES

Lines can be deleted by typing d in various formats:

- The current line can be deleted by typing d.

- A specific line can be deleted by typing the line number followed by d. For example, typing 4d would delete the fourth line in the buffer.

- A range of lines can be deleted by typing the range, separated by a comma, followed by the letter d. For example, typing 1,3d would delete lines 1 through 3 in the current edit buffer. ed will renumber the lines in the buffer after the deletion.

In our example, we will delete the last five lines in the buffer.

```
1,$p
Today was Saturday.  we woke up at 7:00 am, although
we would have preferred to wake up much later.  But
my kid woke up, and we had to feed him.
    So we fed him, and then let
him play by himself,and we think we dozed off again.
    Now it's Sunday.  Although it's Sunday, the funny
thing is, it's just like Saturday.  Exactly!!  The
kid woke up at 7:00 am.  My husband did not budge.
I fed the baby at 7:15.  And then I let him play
in his crib, while I dozed off again.
6,10d
1,$p
Today was Saturday.  we woke up at 7:00 am, although
we would have preferred to wake up much later.  But
my kid woke up, and we had to feed him.
    So we fed him, and then let
him play by himself,and we think we dozed off again.
```

14.13 SAVING CURRENT BUFFER TO DIFFERENT FILE

This feature can take two forms: the entire contents of the current buffer can be saved to another file, or the partial contents can be saved. We describe the former format first.

- A copy of the current file can be saved to another file by typing as follows:

```
w anotherfile
230
```

The above command will write the contents of the current buffer to a file called anotherfile. A number will be displayed underneath the command indicating the number of characters written to it.

- A portion of the current buffer can be written to another file as follows:

```
line1,line2w newfile
```

where `line1` is the starting line number in the current buffer and `line2` is the ending line number. `w` is the write command, and `newfile` is the name of the second file. For example, the following command:

```
1,3w secondfile
146
```

would write lines 1 through 3 of the buffer to `secondfile`. Once again, the number indicates the number of characters written.

Later on in this chapter we will show you a way in which you can actually view the contents of this `secondfile` from within the current ed edit session. For now, let's continue with the discussion.

14.14 SEARCHING FOR PATTERNS

Often we are required to search for specific patterns in large files. Our sample file is small enough not to warrant a search on it. But this capability gains in importance as the size of a file increases. You can search backward or forward from the current position in the buffer. We now describe each method.

- Search forward for a pattern in the current edit buffer by typing as follows:

```
/pattern/
```

The first line, after the current line, that contains the pattern will be displayed. For example, going back to our example, assume that we are currently positioned at the first line. Typing

/we/

will produce the following output.

```
we would have preferred to wake up much later.   But
```

Notice that the line with the match becomes the new current line.

The next match can be instigated without retyping the pattern, since it is the same:

```
//
my kid woke up, and we had to feed him.
```

If no match had been found, then ed would have displayed the familiar question mark:

```
/happy/
?
```

- Search backward in the buffer from the current position by typing as follows:

```
?we?
we would have preferred to wake up much later.   But
```

The only difference between searching backward from forward is that the pattern is enclosed in question marks instead of slashes.

14.15 CHANGING TEXT

There are two ways that existing lines can be changed.

- You can replace a range of existing lines with one or more new lines by using the c command with a range of lines that are to be replaced.

The c command is a combination of delete and append. Here's how it works. First, let's review the edit buffer:

```
1,$p
Today was Saturday.  we woke up at 7:00 am, although
we would have preferred to wake up much later.  But
our kid woke up, and we had to feed him.
    So we fed him, and then let
him play by himself,and we think we dozed off again.
    Now it's Sunday.  Although it's Sunday, the funny
thing is, it's just like Saturday.  Exactly!  The
kid woke up at 7:00 am.  My husband did not budge.
I fed the baby at 7:15.  And then I let him play
in his crib, while I dozed off again.
```

We would like to replace lines 4 and 5, starting with So we fed him, ... with this text: So we fed him his applesauce, he

```
drank his milk, cooed and purred, and then dozed off
again.
```
Here's the syntax of the c command:

```
line1,line2c
<type new text>
.
```

Of course, the syntax makes it seem like a rather difficult command. But let's break it up to show you how it works. `line1` and `line2` indicate the lines of text that are to be replaced. `ed` takes these lines and deletes them from the buffer. Then, you are automatically placed in append mode. Now text can be typed (each line delimited by a carriage return). After the required text has been inserted, type a dot to indicate the termination of input mode. But remember, each part of the command must be on a line by itself. Let's try it now.

```
4,5c
So we fed him his applesauce, he drank his milk,
cooed and purred, and then dozed off again.
.
```

Remember, there are explicit carriage returns at the end of each line. Let's review the edit buffer again.

```
1,$p
Today was Saturday.  we woke up at 7:00 am, although
we would have preferred to wake up much later.  But
our kid woke up, and we had to feed him.
So we fed him his applesauce, he drank his milk,
cooed and purred, and then dozed off again.
   Now it's Sunday.  Although it's Sunday, the funny
thing is, it's just like Saturday.  Exactly!  The
kid woke up at 7:00 am.  My husband did not budge.
I fed the baby at 7:15.  And then I let him play
in his crib, while I dozed off again.
```

■ You can also replace a single line with one or more new lines.

In this case, you simply supply one line number; this is the line to be replaced. The remainder of the command stays the same. Here's sample usage:

```
4c
So we fed him his applesauce.
```

Let's review the first five lines:

```
1,5p
Today was Saturday.  we woke up at 7:00 am, although
we would have preferred to wake up much later.  But
our kid woke up, and we had to feed him.
So we fed him his applesauce.
cooed and purred, and then dozed off again.
```

Notice that the fifth line appears out of context, and should be deleted:

```
5
cooed and purred, and then dozed off again.
d
```

and here are the first five lines of the buffer again:

```
1,5p
Today was Saturday.  we woke up at 7:00 am, although
we would have preferred to wake up much later.  But
our kid woke up, and we had to feed him.
So we fed him his applesauce.
  Now it's Sunday.  Although it's Sunday, the funny
```

14.16 COPYING TEXT

Text can be copied from one location in the edit buffer to another via the t (for transfer) command. Here's the syntax:

```
line1,line2tline3
```

where line1 is the line number to start copying from, line2 is the line up to which the copy is to be performed, and line3 is the line in the edit buffer after which the lines are to be placed. Here's sample usage. (By the way, we deleted the sunday part of the file, because there's really no need for it anymore.)

```
1,$p
```
Today was Saturday. we woke up at 7:00 am, although
we would have preferred to wake up much later. But
my kid woke up, and we had to feed him.
So we fed him his applesauce.
```
1,3t4
```
```
1,$p
```
Today was Saturday. we woke up at 7:00 am, although
we would have preferred to wake up much later. But
my kid woke up, and we had to feed him.
So we fed him his applesauce.
Today was Saturday. we woke up at 7:00 am, although
we would have preferred to wake up much later. But
my kid woke up, and we had to feed him.

Notice that the original lines that are copied remain untouched.

If you need to copy lines to the top of the buffer, enter 0 for
line3:

```
2,4t0
```

If you need to copy lines to the bottom of the buffer, enter $ for
line3:

```
2,4t$
```

14.17 MOVING TEXT

Text can be moved from one location in the edit buffer to the next
via the m (for move) command. Here's the syntax:

```
line1,line2mline3
```

Once again, line1 is line number to start moving from, line2 is
the lower end of the block, and line3 is the line after which the
block will be inserted. Here's sample usage, using the first four
lines of the original file:

```
1,4p
```
Today was Saturday. we woke up at 7:00 am, although
we would have preferred to wake up much later. But
our kid woke up, and we had to feed him.
So we fed him his applesauce.
```
1,2m4
```
```
1,$p
```
our kid woke up, and we had to feed him.
So we fed him his applesauce.

```
Today was Saturday.  we woke up at 7:00 am, although
we would have preferred to wake up much later.  But
```

If you need to move lines to the top of the buffer, enter 0 for line3:

2,4m0

And if you need to move them to the bottom of the buffer, enter $ for line3:

2,4m$

14.18 IMPLEMENTING SYSTEM COMMANDS FROM ED

System commands can be implemented while you are in an ed session by typing as follows:

!command

where command is a valid UNIX command. For example, suppose you needed to know how many other files existed with the prefix new. Here's what you would type:

!ls new*

and the system would respond with the names of those files (if any) whose first three characters matched new. The cursor will reposition where it left off in the buffer and display an exclamation mark on reentry.

Recall that earlier on in the chapter we mentioned that we would show you a way to view the contents of some other file without leaving the current edit session. Well, this is how you do it. Simply type !cat filename or !more filename from within the session, and the requested file, if it exists, will display at the terminal. Once the command is executed, you will once again be placed where you left off in the edit session.

Bourne Shell Implementation

The ed command invoked from the Bourne shell works in the same way as it does in the C shell.

Korn Shell Implementation

The ed command invoked from the Korn shell works in the same way as it does in the C shell.

14.19 OSF/1 CONSIDERATIONS

The ed command works in the same way when invoked from the C, Bourne, or Korn shell in an OSF/1 operating system.

14.20 REVIEW

This chapter described the syntax of the commands that can be used the with ed line editor. You may have realized that the syntax of most of the commands is similar to that in vi. The main difference between the two is that one works with a screen and the other works with lines only. Table 14.1 presents a synopsis of the syntax and description of the ed commands described.

Table 14.1 ed Commands

Command	Syntax	Description
Create file	ed file1	Creates file1.
Exit ed	wq	Writes file and exits.
	q	Exits without saving; warning will be issued.
Input information	a	Appends, before line.
	i	Inserts, after line.
Position on lines	p	Displays current line.
	.=	Displays current line number.
	$=	Displays last line number.
	2	Positions on line 2.
	<Return>, +	Positions on next line.
	-	Positions on previous line.
	.+2	Moves forward 2 lines.
	.-2	Moves back 2 lines.
View buffer	1,$p	Views entire buffer.
	1,5p	Views lines 1 thru 5.
	5p	Views line 5.
Edit lines	s/old/new/	Substitutes old for new.
	1s/old/new/	Substitutes old for new on line 1.
	2,5s/old/new	Substitute old for new for lines 2 through 5.

Table 14.1 ed Command (Contd.)

Command	Syntax	Description
Undo commands	u	Undoes the last command issued.
Change globally	1,$s/old/new/g	Changes all occurrences of old to new.
Delete	s/string//	Deletes string.
	d	Deletes current line.
	2d	Deletes line 2.
	2,5d	Deletes lines 2 through 5.
Load files into current buffer	r filename	Loads filename into current location.
	e filename	Loads filename into current location; deletes current buffer.
Save current file to another	w anotherfile	Writes current file to anotherfile.
	2,5w anotherfile	Writes lines 2 through 5 of current file to anotherfile.
Search for patterns	/pattern/	Searches forward for pattern.
	?pattern?	Searches backward for pattern.
	//	Searches prior pattern.
	??	Searches prior pattern.

Table 14.1 ed Commands (Contd.)

Command	Syntax	Description
Change text	2,5c <new text> .	Deletes lines 2 through 5; inserts new text in that location until dot is encountered.
	2c <new text> .	Deletes line 2; inserts new text in that location until dot is encountered.
Copy text	2,5t8	Copies lines 2 through 5 and inserts them after line 8.
	2,5t0	Copies lines 2 through 5 and inserts them at top of buffer.
	2,5t$	Copies lines 2 through 5 and inserts them at bottom of buffer.
Move text	2,5m8	Moves lines 2 through 5 and inserts them after line 8.
	2,5m0	Moves lines 2 through 5 and inserts at top of buffer.
	2,5m$	Moves lines 2 through 5 and inserts them at bottom of buffer.
Implement system commands from ed	!command	Implements UNIX or user-specified command without leaving ed session.

15

The sed Stream Editor

15.1 INTRODUCTION

The sed utility is called a *stream editor*. The reason why it is called a stream editor is because it is noninteractive. It receives its input from the standard, it operates on the input, and then it sends the resulting stream to the standard output.

Since sed is noninteractive and it operates on every line of the file supplied to it as input, it is particularly useful for performing extensive and global changes on large files. As the editor performs its operations, only a few lines of the file being operated on are kept in memory at one time. Therefore, the size of the file being edited is restricted only by the amount of disk space memory available on the system.

Aside from sed being noninteractive, the syntax of the commands it performs is similar to that of the ed editor in most ways. We now describe in detail how sed is invoked and what parameters it works with.

15.2 INVOKING SED

sed can be used with two main options:

- sed -f script_file source_1 source_2 ... source_n

- sed -e commands source_1 source_2 ... source_n

Both of the above commands can be invoked as indicated and used with the −n option. This option inhibits the normal writing of edited lines. Only those lines are printed which are requested with the p command.   You will understand what we mean as we continue with the chapter.

15.3 INVOKING SED WITH SCRIPT FILE

We now describe the first option.

- sed −f script_file source_1 source_2 ... source_n

The −f option indicates that sed will take the commands that it is to perform from a previously prepared script file. These commands will be performed on one or more named files. sed will operate on each file in the sequence in which it is encountered. In addition to this, it will perform each command it encounters in script_file on every line of the file that it is working with, in the sequence in which these commands are encountered. The script file can be created using one of the standard UNIX editors.

Let's take a look at a source file that is to be operated on.

```
$ cat source
file1
file2
file3.tmp
file4
file5.tmp
file6.tmp
file7
$
```

We would like to delete all lines in this file which contain the string .tmp. We have already said that the commands used by sed are the same as those used by ed (the syntax varies for some commands, these will be described later on in the chapter). Recall that the d command is used to delete lines, and the /pattern/ command is used to search for a pattern. Therefore, first the pattern is specified, and then the command that will operate on the lines that contain that pattern. Here's the command file that will implement the required task:

```
$ cat command_file
/\.tmp/d
$
```

The command above will search for the pattern .tmp, and if this pattern is found, the line will be deleted. Notice that the backslash precedes the dot in .tmp so as to take away the special meaning which is assigned to it. OK. Now let's invoke sed:

```
$ sed -f command_file source
file1
file2
file4
file7
$
```

Notice that the output displays the contents of source, minus the lines that contained the pattern .tmp. Let's take a look at source again, to see if its contents have changed.

```
$ cat source
file1
file2
file3.tmp
file4
file5.tmp
file6.tmp
file7
$
```

As you can see, the contents of the file that is being operated on remain unchanged.

The output for sed could have been redirected to a file, instead of standard output. Here's the command that would have done so:

```
$ sed -f command_file source > output_file
$
```

Notice that this time the system prompt quietly redisplays. Let's take a look at output_file:

```
$ cat output_file
file1
file2
file4
file7
$
```

OK. Looks good. Now what if we were interested in performing a few edit operations on output_file? Suppose all lines that contain the string file were to be changed to document. Let's create another command file to do so. This time the s (for substitute) command will be used to substitute `file` with `document`. Here's the command file:

```
$ cat command_file2
s/file/document/
$
```

Before we continue, we make sure that there is a slash on both sides of the pattern to be substituted. If the slash is missing, then you can expect to see an error message that reads something like this:

```
sed: Ending delimiter missing on substitution :s/file/document
```

Now we will reimplement the prior `sed` command, and pipe its output to another `sed` command that will use `command_file2` as its source, and produce output. Here's the result:

```
$ sed -f command_file source | sed -f command_file2
document1
document2
document3.tmp
document4
document5.tmp
document6.tmp
document7
$
```

And here we have a classic example of a pipe and a filter! The output of one command is piped as input to another, and the filtered output is displayed on standard output. We could have carried the pipe one step further and piped the output to the line printer or a file:

```
$ sed -f command_file source | sed -f command_file2 | lpr
$ sed -f command_file source | sed -f command_file2 > outfile
$
```

If the output is redirected to a file, then that file could be further piped to some other command, blocks of text could be filtered or altered, and the pipeline could continue on and on in this way. The possibilities are confined only by your requirements, and/or your imagination!

15.4 HOW SED WORKS

Since we were more interested in having you understand how sed works, we deliberately kept the source and command files small. However, in order to understand the true power of the sed editor, envision a file that is 50,000 lines long. This could be the output file created by a database program, its contents being the rows or records for a specific table. This table is now being moved to another database. Each record in this table is delimited by the character \n. In order for this table to be loaded into the new database, it must be delimited by a |. sed would be the ideal candidate to perform a global change of all occurrences of \n to |.

And so you may wonder how sed handles such large files without running out of space. It reads one line of the input file at a time, and stores it in memory. Then it scans the command file to find a match so as to execute a command contained therein. If it finds a match, it executes the command, then goes to the next command in the command file. If any subsequent commands result in a change to the modified input line, then they are also performed. After all commands have been read, the input line is output to standard output, or to a file if output was redirected. And then sed reads the next input line.

We now continue with a description of how sed is invoked with the −e option.

15.5 INVOKING SED WITH EDIT COMMANDS

Another way to invoke sed is with the −e option. Here's the syntax:

■ `sed −e commands source_1 source_2 ... source_n`

This syntax indicates to sed that the commands it is to perform on source_1, source_2, ... will not be taken from a script file. Instead, they will be entered right there on the command line.

It makes sense to use sed in this way when only one or two commands are to be performed on the input file, instead of a long sequence of them. We reissue the commands in the prior example using the −e option instead of −f.

`$ sed −e '/\.tmp/d'    source`

Notice that the command to be implemented is enclosed in single quotes. We did not have to do this, but it is good practice to do so. This takes into account any spaces that may exist in the pattern to be matched. Also notice the use of the backslash which precedes the dot (.tmp) to take away the special meaning which is attached to the dot.

15.6 FEATURES OF SED

At the beginning of this chapter we said that sed uses the same commands as the ed editor. That is a true statement. However, sed is different from ed in the following ways:

- sed performs the commands specified on all lines in the source file. It has no concept of current, previous, or next line.

- Input of information to sed is executed via the a, i, and c commands, just as in ed. However, the syntax is slightly different.

- sed contains some commands that do not exist in ed.

- ed contains some commands that do not exist in sed.

  The following should also be noted with reference to sed:

- sed attempts to implement commands based on *addresses*. Addresses can take the form of line numbers, patterns, line ranges, and/or pattern ranges. If no address is specified, then an attempt is made to execute the command(s) on each line in the source file.

- If one address is specified, then sed will implement the command(s) on each line that matches the address.

- If two addresses are specified, then sed will implement the specified command(s) on the group of lines that start with the first address and end with the second address.

- If two addresses are specified and sed cannot find the first address, then the specified command(s) will not be applied to any of the input lines.

- If two addresses are specified and sed cannot find the second address, then the command(s) will be applied from the line containing the first address right through the end of the file.

We now present a variety of examples that illustrate the usage of sed. These examples by no means encompass all commands that can be used with this editor. However, they are sufficient to illustrate the kinds of things that sed can be used for. We expect that you should be able to think up quite a few applications for your installation by the time you conclude this chapter.

15.7 SOME EXAMPLES

All examples will use the following source file:

```
$ cat source
file1
file2
file3.tmp
file4
file5.tmp
file6.tmp
file7
$
```

The instructions will be written to command_file.

Example 1:   Add the string file8 at the end of the file.

```
$ cat command_file
$a\
file8
$
```

Notice that a backward slash follows the standard a (append) command, and the text to be appended appears on the next line. sed requires this syntax for all commands that perform input to a file (that is, the forward slash must be used with the i (insert) and c (change) commands as well.) The text to be added must follow on the next line.

The dollar sign ($) that precedes the a instructs sed to append the string at the end of the file.

And here's the output of sed:

```
$ sed -f command_file source
file1
file2
file3.tmp
file4
file5.tmp
file6.tmp
file7
file8
$
```

We want you to take another look at `command_file`:

```
$ cat command_file
$a\
file8
$
```

We already called your attention to the backward slash that follows the a command. If more than one line is to be appended, then each line must be followed by the backward slash, except the last line. Take a look at this `command_file`:

```
$ cat command_file
$a\
file8\
file9\
file10
$
```

Notice the backward slash at the end of each line except the last line. Here's the output:

```
$ sed -f command_file source
file1
file2
file3.tmp
file4
file5.tmp
file6.tmp
file7
file8
file9
file10
$
```

Example 2:   Add the string file0 to the beginning of the file.

```
$ cat command_file
1i\
file0
$
```

The line number is used explicitly to position on the first line. Then the i command is used to insert the text file0 before the beginning of the first line in the file. Here's the output:

```
$ sed -f command_file source
file0
file1
file2
file3.tmp
file4
file5.tmp
file6.tmp
file7
$
```

Example 3:   Change all occurrences of .tmp to .doc.

```
$ cat command_file
/\.tmp/s/\.tmp/\.doc/
$
```

The backslash is used to take away the special meaning of the dot. First, all lines that contain .tmp are matched via the first part of the command:

/\.tmp/

Next, the s command is used to make the substitution:

...s/\.tmp/\.doc/

For each occurrence of the string .tmp, .doc is substituted:

```
$ sed -f command_file source
file1
file2
file3.doc
file4
file5.doc
file6.doc
file7
$
```

Example 4:   Append the line `This is a temporary file.`
             underneath each occurrence of `.tmp` in the source.

```
$ cat command_file
/\.tmp/a\
'This is a temporary file.'

$ sed -f command_file source
file1
file2
file3.tmp
This is a temporary file.
file4
file5.tmp
This is a temporary file.
file6.tmp
This is a temporary file.
file7
$
```

Example 5:   Write all occurrences of lines ending with `.tmp` to
             a file called `temp`.

```
$ cat command_file
/\.tmp/w temp
$
```

Recall that the w command is used to write to a file. A match is found on all lines that contain the pattern `.tmp`. These lines are written to the file called `temp` via the w command. Here's the output:

```
$ sed -f command_file source
file1
file2
file3.tmp
file4
file5.tmp
file6.tmp
file7
$
```

sed outputs the contents of `source` as is. Now let's see what `temp` looks like:

```
$ cat temp
file3.tmp
file5.tmp
file6.tmp
$
```

Example 6:   Implement the above command, but suppress the
output.

In Example 5, sed created a file called temp and wrote the
appropriate text from source to it. However, it displayed each line
of the source file as it went about its job, a side effect that we really
don't need.   This is where the −n option comes into play.
command_file is still the same. Here's its usage:

```
$ sed −n −f command_file source
$
```

Doing a cat on temp indicates that the file is created as
requested:

```
$ cat temp
file3.tmp
file5.tmp
file6.tmp
$
```

Example 7:   Change all instances of the numbers 1 through 3 in
the source file to their English counterpart.

```
$ cat command_file
/1/s/1/one/
/2/s/2/two/
/3/s/3/three/
$
```

The pattern to be matched is a 1, 2, or 3.   The substitute
command simply substitutes, for the number, its English
counterpart. Here's the output:

```
$ sed −f command_file source
fileone
filetwo
filethree.tmp
file4
file5.tmp
file6.tmp
file7
$
```

Example 8:   Change all instances of digits to the asterisk
character.

```
$ cat command_file
/[0-9]/s/[0-9]/\*/g
$
```

Notice that this substitute command uses metacharacters to search for the pattern that matches the range of digits from 0 through 9:

```
/[0-9]/
```

Once a match is found for any of the digits contained therein, the asterisk is substituted for the digit:

```
...s/[0-9]/\*/
```

And the change is applied globally, that is, to every occurrence of a digit on a line, not just the first:

```
.../g
```

Here's the output:

```
$ sed -f command_file source
file*
file*
file*.tmp
file*
file*.tmp
file*.tmp
file*
$
```

Example 9:   Write lines 1 through 4 to a file called temp.

```
$ cat command_file
1,4pwtemp
$
```

This time sed will be used with the −n option so that it produces no extraneous output, but simply writes the required lines to temp. The range of addresses that are to be operated on consists of line numbers.

```
$ sed -n -f command_file source
$ cat temp
file1
file2
file3.tmp
```

```
file4
$
```

Example 10:   Display the line from the one that contains the
pattern file2 through the one that contains the
pattern file5.

```
$ cat command_file
/file2/,/file5/p
$
```

This time the range of addresses that are to be operated on
comprises string patterns. Here's the output:

```
$ sed -n -f command_file source
file2
file3.tmp
file4
file5.tmp
$
```

Example 11:   Display the source file from line 2 through the
line that contains the pattern file4.

```
$ cat command_file
2,/file4/p
$
```

Notice that this time the range of addresses that are to be
operated on consists of a line number through a string pattern. The
past few examples illustrate the variety of ways in which ranges
can be specified. Here's the output:

```
$ sed -n -f command_file source
file2
file3.tmp
file4
$
```

Example 12:   Delete all blank lines from a file.

We insert a few blank lines in our source file to illustrate this
example:

```
$ cat source
file1

file2
file3.tmp
file4
file5.tmp

file6.tmp
file7
$
```

Here's the command file:

```
$ cat command_file
/^[ ]*$/d
$ sed -f command_file source
file1
file2
file3.tmp
file4
file5.tmp
file6.tmp
file7
$
```

The ^ character is used to specify the beginning of the line. The $ is used to specify the end of the line. The *, as usual, specifies zero or more characters. And the match is specified by the embedded space between the square brackets. The above file will be modified to illustrate how tabs can be removed from text.

Example 13:   Remove all tabs from a file.

This time we insert some tabs into the source file:

```
$ cat source
  file1

  file2
file3.    tmp
file4
  file5.    tmp

file6.tmp
  file7
$
```

Here's the command file:

```
$ cat command_file
/[^I]/s/[^I]//g
$ sed -f command_file source
file1

file2
file3.tmp
file4
file5.tmp

file6.tmp
file7
$
```

A tab is indicated by <Cntrl> I (^I). You can type <Cntrl> I, or simply insert a tab literally within the square brackets. The resulting output indicates that all tabs have been removed from the file. However, the blank lines are still there. You can pipe the output from this example to the command_file from Example 12, and thereby have a file that contains no tabs or blank lines in it.

We have illustrated the usage of the sed editor in a variety of conditions. You now have the knowledge to implement applications that are customized to your installation's specific needs.

Bourne Shell Implementation

The sed editor works in the same way when invoked from the Bourne shell. All examples will produce the same results.

Korn Shell Implementation

The sed editor works in the same way when invoked from the Korn shell. All examples will produce the same results.

15.8 OSF/1 Considerations

The features of the sed editor are the same in an OSF/1 operating system environment. All examples presented in this chapter will produce the same output, regardless of the shell from which they are implemented.

15.9 REVIEW

This chapter described the working of the sed stream editor, and illustrated the powerful capabilities that it can provide. In particular, we learned the following:

- sed can be invoked with a script file that contains the commands that it is to implement, and applied to one or more source files:

  ```
  sed -f command_file source_1 source_2 . . . source_n
  ```

- The commands that are to be implemented by sed can be supplied right on the command line by using the −e option:

  ```
  sed −e commands source_1 source_2 . . . source_n
  ```

- The −n option can be used to suppress normal sed output, and output only those lines that are explicitly specified.

- The output produced by sed can be redirected to a file via the redirection operator:

  ```
  sed -f command_file source_file > output_file
  ```

- For the most part, sed works with the same commands as ed.

- The syntax of the insert commands (a, i, c) varies for sed, in that all text inserted must be followed by a backward slash (except the last line) and the command must be on a line by itself.

- sed works by addresses. Addresses can consist of line numbers, patterns, line ranges, and pattern ranges.

- sed is most suited for implementing global changes on very large files. The reason for this is that it does not place the entire file that it is operating on in memory. Instead, it works on only one input line at a time, does what it has to do, and then proceeds to the next input line in the source file.

Table 15.1 summarizes the syntax of some of the commands presented in this chapter.

Table 15.1 Some Common sed Commands

Command	Syntax	Description
Add strings to end of file	$a\ string1\ string2	$ indicates end of line. a appends to right of text. \ must follow a. Strings must be on lines by themselves, and followed by \.
Add strings to beginning of file	^i\ string1\ string2	^ indicates start of line. i inserts to left of text. All rules listed for a also apply to i.
Substitute for all occurrences of pattern1, pattern2	/pat1/s/pat1/pat2/g	The first /pat1/ finds the pattern. s substitutes. /pat1/ and /pat2/ must be enclosed by slashes. g performs a global change on all occurrences of pat1.
Write all occurrences of pattern1 to another file	/pat1/w file	w writes to file.

Table 15.1 Some Common sed Commands (Contd.)

Command	Syntax	Description
Change all instances of digits to asterisks	/[0-9]/s/[0-9]/*/	[0-9] specifies the range for the pattern. The backslash precedes the * because the * is a special character. \ takes away its special meaning. All special characters must be preceded by \ to take away their special meaning.
Print lines 1 through 5	1,5p	Line number ranges are specified by inserting a comma in between. p prints the line.
Print lines between the strings pat1 and pat2	/pat1/,/pat2/p	Strings specified as ranges must be enclosed between slashes.

Table 15.1 Some Common sed Commands (Contd.)

Command	Syntax	Description
Remove all blank lines from a file	/^[ ]*$/d	^ specifies beginning of line. [ ] specifies match on space. * specifies match on zero or more spaces. d deletes the line that matches the criterion.
Remove all tabs from a file	/[^I]/s/[^I]//g	^I indicates tab character. All other rules are the same as for the removal of blank lines.

16

The ex Line Editor

16.1 INTRODUCTION

The ex is a line editor and is an extension of the ed editor described in Chapter 14. However, ex is considered a little more user friendly because it outputs messages that indicate where you went wrong, instead of the basic question mark (?) that ed displays. In addition to this, the ex editor can be transformed from a basic line editor to a *visual* editor (does vi ring a bell?!). As a matter of fact, you will see a lot of similarities in the commands used in vi, ed, and ex. The reason for this is that the vi editor is based on ex, and ex is based on ed! So if you have developed a familiarity with ed and a liking for vi, then consider yourself fairly well versed in ex as well! Since the commands of each of these editors have been described in detail in prior chapters, we will not go into too much depth here. Each command will be described, but if you require a more in-depth explanation, we refer you to the explanations for the corresponding commands in the prior chapters.

16.2 CREATING A NEW FILE

A new file is created by typing ex followed by the file name:

$ **ex newfile**

As you hit the carriage return key, ex responds as follows:

```
"newfile" [NEW FILE] 1 line, 1 char
:
```

The colon (:) is the ex prompt.

16.3 EDITING A PREEXISTING FILE

A currently existing file can be edited via the ex editor as follows:

```
$ ex file1
"file1" 5 lines, 67 characters
:
```

The system responds with pertinent statistics for the file that is being edited, as in vi.

16.4 EDITING MULTIPLE FILES

Multiple files that have to be edited can be specified on the same command line:

```
$ ex file1 file2 file3
3 files to edit
"file1" 5 lines, 67 characters
:
```

Once file1 has been edited, the next file in the list (file2) can be edited by typing n for next at the colon prompt:

```
:n
"file2" 20 lines, 1023 characters
:
```

16.5 EXITING EX

As with the other editors, there are two ways to exit ex.

- Type :wq to save the file and exit. As you do so, the number of lines and characters contained in the file will be displayed.

- Type :q! to exit the file without saving its contents.

16.6 THE EX ENVIRONMENT

We stated at the beginning of the chapter that the ex editor can be used like the screen editor vi. In order to use ex in screen mode, the current terminal type has to be specified to the system.

There are several ways in which the terminal can be specified to ex. One of them is simply by setting the environment variable TERM to the current terminal type. In some installations, the environment variable EXINIT is used to specify the terminal type. Check with your system administrator for the proper entry. (This entry will vary for different terminal types.) Then use the setenv command to set this variable.

More than one command can be specified in EXINIT, each command separated from the next by a | symbol. EXINIT is, in effect, a startup file that is read in much the same way as .profile, .login, or .cshrc.

If EXINIT is not set, then the system will search for a file called .exrc in your home directory, and consider this as a startup file for the settings for ex. It is necessary that the user invoking ex be the owner of this file, in order for it to be read.

The .exrc file can also be placed in your current working directory. Once created (and owned by you, the user invoking ex), the entries in this file will override all other corresponding entries, if they are set.

You may wonder why a separate file is read on startup of the ex editor. Well, the reason for a separate file is that ex can be used with a variety of options. These options can be specified at the time that ex is invoked, or they can be made permanent by specifying them in the .exrc file. At the beginning of the chapter we mentioned that vi is based on ex. Because of this, if a .exrc file is set up for vi, then the same options will also apply to vi whenever it is invoked. Hence, the .exrc file holds utility for the vi editor as well. We discuss these options next.

16.7 SETTING UP EX (AND VI) ENVIRONMENT VARIABLES

ex and vi environment variable options are set using the set command. The set command is specified by following it with the option that is to be set:

$ **set number**

or by following the variable with the appropriate setting:

```
$ set tabstop=5
```

The variables can be set from within the ex (or vi) session, while in edit mode, by typing a colon followed by the setting:

```
: set number
```

or they can be included as an entry inside the .exrc file.

Settings can be reset as follows:

```
$ set nonumber
```

A brief description of some of the more common variable settings follows.

```
number
```

This instructs the editor to display line numbers in the left-hand margin.

```
tabstop
```

This is the amount of space between tabs.

```
errorbells
```

This specifies that a bell ring each time an error is encountered.

```
ignorecase
```

This specifies that upper- or lowercase should be ignored while searches are being implemented.

```
autoindent
```

This specifies that text entered be automatically indented.

```
terse
```

This specifies that ex messages displayed should be concise.

```
wrapscan
```

This specifies that files should be searched from the current location to the bottom and, if a match is not found, from the start to the current location again.

`report`

This specifies that ex report the number of lines that have been changed, if this number is equal to or greater than what this variable is set to.

`magic`

This specifies retaining the special meanings assigned to special characters such as the dot, comma, question mark, etc.

`autoprint`

This specifies that ex always print any lines that are addressed or changed while in edit session.

16.8 INPUTTING INFORMATION

Information can be entered into a file by typing a (for append) followed by text. As with the other editors, unless you hit the Return key explicitly, ex will consider text to be one line. The a command will insert text after the current line.

Once input is finished, type a dot. Remember, the dot must be on a line of its own, it must be the very first character on the line, and no spaces should precede or follow it.

And now, here's a sample session.

```
$ ex thingstodo
:"thingstodo" [NEW FILE] 1 line, 1 char
:a
Today I have a meeting at 9:30 am.  Then I have
another meeting at 11:00 am.  Then I have another
meeting at 2:00 pm.
Today I promise that I will try not to lose my
cool at these meetings.  I will smile at everyone.
I will try not to doze off.  And I may even chip in
for a few doughnuts for everyone attending.
```

```
:
```

Notice how input is ended via the dot, and the ex prompt (:) redisplays. We now have two options available to us. We can either save the file and exit, or exit without saving. Let's implement the former option first:

`:wq`
```
Wrote "thingstodo"  8 lines, 314 characters
```

Notice how the system responds with relevant statistics for the file being edited. The message displayed at your installation may be different.

We could also have exited without saving the file:

`:q!`
```
$
```

This time the system quietly responds with the system prompt.

Given all of the typing mistakes that have been made, our best option is probably to save the file, and then proceed to edit some of the errors in it. This is how we would proceed:

`:w`
```
Wrote "thingstodo"  8 lines, 314 characters
:
```

The system responds with relevant statistics for the file being edited, and then redisplays the colon prompt, waiting for the next command.

Information can also be input using the i command (for insert). The only difference between a and i is that a inserts text after the current line, while i inserts text before the current line.

16.9 POSITIONING ON LINES

The ex editor follows the same rules as ed when positioning on lines in the edit buffer. These are enumerated now:

- Type p or . to display the current line at which you are positioned.

- Type .= to display the current line number.

- Type $= to display the number of the last line in the buffer.

- Type n to position the cursor at a specific line number, where n is the number.

- Press <Return> or + to go to the next line. Type ++ to go down two lines, and so on.

■ Type − to go back to the previous line. Type −− to go up two lines, and so on.

■ Type .+n to move forward n lines.

■ Type .−n to go back n lines.

16.10 VIEWING THE EDIT BUFFER

The edit buffer is viewed the same way as in ed. The only difference is that commands are typed at the colon prompt in the ex edit buffer.

■ Type 1,$p to display the entire edit buffer.

■ Type range1,range2p to display a range of lines from range1 to range2. The range can consist of numbers or text patterns. For example, the following are valid ranges:

```
1,4p     Lists lines 1 through 4
3,5p     Lists lines 3 through 5
```

■ Type np to display line n only.

In addition to the ed commands, ex has a few of its own:

■ Type the letter l to display any control characters that may exist in the edit buffer. Here's sample usage:

```
1,3l
Today I have a meeting at 9:30 am.   Then I have$
another meeting at 11:00 am.   Then I have another$
meeting at 2:00 pm.$
:
```

Notice the dollar sign at the end of each line. This shows the carriage return at the end of each line at our installation.

■ Type # to display the edit buffer with line numbers:

```
: 1,3#
1 Today I have a meeting at 9:30 am.   Then I have
2 another meeting at 11:00 am.   Then I have another
3 meeting at 2:00 pm.
:
```

Please note that not all versions of ex may have the # feature.

■ Type z to display the current line and a screenfull of lines below it. For example, if you are currently positioned on line 2, then typing z will produce the following output:

```
: z
another meeting at 11:00 am.  Then I have another
meeting at 2:00 pm.
Today I promise that I will try not to lose my
cool at these meetings.  I will smile at everyone.
I will try not to doze off.  And I may even chip in
for a few doughnuts for everyone attending.
:
```

■ Type z- to display the line at the bottom of the screen. A screenfull of text will appear above the current line.

■ Type z= to have the current line display in the middle of the screen.

Please note that not all installations may have the z feature included in the ex editor.

16.11 EDITING LINES

The ex editor supports the s command like ed. The only difference is that in ed the old and new patterns must be delineated with a slash. In ex, you can include or omit the ending slash. We list the possible variations with which the s command can be used:

■ Type s/old/new, to substitute for the first occurrence of old with new on the current line.

■ Type ns/old/new, to substitute for the first occurrence of old with new on line n.

■ Type range1,range2s/old/new, to substitute the first occurrence of old with new for the range specified. Ranges can consist of line numbers or string patterns found within the file.

■ Use metacharacters within ranges, or the patterns to be substituted, as necessary, using the syntax specified above.

In addition to the usual metacharacters that are used within UNIX, `ex` recognizes the following:

- Use \<pat to specify a match of `pat` at the beginning of a word, where `pat` is a pattern comprising one or more characters. Here's sample usage:

:1,3s/\<f/ff

The above command will operate on the range of lines between 1 and 3. It will find a match on all words in these lines that start with the character `f`. If a match is found, then it will substitute for the `f` an `ff`.

- Use pat\> to specify a match of `pat` at the end of a word, where `pat` is a pattern comprising one or more characters. Here's sample usage:

:1,3s/f\>/ff

The above command will also operate on the range of lines betwen 1 and 3. It will find a match on all words in these lines that end with the character `f` and replace them with `ff`.

- Use \u to change the first character of the replacement string to uppercase. Take a look at the output for this command:

:s/file/\u
File
:

Not all installations may have this particular feature.

- Use \l (backslash followed by the letter l) to change the first character of the replacement string to lowercase:

:s/File/\l
file
:

Not all installations may have this particular feature.

- Use \U to change all characters of the replacement string to uppercase:

:s/file/\U
FILE

Not all installations may have this particular feature.

- Use \L to change all characters of the replacement string to lowercase:

```
:s/FILE/\L
file
:
```

Not all installations may have this particular feature.

16.12 EX AND ENVIRONMENT VARIABLE SETTINGS

Earlier on in this chapter we brought to your attention some environment variable settings that affect the way ex works in your environment. We now bring your attention back to some of these settings and illustrate their effect.

16.12.1 The autoindent Variable

If this variable is set, then each line will automatically start at the indentation of the previous line. For example, if you start your first line at column 5 in the buffer, then when you press the Return key, you will be automatically placed at column position 5. You can go back to nonindent mode by typing <Cntrl> D.

Autoindentation becomes significant in ex when you type the a or i command followed by the exclamation mark. The effect of this command is to toggle the current setting of the variable. An example will help you understand what we mean.

Suppose the setting for autoindentations (ai) is turned on as follows:

```
: set ai
```

then, entering a for append will result in autoindent working as specified. However, if you enter a!, then autoindentation will be toggled off.

Similarly, if the setting for ai is turned off as follows:

```
: set noai
```

then entering a will result in no autoindentation. However, inputting information using the syntax a! will toggle it back on.

The i and i! commands can also be used to toggle auto-indentation on and off, as specified, for the insert command.

16.12.2 The ignorecase Variable

If this variable is set, then case is ignored when a search is implemented. If this variable is not set, then the search pattern is taken literally; uppercase is uppercase, and lowercase is lowercase. Here's sample usage:

```
:set ignorecase
:.
file
:s/F/t
:p
tile
:
```

Notice that an uppercase F is replaced by a t. The current line contains a lower case f. However, the substitution is made anyway, since the ignorecase option was set. The substitution would not have been made if the ignorecase settting was like this:

```
:set noignorecase
```

16.12.3 The wrapscan Variable

When this variable is set, like this:

```
:set wrapscan
```

then regardless of the position in the buffer from which a search is made, the entire file will be searched.

If this variable is not set, like so:

```
:set nowrapscan
```

then the search will terminate when the end of the file is reached, and a message stating this will be displayed.

```
Hit bottom without finding RE
```

RE stands for Regular Expression.

16.12.4 The magic Variable

Recall that characters such as a dot, question mark, forward slash, and others have a special meaning for the shell, and are used when searches are made using metacharacters in expressions. When this option is set, if a search is to be issued on these special characters, then they have to be prefixed with a backslash (\) in order to take away their special meaning. Let's illustrate its usage. This variable can be set as follows:

```
:set magic
```

and then a search pattern can be issued as follows:

```
:s/\.tmp/temp
```

The above command will substitute for the first occurrence of the pattern `.tmp`, `temp`. Notice that we had to precede the dot (`.`) with a backslash in order to take away the special meaning that would normally be assigned to it.

On the other hand, the variable could be unset:

```
:set nomagic
```

Now the command illustrated would be issued like this:

```
:s/.tmp/temp
```

Please note that the `nomagic` setting takes away the special meaning assigned to all characters except `^`, which means the beginning of a line, and `$`, which means the end of a line.

16.12.5 The autoprint Variable

If this variable is set, then `ex` will always print any lines that are addressed or changed while in the edit session. You do not have to use the `p` command explicitly. This variable is set as follows:

```
:set autoprint
```

Now take a look at the output for this command:

```
:2
another meeting at 11:00 am.   Then I have another
```

Notice that simply addressing line 2 resulted in its being printed, since the `autoprint` option is set. In `ed`, we would have had to use the `p` command to print it explicitly.

16.13 Undoing Last Command

The last command issued can be undone by typing `u` at the colon prompt.

16.14 Changing All Occurrences of a String

All occurrences of pattern matches can be changed by appending `g` at the end of the substitution command:

`:1,$s/file/tile/g`

The above command will substitute for all occurrences of `file`, `tile` for the complete file being edited.

16.15 Deleting Characters

Characters can be deleted via the `s` command, with a null in the location of the new string:

`:s/old//`

The above command replaces the pattern `old` with a null.

16.16 Deleting Lines

Lines are deleted in `ex` in the same way as in `ed`:

■ Delete the current line by typing `d`.

■ Delete a specific line by typing `nd`, where `n` is the line number.

■ Delete a range of lines by typing `m,nd`, where `m` and `n` specify the range of lines to be deleted.

`ex` provides a few additional deletion capabilities:

- Delete a specified number of lines from the specified range as follows:

`/pattern/d 10`

The above command finds the first occurrence of `pattern` and deletes 10 lines from there, including the line with the pattern in it. This feature may not be available with all installations.

16.17 LOADING FILES INTO CURRENT EDIT BUFFER

Existing files can be loaded into the current edit buffer in several ways:

- Append a file to the existing buffer right after the current line by typing as follows:

`r anotherfile`

`anotherfile` will be read into the buffer right after the current line. For example, if you are currently positioned on line 4 in the buffer, then typing

`:r anotherfile`

will result in `anotherfile` being inserted right after line 4.

- Include another file at a specified line number by typing as follows:

`:nr anotherfile`

where n is the line number. For example, `anotherfile` can be appended after line 3 by typing as follows:

`:3r anotherfile`

- You can replace the current contents of the buffer completely by another by typing as follows:

`:e anotherfile`

If you have not saved the contents of the first file, then `ex` will issue a warning message and give you the option to save it.

16.18 SAVING CURRENT BUFFER TO DIFFERENT FILE

This feature works similarly to that found in `ed`:

- Save the current file under a different file name as follows:

  :w anotherfile

  If the file already exists, then `ex` will issue a message asking you to save to `anotherfile` using the `w!` syntax. (`w!` overwrites the current contents of `anotherfile`.)

- Save a portion of the current file to another file as follows:

  :line1,line2w anotherfile

  where `line1` and `line2` are the line numbers of the current file that are to be written to `anotherfile`.

16.19 SEARCHING FOR PATTERNS

Patterns are searched as in `ed`, with the exception that the last slash that delineates the pattern string need not be inserted in `ex`. We now list the major pattern search capabilities of `ex`:

- Implement a forward search by typing as follows:

  /pattern

- Implement a backward search by typing as follows:

  ?pattern

- Specify metacharacters within pattern strings, if necessary. Take a look at the following examples:

  /pat*/

This searches for the first occurrence of a string that starts with `pat` and ends with zero or more characters.

  /pat?/

This searches for the first occurrence of a string that starts with `pat` and ends with just one character.

```
/[A-Za-z]*/
```

This searches for the first occurrence of a string that starts with any character in the range A to Z or a to z and ends with zero or more characters.

- Specify the prior search pattern again simply by typing two forward slashes (//).

16.20 GLOBAL SEARCHES

Global searches are instigated in the same way in ex as in ed. There are two ways to implement these.

- The first method works by entering g followed by the search pattern. This syntax results in all occurrences of the pattern being matched in the file. Here's sample usage:

  :g/pattern/p

  If you do not enter the p, then only the last line with the match will display. If you do enter the p, then all lines with the match will display.

- The flip side of the coin would be to do a global search for all lines within the file that do not contain the pattern specified. This is specified as follows:

  :g!/pattern/p

16.21 CHANGING TEXT

The c command in ex works the same way as in ed. There are two ways that this command can be used:

- Replace a range of lines with one or more lines as follows:

  m,nc
  <new text>
  .

  where m through n is the range of lines, c is the change command, <new text> is the new text that you want inserted in that location. Don't forget to exit out of input mode by typing

a dot on a new line by itself!
If you specify a range like this:

```
1,3c
hello
.
```

then lines 1 through 3 will be deleted, and only one line with the
characters `hello` will be inserted in their place.

16.22 COPYING TEXT

`ex` uses the same commands as `ed` to copy text.

■ Text can be copied from one location to the next as follows:

```
line1,line2 t line3
```

where `line1` is the line number to start copying from, `line2`
is the line up to which the copy will be performed, and `line3`
is the line after which the lines will be inserted.

Lines can be copied above the first line in the file by setting
`line3` to 0. Lines can be copied after the last line in the file by
setting `line3` to $.

In addition to the `t` command, `ex` supports the `co` command,
which inherently works the same way as the `t` command. Only, we
somehow feel that `co` conveys what's going on a little bit better
than `t`. We now present some examples that illustrate sample
usage of the various forms of the copy command.

■ Copy text from one location to the next using the same syntax
as the `t` command, except replace the `t` with a `co`. Here's
sample usage:

```
:1,5co6
```

The above command copies lines 1 through 5 and places them
after line 6.

■ Copy text from one location to the next using the yank and put
commands. The yank (`ya`) command puts the specified lines into
a buffer. The put (`pu`) command places them back into the
specified location. The lines that are yanked are not deleted
from the original buffer. Here's sample usage:

```
:1,5 ya
:8
:pu
```

The above sequence of commands will yank lines 1 through 5 into the buffer. Then line number 8 is set to the current line, and lines 1 through 5 are copied back after line 8.

16.23 MOVING TEXT

Text is moved from one location to the next in the same way in ex as in ed. Here's the syntax:

```
line1,line2,m line3
```

The range of lines from line1 through line2 is moved to after line3.

If you need to move lines to the top of the buffer, enter 0 for line3. If you need to move lines to the bottom of the buffer, enter $.

16.24 IMPLEMENTING SYSTEM COMMANDS

System commmands are implemented in the same way from ex as from ed:

```
:!command
```

The command specified is implemented as if it were typed from the command line prompt, without your having to leave the edit session.

16.25 INVOKING VI FROM EX

Earlier on in the chapter we mentioned that ex can be invoked like vi, and it can be transformed into a screen editor in this way. Well, this is how you do it. Simply type as follows:

```
:vi
```

Yes, you saw right. Just invoke vi from ex, and then you are operating ex in vi mode! Type Q when you want to switch out of vi and back to line mode in ex.

Bourne Shell Implementation

The `ex` editor works in the same way when invoked from the Bourne shell as from the C shell. All examples will produce the same results. However, remember, that the syntax for setting environment variables is different in this shell. The `set` keyword is omitted. Here's a refresher on how to set one of the environment variables:

`:tabstop=4`

The above setting sets the number of spaces between tabs to 4.

`:number`

The above setting sets line numbering on.

Aside from this, all examples will produce the same results.

Korn Shell Implementation

The Korn shell sets environment variables in the same way as the Bourne shell. All examples will produce the same result when run from this shell as from the Bourne shell.

16.26 OSF/1 Considerations

Everything said about the `ex` editor in this chapter holds true for this editor in the OSF/1 environment. All examples will produce the same results when run from the different shells available in this environment.

16.27 Review

This chapter described the features of the `ex` editor. Along the way, it pointed out the similarities and differences between this editor and `ed`, the other line editor available in the UNIX environment. `ex` can be considered a superset of `ed`, providing support for all of its basic commands, plus a whole bunch of additional features that make it more powerful and user friendly than `ed`.

Table 16.1 presents the syntax and description of some of the more common environment variable settings that affect the behavior of ex. Abbreviations of some of these variables are also provided, for your easy reference.

Table 16.1 ex and vi Environment Variable Settings

Command	Description
set number	Displays line numbers in the left margin.
set nonumber	Does not display line numbers. This is the default.
set tabstop=4	Sets tabs at 4 spaces each.
unset tabstop	Sets tabs to default setting of 8 spaces.
set errorbells	Rings a bell if an error is made. This is the default setting.
set noerrorbells	Does not ring a bell in case of an error.
set ignorecase	Ignores upper- or lowercase when implementing searches.
set noignorecase	Does not ignore case when implementing searches. This is the default.
set autoindent set ai	Sets automatic indentation of lines during text entry.
set noautoindent set noai	Does not set automatic indentation of lines during text entry. This is the default.

Table 16.1 ex and vi Environment Variable Settings (Contd.)

Command	Description
set terse	Reduces length of messages from ex.
set noterse	Displays the full ex message. This is the default.
set wrapscan set ws	Searches from current location in file to the end. If pattern not found, then searches from the beginning to current location. This is the default.
set nowrapscan set nows	Searches from current location to end of file only. Does not wrap around.
set magic	Retains special meaning assigned to metacharacters used in expressions.
set nomagic	Takes away special meaning of all metacharacters used in expressions except ^ (beginning of line) and $ (end of line).
set autoprint	Automatically prints lines which are addressed and/or changed.
set noautoprint	Does not print lines which are addressed and/or changed, unless explicitly specified.
set report=30	Reports if 30 or more changes have been made to the file being edited.

File/Text
Manipulation Tools

Commands for
Manipulating Files

17.1 INTRODUCTION

This chapter describes those commands that are used to manipulate files. The following commands will be discussed:

- `sort`
  This command is used to sort files based on specified criteria.

- `diff`
  This command is used to track differences between files on a line-by-line basis. Two commands that are related to `diff` will also be described.

- `cmp`
  This command compares files on a byte-by-byte basis.

- `comm`
  This command is used to find the similarities between files.

- `split`
  This command is used to split up files.

- `lpr`
  This command is used to print files.

- `pr`
  This command is used to prepare files for printing.

17.2 THE SORT COMMAND

This command is used to sort files into alphabetical or numerical order on a line-by-line basis. You have encountered the use of this command in pipes created in prior chapters. We now describe some of its more useful options. The following source file will be used to illustrate its use:

```
$ cat names
Ron Sirvent hired 1986
William Boyd hired 1987
Jessica Boyd hired 1989
Nevine Abdel-Wahab hired 1988
Saba Zamir hired 1989
$
```

Before continuing with Section 17.2.1, keep in mind that the sort command divides the source file that it operates on into logical fields. Each field is separated from the next by a tab or white space. Files are sorted in different ways based on the options that are (or are not) supplied. The above source file is consistent in its line format; each line contains four fields. The fourth field is a number.

17.2.1 Sorting in Alphabetical Order

Using the sort command without any options results in the file being sorted in alphabetical order by its first field. Let's try it now:

```
$ sort names
Jessica Boyd hired 1989
Nevine Abdel-Wahab hired 1988
Ron Sirvent hired 1986
Saba Zamir hired 1989
William Boyd hired 1987
$
```

17.2.2 Sorting by Skipping Fields

Since files which contain names of people are usually sorted by last name, and our source file happens to contain the last name in the second field, let's sort it accordingly. Here's how this works:

```
$ sort +1 names
Nevine Abdel-Wahab hired 1988
```

```
William Boyd hired 1987
Jessica Boyd hired 1989
Ron Sirvent hired 1986
Saba Zamir hired 1989
$
```

As you can see, now the file is sorted by last name, which is actually the second field in each line. The +1 (that's the number 1) option indicates to the `sort` command to skip the first field before implementing the `sort`.

17.2.3 Sorting Through Specific Fields

Take another look at this part of the output from the last example:

```
William Boyd hired 1987
Jessica Boyd hired 1989
```

Although the lines have been placed in the correct order if only the second field is taken into consideration, the truth of the matter is that Jessica Boyd should appear before William Boyd because a J precedes a W. The reason why this happened is because we instructed the sort to skip the first field, and then sort the remaining fields in the file. In those instances where the second field is the same, the `sort` utility tries to sort by the following field, which is `hired`. This field is the same for both files, so now the `sort` takes a look at the next field, which consists of the numbers 1988 and 1989. These numbers are read as ASCII characters (since we have not instructed `sort` to treat them as numbers). The first three characters of the year are once again the same. Hence, the lines are placed in the order in which they appear based on the last digit in the year, which is a 7 and a 9. This is why `William Boyd` appears before `Jessica Boyd`.

This problem can be fixed as follows:

```
$ sort +1 -2 +0 -1 names
Nevine Abdel-Wahab hired 1988
Jessica Boyd hired 1989
William Boyd hired 1987
Ron Sirvent hired 1986
Saba Zamir hired 1989
$
```

The above command instructs `sort` to skip the first field (+1), and stop sorting after the second field (that's the −2 option). Once this is done, then `sort` may or may not have groups of similar second fields together. If it does, then the +0 option instructs it to sort the resulting output by skipping zero fields, and to stop sorting after the first field (−1 option).

17.2.4 Sorting by Numeric Fields

Let's sort the names file by the fourth field, which is the year in which these people were hired:

```
$ sort +3 names
Ron Sirvent hired 1986
William Boyd hired 1987
Nevine Abdel-Wahab hired 1988
Jessica Boyd hired 1989
Saba Zamir hired 1989
$
```

The +3 option is used to skip the first three fields and sort by the fourth, which is the year. Although the output indicates that perhaps the sort did what we instructed it to do, the truth of the matter is that the sort read the numbers as ASCII characters, and since 6 appears before 7 in the ASCII table, and 8 before 9, the output is as we expected. Let's sort a different source file instead:

```
$ cat numbers
   235
32
   228
$
```

We deliberately placed a few spaces inside each field of the file, and you will know the reason why in just a minute. Let's sort this file now:

```
$ sort numbers
   235
   228
32
$
```

As you can see, the numbers have not been sorted properly this time. This is because they are being read in as ASCII characters. The ASCII character 2 occurs before the 3, and therefore number 235 appears before number 32. But how do we explain the 235 before the 228? Well, we really should have mentioned at the beginning of the chapter that spaces are *not ignored* when a field is read. In the numbers file, the spaces are considered as part of the field. If a file contains more than one field, such as this:

```
Ron Sirvent hired 1986
```

then "Ron" is the first field, " Sirvent" is the second field, the third field is " hired", and so on. The leading spaces are considered as part of the field, regardless of how many there may be.

To go back to our example, we now show you how to indicate to sort that the field that is being sorted is numeric. Use the −n option to indicate that a specific field is a number. Here's sample usage:

```
$ sort −n numbers
32
   228
    235
$
```

That's much better. However, the embedded blanks don't look that great. The next section explains how embedded blanks can be ignored.

17.2.5 Removing Blanks

Let's take another look at the output of the numbers file, without the −n option:

```
$ sort numbers
     235
     228
32
$
```

As stated previously, numerical digits will be treated as ASCII characters by the sort utility, and operated on accordingly, unless the −n option is used to indicate that they are numbers. If the −n option is not used, then the leading spaces between uneven length numbers, such as 235, 228, and 32, will be treated as part of the field, and thus the sort will not work the way you may expect it to.

On the other hand, you can remove blanks from the field that is being sorted by using the −b option. Let's try it now:

```
$ sort −b numbers
   228
    235
32
$
```

As you can see, the 228 appears before the 235, and 32 is still at the bottom. Since sort has been instructed to ignore the leading spaces, they are not included as part of the field, and thus 228 appears before 235. However, since we did not use the −n option, sort still reads the numbers as ASCII characters, and that is why the 3 in the 32 appears after the 2 in the 228 and 235.

17.2.6 Redirecting Output

The output of the sort command can be redirected to a file instead of standard output by using the −o option. This option must be immediately followed by the name of the file that output is to be redirected to. Here's sample usage:

```
$ sort -o outfile names
$ cat outfile
Jessica Boyd hired 1989
Nevine Abdel-Wahab hired 1988
Ron Sirvent hired 1986
Saba Zamir hired 1989
William Boyd hired 1987
$
```

And of course, you can always use the redirection operator (>) to explicitly pipe the sorted output to some file.

```
$ sort names > outfile
```

17.2.7 Sorting Multiple Files

Multiple file names can be supplied to the sort command and output redirected to one file. The result will consist of the contents of all files in the sorted order specified. We are going to sort the names file and another one called occupation. Here's the output:

```
$ cat occupation
Programmer(s):
Analyst(s):
Database designer(s):
Project manager(s):
Systems architect(s):
$ sort names occupation
Analyst(s):
Database designer(s):
Jessica Boyd hired 1989
Nevine Abdel-Wahab hired 1988
```

```
Programmer(s):
Project manager(s):
Ron Sirvent hired 1986
Saba Zamir hired 1989
Systems architect(s):
William Boyd hired 1987
$
```

If the files are already presorted before they are supplied to sort as arguments, then the —m option can be used to save the utility from resorting them before producing the final output. This is a good time saver when very large files are involved. Here's sample usage:

```
$ sort names > outnames
$ sort occupation > outoccupation
$ sort -m outnames outoccupation
Analyst(s):
Database designer(s):
Jessica Boyd hired 1989
Nevine Abdel-Wahab hired 1988
Programmer(s):
Project manager(s):
Ron Sirvent hired 1986
Saba Zamir hired 1989
Systems architect(s):
William Boyd hired 1987
$
```

17.2.8 Removing Duplicate Lines

If two files are sorted together and both files contain the same lines, then the two lines will appear as duplicates in the final output. Take a look at this example:

```
$ cat file1
one
two
$ cat file2
two
three

$ sort file1 file2
one
three
two
two
$
```

Duplicate lines can be eliminated by using the −u option:

```
$ sort −u file1 file2
one
three
two
$
```

17.3 THE DIFF COMMAND

This command is used to list the differences, if any, between two files. We will use the diff command on file1 and file2. For illustration purposes, the same line is inserted in line 3 for both of these files.

Here are file1 and file2 presented side by side:

$ cat file1	$ cat file2
one	two
two	three
four	four
five	fine

and here's the diff command and its output:

```
$ diff file1 file2
1 d 0
< one
2 a 2
> three
4 c 4
< five
---
> fine
$
```

Although the output may appear difficult to comprehend at first glance, it's really not that bad. Before we describe each line of output, let's get the generalities out of the way.

The d indicates that a line has been deleted.

The a indicates that a line has been added.

The c indicates that a line has been changed

The text following the < symbol is the old version of the line, or the lines in the first file which do not appear in the second.

The text following the > symbol is the new version of the line, or the lines in the second file that do not appear in the first.

Exactly which file is being referenced is indicated by the symbol contained in the line that displays the old or new versions of the text. You will understand when we explain the current output.

Based on what we have just said, the order in which the files are supplied as arguments to diff is obviously important. Later on in this chapter we will change the order, and you will see a different output. But first, let's understand the current output.

1 d 0	The output indicates that line 1 in file1 has been deleted from file2. Or, in other words, line 1 in file1 does not exist anywhere in file2. We understand that line 1 has been deleted from file1 and not file2 because the line that follows contains the less than symbol: <. The text that follows this symbol displays the *old* version of the line in file1.
< one	The text to the right of < is the old version of the text in file1, that does not exist in file2.
2 a 2	Line 2 in file2 has been added, and it appears as line2 in that file. We understand that line 2 has been added to file2 and not file1 because the following line contains the greater than symbol: >. This symbol is used to display the *new* version of the line in file2.
> three	The text to the right of > is the new version of the text in file2 that does not exist in file1.
4 c 4	Line 4 in both file1 and file2 has changed. We understand that both files are affected because text appears to the right of both the < and the > symbols. These display the old and the new versions for the same line number in both files.
< five	The text to the right of < is the old version of the text in file1.
---	The dashed line delineates the old and new versions of the changed lines which are displayed.

> fine   The text to the right of > is the new version of the text in `file2`.

The output should make more sense now. The next section goes into further details with reference to the output of `diff`.

17.3.1 The Syntax of Output for diff

Each line in `file1` is compared with each line in `file2`. If there are any differences, then the nature of the difference is listed in specific ways. Some variations to the output just described are now presented.

- `line_a, line_b a line_x, line_y`

The syntax listed indicates that the range of lines from `line_a` through `line_b` is different from the range of lines from `line_x` through `line_y`, and the difference exists because lines a through b have been appended to `file2`.

- `line_a, line_b c line_x, line_y`

The syntax listed indicates that the range of lines from `line_a` through `line_b` is different from the range of lines from `line_x` through `line_y`. The differences are indicated by the lines that follow it in the output. The lines preceded by the < symbol are the old version. The text following the > is the new version.

- `line_a, line_b d line_x, line_y`

The syntax listed indicates that the range of lines from `line_a` through `line_b` is different from the range of lines from `line_x` through `line_y`, and the difference exists because lines a through b have been deleted in `file2` and not in `file1`. The old version of the deleted line which still exists in `file1` will be displayed, preceded by the < symbol.

As indicated previously, the actual lines which are different in one or the other or both files are also listed in the output for `diff`. These lines are preceded by either the less than symbol (<) or the greater than symbol (>). The less than symbol displays the line or lines from `file1`, and the greater than symbol indicates the line or lines from `file2`.

We will now change the order of the files sent as arguments to `diff`.

17.3.2 Ordering of Files Being Compared

Based on what has just been said, it should be obvious to you that the order in which the two file names are supplied to diff can result in varying output. For example, consider the two files:

```
$ diff file2 file1
0 a 1
> one
2 d 2
< three
4 c 4
< fine
---
> five
$
```

Here are file2 and file1, once again presented side by side:

$ cat file2	$ cat file1
two	one
three	two
four	four
fine	five

This time the output indicates as follows:

```
0 a 1
> one
```

The line containing the text one has been added to file1, and this line does not exist in file2.

```
2 d 2
< three
```

The line containing the text three has been deleted from file1.

```
4 c 4
< fine
---
> five
```

Line 4 in both files has changed. This line exists as fine in file2, and it exists as five in file1.

As you can see, the ordering of the files is very important. The entire perspective changes, based on the order of the arguments sent to diff.

17.3.3 Suppressing Blanks in Comparison

The utility diff displays all differences between two files. Take a look at this sequence of commands:

```
$ cat file3
A file
$ cat file4
A    file
$ diff file3 file4
1 c 1
< A file
---
> A    file
$
```

As you can see, the two files are interpreted as being different, although the only difference between them is the extra blanks between A and file in file4. Blanks can be suppressed in the comparison of two files by using this utility with the −b option. Let's try it now:

```
$ diff −b file3 file4
$
```

There is no output, indicating that there is no difference between the two files.

Please note that the −b option disregards blanks, tabs, or other forms of white space only within lines. If the blanks or tabs appear at the beginning of the line, then they will be reported as a difference by diff.

17.4 THE CMP COMMAND

The cmp command is used to compare files on a byte-by-byte basis. (Keep in mind that each character in a file occupies one byte.) diff does a comparison on a line-by-line basis, without actually indicating what character in the line is different. cmp points out the first difference that it finds, and then stops execution. Here's sample usage using file1, file2, file3, and file4 from the prior examples:

```
$ cmp file1 file2
file1, file2 differ at char1, line1
$ cmp file3 file4
file3, file4 differ at char3, line1
$
```

17.4.1 Displaying All Differences

All differences (on a byte basis) can be displayed in a file by using the cmp command with the −l option. Here's sample usage using two files called first and last:

```
$ cat first
one
two
three
$ cat last
one
twenty
thirty
$ cmp −l first last
7:   0x6F 0x65
8:   0x0A 0x6E
10:  0x68 0x79
11:  0x72 0x0A
12:  0x65 0x68
13:  0x65 0x68
14:  0x0A 0x69
$
```

The numbers in the output are displayed in three columns. The first column indicates the position of the byte in the file called first (in decimal), the second column displays the hexadecimal value of that byte in first, and the third column displays the octal or hexadecimal value of the byte in the file called last.

17.5 THE COMM COMMAND

The comm command is used to display the similarities between two files. Its output comprises all lines that are identical in the two files that are supplied to it as arguments. Here's sample usage:

```
$ comm first last
          one
    twenty
    thirty
two
three
$
```

The output for the `comm` command also appears in columnar format. The first column indicates the lines that appear in `file1` but not in `file2`. The second column indicates the lines that appear in `file2` but not in `file1`. The third column displays the lines that are common to both files.

17.6 THE SPLIT COMMAND

This command is used to split large files into smaller chunks. There can be several reasons for needing to do so. For instance, there may be insufficient disk space to perform operations on a very large file. However, this task may be implemented successfully if the file is split up into chunks, and then each chunk is operated on separately. Later, the `cat` command can be used with the redirection operator to merge the chunks back into one file. The syntax for this command follows:

```
$ split bigfile
$
```

The default for the split size is 1000 lines in each section. The name of each chunk is also automatically generated; it is an `x` followed by two sequential letters. Let's do a `ls` on `x*` to see how `bigfile` was split up:

```
$ ls x*
xaa     xab     xac
$
```

If `bigfile` comprises, say, 2600 lines, then `xaa` and `xab` will be 1000 lines each. The file `xac` will be 600 lines long.

The size of each chunk can also be specified explicitly like this:

```
$ split -300 bigfile
$ ls x*
xaa     xab     xac     xad     xae     xaf    ...
$
```

Once you are done processing the chunks, use the `cat` command to concatentate all files back into `bigfile`:

```
$ cat x?? > bigfile && rm x??
$
```

The above command writes all files beginning with an `x` and followed by two characters to `bigfile`. If this command executes successfully, then all these files are removed using the `rm` command.

17.7 THE LPR COMMAND

The `lpr` command is used to print files. But in order for several print commands to execute without conflicting with each other (perhaps by different people using the system), it is necessary to spool the requests to a printing device. The spooling mechanism allows requests for printouts to be queued, if the printer is busy printing some other request. Once the current print jobs are done, then the next request in the queue is honored. The command that spools requests to the printer is `lpr`. Here's sample usage:

```
$ lpr file1
$
```

The above command will queue the request to the spooler if necessary. Otherwise it will produce a hard copy of the file via the line printer.

A few useful options to the `lpr` command follow.

17.7.1 Printing Several Files

Several files can be printed in the same command line:

```
$ lpr file1 file2 file3 file4
$
```

17.7.2 Printing Multiple Copies

Multiple copies of the same file can be printed via the −n option followed by the number of copies:

```
$ lpr −n5 file1
$
```

The above command will print five copies of `file1`.

17.7.3 Outputting a Message after Printout

In a working environment, not too many people are fortunate enough to have the line printer within a five-foot radius of where they work. The –m option is used to mail a message to the user after successful printout of the requested file. Here's sample usage:

```
$ lpr —m file1
$
```

The –w option can be used instead of –m to write the message to your terminal, instead of having it sent to you via electronic mail.

17.8 THE PR COMMAND

The `pr` command is used to prepare a file before it is printed. By preparation is meant various things, such as paginating it, adding headers and footers, and doing other neat little things that make it more presentable and pleasing to the eye. Here's sample usage:

```
$ pr file1

May 17 18:43 1992   file1   Page 1, line 1


one
two
four
five



$
```

Enough blank lines are inserted at the bottom of the document (if it does not fill the entire page) to fill a standard-size page. We do not show all of the blank lines in the interest of saving space.

The `pr` command can be used with various options. We describe these next.

17.8.1 Displaying Headers

Headers can be added to files via the −h option followed by the header enclosed in double quotes. Here's sample usage:

```
$ pr -h "THIS IS FILE 1" file1

May 17 18:43 1992  THIS IS FILE 1  Page 1, line 1


one
two
four
five



$
```

The double quotes are required so as not to confuse pr if there are embedded spaces in the header.

17.8.2 Displaying Line Numbers

Line numbers can be appended to each line via the −n option:

```
$ pr -n file1


May 17 18:50 1992  file1  Page 1, line 1


  1:one
  2:two
  3:four
  4:five



$
```

17.8.3 Suppressing Header and Trailer

The header and trailer that normally display with the pr command can be suppressed via the −t option:

```
$ pr -t file1
one
two
four
five

$
```

17.8.4 Adjusting Page Length

The normal default page length of 66 lines can be overridden via the −l (that's the letter l) option. Here's sample usage:

```
$ pr -124 file1
$
```

    The above command instructs pr that the length of the page is 24 lines, instead of the default page length of 66. This is useful when pr outputs to the screen, and we don't want the output to run off the screen.

17.8.5 Adjusting Left Margin Size

The left margin can be explicitly specified (if your printer does not automatically do so) via the −o option followed by a number indicating the number of characters to indent. Please note that this option may not be available with all installations.

17.8.7 Piping to a Printer

The pr command is usually used in conjunction with the lpr command. Its output is simply piped to lpr via the | symbol:

```
$ pr file1 | lpr
$
```

Bourne Shell Implementation

All commands described in this chapter work the same way and will produce the same output when run from a Bourne shell environment.

Korn Shell Implementation

All commands described in this chapter work in the same way and will produce the same output when run from a Korn shell environment.

17.9 OSF/1 CONSIDERATIONS

All commands described in this chapter work the same way and will produce the same output when run from any of the supported shells in an OSF/1 environment.

17.10 REVIEW

This chapter described some general all-purpose commands that are used to manipulate preexisting files. The following utilities were discussed:

- The `sort` command, which sorts the files supplied to it as arguments.

  Table 17.1 summarizes the options available with the `sort` command.

- The `diff` command, which lists the differences, if any, between files. The order of the files supplied to it as arguments is important, the output will differ based on this order. The output of the `diff` command has a syntax all its own.

  `diff` can be used with the –b option to disregard blanks in the comparison.

  Table 17.2 summarizes the features of this syntax.

Table 17.1 The sort Command

Command	Syntax	Description
Sort alphabetically	sort file1	Sorts file1 in alphabetical order.
Sort by specific field	sort +1 file1	Skips field 1, and starts sort at field 2.
Inhibit sort at specific field	sort -2 file1	Stops sorting after field 2; restarts sorting at field 1.
Sort on numeric value	sort -n file1	Sorts field as numeric, not ASCII characters.
Remove leading blanks	sort -b file1	Removes leading blanks from field before sorting.
Redirect output	sort -o ofile file1	Redirects sorted output to ofile.
Redirect output	sort file1 > ofile	Redirects sorted output to ofile via redirection.
Sort multiple files	sort file1 file2	Sorts file1 and file2, and produces 1 output file.
Sort presorted files	sort -m file1 file2	Sorts file1 and file2. Assumes they are presorted.
Remove duplicate lines	sort -u file1 file2	Removes duplicate lines from the output.

Table 17.2 Syntax of Output of the diff Command

Syntax	Description
d	Line has been deleted.
a	Line has been added.
c	Line has been changed.
< text	Old version of text.
> text	New version of text.
----	Delineates old and new versions of changed text.

- The cmp command, which compares files on a byte by byte basis, and displays the line and character with the first difference in it.

- The comm command, which displays the similarities between 2 files.

- The split command, which splits large files into smaller ones.

- The lpr command, which spools requests to print one or more files.

- The pr command, which prepares a file before it is printed.

Table 17.3 summarizes the options described in this chapter which are used in conjunction with these commands. The pr command is presented first.

Table 17.3 Miscellaneous File Manipulation Commands

Syntax	Description
The pr command:	
pr file1	Outputs headers, footers, etc., and writes to file1.
pr -h "FILE1" file1	Writes header "FILE1" on each page of file1.
pr -n file1	Writes line number for each line in file1.
pr -t file1	Suppresses header and trailers in file1.
pr -l 24 file1	Adjusts default page length of 66 to 24.
pr -o5 file1	Explicitly sets left margin to 5 columns.
pr file1	lpr	Pipes output produced by pr to line printer.

Table 17.3 Miscellaneous File Manipulation Commands (Contd.)

Syntax	Description
The cmp command:	
cmp file1 file2	Compares file1 with file2 on a byte-by-byte basis. Stops execution after pointing out the first difference.
cmp -l file1 file2	Displays all differences in hexadecimal between the two files.
The comm command:	
comm file1 file2	Displays similarities between two files in columnar format: Col 1: Lines in file1, not in file2. Col 2: Lines in file2, not in file1. Col 3: Lines in both files.
The split command:	
split bigfile	Splits bigfile into 1000-line chunks. Each subfile is named x followed by the sequence of alphabetic characters aa, ab, and so on.
split -100 bigfile	Splits bigfile into 100-line chunks.
The lpr command:	
lpr file1	Queues request to print file1 to the spooler. Prints file1.
lpr file1 file2 file3	Prints multiple files in specified sequence.
lpr -n4 file1	Prints 4 copies of file1.
lpr -m file1	Mails message to user after printout.

Finding Text Patterns
Using grep, fgrep, and egrep

18.1 INTRODUCTION

You have encountered the use of `grep` in prior chapters, and you have an idea of what it does. It is used to find the pattern specified in one or more files. Often it is used in pipelines, where it uses the output of one command as its input, and its output is further filtered as input to some other command, and so on. We now describe the options available with `grep` and its two derivative utilities, called `egrep` and `fgrep`. As you read this chapter, you will realize that `grep` can combine the file matching capabilities found in the shell with the string matching capabilities utilized by the system editors described in prior chapters. The commands found in this chapter will most likely be familiar to you; they follow the same syntax for the matching capabilities just listed.

18.2 GREP, A REVIEW

`grep` is a utility that will search for a specified string pattern in one or more files. The string to be searched for may appear as is, or may be enclosed in single or double quotes. The reason for enclosing the string to be searched for in single or double quotes is so that the shell does not interpret any special characters that may be a part of the string (like the question mark (?), the dot (.), and so on) literally. Keep in mind that any character enclosed in single quotes loses its special meaning. The dollar sign ($), backslash (\), and back quote (') retain their special meaning inside double quotes.

Here's sample usage of all three:

```
$ grep hello file1
hello
$ grep "hello" file1
hello
$ grep 'hello' file1
hello
$
```

The output is self-explanatory. grep outputs the line containing the specified string pattern in all three cases. Now let's throw in a few special characters and see what happens. But first, we have to set up the test. Take a look at the revised version of file1:

```
$ cat file1
The message said NOWAY
$
```

And now we are going to set up a local variable called sign:

```
$ set sign=NOWAY
$ echo $sign
NOWAY
$
```

OK. Let's try all three formats:

```
$ grep The message said $sign file1
Cannot open message
$
$ grep "The message said $sign" file1
The message said NOWAY
$
$ grep 'The message said $sign' file1
$
```

In the first instance, since the string contains embedded blanks, grep thought that the string to be sought was The and the files in which it is to be searched were message, said, $sign and file1. Since there happens to be no file called message in our current working directory, the error message Cannot open message displays, and that's the end of that.

In the second case, the whole string is enclosed in double quotes. The $ sign retains its special meaning within the double quotes. Therefore, the value stored inside the local variable $sign (NOWAY) is substituted in its place, and grep tries to find a match on the string The message said NOWAY.

Since the string pattern is found in the specified file, which is file1, grep outputs the string, indicating a match.

In the third case, the string is enclosed in single quotes. That means all special characters lose their special meanings. Hence, the string that is matched on is.

```
The message said $sign
```

and since file1 does not contain this pattern, the system prompt simply redisplays.

You should now be clear as to when patterns to be matched on should be enclosed in single, double, or no quotes.

18.3 MATCHING ON MULTIPLE FILES

Before we get into details of how patterns can be specified to grep, keep in mind that multiple file names can be supplied as arguments to grep:

```
$ grep "Hello" file1 file2 file3 file4 file5
```

The above command would try to find a match on Hello in file1, file2, file3, file4, and file5. It will search the files one by one in the sequence in which they appear. If it finds a match in one of the files, then the name of the file will precede the string with the match. The following example illustrates what has just been said.

```
$ grep "The" file1 file2 file3 file4 file5
file1: The message said NOWAY
$
```

As you can see, the name of the file that contains the match precedes the match string.

18.4 USING METACHARACTERS IN FILE NAMES

We could have issued the command in the prior example like this:

```
$ grep "The " file?
file1: The message said NOWAY
$
```

Notice that we substituted the question mark (?) into the last character of file, thereby utilizing this metacharacter to search for all files that start with the string file and end with one character.

As a matter of fact, you can use any of the metacharacters that were introduced in Chapter 6 ("UNIX Directories and Metacharacters") in the file names specified. For example, if you wanted to find a match for the string specified for all files in the current working directory, then the following command would be issued:

```
$ grep "Hello" *
```

If you wanted to match file names that end with .doc only, then specify as follows:

```
$ grep "Hello" *.doc
```

If you wanted to match file names that start with the first three characters of the alphabet, upper- or lowercase, then the command would look like this:

```
$ grep "Hello" [ABCabc]*
```

or, if you prefer this syntax,

```
$ grep [A-Ca-c]*
```

and so on. Refer to Chapter 6 for further matching capabilities offered by the system.

18.5 USING METACHARACTERS IN REGULAR EXPRESSIONS

We now describe the string matching capabilities available to grep (as opposed to the file matching capabilities just described in Section 18.4). Complex string patterns can be specified to grep; these are called *regular expressions*. The following source file will be used by all examples in this section:

```
$ cat file1
This is line 1.
this is line 2.

And now let's make this little bit more interesting!
So what were you up to last night????
Catching up on your ZZZZZZZ's?
```

```
Or what!
$
```

18.5.1 Matching on Beginning of Line

`grep` can be instructed to find a match on one or more characters that must appear in the beginning of the line by using the caret (^) followed by the character or string:

```
$ grep "^this" file1
this is line 2.
$
```

A match is found on line 2 only, although `this` is also found in the fourth line.

18.5.2 Matching on End of Line

A match can be found for one or more characters that are found at the end of a line by writing the character or string followed by the dollar sign:

```
$ grep '\.$' file1
This is line 1.
this is line 2.
$
```

There are only two lines in `file1` which end with a period, and they are displayed. This example presents a few interesting features. First of all, notice that single quotes enclose the string pattern to be matched. Double quotes will not work, since the shell will attach the special meaning to the dollar sign, and expect a variable name to follow it. Next, notice the forward slash before the period. This is necessary in order to take away the special meaning of the dot that the shell attaches to it. Finally, the dollar sign terminates the string, indicating that the period must be at the end of the string. The output indicates a successful search.

18.5.3 Matching on Beginning and End of Line

A match can be found on lines containing nothing but the specified pattern by combining the syntax of the two metacharacters just described:

```
$ grep '^Or what!$' file1
Or what!
$
```

The output is self-explanatory. If you were to take the time to insert an "Or what!" somewhere in the middle of some other line and rerun this command, then you would see that that string would not be picked up.

18.5.4 Matching on Any Character

Any character can be matched by placing a dot (.) in the location where the match is to be found:

```
$ grep 'O.' file1
Or what!
$
```

The dot works similar to a question mark. It matches one character.

18.5.5 Matching on Zero or More Characters

Zero or more characters are matched with the asterisk:

```
$ grep "this*" file1
this is line 2.
And now let's make this little bit more interesting!
$
```

The first line that displays starts with the string this and is followed by zero or more characters. The second line contains this in the middle of the string; hence the match.

18.5.6 Matching on Ranges

Matches can be found on ranges by enclosing them within square brackets. The range follows the order in which characters appear in the ASCII table. This table is reproduced in Chapter 6 ("UNIX Directories and Metacharacters"); refer to it if necessary.

```
$ grep '[A-Z]' file1
This is line 1.
```

```
And now let's make this little bit more interesting!
So what were you up to last night????
Catching up on your ZZZZZZZ's?
Or what!
```

The above command specifies that grep is to find a match on all lines that contain any character between uppercase A and z. The output indicates that line 2 is dropped from the output, since it contains no uppercase letters.

```
$ grep '^[a-z]' file1
this is line 2.
$
```

The above command instructs grep to find a match on all lines that begin with lowercase a through z. (The caret results in a match being found at the beginning of the line.) This command catches line 2 only.

```
$ grep '[A-z]' file1
This is line 1.
this is line 2.
And now let's make this little bit more interesting!
So what were you up to last night????
Catching up on your ZZZZZZZ's?
Or what!
$
```

This time we caught all lines in the file, since they contain either upper- or lowercase letters. Take a look at this variation:

```
$ grep '[z-A]' file1
$
```

This time we didn't catch anything. This is because the range is specified the other way round, and the shell is probably far too confused to produce any output. Hence, the friendly advice from the authors of this book: stick to logical ranges, or you will end up with unpredictable results.

18.5.7 Negating the Match Criterion Specified

grep can be instructed to find a match on everything except the pattern specified by including the caret character (^) inside the brace that contains the match. Here's sample usage:

```
$ grep "[^Or what]" file1
This is line 1.
this is line 2.
And now let's make this little bit more interesting!
So what were you up to last night????
Catching up on your ZZZZZZ's?
Or what!
$
```

The output isn't quite what we expected. The last line Or what! still displays. Well, the reason for this output is that we instructed grep to find a match on all lines that contain anything but the string Or what. However, we didn't account for the exclamation mark at the end of the line, so it found a match on that character, and therefore the line displayed anyway! The problem could be fixed as follows:

```
$ grep "[^Or what\!]" file1
This is line 1.
this is line 2.
And now let's make this little bit more interesting!
So what were you up to last night????
Catching up on your ZZZZZZ's?
$
```

The output indicates that a match is found on all lines in the file that do not contain the pattern Or what!. Notice that we were obliged to place a backslash before the exclamation mark in order to take away the special meaning that it has for the grep utility.

18.6 OPTIONS AVAILABLE TO GREP

We now describe the options which can be used with grep to modify its output. Here's the source file again, so you don't have to keep flipping back to refer to it:

```
$ cat file1
This is line 1.
this is line 2.

And now let's make this little bit more interesting!
So what were you up to last night????
Catching up on your ZZZZZZ's?
Or what!
$
```

18.6.1 Omit File Header

A file header displays each time grep is supplied multiple file names. This file header can be omitted from the output by issuing it with the −h option:

```
$ grep −h 'Or what!' file*
Or what!
$
```

18.6.2 Display Count

grep can be asked to display a count of matching lines, without displaying the lines themselves, via the −c option:

```
$ grep −c 'line' file1
2
$
```

The output indicates that there are 2 lines that contain the string line.

18.6.3 Ignore Case

Upper- or lowercase can be ignored via the −i option:

```
$ grep −i 'this' file1
This is line 1.
this is line 2.
And now let's make this little bit more interesting!
$
```

Please note that this option may not be available at all installations.

18.6.4 Display Line Number

The line number of the line which contains the match can be displayed via the −n option:

```
$ grep −n '^$' file1
3
$
```

The regular expression instructs grep to find a match on all lines that contain nothing in them, that is, blank lines. (There are no characters between the start and end of line delimiters, ^ and $.) The −n option asks grep to list the line number, since the output will be a blank otherwise, and could be confusing. The third line is a blank line. Here's another example:

```
$ grep −n 'this' file1
2:   this is line 2.
4:   And  now  let's  make  this  little  bit  more
interesting!
$
```

As you can see, not only the line number outputs, but also the line itself.

18.6.5 Invert Search Pattern

grep can be instructed to match all lines except the one specified via the −v option. Here are a few examples and output:

```
$ grep −v "line" file1
And now let's make this little bit more interesting!
So what were you up to last night????
Catching up on your ZZZZZZZ's?
Or what!
$
```

The above command finds a match on all lines in the file specified except those that contain the pattern line in them.

Since regular expressions which indicate search patterns can be quite confusing to the novice UNIX system user (and even you might look at one with a blank stare one day, many months after you wrote it), we suggest that you keep the regular expressions simple. There is no need to prove to the system, or yourself, just how clever you can be. A straightforward expression says more for the person who created it than a convoluted one.

18.6.6 List File Names

The −l (that's the letter l) option is used to list file names. It is useful when multiple files are supplied as arguments to grep. It is used to list the file name only, if a match is found, instead of each line that contains the match. Here's sample usage:

```
$ grep -l 'Or what!' file1 file2
file1
$
```

Since `file2` did not contain the pattern specified, it was not listed in the output.

18.7 FGREP, A FASTER GREP

`fgrep` implements commands in the same way as `grep`, except that it offers fewer capabilities in that it is unable to interpret metacharacters. It performs searches on fixed strings only. For this reason, it is considerably faster than its counterpart. Here's sample usage:

```
$ fgrep "Or what!" file1
Or what!
$
```

If a metacharacter is included in the pattern, then `fgrep` considers it part of the string to be searched for, and if that string does not appear literally in any file, then it produces no output. Take a look at this sample usage:

```
$ fgrep '[T]' file1
$
```

Keep in mind, however, that you can still use metacharacters within the file names. The following command is perfectly legal:

```
$ fgrep 'Or what!' file*
```

`fgrep` will try to find a match on the fixed string `Or what!` in all files in the current working directory that start with the string `file` and end with zero or more characters.

18.7.1 Matching on Beginning and End of Line

Just as the `^text$` combination is used to find lines that contain only the pattern `text` in them, the `-x` option can be used with `fgrep` to produce the same result. We add an `Or` to `file1` as the last line to illustrate this particular option:

```
$ cat file1
This is line 1.
```

```
this is line 2.

And now let's make this little bit more interesting!
So what were you up to last night????
Catching up on your ZZZZZZZ's?
Or what!
Or
$
```

And now here's sample usage of the command, using both methods:

```
$ fgrep -x '^Or$' file1
Or
$ fgrep -x 'Or' file1
Or
$
```

The last line only displays in the output, although the string Or is also contained in the line just before the last one.

Please note that this option can also work with the grep utility.

18.7.2 Supplying File Containing Patterns

fgrep can be supplied a file that contains the list of patterns that it is to find a match on via the -f option. Each pattern must be a fixed string, and on a separate line by itself. Here's sample usage:

```
$ cat matchfile
line
what
$ fgrep -f matchfile file1
This is line 1.
this is line 2.
So what were you up to last night???
Or what!!
$
```

Please note that this option can also be used with the grep utility.

18.8 EGREP, AN EXTENDED GREP

egrep stands for *extended grep*. It implements commands as grep does, but allowing for more extensive and complex pattern matching capabilities in regular expressions than grep. For example, egrep can be instructed to find a match on all lines that contain this pattern or that pattern. An expression such as this would be separated by the or symbol (|) and enclosed in parentheses in order to group the choices together. Here's an example:

```
$ egrep '(line 1|line 3)' file1
This is line 1.
$
```

The above command instructs egrep to find a match on all lines that contain the pattern line 1 or line 3 in them.

What do you think would happen if egrep found a match on both choices? Let's try it now:

```
$ egrep '(line 1 | line 2)' file1
This is line 1.
this is line 2.
$
```

Bourne Shell Implementation

The grep, fgrep, and egrep commands work in the same way when implemented from the Bourne shell as from the C shell. All examples illustrated in this chapter will produce the same result.

Korn Shell Implementation

The grep, fgrep, and egrep commands work in the same way when implemented from the Korn shell as from the C and Bourne shells. All examples illustrated in this chapter will produce the same result.

18.9 OSF/1 CONSIDERATIONS

The utilities grep, fgrep and egrep are similar in that they work in an OSF/1 environment in the same way as they would in UNIX. However, keep in mind that it is possible that the system has been configured for some other locality (refer to chapters on the shell environment, Part 2 of the book, for further details). If this is the case, then different rules can apply to any ranges specified via metacharacters. Please refer to the specific prior chapters that deal with these subjects for the variations found in an OSF/1 environment.

18.10 REVIEW

In this chapter we described three utilities that find text patterns in files and work in inherently the same way: grep, fgrep, and egrep. Some of the main differences between these utilities are that grep can be used with metacharacters that are used within regular expressions to specify search patterns; fgrep cannot, and therefore is a somewhat faster version of grep. egrep is an extension of grep, and allows advanced capabilities that allow specification of alternative search patterns.

Table 18.1 provides a synopsis of the major features of grep.

Table 18.1 grep Commands

Command	Syntax	Description
Find pattern in file	grep pattern file1	Finds match on pattern in file1.
	grep "pattern" file1	Finds match on pattern in file1. $, \, and ' retain their special meaning.
	grep 'pattern' file1	Finds match on pattern in file1. All special characters lose their special meaning.
Find pattern in multiple files	grep pattern file1, file2, ... ,filen	Finds match on pattern in file1, file2, up to filen.
Use meta-characters in file names	grep pattern file*	Finds match on pattern in all files that start with file and end in zero or more characters.
	grep pattern [a-z]file	Finds match on pattern in all files that start with any letter between lowercase a and z, and end with file.

Table 18.1 grep Commands (Contd.)

Command	Syntax	Description
Use meta-characters in regular expressions	grep '^pattern' file1	Matches on pattern if it is found at beginning of line.
	grep 'pattern$' file1	Matches on pattern if it is found at end of line.
	grep '^pattern$' file1	Matches on pattern if it is the only string found in a line.
	grep '.' file1	Matches on any single character in location specified.
	grep 'pattern*' file1	Matches on zero or more characters in location of asterisk.
	grep '[a-z]pattern' file1	Matches on range specified within square brackets in location specified.
	grep '[^pattern]' file1	Matches on anything except pattern.
	grep '[^A-B]pattern' file1	Matches on anything except range specified in brackets. pattern must be part of the match as is.

Table 18.1 grep Commands (Contd.)

Command	Syntax	Description
Using options with grep	grep -h 'pattern' file1	Omits file header that displays when a match is found.
	grep -c 'pattern' file1	Displays count of matching lines, instead of lines themselves with match.
	grep -i 'pattern' file1	Ignores case while finding a match.
	grep -n 'pattern' file1	Displays line number of match.
	grep -v 'pattern' file1	Finds match on everything except pattern.
	grep -l 'pattern' file1	Lists names of files with match instead of lines which contain the match.

Text Manipulation
Using awk

19.1 INTRODUCTION

awk can be considered a text manipulation language, not far
different from grep and sed, that allows you to manipulate specific
text patterns in files and produce the required output. However, it
provides enhanced capabilities over the two utilities just mentioned,
allowing you to perform different types of actions on the lines
selected. It is named after the initials of the three people that
created it: A. *Aho*, P. *Weinberger*, and B. *Kernighan* (and for the C
programmers in our audience, yes, that's the same Kernighan from
the Kernighan and Ritchie book *The C Programming Language*).
This chapter describes the main features of this language.

19.2 AWK BASIC SYNTAX AND OPERATION

The basic syntax of awk is as follows:

```
awk pattern {action}
```

pattern is the pattern that is matched in the file. action is
the action performed on the line or lines that contain a match for
pattern. The action must always be enclosed within curly braces.
Now the interesting thing about awk is that the specification of
pattern is optional, and so is action. However, one or the other
must exist in order to do something with the file named. (Typing
awk followed by a file name will not produce an error message. It

will simply be a do-nothing command.) If `pattern` is omitted, then the action specified will be performed on all lines within the file named. If `action` is omitted, then the output for `awk` will be only those lines that contain the pattern specified; the output file will be a filtered version of the original. If both options are present, then the file will be searched for a match on `pattern`. If a match is found, then `action` will be performed on that line, and this will be the ouput.

As with other UNIX commands, the output produced by `awk` can be redirected to another file using the redirection operators (> or >>) as necessary, or piped as input to another command.

`awk` can be invoked at the command line, or supplied a file which will contain a list of instructions. Regardless of the format in which `awk` operates, the list of instructions that it is supplied is called a program. `awk` reads the program and checks for any syntax errors. If there are none, then it reads the first record in the file on which it is to operate, goes through the list of actions specified in the command file, and performs the related actions if a match is found. Once the list is exhausted, it proceeds to read the next line of the file, and continues in the same way.

Before we proceed to describe features of `awk`, here is the source file that we will be using in the examples that follow:

```
$ cat textfile
It took me 33 years to get this far.
I'm not going to give it up for anything,
including you!
$
```

`awk` considers each line in this program a record. Each record comprises fields which are separated from each other by white space. Hence, each word within a record is a field that can be operated on, as far as `awk` is concerned. For example, the last line in the file,

```
including you!
```

comprises two fields. `awk` can be used to perform complex operations on fields, which the other text formatting utilities cannot.

The source file is perhaps a little strong in its statement of intent. But trust us, it's going to be converted to nothing less than sugar and spice by the time we are done with it!

19.3 SPECIFYING TEXT PATTERNS

Text patterns are specified to awk by enclosing them within slashes.
Take a look at this command and its output:

```
$ awk /"I'm"/ textfile
I'm not going to give it up for anything,
$
```

The pattern to be searched for is enclosed within slashes and
double quotes. The quotes, once again, are necessary in order to
take away the special meaning that the shell would assign to the
apostrophe in I'm. Since no action is specified (there are no
instructions enclosed), all that awk does is search for one or more
lines that contain the pattern and output them to standard output.

As indicated in the last paragraph, double and single quotes are
still required (as in sed and grep) to enclose patterns that contain
special characters. You see, not only are there special characters
that mean something to the shell, but there are also special
characters that mean something to awk. It is best to enclose all
your patterns within single quotes, which take away the meaning
of all special characters, regardless of who they are interpreted by
(the shell or awk). The quotes must be inside the slashes and
enclose the pattern only.

19.4 SPECIFYING ACTIONS ONLY

Take a look at this example in which no pattern is specified, only
an action:

```
$ awk {print} textfile
It took me 33 years to get this far.
I'm not going to give it up for anything,
including you!
$
```

The print statement is a *built-in* component of the awk
language. It simply prints its argument to standard output (unless
redirected elsewhere). The above command specifies no pattern.
Hence, the action (which is a print) applies to all lines (or records)
in the file, and the file is displayed on the terminal. Please note
that the {print} command must not be enclosed in single quotes,
but needs curly braces, since this is an action, not a pattern
specification.

19.5 SPECIFYING COMMAND FILES

Since awk is considered a programming language, more often than not a list of instructions is supplied to it, instead of just one command. These instructions can be written to a file, and the file supplied to awk as an argument via the −f option. This is a much better way of working with awk, since all commands are saved to a file, and can be modified as necessary. Henceforth, all of our commands will be written to a file called cmd_file (command file). Here's sample usage:

```
$ cat cmd_file
/going/ {print}
$ awk -f cmd_file textfile
I'm not going to give it up for anything,
$
```

19.6 SPECIFYING MULTIPLE FILES

Multiple files can be supplied as arguments to awk simply by listing them one after another. Also, metacharacters can be used within file names; the shell will apply its file matching capabilities, and awk will process the commands specified on each file found. Here's an example that illustrates this:

```
$ awk -f cmd_file file*
```

The above command will execute the commands listed in cmd_file on each file in the current working directory that starts with the string file and ends with zero or more characters.

OK. Now that you know the basics, let's get into details of the various ways in which pattern and action can be specified.

19.7 PATTERN SPECIFICATION

Patterns can be specified in any of the following ways:

- Fixed strings

- Numbers

- Fields

- Variables (built-in and assigned)

- Regular expressions

- Combinations of any of the above patterns using the logical or (| |), and (& &), and not (!) operators

- Combinations of any of the above patterns using relational operators

- Combinations of numbers, fields, and numeric variables using operators such as plus (+), minus (−), etc.

We now describe the usage of each of these patterns, except the last two. These will be described after the section on control structures, since these combinations are used within these structures.

For now, the action will be limited to a simple `print` statement. The source file is redisplayed for your convenience.

```
$ cat textfile
It took me 33 years to get this far.
I'm not going to give it up for anything,
including you!
$
```

19.7.1 Fixed Strings

The usage of fixed strings has already been illustrated. Don't forget to enclose the pattern to be searched for within slashes. Here's an example:

```
$ cat cmd_file
/years/ {print}
$ awk −f cmd_file textfile
It took me 33 years to get this far.
$
```

19.7.2 Numbers

Numbers can be matched in the same way as fixed strings. Remember that numbers are interpreted simply as ASCII characters. Therefore, a match on /33/ is not the same as a match on /33 /, since the last match has a space at the end. Here's sample usage:

```
$ cat cmd_file
/33/ {print}
$ awk -f cmd_file textfile
It took me 33 years to get this far.
$
```

On the other hand, numbers are interpreted as just that when they are combined with relational operators. We defer further discussion of the subject until that section, which is presented later on in this chapter.

19.7.3 Fields

Individual fields are referenced within awk programs by preceding the number of the field (starting with 1) with a *dollar sign*. For example, the first field in a line will be referenced as $1, the second field as $2, and so on.

Referencing fields becomes significant when they are combined with relational operators and tested within control structures. We defer further discussion of fields until later.

19.7.4 Variables

You have already encountered the use of locally and globally assigned shell variables. In this chapter we introduce you to variables which are called *awk built-ins*. These variables add much versatility to the kind of text manipulation that can be performed with awk.

The variables listed below are recognized by awk as having a special meaning.

$n
This is the contents of the nth field in the current record.

$0
This is the current record.

FILENAME
This is the name of the current file that is being operated on.

NR
This is the number of the record that is currently being operated on; the first record starts with the number 1.

`NF`
This is a count of the total number of fields in the current record.

`FS`
This is the character or expression used as a field separator for the input file.

`RS`
This is the character used as the record separator for the input file.

`OFS`
This is the character used as the field separator for the output produced by `awk`. It defaults to a space.

`ORS`
This is the character used as the record separator for the output produced by `awk`. It defaults to a space.

Referencing `awk` built-ins becomes significant when they are combined with relational operators and used within control structures. We defer further discussion of these variables until later on in this chapter.

19.7.5 Regular Expressions

Regular expressions can be used inside a pattern. These regular expressions are specified in the same way as they are for `grep`. `awk` can also handle expanded and more complex regular expressions than `egrep` is capable of handling. Please refer to Chapter 18 ("Finding Text Patterns Using `grep`, `fgrep`, and `egrep`") for a detailed discussion of the types of expressions that can be specified. We present just a couple of illustrative examples here:

```
$ cat cmd_file
/^[I]/{print}
$ awk -f cmd_file textfile
It took me 33 years to get this far.
I'm not going to give it up for anything,
$
```

The above command instructs `awk` to find a match on all lines that begin with uppercase `I`, and print them. Regular expressions must not be enclosed in quotes.

```
$ cat cmd_file
/far.$/{print}
$ awk -f cmd_file textfile
It took me 33 years to get this far.
$
```

awk is instructed to find a match on all records in textfile that end with the string far.. awk produces the expected output.

19.7.6 Combining Patterns Using ||, &&, and ! Operators

A single pattern can be specified by combining multiple specifications using the logical or (||), and (&&), and not (!) operators. Consider the following examples, which combine fixed strings to come up with the required pattern:

```
$ cat cmd_file
/33/ || /43/ {print}
$ awk -f cmd_file textfile
It took me 33 years to get this far.
$
```

The above command instructs awk to find a match on all records that contain either the string 33 or the string 43 in them. It is necessary that both patterns that are or'ed be individually enclosed in slashes, or this pattern specification will not work. awk outputs the record with 33 in it. If we were to append textfile like this:

```
$ cat textfile
It took me 33 years to get this far.
I'm not going to give it up for anything,
43 including you!
$
```

then we receive the following output:

```
$ awk -f cmd_file textfile
It took me 33 years to get this far.
43 including you!
$
```

Let's change the || to an && and see what happens:

```
$ cat cmd_file
/33/ && /43/{print}
$ awk -f cmd_file textfile
$
```

This time awk did not find a match. This is because the and
condition implies that the two patterns must be contained in the
same line (record). Let's change cmd_file accordingly:

```
$ cat cmd_file
/33/ && /get/ {print}
$ awk -f cmd_file textfile
It took me 33 years to get this far.
$
```

You should now be able to understand the output.
We continue with the examples.

```
$ cat cmd_file
!/33/{print}
$ awk -f cmd_file textfile
I'm not going to give it up for anything,
including you!
$
```

This time awk is instructed to find a match on all patterns
except those that contain a 33 in them. The ! operator is used to
negate the match for the pattern contained within the slashes.
Please note that this operator must be outside the slashes in order
for this to work.

Now we use these operators to come up with a customized
pattern using regular expressions:

```
$ cat cmd_file
/^It/ && /far.$/ {print}
$ awk -f cmd_file textfile
It took me 33 years to get this far.
$
```

awk is instructed to find a match on all records that contain the
string It at the beginning of the line, and far. at the end of the
line. The && in between the two matches ensures that a match
should be found if and only if the first word is It and the last word
in the record is far..

```
$ cat cmd_file
/^It/ || /ding/ {print}
$ awk -f cmd_file textfile
It took me 33 years to get this far.
including you!
$
```

This time awk is instructed to list all records that start with the
string It, or contain the string ding. awk finds a match on two
lines.

As you can see, logical operators can be combined and complex conditions can be created, the complexity of which is limited only by your needs or your ability to create them.

19.8 CONTROL STRUCTURES UTILIZED BY AWK

awk supports control structures, just like any other programming language. The control structures are similar to the ones found in the C language. We list them now in *pseudocode* only (English-like syntax). Examples using these control structures will be presented in the next section, which describes the operators supported by awk. The "truth" of a condition is the duration that the condition being tested holds true.

- The if construct

  This is the simplest form of conditional execution. It can be represented as follows:

  ```
  if (expresssion is true)
     {
     do this
     and this
     }
  ```

- The if-else construct

  The if-else construct is a derivative of the if construct.

  ```
  if (expression is true)
     {
     do this
     and this
     }
  else
     {
     do this
     and this
     }
  ```

- The while construct.

  The while construct provides looping for the same set of instructions while the condition specified holds true.

```
while (this condition is true)
   {
   do this
   and this
   }
```

- The `for` construct

The `for` construct provides another means of looping, like the `while`. This loop, however, allows initialization, testing, and reevaluation of the condition all within the same statement.

```
for (expression 1; expression 2; expression 3)
   {
   do this
   and this
   }
```

Expression 1 contains the initialization of the variable or variables being tested. Expression 2 contains the conditional test. While expression 2 holds true, the statements within the braces will be executed. Expression 3 reevaluates the conditional test.

19.9 COMBINING PATTERNS USING RELATIONAL OPERATORS

In this section and the next we describe the use of relational and regular operators and illustrate their use via the control structures just described.

The patterns described in Section 19.7 can be combined with relational operators to test for conditions and perform actions based on the results. A list of the relational operators that are recognized by `awk` follows, along with simple examples that illustrate their usage. As you read the descriptions, keep in mind that the terms `expr1` and `expr2` can be any of the patterns listed in the prior sections (fixed strings, numbers, fields, variables, regular expressions), unless noted otherwise.

- `expr1 == expr2`

`expr1` is checked to see if it is equivalent to `expr2`.

Usage of the above expression will be illustrated via examples utilizing the `if` construct. Once again, the source file is `textfile`, and the commands are written to `cmd_file`.

```
$ cat textfile
It took me 33 years to get this far.
I'm not going to give it up for anything,
including you!
$ cat cmd_file
{
if ($2 == "took")
   {
   print
   print $3
   }
}
```

Before we present the output for this command file, make a note of the following. First, recall what we said at the beginnning about the basic syntax of awk:

```
pattern {action}
```

As you can see, anything enclosed within curly braces is an action that is implemented on each record of the source file, unless a pattern is specified before it. In this case, the action will be performed only on those records that match the pattern. Now take another look at the first and last lines in cmd_file:

```
{
...
}
```

The contents of cmd_file contain no pattern specification, only an action which is enclosed within the first set of curly braces. Hence, the action specified will be performed on all records. Now take a look at the output:

```
$ awk -f cmd_file textfile
It took me 33 years to get this far.
me
```

The output can be explained in terms of the action requested:

```
if ($2 == "took")
   {
   print
   print $3
   }
```

awk is instructed to test if the second field in the record matches the string took. The awk built-in variable $n is used to test the contents of a specific field, the second one. The equivalence operator (==) is used to check the equivalence of the two strings. If they are equivalent (which they are for the second record in the source file), the statements within the braces are executed. The first statement instructs awk to print the entire record. The second statement instructs awk to print only the third field. Hence, the output as it displays.

We will now specify a pattern within cmd_file:

```
$ cat cmd_file
/^[Ii]/
{
if ($2 == "took")
   {
   print $3
   }
}
$
```

OK. Let's take a moment to understand this. awk is instructed to find a match on all records that start with an I (upper- or lowercase). The ^ is used to indicate that the match must exist at the start of the line. The square brackets are used to specify the match characters. The entire pattern is enclosed within the slashes, which is required. If a match is found, then awk will simply output the line. But in addition to this default output, awk is instructed to print the third field of those lines whose second field matches took. Here's the output:

```
$ awk -f cmd_file textfile
It took me 33 years to get this far.
me
I'm not going to give it up for anything,
including you!
$
```

The output is self-explanatory. Let's continue with the remaining relational operators:

- expr1 != expr2

  expr1 is checked to see if it is not equivalent to expr2.

```
$ cat cmd_file
{
   if ($1 != "I")
     print $1
}
```

The above command file instructs awk to print the first field of all those records whose first field is not an I.

Here's the output produced when the command executes:

```
$ awk -f cmd_file textfile
It
I'm
including
$
```

The output is self-explanatory.

■ expr1 <   expr2

expr1 is checked to see if it is less than expr2.

■ expr1 >   expr2

expr1 is checked to see if it is greater than expr2.

■ expr1 <= expr2

expr1 is checked to see if it is less than or equal to expr2.

■ expr1 >= expr2

expr1 is checked to see if it is greater than or equal to expr2.

Here are some examples that illustrate their usage:

```
$ cat cmd_file
{
  i = 1
  while (i <= NF)
     {
     print $i, "|"
     i = i+3
     }
}
```

This command file presents a few interesting features. First, notice that a temporary variable called i is set equal to 1. awk allows the use of variables; the data type of these variables is not explicitly declared. Instead, it is implied by the context in which it is used. For example, in the above example, i is understood to be an integer. It would be understood to be a literal string if it had been declared like this:

```
i = "string"
```

The next thing to notice is the `print` statement, which prints not only the contents of the current field, but also the literal string `"|"` afterwards. Finally, the variable i is incremented by 3 so that the `while` does not turn into an infinite loop. The logical increment of i would have been 1, so that each field in the record would be printed, and terminated by a |. However, we don't want the output to be too long; you'll get the idea! Summarizing, awk is instructed to print every third field followed by | while the number of the current field is less than or equal to the total number of fields in that record (the awk built-in NF). Let's take a look at the output:

```
$ awk -f cmd_file textfile
It |
33 |
get |
I'm |
to |
up |
including |
$
```

Finally, take a look at the last two relational operators:

- expr1 ~   expr2

expr1 and/or expr2 are regular expressions. expr1 is compared with expr2 to see if they match.

- expr1 !~ expr2

expr1 and/or expr2 are regular expressions. expr1 is compared with expr2 to see if they do not match.

And now, a few illustrative examples:

```
$ cat cmd_file
{
  i = 1
  if ($i ~ /[A-Ga-g]/)
    {
    print $i
    }
}
```

The variable i is set to 1. Next, the first field is checked to see if it contains uppercase A through G, or lowercase a through g. If it does, then it is printed. Here's the output:

```
$ awk -f cmd_file textfile
including
$
```

As you can see, a match is found on the third line in the file, on the g in including, and that field is displayed.

In ways such as these, you can produce filtered output. This filtered output can be further filtered or piped as necessary. Perhaps ideas are now starting to emerge in your mind with reference to the little and big things that you would like to do at your installation. You should now be starting to get an assessment of the power that is placed at your fingertips with this text formatting language.

The !~ works similar to ~, only it checks that the regular expressions provided on one or both sides of the operator do not match.

19.10 COMBINING PATTERNS USING MATH OPERATORS

We now continue with our discussion on some regular operators that are recognized by awk. The operators you find listed in this section are the same as in C. As you read through the list, keep in mind that expr1 and expr2 can be numbers, fields, or variables that contain numeric values.   Here's the list, and a brief description:

- expr1 + expr2

expr1 is added to expr2.

- expr1 - expr2

expr1 is subtracted from expr2.

- expr1 * expr2

expr1 is multiplied by expr2.

- expr1 / expr2

expr1 is divided by expr2.

- `expr1 % expr2`

`expr1`is divided by `expr2` to obtain the remainder.

- `expr1++`

Increment the value stored in `expr1` by 1, after evaluating the contents of `expr1`.

- `++expr1`

Increment the value stored in `expr1` by 1, before evaluating the contents of `expr1`.

- `expr1--`

Decrement the value stored in `expr1` by 1, after evaluating the contents of `expr1`.

- `--expr1`

Decrement the value stored in `expr1` by 1, before evaluating the contents of `expr1`.

- `expr1 += expr2`

Set `expr1` = `expr1` + `expr2`.

- `expr1 -= expr2`

Set `expr1` = `expr1` - `expr2`.

- `expr1 *= expr2`

Set `expr1` = `expr1` * `expr2`.

- `expr1 /= expr2`

Set `expr1` = `expr1` / `expr2`.

- `expr1 %= expr2`

Set `expr1` = `expr1` % `expr2`.

Usage of the operators +, −, *, and / should be familiar to you. For those of you who are not C programmers, we illustrate the usage of the remaining operators via this very simple example.

```
$ cat cmd_file
/[0-9]/
{
   for (i=1; i <= NF; i++)
      {
      if ($i ~ /[0-9][0-9]/)
         {
         var = $i + 20
         print var
         var = $i - 20
         print var
         var = $i * 5
         print var
         var = $i / 2
         print var
         var = $i % 2
         print var
         }
      }
}
```

There are several points of interest in this very simple example. First of all, this time we decide not to go through every single record in the source file. Instead, we will operate only on those records that contain a digit in them (that's the range specification from 0 through 9). This cuts down on the total time it takes to process a file, since we are no longer processing every record anymore.

Next, notice the for loop:

```
for (i=1; i <= NF; i++)
   {
   .
   .
   .
   }
```

The first part of the for loop consists of the initialization. The variable i is initialized to 1. Next comes the conditional test. Here we compare the value stored in i with the total number of fields in the record. If i is less than or equal to this number, then the statements contained within the curly braces are executed. The third part of the for loop reevaluates the value contained in i. As you can see, i is incremented via the increment operator:

```
i++
```

Now i is set to 2 (we are at the second iteration of the loop). If the number 2 is still less than or equal to the total number of fields in that record, then the set of instructions contained within the curly braces is once again implemented.

OK. Now let's take another look at that set of instructions:

```
if ($i ~ /[0-9][0-9]/)
   {
      var = $i + 20
      print var
      var = $i - 20
      print var
      var = $i * 5
      print var
      var = $i / 2
      print var
      var = $i % 2
      print var
   }
}
```

The current field is compared to any two-digit number. If a match is found, then the set of instructions within the curly braces is executed.

The first statement looks like this:

```
var = $i + 20
```

Given that a match is found on the field 33, this is actually what happens:

```
var = 33 + 20
```

Therefore, 20 is added to 33, and the result, which is 53, is stored in that var. We now present the complete output of this command file.

```
$ awk -f cmd_file textfile
It took me 33 years to get this far.
53
13
165
16
1
$
```

Take a few moments now to work through the numbers of the output, so that you understand this example fully.

Before we proceed to the next section, we need to point out a very important feature of the increment or decrement operators. Let's review what we said about the increment operator:

```
expr1++
```

Increment the value stored in `expr1` by 1, after evaluating the contents of `expr1`.

```
++expr1
```

Increment the value stored in `expr1` by 1, before evaluating the contents of `expr1`.

Now take a look at its usage in the `for` loop:

```
for (i=1; i<NF; i++)
```

Notice that we use the `post++` as opposed to the `pre++`. We had good reason to do so. If the `for` loop was formulated like this:

```
for (i=1; i<NF; ++i)
```

then `i` would have been initialized to 1, as usual. However, `i` would be incremented by 1 and set to 2 before the test condition was evaluated. Although the condition within the test would result in the body of the `for` loop being implemented, `i` would be set to 2, and therefore field number 1 would never be evaluated. Therefore, the `pre++` syntax will not work correctly in this particular condition.

19.11 FUNCTIONS IN AWK

Following is a list of some of the more commonly used built-in functions that are recognized by `awk`.

- `index(string1, string2)`

This function returns the character position of `string2` in `string1`. If `string2` does not exist in `string1`, then a zero is returned.

For example, the statement

```
i = index("Hello there", "l")
```

will store the value 3 in i, since l (that's the letter l) occurs in the third position of the string Hello there. As you can see, only the first occurrence of the search string is taken into consideration. If the statement read like this:

```
i = index("Hello there", "q")
```

then i would contain a zero, since it could not find the specified letter. Here's sample usage:

```
$ cat cmd_file
{
   i = index($2, "o")
   print i
}
$ awk -f cmd_file textfile
2
2
2
$
```

We receive a 2 in each line of the output, since an o is encountered in the second location of the second field for each line (took, not, and you!). Let's search for a u instead and see what happens:

```
$ cat cmd_file
{
   i = index($2, "u")
   print i
}
$ awk -f cmd_file textfile
0
0
3
$
```

The first two lines do not contain a u in their second fields; hence a zero is stored in i. However, a u is found in the third location of this field for the third record; hence a 3 is stored inside i.

■ substr(string1, pos_x, n)

This function substrings n characters of string1, starting at the number indicated in pos_x, and returns this substring. If string1 does not contain n characters, then the remainder of the string is returned anyway. The statement

```
x = substr("Hello there", 3, 3)
```

will store the string llo in x. Let's use it with textfile now:

```
$ cat cmd_file
{
   x = substr($2, 3, 3)
   print x
}
$ awk -f cmd_file textfile
ok
t
u!
$
```

The second field in the first record is took. The next 3 characters, starting from position 3, are stored inside x. However, there are only 2 characters left (the space that follows took is not a part of this field), and that is why the ok displays.

In the second record, only t is stored inside x, and a u! is stored for the last line.

■ length

This function returns the length in characters of the current record.
The statement

```
x = length("Hello there")
```

will store 11 in x. We now display sample usage for textfile:

```
$ cat cmd_file
{
   x = length($0)
   print x
}
$ awk -f cmd_file textfile
36
41
14
$
```

Notice the use of the awk built-in variable $0. This stands for the current record. cmd_file is set up to count the number of characters in each record in the file. If you take the time to verify the results (as we did, in our laborious efforts to make this a good book), you will see that we do indeed have the correct length of each line.

■ `print string_1 string_2 ... string_n`

This function prints each string specified. All strings are concatenated together if they are not separated by commas. Here's sample usage:

```
$ cat cmd_file
{
  print $1, $2
}
$ awk -f cmd_file textfile
It took
I'm not
including you!
$ cat cmd_file
{
  print $1 $2
}
$ awk -f cmd_file textfile
Ittook
I'mnot
includingyou!
$
```

■ `printf "format", string1, string2, ...`

This function works similar to the `printf()` function in C. It formats its arguments `string1`, `string2`, etc., as specified by `format`, (which must be enclosed in double quotes), and displays the arguments accordingly.

The statement

```
printf "Total: %d \n", 1+3
```

will display

```
Total: 4
```

for each line in the file. Notice the backslash n (\n) at the end of the format statement. This is necessary in order to place a newline character, or a carriage return, at the end of each line of output.

We could just have used fields within our arguments, given that they contain numeric values:

```
printf "Total: %d", $1 + $2
```

If you apply the total function to nonnumeric fields, then you will get zeros for it.

Format, as mentioned previously, contains the specification of the format of its corresponding argument. Format is specified via the % symbol followed by an optional number, which indicates the required length of the output. The character that follows indicates the data type of the argument being printed. In this case, the d indicates that the corresponding argument should be output as a decimal number. Also notice that arbitrary text can be made a part of the output by enclosing it in double quotes ("Total:") in this example.

Increasing the complexity of the statement a bit, take a look at cmd_file and its output:

```
$ cat cmd_file
{
    printf "String: %.4s | Num of fields: %d | \
    Current record: %d \n", $0, NF, NR
}
$ awk -f cmd_file textfile
String: It t | Num of fields: 9 |
Current record: 1
String: I'm  | Num of fields: 9 |
Current record: 2
String: incl | Num of fields: 2 |
Current record: 3
$
```

We specify that the current record should output a 4-character string; the format specification looks like this:

```
%.4s
```

The % qualifier is required to indicate that a format specification is to follow. The dot right after (.) has to do with the precision of the format specification – what it does is specify the exact length of the string being operated on that we want displayed. If we had not included the dot, like this:

```
%4s
```

then the entire string would have been displayed, although we asked printf() to print only 4 characters. This is because the string to be output is longer than 4 characters; hence printf() simply disregards the preceding length specifier. Why does printf() do this? printf() is a function that is derived from the C language. It is beyond the scope of this book to get into details about this, we refer you to a book on C for further details.

Continuing with the example, the | symbol is used to separate the next format specification. At the end of the line, notice the sole backslash:

```
printf "String: %.4s | Num of fields: %d | \
```

This is an escape character. We were required to place this backslash here in order to continue the printf() statement on the next line. This slash allows us to take away the special meaning assigned to the carriage return which immediately follows it, so that awk understands that the printf() statement is not complete yet. Recall that this is the same way we are able to specify UNIX commands that span multiple lines.

It is beyond the scope of this book to explain the full set of formatting features available with the printf() statement. Please refer to an appropriate book on the C programming language for further details.

19.12 PREDEFINED STATEMENTS IN AWK

awk performs specific actions if it encounters any of the following statements in its code:

■ next

awk drops the current record when it encounters a next statement, and picks up with the next record. All commands are executed for the next record picked up. We illustrate its sample usage:

```
$ cat cmd_file
{
  print
  if ($1 ~ /Third/)
    next
  print $1
}

$ awk -f cmd_file textfile
First line
First
Second line
Second
Third line
Fourth line
Fourth
Fifth line
Fifth
$
```

Notice that the first field for the third record is not displayed, since the third record is dropped as soon as the keyword `next` is encountered.

In addition to the statements just described, awk supports the following statements, which behave like their C language counterparts. But for non-C programmers, here are brief descriptions and sample usage.

- break

This statement causes awk to immediately exit from an enclosing `for` or `while` loop, regardless of the number of iterations that may still need to be implemented. For example, consider the following command file:

```
$ cat cmd_file
{
  i = 0
  while (i < 5)
    {
    print $0
    i = i + 1
    break
    }
}
```

Under normal circumstances, each statement in the file would have printed 5 times, since there are 5 iterations in the loop. However, immediately after the first iteration (i is equal to 0), awk finds a break, and exits out of the `while` loop. In this example, the statements contained within the `while` are executed only once, and here's the output:

```
$ awk -f cmd_file textfile
First line
Second line
Third line
Fourth line
Fifth line
$
```

- continue

This statement causes awk to perform the next iteration of the `while` or `for` loop without implementing any remaining statements that may exist within the loop. Consider the following program:

```
$ cat cmd_file
{
   for (i=1; i<3; i++)
     {
     if ($1 ~ /Second/)
        continue
     print $0
     }
}
$ awk -f cmd_file textfile
First line
First line
Third line
Third line
Fourth line
Fourth line
Fifth line
Fifth line
$
```

When the second line in the source file is encountered, its first fields matches the string Second, and so the continue statement is executed. This results in all subsequent commands in the for loop being skipped for this particular record, and this is why it is not printed. However, awk continues with the next iteration, instead of exiting completely from the loop, and so the third record in the source file is read, and the enclosed commands executed. Each line is printed twice, because the print statement is inside the loop which executes twice.

■ exit

This statement provides immediate unconditional exit from anywhere in the awk program.

■ Comments

And last, but certainly not least (as a matter of fact, we feel quite guilty that this topic was not presented earlier on in the chapter), use the # symbol to precede all comments in the program. Use comments to describe the overall function of the awk program, and describe what is going on, instead of how. Comment where necessary; don't overdo it, but please don't skip the comments altogether. Furthermore, make sure that your comments are true, and not misleading. The prior example is presented with comments:

```
$ cat cmd_file
# action follows
{
    # print only those records that do not start with
"Second".
    # process only the first three lines or records.
    for (i=1, i<=3; i++)
        {
        if ($1 ~ /Second/)
            continue
        print $0
        }
}
# action ends
$
```

Bourne Shell Implementation

awk will produce the same results when implemented from the Bourne shell as illustrated within the C shell. All examples will produce the same output.

Korn Shell Implementation

awk will produce the same results when implemented from the Korn shell as illustrated in this chapter. All examples will produce the same output.

19.13 OSF/1 CONSIDERATIONS

awk behaves in the same way when executed from an OSF/1 environment as in UNIX. All examples in this chapter will produce the same result.

19.14 REVIEW

This chapter presented an in-depth discussion of the powerful document formatting utility/language called awk. Table 19.1 presents a synopsis of the major features of this language.

Table 19.1 awk Commands
Basic Syntax and Pattern Specification

Syntax	Description
Basic syntax of awk	
awk /pattern/ {action}	awk performs action on records that contain pattern.
awk -f cmd_file source	awk performs commands contained in cmd_file on file called source.
awk /pattern/	awk finds records matching pattern, and prints them. No action is performed on these lines.
awk {action}	awk performs action on all records.
awk /pattern/ cmd_file source1 source2 source3	awk performs action on records with pattern in multiple files.
Pattern specification	
awk /fixed string/	fixed string must be enclosed within slashes.
awk /33/	Numbers can be specified within pattern.
awk /$1/	The number of the field referenced must be preceded by a dollar sign.
awk /$var1/	Locally or globally assigned variables can also be specified as pattern.

Table 19.1 awk Commands
Basic Syntax and Pattern Specification (Contd.)

Syntax	Description
Pattern specification (continued)	
awk /awk_builtin/	awk_builtins are variables recognized by awk; they are referenced as follows:
$n	$n references field, where n is field number.
$0	$0 references current record.
FILENAME	FILENAME references current file being processed.
NR	NR references number of record being processed.
NF	NF references total number of fields in current record.
FS	FS references field separator.
RS	RS references record separator.
OFS	OFS references output field separator.
ORS	ORS references output record separator.
awk /regular expresson/	regular expression can be any expression which utilizes metacharacters.
awk /pat1/ && /pat2/	pat1 and pat2 can be any valid patterns recognized by awk. Two (or more) patterns can be combined via && to specify that both patterns must hold true for a valid match.

Table 19.1 awk Commands
Basic Syntax and Pattern Specification (Contd.)

Syntax	Description
Pattern specification (continued)	
awk /pat1/ || /pat2/	pat1 and pat2 can be any valid patterns recognized by awk. Two (or more) patterns can be combined via || to specify that one or the other pattern must hold true for a valid match.
awk !/pattern/	A ! before pattern instructs awk to match on anything but the pattern specified.
Pattern specification using relational operators (expr1 and expr2 can be any pattern recognized by awk)	
expr1 == expr2	expr1 is equal to expr2.
expr1 != expr2	expr1 is not equal to expr2.
expr1 < expr2	expr1 is less than expr2.
expr1 > expr2	expr1 is greater than expr2.
expr1 <= expr2	expr1 is less than or equal to expr2.
expr1 >= expr2	expr1 is greater than or equal to expr2.
expr1 ~ expr2	expr1 matches regular expression expr2.
expr1 !~ expr2	expr1 does not match regular expression expr2.

Table 19.1 awk Commands
Basic Syntax and Pattern Specification (Contd.)

Syntax	Description
Pattern specification using math operators expr1 and expr2 can be numbers, fields, and variables that contain numeric values.	
expr1 + expr2	expr1 is added to expr2.
expr1 - expr2	expr2 is subtracted from expr1.
expr1 * expr2	expr1 is multiplied by expr2.
expr1 / expr2	expr1 is divided by expr2.
expr1 % expr2	expr1 is divided by expr2 to obtain remainder.
expr1++	expr1 is incremented .by 1 after expr1 is evaluated.
++expr1	expr1 is incremented by 1 before expr1 is evaluated.
expr1--	expr1 is decremented by 1 after expr1 is evaluated.
--expr1	expr1 is decremented by 1 before expr1 is evaluated.
expr1 += expr2	expr1 = expr1 + expr2.
expr1 -= expr2	expr1 = expr1 - expr2.
expr1 *= expr2	expr1 = expr1 * expr2.
expr1 /= expr2	expr1 = expr1 / expr2.
expr1 %= expr2	expr1 = expr1 % expr2.

Table 19.2 presents the control structures recognized by awk.

Table 19.2 Control Structures Recognized by awk

Construct	Description
The if construct	

if (expression is true)
  {
  do this
  and this
  }
	This is the simplest form of conditional execution.
	Braces are optional if there is only one enclosed statement.

The else construct	

if (expression is true)
  {
  do this
  and this
  }
else
  {
  do this
  and this
  }
	This is a derivative of the if construct.
	Braces are optional if there is only one enclosed statement.

The while loop	

while (condition is true)
  {
  do this
  and this
  }
	There should be some statement within the loop that will change the status of the condition; otherwise the loop will execute forever.

The for loop	

for (initialize; test;
    reevaluate)
  {
  do this
  and this
  }
	The for loop is a more concise derivative of the while loop. Initialization, testing, and reevaluation are all contained within one statement.

Table 19.3 summarizes the functions recognized by awk.

Table 19.3 Functions Recognized by awk

Function	Description
index (string1, string2)	Returns character postion of string2 in string1. Returns 0 if string2 does not exist in string1.
substr(string1, pos, n)	Returns substring of string1, starting at position pos. n characters are returned.
length(string)	Returns length of argument string.
print string1 string2 ...	Prints each argument specified. Concatenates arguments if they are not separated by commas. Uses value stored in OFS (output field separator) as field delineator if commas exist between arguments.
printf "format", string1, string2 ...	Formats arguments string1, string2, ... as specified in format.

Table 19.4 summarizes the built-in statements recognized by awk.

Table 19.4 Predefined Statements in awk

Statement	Description
next	Discards current record being processed and picks up the next one. Processing starts from the first command, instead of the next command after next.
break	Immediately exits from enclosing for or while loop, regardless of number of iterations still required within the loop.
continue	Performs next iteration of the loop, without implementing any subsequent statements that may appear.
exit	Immediately unconditionally exits from the program.
#comment	Recognizes the text that follows to be a comment.

Miscellaneous File Commands

20.1 INTRODUCTION

In this chapter we present some more useful commands that reference files. The following will be discussed:

- `find` - This command searches recursively for the file specified, either by its name or by some other characteristic.

- `whereis` - This command returns the location of the source, binary, and manual pages of system command files.

- `wc` - This command returns a count of the total number of lines, words, and characters in a file.

- `cut` - This command does a "cut" of a file (as in cut and paste). It extracts selected fields from its argument.

- `paste` - This command joins lines in one file, or corresponding lines in several files.

- `tr` - This command translates one or more characters in the source file, to one or more characters in the destination file. Keep in mind that source and destination files can be standard input and output.

20.2 THE FIND COMMAND, OVERVIEW

This command searches recursively for the file specified, either by its name or by some other characteristic. By a recursive search is meant that it will search all subdirectories within a directory before it proceeds to the next one. Its basic syntax is

```
find path_list options filename(s) action
```

The `path_list` specifies the directories to be searched. The options specify the characteristic of the file by which the search is to be implemented. Some of the more commonly used criteria are by

- The name of the file

- Its owner

- Group name

- Size

- Time last accessed

- Time last modified

The `path_list`, at least one option, and a file name must be specified, in order for `find` to do some kind of work.

The `find` command works in silent mode. That is, it may or may not find the file specified, and you may never know what it did! And of course, this may lead you to wonder what value this command can have for you. Well, for this reason you can also direct `find` to display its results by specifying an action, like print to the terminal or redirect elsewhere.

Here we issue the `find` command to search for a file called `mystery`:

```
$ pwd
/home/whales/zamir
$ find /bin /usr -name mystery -print
$
```

Before we explain the output, take a few moments to understand the command. A `find` is issued for the file named `mystery`. The directories `/bin` and `/usr` (and all subdirectories within them) are searched for this file. The `-print` option instructs `find` to display its findings to standard output.

As you take a look at the output, you see that there is none. This is because find could not find the file name in the directories specified.

Before continuing, notice that a pwd command is issued so that you understand your current location in the system. As you can see, no subdirectories within the current location are specified to be searched. Let's reissue the find command to search within this area of the file system as well.

```
$ find /bin /usr . -name mystery -print
find: cannot chdir to ./temp/REDHOT/sally: Permission denied
```

No luck this time either. However, we do receive a message stating that a search could not be conducted on Sally's directory in the REDHOT subtree. If you do not have permission to traverse certain directories, then the file system will inform you as such.

Notice that a dot is used to specify the current working directory. Since we have not succeeded in locating the file as yet, let's just search starting from root. Here's the command:

```
$ find / -name mystery -print
/test/mystery
$
```

OK. We finally found the mystery file. Notice how the complete path is output for this file. Although starting from root will result in the file being found if it exists anywhere in the file system (unless you don't have permission to traverse a directory), keep in mind that this kind of search will take a while. After all, the entire file system is searched. It is best to issue a find command such as this in the background (using the & symbol), and redirect the output to a file, like this:

```
$ find / -name mystery -print > outfile &
$
```

It is necessary to redirect the output, otherwise find will display each location where it finds the file throughout the remainder of your session, while it executes. This could throw off the screen display a little bit. A cat to outfile will display the location of mystery:

```
$ cat outfile
/test/mystery
$
```

Before proceeding to the next section, keep in mind that the usual rules for using metacharacters for wildcard searches can also be utilized when issuing the find command. For example, the command:

```
$ find / -name "*.doc" -print
```

will traverse the entire file system for all files that start with zero or more characters, and end with a .doc. The usual rules apply when enclosing names that utilize metacharacters within single or double quotes.

We now continue to describe the usage of the find command with some of the more commonly used options.

20.2.1 Using find with Owner Name Option

You can issue a find for all files that are owned by somebody, within the specified directories. The -user option, followed by the user name, indicates this. Here's sample usage:

```
$ find . -user zamir -print
.
./file1
./document
./backup/file1
./file2
$
```

If you do an ls -l on any of the files displayed, you will see that they are indeed owned by username zamir. What is interesting about this output is the first line:

```
.
```

Recall that a dot (.) indicates the current working directory. Its display in the output indicates that the current working directory is owned by user zamir. Also notice the path:

```
./backup/file1
```

Apparently, backup is a directory with a file called file1. Apparently, both the directory and the file contained in it are owned by zamir.

20.2.2 Using find with Group Name Option

You can issue a find for all files that belong to a certain group by using the -group option followed by the group name:

```
$ find . -group team1 -print
./file1
./file2
./file3
$
```

The output displays the files in the current working directory which are owned by the group team1.

20.2.3 Using find with Size Option

You can issue a find for files that are a specific size via the -size option. Size is specified in blocks; 1 block is 512 bytes long. The following command searches for all files that are 5 blocks long:

```
$ find . -size 5 -print
$
```

Apparently, there are no files which are five blocks long.

20.2.4 Using find by Time Last Accessed

A find can be issued for all files that were accessed in the last n days, where n is a number. This is done via the -atime option, followed by a number which specifies the number of days from the current system time. Here's sample usage:

```
$ find . -atime 0 -print
.
./document
./backup
./file1
$
```

The output for the command displays all files and/or directories that were accessed in the last day, counting back from the current system time.

20.2.5 Using find by Time Last Modified

A `find` can also be issued for all files that have been modified in the last *n* days, where *n* is a number. Use the `-mtime` option followed by a number indicating the number of days. The command that follows asks `find` to list those files that have been modified in just the last day:

```
$ find . -mtime 0 -print
.
./file1
$
```

Apparently, `file1` in the current directory has been modified in the current day. Notice how the dot also displays for the current directory. This makes sense, since this directory contains `file1`.

Please note that the term "access" includes files that have been modified, because you have to access something before you can modify it. Hence, all files that displayed in this example also displayed in the example in the prior section.

20.2.6 Issuing System Commands on Files Found

You can run a regular UNIX system command on the files found via the `-exec` option followed by the command. We can instruct it to copy the file found to a specified directory, like so:

```
$ find . -name "*.doc" -exec cp {} document \;
$
```

The `-exec` command indicates that we wish to issue a system command on the files found. The command issued is a copy (`cp`) to the directory `document`. The curly braces (`{}`) are required, instructing `find` to substitute the name of the file in this location. The semicolon is also required, in order for the command to be executed. However, it must be preceded by the escape character `\`, so as to take away its special meaning for the `find` command.

20.2.7 Reaffirming Execution of System Commands

You can use the `-ok` option to have the system reaffirm the system command that it is to execute, before it does so. For example, this option should prove useful with the `rm` command:

```
$ find . -name "*.doc" -ok rm {} \;
rm ./file1.doc? y
rm ./file2.doc? y
rm ./fanouts.doc? n
$
```

You need to enter a y before the file will be removed from the directory.

20.3 THE WHEREIS COMMAND

This command is similar to find, in that it finds the location of files. However, the file names that it accepts as arguments are UNIX system commands, such as ls, pwd, etc. It finds the location of the source, the binary, and the manual pages for the specified command. Let's try it now:

```
$ whereis who
who: /usr/bin/who /usr/man/man1/who.1
```

Apparently, the source file exists in /usr/bin and the manual pages are located in /usr/man/man1/who.1. Now how did we know that who.1 contains the manual pages? Well, if you take a brief moment now to take a look at the available UNIX Commands Reference Manuals, you will notice that they are divided into several volumes. who.1 is the manual page for who, which exists in volume number 1 (the .1 after the command name indicates this). who.1 exists in the subdirectory man1, whose parent is man. The man directory also contains subdirectories man2, man3, and so on, for each existing volume of the UNIX Commands Reference Manuals.

We now issue the whereis command for a nonexistent UNIX command:

```
$ whereis how
how:
$
```

As you can see, no text is generated for nonexistent UNIX commands supplied as arguments. Assume that there is a user-created executable file called xx, which looks like this:

```
$ cat xx
cd ~
ls -l
$
```

Let's try a whereis on this file:

```
$ whereis exec
xx:
$
```

The output indicates that whereis works only with standard UNIX commands.

20.3.1 Locating Binary File Only

The whereis command can be used with the –b option to locate the binary file only. Here's sample usage:

```
$ whereis -b who
who: /usr/bin/who
$
```

The binary file exists on /usr/bin.

20.3.2 Locating Manual Pages Only

The whereis command can be used with the –m option to locate the manual pages only. Here's sample usage:

```
$ whereis -m pwd
who:   /usr/man/man1/who.1
$
```

20.4 THE WC COMMAND

The wc command gives a count of the total number of lines, words, and characters in a file. Take a look at this file, and then vital statistics for it:

```
$ cat source
Sometimes you need to count some words some of the time.
And sometimes you need to count some words all of the time.
But you never need to count all of the words all of the time.
$ wc source
   3  37   179  source
$
```

The first number (3) is a count of the number of lines in the file. The second number (37) displays the word count, and the third number (179) is the character count. The name of the file displays at the end.

20.4.1 Counting Lines, Words, or Characters Only

Use wc with the −l option to display number of lines only. Use wc with the −w option to display number of words only. Use wc with the −c option to display number of characters only. Here's sample usage:

```
$ wc -l source
   3    source
$ wc -w source
  37    source
$ wc -c source
 179      source
$
```

20.5 THE CUT COMMAND

The cut command is used to extract specified fields of data from the argument supplied to it. This argument can be a file name or the output of a filter or pipe. The command can take two general forms:

```
cut -cnum filename

cut -fnum filename
```

In the first instance, the −c option specifies that characters are to be extracted. num indicates the column numbers. In the second instance, fields are extracted. We now discuss each in detail.

20.5.1 Specifying Characters

We use the same source file to illustrate sample usage of the cut command that operates on columns:

```
$ cat source
Sometimes you need to count some words some of the time.
And sometimes you need to count some words all of the time.
But you never need to count all of the words all of the time.
$
```

```
$ cut -c5 source
t
s
y
$
```

As you can see, the cut command operates as specified on each line of the argument file supplied to it. The fifth character of each line is displayed.

Ranges can be indicated via the dash (–). A dash between two integer numbers (which must be in ascending order) specifies the range from the number on the left to the one on the right:

```
$ cut -c4-9 source
etimes
 somet
 you n
$
```

As you can see, the space is considered a column.

If the dash appears on the left only, then character position 1 is taken as the default for the number to the left of the range:

```
$ cut -c-5 source
Somet
And s
But y
$
```

If the dash appears on the right only, then the last character in each line is taken as the default:

```
$ cut -c4- source
etimes you need to count some words some of the time.
 sometimes you need to count some words all of the time.
 you never need to count all of the words all of the time.
$
```

Multiple specifications and/or ranges can be specified, each separated by commas, but make sure there are no embedded spaces between the commas:

```
$ cut -c4,7-9,13 source
emesu
 mets
  u nr
$
```

Notice how the characters extracted are concatenated together.

20.5.2 Specifying Fields

Specific fields, and field ranges, can be extracted via the −f option:

```
$ cut −f4 source
Sometimes you need to count some words some of the time.
And sometimes you need to count some words all of the time.
But you never need to count all of the words all of the time.
$
```

Well, the output isn't exactly what we expected! No extractions were performed because the cut command extracts the specified fields only if they are separated by tabs. Since the fields in the source file are separated by spaces, we would need to reissue the cut command with the −d option. Here's sample usage:

```
$ cut −d ' ' −f4 source
to
need
need
$
```

Notice how the field delimiter, which is a space, is enclosed within single quotes. This is necessary in order to take away the special meaning assigned to it.

Ranges for fields can be extracted like characters, and multiple fields and/or ranges can also be specified, with the −f option. But remember not to embed spaces between the ranges:

```
$ cut −f3,5−9 source
need count some words some of
you to coun some words all
never to count all of the
$
```

20.6 THE PASTE COMMAND

The paste command is used to join columns together in one or more files. The format of the paste command looks like this:

```
paste file1 file2
```

Consider the following two files:

```
$ cat file1
1
2
3
```

```
$ cat file2
One
Two
Three
$
```

Each line in the first file can be joined with the corresponding line in the second file via the `paste` command:

```
$ paste file1 file2
1 One
2 Two
3 Three
$
```

The order of the files determines the order in which the lines are joined together:

```
$ paste file2 file1
One 1
Two 2
Three 3
$
```

What if one file has more lines than the other?

```
$ cat file1
1
2
3
4
$
$ cat file2
One
Two
Three
$ paste  file1 file2
1 One
2 Two
3 Three
4
$
```

As many files can be pasted together as necessary. Simply separate each file name by a space.

20.6.1 Specifying Delimiter/Join Field

Under normal circumstances, lines pasted together are separated by a space. You can use the −d option to change this field to anything else. This option is followed by the alternative delineator, comprising one or more characters. Here's sample usage:

```
$ paste −d+ file1 file2
1+One
2+Two
3+Three
$
```

20.6.2 Pasting from One File Only

The −s option is used to indicate that lines of the same file are to be pasted together. Here's sample usage:

```
$ paste −s file1
1  2  3
$
```

20.7 THE TR COMMAND

This command is used to translate characters from a file or standard input. The general syntax of the command looks like this:

```
tr from to
```

The from indicates what characters are to be translated. The to indicates what they are to be translated to. tr can translate the output from some filter and perform translations on it, like so:

```
$ ls | sort | tr H h
```

The above command performs a listing of the current directory, sorts it, and then pipes the sorted output to tr, which translates all occurrences of an H to h.

tr can also take a file as an argument on which the translations are to take place. In this case, the syntax of the tr command looks like this:

```
tr from to < file
```

The < operator is used to redirect the contents of the file via standard input to `tr`. The use of this operator is necessary because `tr` always expects its input to come from standard input, and this operator makes it believe such is the case. Here's sample usage:

```
$ cat file
Hello
$ tr H h < file
hello
$
```

The output of the `tr` command goes to standard output, or it can be redirected to a file. If it is redirected to a file, then the syntax would look like this:

```
tr from to < file > outfile
```

Here's sample usage:

```
$ tr H h < file > outfile
$ cat outfile
hello
$
```

The `to` part of the `tr` command can contain octal representations of special (or regular) characters found in the ASCII table. Octal numbers must be preceded with a backslash in order to be inter-preted as such. Following is the octal representation of a tab:

```
\11
```

The following command will translate all the 1 characters to tabs:

```
$ tr 1 '\11'< file
He      o
$
```

The single quotes are required to take away the special meaning of the backslash.

The `to` and `from` parts of the `tr` command can also contain ranges. A range is separated by a dash, as usual, and enclosed within square brackets. Here's sample usage:

```
$ tr [a-z] [A-Z] < file
HELLO
$
```

The above command changes all occurrences of lowercase letters to uppercase.

20.7.1 Deleting Multiple Occurrences of Characters

Multiple subsequent occurrences of characters can be extracted from the final output via the −s option. For example, if a file contains lots of embedded spaces, like this:

```
$ cat space
This      file contains     tons      of spaces.
$
```

then the file can be translated like this:

```
$ tr -s ' ' ' ' < space
This file contains tons of spaces.
$
```

20.7.2 Deleting Any Occurrence of Characters

Characters can be deleted via the −d option used with the tr command. For instance, all tabs can be deleted from a file like this:

```
$ cat tabs
This    file       contains lots   of tabs.
$
$ tr -d '\11' < tabs
Thisfilecontainslotsof tabs.
$
```

The last field is preceded by a space instead of a tab, and this is why it remains unaffected by the tr command.

Bourne Shell Implementation

All commands presented in this chapter behave the same way when implemented from the Bourne shell. All examples will output the same result.

Korn Shell Implementation

All commands presented in this chapter behave the same way when implemented from the Korn shell. All examples will output the same result.

20.8 OSF/1 CONSIDERATIONS

All commands presented in this chapter behave the same way when implemented from any of the shells in an OSF/1 environment. All examples will produce the same output.

20.9 REVIEW

This chapter described some more helpful commands that are used to manipulate files. Tables 20.1 through 20.4 present a synopsis of each command, its options, and the syntax.

Table 20.1 The find Command

Command	Syntax	Description
find	find path options file(s) action	Searches recursively for file(s) specified in path, applies options, and performs action.
Options available with find:		
By user name: find path -user user1 -print		Finds all files in path that are owned by user user1 and displays to standard output.
By group name: find path -group group1 -print		Finds all files in path that are owned by group group1 and displays to standard output.
By size in blocks: find path -size num -print		Finds all files in path that are num (a number) blocks long (1 block is 512 bytes), and displays.
By time last accessed: find path -atime num -print		Finds all files in path that were accessed in the last num (a number) days, and displays.
By time last modified: find path -mtime num -print		Finds all files in path that were modified in the last num (a number) days, and displays.
Issuing system commands on files found: find . -name file -exec cmd {} \; find . -name file -exec -ok cmd {} \;		Implements command (cmd) on each file found. Asks for reaffirmation with ok option.

Table 20.2 whereis and wc Commands

Command	Syntax	Description
whereis	whereis cmd	Locates source, binary, and manual pages of system command cmd.
Options available with whereis:		
Binary file: whereis -b cmd		Locates binary file only.
Manual pages: whereis -m cmd		Locates manual pages only.
wc	wc file	Gives count of total number of lines, words, and characters in file.
Options available with wc:		
Lines only: wc -l file		Counts lines only.
Words only: wc -w file		Counts words only.
Characters only: wc -c file		Counts characters only.

Table 20.3 The cut Command

Command	Syntax	Description
cut	cut -cnum file cut -fnum file	Extracts specified characters or fields from each line of file.
Options available with cut		
Specifying characters: cut -cnum file		Extracts character number num from file.
cut -cm-n file		Extracts characters from range m through n.
cut -c-n file		Extracts characters 1 through n.
cut -cm- file		Extracts characters from range m through the end of the line.
cut -cnum,m-n file		Extracts character number num and range m through n.
Specifying fields: cut -fnum file		Extracts field number num from file.
cut -fm-n file		Extracts fields from range m through n.
cut -f-n file		Extracts fields 1 through n.
cut -fm- file		Extracts fields from range m through the end of the line.
cut -fnum,m-n file		Extracts field number num, and range m through n .

Table 20.4 The paste and tr Commands

Command	Syntax	Description
paste	paste file1 file2	Joins corresponding lines in file1 with file2 and writes to standard output.
Options available with paste		
Specifying join field: paste -dfield file1 file2		Specifies field as join field, instead of the default space.
Pasting from one file only: paste -s file1		Joins all lines of file1 together.
tr	tr cr1 cr2	Translates character(s) cr1 to character(s) cr2. cr1 and cr2 can be character ranges.
Options available with tr		
Deleting multiple occurrences of characters: tr -s cr1 cr2		Translates character(s) cr1 to character(s) cr2, and deletes multiple subsequent occurrences of them in the process.
Deleting any occurrence of character(s): tr -d cr1		Deletes all occurrences of character(s) cr1

Document Formatting Utilities

Chapter

21

Formatting Using
nroff

21.1 INTRODUCTION

`nroff` is a *text formatter* that has the capability to produce
documents that appear to be professionally typeset. Typesetting
using a text formatter is different from that achieved with a word
processor. Word processors allow you to italicize, underline, indent,
or whatever simply with a keystroke or two. The specific instructions that produce the result are transparent to you. On the other
hand, typsetting using a text formatter could pretty much be
considered a two- or three-step process, depending on which way
you do it. First, you create a document using one of the system
editors. Next, you insert commands within the document that give
specific instructions to the formatter on what to do. (This could be
considered as part of the first step.) Finally, you provide this file
as an argument to the text formatter, which typesets it as per your
instructions and let's you marvel at what a good job it did! This
chapter goes into details of how documents can be typeset using
`nroff`.

UNIX provides another popular document formatting utility
called `troff`. This utility is described briefly in the next chapter.
As you read this chapter, keep in mind that `troff` is like a
superset of `nroff`. All commands that you read about in this
chapter can be implemented using `troff` as well. Only a few of
these commands may produce a different kind of output. The
difference between the two utilities is that `nroff` is primarily
geared towards letter-quality printers. `troff`, on the other hand,
was originally created for a typesetting device called C/A/T. This

device is practically obsolete now, and for this reason options have been added to troff to allow it to drive other kinds of devices.

We now continue with our discussion on nroff.

21.2 NROFF, THE BASICS

As indicated in the introduction, instructions to nroff are embedded within the text itself. Each instruction must appear on a line by itself. Usually, each instruction immediately precedes the line or paragraph that needs to be formatted a certain way. The format of these instructions is a dot (.) or single quote (′), followed by one or two characters. Instructions can be followed by one or more arguments which modify the output of the instruction in some way. Just to get you started, here's a one-line text document, preceded by an nroff instruction:

```
$ cat text1
.ul
You'll never believe what we have in store for you!
$
```

As you can see, the first line in text1 contains three characters which could be considered to be Greek by some, but are really an embedded instruction to nroff. The .ul command instructs nroff to underline the line that follows it. The file text1 will be supplied as an argument to nroff, and the output piped to a file or the line printer. If the output is not piped, then the result will be displayed to standard output. We will redirect output to the line printer.

```
$ nroff text1 | lpr
$
```

The output file will look like this:

You'll never believe what we have in store for you!

Now if you had two lines of text, and if both lines were to be underlined, then the number 2 can be appended to .ul. (A space may or may not be embedded in the instruction, and the argument supplied to it. We will use spaces because it's easier to follow.) Now text1 would look like this:

```
$ cat text1
.ul 2
You'll never believe what we have in store for you!
Not in your wildest dreams!!
$ nroff text1 | lpr
$
```

and the output document would look like this:

<u>You'll never believe what we have in store for you!</u> <u>Not in your wildest dreams!!</u>

Notice how the second line got squeezed into the first. This feature of nroff is called *filling*. nroff will automatically fill lines with as many words as it can place on each line. Line breaks can be specified explicitly by inserting the .br command after the line. Here's how the file would look now:

```
$ cat text1
.ul 2
You'll never believe what we have in store for you!
.br
Not in your wildest dreams!!
$
```

and the output would look like this:

<u>You'll never believe what we have in store for you!</u>
<u>Not in your wildest dreams!!</u>

We can go one step further, and precede the number that follows the instruction with a plus or minus sign. In this case, the output of the instruction is modified that many times relative to the current setting. For example, the instruction .in is used to indent a line by a number of spaces. Take a look at the modified version of text1:

```
$ cat text1
.in 3
You'll never believe what we have in store for you!
.in +3
Not in your wildest dreams!!
.in -1
Unless your dreams lead you far beyond.
$
```

The first instruction indents the line that follows it by 3 columns. The next instruction indents the line 3 spaces relative to the current setting. The next line in the document, therefore, is in effect indented 6 columns. The indent is decreased by 1 column relative to the current setting for the last line. Here's how the output file would look:

```
$ nroff text1 | lpr
    You'll never believe what we have in store for you!
        Not in your wildest dreams!!
        Unless your dreams lead you far beyond.
$
```

Not only can you issue instructions to nroff, but you can give a name to a group of instructions, and insert this name anyplace in your document. Now each time nroff encounters this name, it will execute that set of instructions. This is called a *macro*. Macros can get as complicated and sophisticated as you can make them. You can also use some predefined macros that exist in the UNIX system, one of the more popular ones being ms (we devote a full chapter to this one later on in the book). By convention, macro names are uppercase letters, to distinguish them from nroff instructions, which are always lowercase. But aside from this distinction, macro references are similar to nroff instructions. They are preceded by a dot, and can be one or two characters long. This is how a macro reference would look in a text file:

```
$ cat somefile
.ul
You'll never believe what we have in store for you!
.PW
$
```

The last line is a macro reference. We describe how macros are created later on in this chapter. For now, assume that the .PW macro implements a group of instructions that perhaps insert a footer, number the page, draw a horizontal line at the bottom of the page, and so on.

In addition to what we have mentioned so far, nroff provides another rather nice feature which results in lines of unequal length being automatically filled in (unless specified otherwise). An example will clarify what has just been said. Consider the following text.

```
$ cat text1
Some lines are short.
Most lines are of average length.
And a few lines are longer than the short and the mediums.
$
```

Assuming that the length of a line is set to 55 characters (which incidentally is set via the command `.ll  55`), then `nroff` will reformat `text1` like this:

```
Some lines are short.  Most lines are of average length. And a
few lines are longer than the short and the mediums.
```

Notice that `nroff` inserted two spaces between each period and the next sentence.

21.3 THE INITIAL DESIGN STAGE

Before you insert `nroff` instructions into the text, take a few moments to visualize the format of the finished document. This, of course, probably depends on the kind of document that is being produced. For example, if you are writing a letter, then your address could be in the top right corner of the page. The address of the person to whom the letter is addressed could be flush left. If this letter is in reference to something, then the `Re:` could appear in bold and/or underlined. The first line of each paragraph could be indented. Based on the text, certain words could be italicized, and so on. And since we just spent the last nine lines of this section describing the format of a probable letter, let's write one now and then format it as indicated.

At the beginning of the chapter, a file called `text1` was formatted. Let's take another look at the output produced:

```
You'll never believe what we have in store for you!
  Not in your wildest dreams!!
Unless your dreams lead you far beyond.
```

Well – we weren't kidding. We're going to format a love letter! And a very sweet one, at that!! The letter will be written to a file called `letter1`. First, we will display the text without any `nroff` commands in it. Then, instructions to `nroff` will be inserted as necessary. The output of each part of the letter will be displayed before the next part is presented.

OK. First things first. The letter is being addressed to Miss Medora Blackwell. Her lost lover's name is Luke Valentino. Let's take a look at the introduction of the letter:

```
$ cat letter1
Luke Valentino
100 Lost Haven Drive
Starry Town, NY 12399

April 25, 1992
```

```
Miss Medora Blackwell
69 East 96 West, Apt. X
New York, NY 10017
```

All right. As we said before, Luke's address will appear in the top right-hand corner of the page. But before text can be formatted, instructions must be given to specify the top, bottom, left, and right margins. Then, Luke's address can be indented accordingly.

21.4 SETTING LEFT MARGIN

The .po command is used to specify the page offset, or the distance from the left edge of the paper at which the document is to be printed. For example, the command

```
.po 5
```

will set the left margin to five columns from the left of the page.

The default setting is 0. This means that unless you specify otherwise, nroff will print the document with no left margin.

As indicated previously, the page offset can be reset relative to its current position by preceding the number with a plus or minus sign. For example, the command .po +4 will reset the page offset to 9. The command .po −6 will reset it to 3.

21.5 SETTING RIGHT MARGIN

The right margin can be set by specifying the page offset in conjunction with the line length. The default width of a page is 65 characters. So if the page offset is 5 and the page width is 65, then setting the line length to 60 will result in a left margin of 5 columns (65-column page - 5-column offset equals line length of 60 columns). Line length is set via the .ll command:

```
.ll 55
```

The above command will set line length to 55. Once again, the + and − symbols can be used to readjust the margin as necessary. Typing .ll by itself resets the line length to the last set value.

21.6 Setting Top and Bottom Margins

The top and bottom margins are set by setting the number registers. Number registers are described in detail in Chapter 23, "The ms Macro Package." We will defer further discussion of these settings until then. For now, we're going to take the easy way out, and simply insert a number of blank lines at the top of the document, thereby achieving the required space at the top of the page. Blank lines are inserted via the `.sp` command. The `.sp` command by itself results in one blank line being inserted. This command can be followed by a number to indicate the number of additional blank lines. The following command inserts 5 blank lines in the location where it is encountered in the document:

```
.sp 5
```

21.7 Setting Indents

Luke's address has to be towards the right edge of the page. We can position it here by setting the indent relative to the current position. The `.in` command is used to set the indent:

```
.in +30
```

The above command will result in subsequent text being indented to column 35 (5 spaces for the left margin + 30 for the indent).

Typing `.in` by itself will result in the indent being set to the last value stored in it.

We will insert 8 blank lines for the top margin, and 3 blank lines right after the date.

21.8 Adding Comments

Comments can be inserted after `nroff` commands as follows:

```
.sp \" Insert blank line
```

The backslash followed by a quotation mark instructs `nroff` to disregard the remainder of the line and not display it in its output. We will comment the final version of the letter that Mr. Valentino will be sending to Miss Blackwell. For now, let's continue with the letter.

21.9 FIRST TEST RUN

OK. Now it's time to insert the commands in the text file. We set the line length to 65 and indent 40 characters for this example.

```
$ cat letter1
.po 5
.ll 55
.in +40
Luke Valentino
.br
100 Lost Haven Drive
.br
Starry Town, NY 12399
.sp 1
April 25, 1992
.in
.sp 3
Miss Medora Blackwell
.br
69 East 96 West, Apt. X
.br
New York, NY 10017
.br
$
```

Let's give it a test run though `nroff`. Here's the output:

<pre>
                                        Luke Valentino
                                        100 Lost Haven Drive
                                        Starry Town, NY 12399

                                        April 25, 1992

        Miss Medora Blackwell
        69 East 96 West, Apt X
        New York, NY 10017
</pre>

So far, so good. We only display half the page. We will not display the output text of the letter in a different font (the font we use to display command output in), since the actual output resembles the font that you are reading. However, embedded nroff commands will be displayed in the program font, since this will help make the instructions stand out. We will abide by these rules in the remaining chapters in Part 5. Let's continue with the letter.

By the way, if we had indented deeper than the width of the page, then text would wrap around, and nroff would insert a hyphen within words, if necessary. For example, inserting the following instruction instead of `.in +40`:

```
.in +50
```

would have resulted in the following output for Mr. Luke Valentino's address:

                              Luke
                              Valen-
                              tino
                              100
                              Lost
                              Haven
                              Drive
                              Star-
                              ry
                              Town,
                              NY
                              12399

                              April
                              25,
                              1992

21.10 Adjusting and Filling Lines

Let's continue with the text of the letter.

It was three years ago today that I first met you in a crowded, hazy
bar down on Main Street. It was a hot, sticky, humid summer
night; it had been that way for many weeks. The sun had been
merciless; there was no escaping the heat!
.br
As I walked into that bar, thirsting for an ice cold drink,
I noticed you sitting alone with a drink in your hand.
I followed the silhouette of your body and then looked up at your
eyes.
.br
I had never seen eyes such as yours. There is a color called
ice-blue; I have seen it in the rivers that cascade from the
mountain peaks across huge boulders strewn over the landscape
by the glaciers in the Himalayas. Your eyes were an
incredible ice-blue. And yet your aura was such that it
could set fire to this ice.

21.10.1 Default Justification of Lines

OK. Let's take a breather (or cold shower) and review the
document. As you can see, the lines are of uneven length. The left
border is even, and the right is what is called *ragged*. `nroff`
automatically adjusts the borders so that they are both even, unless
specified not to do so. This is how the paragraph will look if it is
"nroffed":

It   was three   years   ago today   that   I first   met   you in   a
crowded   hazy   bar down   on Main Street. It was a   hot, sticky,
humid summer night;it had been that way for many weeks. The sun
had been merciless; there was no escaping the heat!
As I walked into that bar, thirsting   for an ice cold drink, I
noticed you sitting alone with a drink in your hand. I followed
the silhouette of your body and then looked up at your eyes.
I had never seen eyes such as yours. There is a color called
ice-blue; I have seen it in the rivers that cascade from   the
mountain peaks across huge boulders strewn over the landscape

by the glaciers in the Himalayas. Your eyes were an incredible
ice-blue. And yet your aura was such that it could set fire to this
ice.

You can instruct `nroff` not to justify margins like this:

```
.na
```

This is how the paragraph will look if it is preceded by `.na`:

It was three years ago today that I first met you in a crowded,
hazy bar down on Main Street. It was a hot, sticky, humid summer
night; it had been that way for many weeks. The sun had been
merciless; there was no escaping the heat!
As I walked into that bar, thirsting for an ice cold drink, I
noticed you sitting alone with a drink in your hand. I followed
the silhouette of your body and then looked up at your eyes.
I had never seen eyes such as yours. There is a color called
ice-blue; I have seen it in the rivers that cascade from the
mountain peaks across huge boulders strewn over the landscape by
the glaciers in the Himalayas. Your eyes were an incredible ice-
blue. And yet your aura was such that it could set fire to this
ice.

21.10.2 Line Filling

As you can see, although the right margins are still ragged, lines
are filled with words if there are enough spaces to fit a word in.
Therefore, filling is also an automatic feature of `nroff`. You can
turn filling off with this command:

```
.nf
```

Doing so would result in no difference between the way text is entered and the way it will display after being typeset. Filling can be turned on again via this command:

```
.fi
```

21.10.3 Hyphenation

As `nroff` fills lines, it will insert a hyphen if it encounters a long word at the end of a line. This is another default feature of `nroff`. However, automatic hyphenation can be turned off as follows:

```
.nh
```

Only those words which you choose to do yourself will now be hyphenated. Automatic hyphenation can be turned back on as follows:

```
.hy
```

21.10.4 Flush Left, Ragged Right

Flush left and ragged right is the same as the `.na` command with filling. The `.ad` command is the instruction to adjust:

```
.ad l
```

21.10.5 Ragged Left, Flush Right

Ragged left and flush right lines can be obtained with this instruction:

```
.ad r
```

And here's how the output would look:

It was three years ago today that I first met you in a crowded,
hazy bar down on Main Street. It was a hot, sticky, humid summer
night; it had been that way for many weeks. The sun had been
merciless; there was no escaping the heat!
As I walked into that bar, thirsting for an ice cold drink, I noticed you sitting alone with a drink in your hand. I followed
the silhouette of your body and then looked up at your eyes.
I had never seen eyes such as yours. There is a color called
ice-blue; I have seen it in the rivers that cascade from the
mountain peaks across huge boulders strewn over the landscape by
the glaciers in the Himalayas. Your eyes were an incredible ice-
blue. And yet your aura was such that it could set fire to this
ice.

21.10.6 Centering Lines

Lines can be centered by supplying c as an argument to the adjust
command. Here's the command and subsequent output:

```
.ad c
```

It was three years ago today that I first met you in a crowded,
hazy bar down on Main Street. It was a hot, sticky, humid summer
night; it had been that way for many weeks. The sun had been
merciless; there was no escaping the heat!
As I walked into that bar, thirsting for an ice cold drink, I noticed you sitting alone with a drink in your hand. I followed
the silhouette of your body and then looked up at your eyes.
I had never seen eyes such as yours. There is a color called
ice-blue; I have seen it in the rivers that cascade from the
mountain peaks across huge boulders strewn over the landscape by
the glaciers in the Himalayas. Your eyes were an incredible ice-
blue. And yet your aura was such that it could set fire to this
ice.

21.10.7 Line Spacing

The default condition for nroff is single spacing. However, any kind of spacing can be specified via the .ls command. For example, the following command makes the file double spaced:

```
.ls 2
```

21.11 INDENTING PARAGRAPHS

There are two main ways in which text can be indented. You can either indent all lines that follow by a certain number of characters. Or, you can simply indent the first line of a paragraph. As explained earlier in this chapter, text can be indented by the .in command followed by a plus or minus sign and a number. The indentation is performed relative to the current position. For example, if the current left margin is set at column 5, then the command

```
.in +5
```

will result in subsequent text starting at column 10.

A single line can be indented via the .ti command. The remaining lines continue to be indented to the current setting.

Mr. Blackwell is interested in indenting the first line of each paragraph by 3 spaces. A .ti 3 command will be inserted in the text just before each paragraph. Here's how the source file looks:

```
.ti 3
```
It was three years ago today that I first met you in a crowded, hazy bar down on Main Street. It was a hot, sticky, humid summer night; it had been that way for many weeks. The sun had been merciless; there was no escaping the heat!
```
.ti 3
```
As I walked into that bar, thirsting for an ice cold drink,
I noticed you sitting alone with a drink in your hand.
I followed the silhouette of your body and then looked up at your eyes.
```
.ti 3
```
I had never seen eyes such as yours. There is a color called ice-blue; I have seen it in the rivers that cascade from the

mountain peaks across huge boulders strewn over the landscape
by the glaciers in the Himalayas. Your eyes were an
incredible ice-blue. And yet your aura was such that it
could set fire to this ice.

And this is how it looks after being formatted by `nroff`:

It was three years ago today that I first met you in a crowded,
hazy bar down on Main Street. It was a hot, sticky, humid summer
night; it had been that way for many weeks. The sun had been
merciless; there was no escaping the heat!

As I walked into that bar, thirsting for an ice cold drink, I
noticed you sitting alone with a drink in your hand. I followed
the silhouette of your body and then looked up at your eyes.

I had never seen eyes such as yours. There is a color called
ice-blue; I have seen it in the   rivers that cascade from the
mountain peaks across huge boulders strewn over the landscape by
the glaciers in the Himalayas. Your eyes were an incredible
ice-blue. And yet your aura was such that it could set fire to
this ice.

21.12 INSERTING BLANK LINES

Mr. Valentino would like to insert a blank line between each
paragraph. `nroff` can be instructed to insert blank lines via the
`.sp` command. For example, five blank lines could be inserted like
this:

```
.sp 5
```

Blank lines can also be inserted simply by hitting the carriage
return key without typing any text. This is a literal insertion.

Mr. Valentino will insert a `.sp` instruction just before each
paragraph.

21.13 KEEPING BLOCKS OF TEXT ON ONE PAGE

Let's complete the letter before continuing with this section. Here's the remaining text:

And now, after all these years, I know it was destined to
be. There is nothing I would like more than to be able to
look into your eyes each morning as you wake up from your
restful sleep, and watch them close again at night,
as you snuggle up under the covers, beside me.
I love you.
Will you marry me?
Yours,
Luke.

Very touching, indeed. We take a brief moment to wipe the
tears from our eyes before continuing with this chapter.

Since this letter is now long enough to span two pages, Mr.
Valentino is concerned that its impact will be lost if a page break
occurs somewhere in between the last paragraphs. The `.ne`
command followed by a number can be used to specify the number
of lines that must appear on the same page. For example, the
command

```
.ne 4
```

specifies that the next four lines must appear on the same page. If
a page break were to occur at the second line, then the four lines
will be displayed on the next page.

21.14 SPECIFYING PAGE BREAKS

Page breaks can be inserted manually by inserting the `.bp`
command in the appropriate locations.

21.15 CENTERING TEXT

The second to last line (`I love you`) requires further emphasis. Mr. Valentino decides that he would like this line centered. `nroff` will center a line via the `.ce` command. If this instruction is followed by a number, then that many lines will be centered. For example, the instruction

```
.ce 4
```

will center the next four lines.

Mr. Valentino inserts a `.ce` command just before the `I love you` line.

21.16 UNDERLINING TEXT

The last line (`Will you marry me?`) also requires further emphasis. Mr. Valentino decides to center and underline it. We illustrated the use of the `.ul` command, which is used to underline text. It can be used in conjunction with `.ce` to center and underline. For example, the following sequence of instructions will center and underline the required line:

```
.ce
.ul
Will you marry me?
```

The output would, however, result in each word being underlined separately:

<u>Will</u> <u>you</u> <u>marry</u> <u>me?</u>

You can underline the complete line via the `.cu` command. Here's how the source would look:

```
.ce
.cu 1
Will you marry me?
```

and the output looks like this:

<u>Will you marry me?</u>

Mr. Valentino prefers the latter style over the former.

21.17 MACROS

All that is left to be done now is to format the last two lines of text in the document (Yours and Luke). Both of these lines are to be indented the same number of columns as Luke's address, which was 40 characters to the right of the current location. Three blank lines must also be inserted. Furthermore, the two lines of text with two blank lines in between and the three preceding blank lines must all fit on the same page. Mr. Valentino decides to create a macro to do the job.

As indicated previously in this chapter, a macro is a collection of instructions that can be implemented simply by referencing the macro name. Macros are best utilized if a complicated set of instructions is to be implemented frequently in one document. They incorporate consistency into your document. In this particular case, a macro is really not necessary, since only a couple of instructions will be embedded in it, and the macro will be referenced only once. However, the example is comprehensive enough to have you understand how a macro is created, and then referenced. Also, more likely than not, you will be using predefined macros that already exist in the system (we devote a complete chapter to ms later on in the book).

21.17.1 Creating and Referencing Macros

Macros are created as follows:

```
.de AB
```

The above command defines a macro called AB. Once a macro has been defined, a group of nroff instructions is placed in it. Two dots are used to end the set of instructions that comprise that macro. Here's our macro definition:

```
.de AB
.in +30
.ne 8
.sp 3
..
```

Once the macro has been defined, it can be referenced simply via its name:

```
.AB
```

21.17.2 Macros and Traps

We mentioned in the prior section that macros are most useful for a set of instructions that is to be executed frequently throughout the document. For example, a useful application for a macro would be one that displays the page number and chapter title in a book. Let's assume we create a macro called .PG which does just this. If the book happens to be 100 pages long, then this macro would be called 100 times. However, after the book has been written, it will be edited, lines deleted, lines added, and so on. This will result in the placement of the call to .PG changing with each edit. This is where a trap comes to the rescue.

A trap is used to define the location in a page (by line number) at which the macro will always be called. The macro which it references must be defined prior to this instruction. For example, it would be appropriate to set a trap for the .PG macro at line 1 of each page. This is how the command would look:

```
.wh 1 .PB
```

The above instruction will call the .PB macro at line 1 of each page. A positive number starts the count from the top of the page. A negative number can also be specified. This will result in the line count starting from the bottom of the page. For example, the command

```
.wh −5 .AB
```

will call the macro .AB 5 lines from the bottom of the page.

Mr. Valentino is writing a simple 2-page letter; he does not need to use the trap command.

In the next section we present the complete source document with embedded nroff instructions, and the output.

21.18 THE COMPLETE DOCUMENT

All that is left now is the end of the letter which contains his name. Here's the text, all in one place, with all of the instructions embedded in it:

```
$ cat letter1
.po 5      \" Set left margin at 5 columns
.ll 55     \" Set page length to 55 lines
.in +40    \" Indent 40 columns
```

```
Luke Valentino
.br      \" Break line
100 Lost Haven Drive
.br
Starry Town, NY 12399
.sp 1      \" Insert 1 blank line
April 25, 1992
.in                \" Set indent to what it was originally
.sp 3                \" Insert 3 blank lines
Miss Medora Blackwell
.br
69 East 96 West, Apt. X
.br
New York, NY 10017
.br
.sp 4
.ti 3                \" Indent next line 3 more columns
It was three years ago today that I first met you in a crowded, hazy
bar down on Main Street.  It was a hot, sticky, humid summer
night; it had been that way for many weeks.  The sun had been
merciless; there was no escaping the heat!
.ti 3
.sp 1
As I walked into that bar, thirsting for an ice cold drink,
I noticed you sitting alone with a drink in your hand.
I followed the silhouette of your body and then looked up at your
eyes.
.sp
.ne 6                \" Keep next 6 lines together
.ti 3
I had never seen eyes such as yours.  There is a color called
ice-blue; I have seen it in the rivers that cascade from the
mountain peaks across huge boulders strewn over the landscape
by the glaciers in the Himalayas.  Your eyes were an
incredible ice-blue.  And yet your aura was such that it
could set fire to this ice.
.sp 1
.ti 3
And now, after all these years, I know it was destined to
be.  There is nothing I would like more than to be able to
look into your eyes each morning as you wake up from your
restful sleep, and watch them close again at night,
as you snuggle up under the covers, beside me.
.sp 1
.ce 2                \" Center next 2 lines
I love you.
.sp 1
.cu 1                \" And underline
Will you marry me?
```

```
.sp 3
.in +40
Yours,
.sp 2
Luke.
$
```

Here's the command that will produce the output to the line printer:

```
$ nroff letter | lpr
```

The output letter is presented on the next page.

Luke Valentino
100 Lost Haven Drive
Starry Town, NY 12399

April 25, 1992

Miss Medora Blackwell
69 East 96 West, Apt X
New York, NY 10017

It was three years ago today that I first met you in a crowded hazy bar down on Main Street. It was a hot, sticky, humid summer night;it had been that way for many weeks. The sun had been merciless; there was no escaping the heat!

As I walked into that bar, thirsting for an ice cold drink, I noticed you sitting alone with a drink in your hand. I followed the silhouette of your body and then looked up at your eyes.

I had never seen eyes such as yours. There is a color called ice-blue; I have seen it in the rivers that cascade from the mountain peaks across huge boulders strewn over the landscape by the glaciers in the Himalayas. Your eyes were an incredible ice-blue. And yet your aura was such that it could set fire to this ice.

And now, after all these years, I know it was destined to be. There is nothing I would like more than to be able to look into your eyes each morning as you wake up from your restful sleep, and watch them close again at night, as you snuggle up under the covers, beside me.

I love you.

Will you marry me?

Yours,

Luke

Bourne Shell Implementation

All `nroff` commands are the same, and produce the same output, regardless of the shell from which they are implemented.

Korn Shell Implementation

All `nroff` commands are the same, and produce the same output, regardless of the shell from which they are implemented.

21.19 OSF/1 CONSIDERATIONS

The `nroff` utility works in the same way in an OSF/1 operating system as in UNIX. All commands are also the same.

21.20 REVIEW

This chapter described some of the fundamental commands that can be used in `nroff` to format documents. The next chapter goes into further details of some additional `nroff` commands and options that they can be used with. Table 21.1 presents a synopsis of `nroff` commands presented in this chapter.

Table 21.1 nroff Commands

Command	Syntax	Description
Set page offset or left margin	.po num	Sets page offset to num columns from left edge of page. + or - before num sets offset relative to current position.
Set right margin	.po num1 .ll num2	Sets page offset in conjunction with line length to num1 and num2.
Set indent	.in num	Sets indent to num. + or - sets indent relative to current setting.
Insert blank line	.sp num	Inserts num blank lines.
Add comments	\"	nroff ignores remainder of line.
Set off right justification	.na	nroff automatically right justifies. This command turns this feature off.
Set off line filling, turn it back on	.nf	nroff automatically fills lines. This command turns this feature off.
	.fi	Turns filling back on.
Set hyphenation off and on	.nh	nroff automatically hyphenates. This command turns this feature off.
	.hy	Turns hyphenation back on.
Flush left, ragged right	.ad l	Adjusts justification as indicated.
Ragged left, flush right	.ad r	Adjusts justification as indicated.

Table 21.1 nroff Commands (Contd.)

Command	Syntax	Description
Center lines	.ad c	Adjusts lines as indicated.
	.ce num	Centers num lines.
Set line spacing	.ls num	Sets line spacing to num.
Indent single lines	.ti num	Indents following line by num columns.
Insert blank lines	.sp num	Inserts num blank lines.
	Carriage return	Inserts blank line.
Keep blocks on same page	.ne num	Keeps next num lines on same page.
Specify page breaks	.bp	Inserts page break in that location.
Center text	.ce num	Centers the next num lines.
Underline text	.ul num	Underlines each word of the next num lines.
	.cu num	Underlines the complete line.
Define macro	.de XY <instruction s> ..	Defines macro called XY, which contains a group of nroff instructions. The ".." ends the definition.
Reference macros	.XY	Executes a group of instructions contained in macro XY.
Define trap	.wh +num XY	Executes macro XY at num lines from top of each page in document.
	.wh -num XY	Executes macro XY at num lines from bottom of each page in document.

nroff Continued
and troff

22.1 INTRODUCTION

In this chapter we describe some more `nroff` commands and their
options. Next, we describe some basic `troff` commands. The
reason why we are combining the two topics is that commands
issued to `troff` in its *raw* format are almost exactly the same as
those found in `nroff`. You may be wondering why we used the
word "raw" – well, the capabilities offered by `nroff` and `troff`
can be greatly enhanced, and a lot of the irksome *housekeeping*
required in these two utilities can be eliminated when they are used
in conjunction with one of the available macro packages such as ms
or mm. These will be discussed in the next chapter. For now, let's
turn our attention back to `nroff`. We will use `troff` to format
Miss Medora Blackwell's response to Luke Valentino. (For those of
you who did not read the last chapter, take a few moments now to
flip back and read this letter. You won't regret it.)

22.2 TITLES IN NROFF

`nroff` allows you to format titles. Titles can consist of three fields,
left, center, and right. All three of these fields can exist, or two, or
just one. Take a moment now to flip to the next page of this
chapter and look at the top. Depending on whether it is an even or
an odd page, the page number displays on either the left edge of the
page or the right. The chapter title or the part title displays on the
other edge. Now picture a title in the center, and perhaps you can

understand why titles can be supplied to `nroff` in three parts. We continue to elaborate on this in the remainder of this section.

22.2.1 Specifying Titles

Titles are specified as follows:

```
.tl 'left heading'center heading'right heading'
```

The left heading is left justified, the center heading is centered, and the right heading is right justified. They must be separated from one another by single quotes. If there are left and right headings, then the center heading will center between them. It will adjust as necessary if the heading on the left or right is blank. As indicated previously, any one of these fields can be blank. Here's sample usage:

```
.tl 'Chapter 22'nroff and troff'Part III'
```

and this is how the output would look:

```
Chapter 22          nroff and troff          Part III
```

Suppose one of the fields is blank:

```
.tl 'Chapter 22'nroff and troff''
```

The output would change as follows:

```
Chapter 22          nroff and troff
```

As you can see, the blank field must be specified with a single quote, although it does not contain anything.

Suppose the titles contain the potential of overlapping:

```
.tl 'Chapter 22'nroff, troff, and Miscellaneous Commands'Part III'
```

These actually will overlap. `nroff` simply overwrites the long fields. It is your responsibility to ensure that the fields do not overlap.

22.2.2 Specifying Page Numbers in Titles

At the beginning of the chapter we gave you a hint of how page numbers can be incorporated as either the left or right field of the title. We now describe how this can be done. Here's the syntax:

```
.tl 'Page %''Chapter 22'
```

The percent sign (%) within the single quote of the title command results in the current page number being substituted in its place. This value is obtained by accessing the contents of a register in the system called the page number register. Page numbers can be specified explicitly via the .pn command, followed by a number. This setting takes effect on the next page.

22.2.3 Specifying Title Length

The default length of a title is the width of the page between the left and right margins. However, length can be specified explicitly and any restrictions bypassed via the .lt command. Here's sample usage:

```
.lt 60
```

The above command specifies the length of the title as 60 characters.

22.3 SPECIAL CASES IN NROFF

We conclude our discussion on nroff commands by describing some of the special case situations that can occur. These are:

- Underlining specific characters only in words.

- Embedding nroff commands which are to be interpreted literally.

- Keeping blocks of words together on the same line.

Each of these cases can be handled via special character sequences available in nroff. A discussion of each case follows.

22.3.1 Underlining Specific Characters Only

If you have worked with dialog boxes in a window environment, then you must have noticed that the first letter of each menu option is underlined, indicating that the option can be executed simply by depressing that letter. (For those of you who have not encountered screens such as these, never mind; it doesn't matter.) For example, suppose only the first letter of this line is to be underlined:

```
Main Menu
```

In Chapter 21 we indicated that the `.ul` command underlines words only. Inserting a `.ul` before the required word, like this:

```
.ul
Main
Menu
```

will result in the following output:

<u>Main</u> Menu

As you can see, the whole word is underlined. This won't do. You can instruct `nroff` to underline one or more characters in a word only by inserting the `\c` command after the characters to be underlined. Here's sample usage:

```
.ul
M\c
ain Menu
```

The output would look like this:

<u>M</u>ain Menu

What happens is that the `\c` instructs `nroff` that the characters on the following line are a part of the same word; hence `nroff` should not insert a space between its two parts. If more than one character was to be underlined, then those characters would simply be placed on a line by themselves, and the `\c` appended to them.

22.3.2 Embedding nroff Commands as Literal Text

Suppose your document contained text that contained `nroff` commands that were not to be interpreted as such. Consider the following example:

.ce The Center Command
The Center Command is used to center text.

nroff will output this as follows:

The Center Command is used to center text.

The problem here is that nroff did not display the text line

. ce The Center Command

It read the first three characters of that line, and understood it to be an instruction to center the line that follows it. This problem can be alleviated by inserting a \& just before the line with the special characters. This is called the *zero width* character. Here's sample usage:

\ & . ce The Center Command
The Center Command is used to center text.

The output will look like this:

.ce The Center Command
The Center Command is used to center text.

22.3.3 Keeping Blocks of Words Together

Sometimes the impact of text can be lost if some key words are spread out over two lines. For example, consider the following example of formatted text:

You need to make a right at the light and then continue to
First River Drive. From there, make a left and then a right by
Second and Fourth (that's a neighborhood grocery store). And
"Le Chic Le La" is located right there.

When formatted, the above text will be filled and justified to produce the following output:

You need to make a right at the light and then continue to First River Drive. From there, make a left, and then a right by Second and Fourth (that's a neighborhood grocery store). And "Le Chic Le La" is located right there.

The above text would perhaps look better if the groups of words contained in First River Drive, Second and Fourth, and Le Chic Le La were kept together on the same line. We can instruct nroff to keep words together via the unpaddable space character; this is the backslash followed by a space. Here's how the text would look before being formatted:

You need to make a right at the light and then continue to
First\ River\ Drive. From there, make a left and then a right by
Second\ and\ Fourth (that's a neighborhood grocery store). And
"Le\ Chic\ Le\ La" is located right there.

And this is how it would look when formatted:

You need to make a right at the light and then continue to First River Drive. From there, make a left and then a right by Second and Fourth (that's a neighborhood grocery store). And "Le Chic Le La" is located right there.

22.4 OPTIONS TO NROFF

So far we have been describing only those commands which are used to specify how `nroff` is to format a document. Once the document has been formatted, `nroff` can be run with several options that are specified at the command line. It is beyond the scope of this book to describe all of the options available. We describe some of the more useful ones, which are:

- Print specific pages only.

- Stop at every n pages, where n is a number.

- Specify starting page number.

- Produce equally spaced words in adjusted lines.

- Use macro package.

22.4.1 Print Specific Pages Only

`nroff` can be instructed to print specific pages of the formatted text via the −o option followed by either the page number or the range of page numbers to be printed. Here's sample usage:

```
$ nroff -o5 file1 | lpr
$ nroff -o5-15 file1 | lpr
$
```

The first command prints page 5 of the formatted document called `file1`. The second command prints pages 5 through 15.

Specific page numbers and ranges can also be specified on the same command line by separating them with commas. Here's an example in which fields overlap:

```
$ nroff -o6,8-10,9 file1 | lpr
$
```

This command produces no output. Overlapping fields don't work.

If the first number in a range is omitted, then the default output will start from page 1. If the last number in a range is omitted, then the output will continue until the last page. The following examples illustrate these two cases:

```
$ nroff -o-6 file1 | lpr
$ nroff -o7- file1 | lpr
$
```

22.4.2 Stop at n Pages

nroff can be instructed to pause after printing a specified number of pages via the -s option. This feature is handy when a large size document is being formatted, and the output needs to be checked in the middle for some reason, paper needs to be added, etc. The following command will cause nroff to pause after 5 pages:

```
$ nroff -s5 file1 | lpr
```

and this one will make nroff pause after each page:

```
$ nroff -s file1 | lpr
```

22.4.3 Specify Starting Page Number

nroff can be instructed to number the starting page with something other than the default of 1 via the -n option. An application for which this option should prove useful is when a large document containing several sections has been written to separate files. When section 2 is output, it will start from the page following the last page of section 1, instead of page 1. Here's sample usage:

```
$ nroff -n23 section2 | lpr
```

The first page of the file called section2 will be numbered 23 instead of 1.

22.4.4 Use Macro Packages

We have referred to the use of macro packages now and then in this and the prior chapter. A complete discussion of some macro packages that can be used with nroff (and troff) is given in the next chapter. The -m option followed by the macro name results in that predefined macro package being called up.

```
$ nroff -mm file1 | lpr
```

Predefined macro packages reside in the directory /usr/lib/tmac, and they all begin with the letters tmac.. In addition to using the predefined macro packages that come with the system, you may create your own. However, in order to be used, they must be placed in the same directory as the others (/usr/lib/tmac) and begin with the prefix tmac..

22.5 MISCELLANEOUS FEATURES OF NROFF

There are a few more useful features that we will describe before wrapping up our discussion on nroff. These features are:

- Specifying multiple files as input to nroff at the command line.

- Specifying multiple files as input to nroff within the document being formatted.

- Switching to standard input from within the document being formatted.

- Specifying arguments in inches or centimeters.

22.5.1 Specifying Multiple Files on Command Line

Multiple files can be supplied as arguments to nroff on the same command line. For example, the commands

```
$ nroff file1 file2 file3 | lpr
$ nroff file[1-3] | lpr
```

result in file1, file2, and file3 being formatted and output to the line printer. There are a few problems associated with specifying multiple files on the same command line. This is due to the fact that all files are concatenated into one before being fomatted. Hence, instructions which are relative to the current position in the second file will be formulated from the last current position in the first file. For example, the instruction

```
.po 5
```

will set the page offset at five columns. The instruction

```
.po +5
```

in `file2` would result in the page offset being set to 10 columns!
Second, since all files are concatenated into one, `file2` will output
from where `file1` ends; this may not necessarily be a new page!
Inserting a `.bp` at the beginning of each file would be a possible
solution for this problem.

22.5.2 Specifying Multiple Files from within Text

`nroff` can be instructed to read its input from a different file via
the `.so` instruction. Here's sample usage:

```
.so otherdoc
```

   `nroff` will temporarily exit from the current text file to read
input from the file `otherdoc`, in the location indicated. This is
almost like inserting `otherdoc` into the current document at this
location.

   As far as the contents of `otherdoc` are concerned, it can be
simply another text file that may or may not contain embedded
`nroff` instructions, or it may be one or more files that contain
groups of instructions that are macro definitions. Hence, these
macros can be used by different documents, instead of just the file
in which they are defined. Here's the source file:

```
$ cat file1
You need to make a right at the light and then continue to
First River Drive.  From there, make a left and then a right by
Second and Fourth (that's a neighborhood grocery store).  And
"Le Chic Le La" is located right there.
.so file2
$
```

   This is what `file2` looks like:

```
$ cat file2
This is a line in which automatic filling is turned on.
$
```

   Notice the call to `file2` via the `.so` instruction in `file1`. Now
let's send the file as an argument to `nroff`:

```
$ nroff file1|lpr
```

   Here's the file that is output to the printer:

You need to make a right at the light and then continue to First River Drive. From there, make a left and then a right by Second and Fourth (that's a neighborhood grocery store). And "Le Chic Le La" is located right there. This is a line in which automatic filling is turned on.

Notice how `file2` starts from where `file1` ends. The second file is concatenated, and all text is justified and filled.

22.5.3 Switching to Standard Input from within Text

`nroff` can be instructed to take its input from standard input via the `.rd` command, which may or may not be followed by some text.

If you issue this instruction without an argument, a beep will sound at the terminal, and `nroff` will wait for you to type some text, followed by two carriage returns, before it goes back to the original document. Whatever you type will become part of that document at that location.

Issuing this instruction followed by an argument will result in that text being displayed at the terminal, and `nroff` will wait for you to type something in response to that prompt. Here's sample usage:

```
.rd address:
```

When `nroff` encounters the `.rd` command, it will exit from the text file and display the prompt at the terminal:

```
address:  100 East 76th Street
New York, NY 10017
<Return>
<Return>
```

The text that you type will be formatted based on the instructions preceding the `.rd` command, and displayed in the output accordingly.

22.5.4 Specifying Arguments in Inches/Centimeters

Throughout our discussion on nroff, we have been describing instructions whose arguments are numbers specifying rows or columns. Arguments can be specified to nroff in inches or centimeters instead of columns or rows. Inches are specified by appending i to the number in the argument:

```
.po 1i
```

The above command sets the page offset to 1 inch.

Centimeters can be specified by appending c to the number in the argument:

```
.po 2.5c
```

The above command sets the page offset to 2.5 centimeters. Requests such as these are said to be *dimensioned*.

There could be several reasons for specifying dimensioned arguments. Sometimes it's just easier to specify offsets and indents in terms of inches or centimeters.

Another reason for using dimensioned arguments is that one day your document may be formatted using troff instead of nroff. troff is a variation of nroff, and understands all nroff commands described in prior chapters. The difference is that nroff was originally designed for line printers and letter-quality printers. troff is more oriented towards typesetter devices. Hence, there will be a difference in the appearance of the final document. Dimensioned arguments have the advantage of producing the same output, regardless of the type of output device.

We now continue the chapter with a discussion of troff.

22.6 TROFF, AN INTRODUCTION

As indicated in the prior section, troff is a variation of nroff, primarily oriented towards typesetter devices. troff understands all nroff commands. However, troff provides enhanced capabilities over nroff. It is these commands that we describe in this chapter. We will also reference some commands that are interpreted differently by troff. If you did not read Chapter 21, please refer to it now for detailed descriptions of nroff commands. These commands provide the same functionality for files that are supplied as input to troff.

22.7 NROFF COMMANDS INTERPRETED DIFFERENTLY BY TROFF

The following commands have the same syntax, but produce different results, depending on whether `nroff` or `troff` is used to format the text.

- The `.ul` command results in text being underlined by `nroff`. `troff` italicizes text instead.

- Arguments with no dimensions produce different results in `nroff` and `troff`. For example, to take a horizontol command, `.in 4` (indent 4), will result in four *character* spaces being indented, all characters being the same width. `troff` will indent by four m character spaces. The m character space is the default. This default can be changed by specifying n character spaces:

```
.in 5n
```

The above command will indent by 5 n character spaces in `troff`. Specifying n characters as opposed to m characters results in a tighter output, since an n character is narrower than an m character.

As an example of a command with vertical line spacing, `.sp 4` (insert 4 blank lines) will result in four blank rows being inserted by `nroff`. However, in `troff`, the line depth can be changed. The command `.sp 4` will result in 4 blank rows of the current line depth being inserted by `troff`. The v suffix specifies vertical spacing.

22.8 SPECIFYING POINT SIZE

`troff` allows you to specify the size of the text (this is called point size) via the `.ps` instruction:

```
.ps 14
```

The command above results in all subsequent text being displayed in point size 14. Issuing `.ps` with no arguments results in the point size being reset to its prior value.

22.9 SPECIFYING FONT

`troff` also allows you to specify fonts via the `.ft` command. For example, the command

```
.ft R
```

will set the font of all subsequent text to Times Roman style. It is important to note that the device to which the output will be sent needs to be aware of the font specified, and different fonts will be mounted on different installations. Consult your systems administrator as to what fonts are available on your system.

22.10 SPECIFYING VERTICAL SPACING

In Section 22.7 we briefly mentioned vertical spacing. This instruction is specified via the `.vs` command. It changes the height of subsequent rows in the document. A `.vs` without any arguments will result in vertical spacing reverting to the prior setting. Here's sample usage:

```
.vs 0.15i
```

The above command sets the height of one row to .15 inch.

22.11 TROFF IN CONJUNCTION WITH MACRO PACKAGES

So far we have been describing some basic formatting commands that allow you to produce fairly decent looking documents. However, *high-level* formatting constructs are often required to produce certain types of results that cannot achieved with the *low-level* commands described so far. These formatting constructs can be incorporated inside `troff` by using it in conjunction with predefined macros. The next chapter describes the `ms` macro package used in conjunction with `troff`.

22.12 SAMPLE USAGE OF TROFF COMMANDS

We now format Miss Medora Blackwell's response to Mr. Luke Valentino's letter using `troff` commands:

```
$ cat letter
.po 5     \" Set left margin at 5 columns
.ll 55    \" Set page length to 55 lines
.in +40   \" Indent 40 columns
```
Medora Blackwell
```
.br
```
69 East 96 West, Apt. X
```
.br
```
New York, NY 10017
```
.sp 1
```
May 9, 1992
```
.in
.sp 3
```
Mr. Luke Valentino
```
.br
```
100 Lost Haven Drive
```
.br
```
Starry Town, NY 12399
```
.br
.sp 4
.ti 3
```
Dear Mr. Valentino,
```
.sp 1
.ti 3
```
Thank you for your letter dated April 25, 1992. I apologize
for not being able to respond to you sooner. Work has been
really hectic; I have been placed in charge of the
Mitsufushi account, and expect to be traveling to Japan some
time next month to seal the deal. There is no end to the
paperwork involved!
```
.sp
.ti 3
```
I don't quite remember, but I think I have mentioned to you
that Mitsufushi has been our primary target customer for
the past five months. Their acceptance of our product is
one of the key factors that will influence the future growth
of our company.
```
.sp
.ti 3
```
There were at least five people vying for the position that I
now have. The difficulties were compounded by the fact that
I am a woman, and Japanese men are not used to women being
placed in the lead. I used what leverage I had to get this
spot, and created leverage where I had none. And finally I
succeeded, because I persevered and overcame obstacles as
intelligently as my mind would allow, and I never gave up.
```
.sp
.ti 3
```
Do you understand where I'm coming from, Luke? I think I

am too set in my ways, too career-oriented, and far too ambitious
to ever let go of my own dreams. I don't know how I could
ever become a part of yours. You are much too sweet a
man for one as relentless as me.
```
.sp
.ti 3
```
Maybe, one day, I will tire of the never-ending deadlines,
the politics, the red tape, the rat race. But now is
not the time.
```
.sp 3
```
Yours,
```
.sp 2
```
Medora.
```
$
```

Bourne Shell Implementation

All commands described in this chapter will produce the same
result if `nroff` or `troff` is invoked from the Bourne shell. `nroff`
and `troff` are standard utilities; it does not matter what shell they
are invoked from.

Korn Shell Implementation

All commmands described in this chapter will produce the same
result if `nroff` or `troff` is invoked from the Korn shell.

22.13 OSF/1 CONSIDERATIONS

The `nroff` and `troff` document formatters behave in the same
way when they are run in an OSF/1 environment. All instructions
and options will produce the same results.

22.14 REVIEW

This chapter described a few more features of `nroff`. Table 22.1
summarizes these features.

Table 22.1 nroff Commands and Options

Command	Syntax	Description
Specify titles	.tl 'l'c'r'	Specifies left (l), center (c), and right (r) titles on top of page. Any one of these fields can be blank; quotes must exist.
Specify page #s in title	.tl 'Page %'"	Substitutes page number in % field, displays at left edge of page.
Specify title length	.lt 60	Specifies title length of 60. Overrides margin settings.
Underlines characters in words	.ul M\c ain	Underlines the M in text Main only.
Embed nroff commands in text	\&.ce	Use zero width character \& to take away special meaning of nroff command.
Keep blocks of words together	Main\ Menu\ Options	Use backslash followed by a space ("\ "), the unpaddable space character, to keep groups of words together.
Switching to input from another file	.so otherfile	Input is read from otherfile and then nroff returns to current file.
Switching to standard input	.rd .rd address:	System beeps and waits for you to input something at the terminal. Terminate input by 2 carriage returns. System displays prompt "address:" instead of beeping.
Specify dimensional arguments	.po 1.3i .po 2.5c	Page offset is set to 1.3 inches. Page offset is set to 2.5 centimeters.

Table 22.2 summarizes some more commonly used nroff options.

Table 22.2 Options Supplied to nroff

Option	Syntax	Description
Print specific pages	nroff -o4 file|lpr nroff -o2-4 file|lpr nroff -o-3 file|lpr nroff -o5- file|lpr	Prints page 4. Prints pages 2 through 4. Prints pages 1 through 3. Prints pages 5 through end.
Stop at specific page	nroff -s5 file|lpr	Stops at page 5 of each document.
Specify start page #	nroff -n23 file|lpr	First page number starts at 23.
Produce equal space words	nroff -e file|lpr	All words are equally spaced.
Use macro packages	nroff -mname file|lpr	Uses macro package "name" with nroff.

Table 22.3 describes the additional commands that are available in troff only.

Table 22.3 troff Commands (Different from nroff)

Command	Syntax	Description
Italicize text	.ul	Italicizes text, instead of underlining it like nroff.
Specify dimension arguments	.in 5m .in 5n	Indents by 5 m characters. Indents by 5 n characters.
Specify point size	.ps 14	Sets point size to 14.
Specify font	.ft R	Sets font to Times Roman.
Specify vertical spacing.	.vs 0.5c	Sets height of row to .5 centimeter.

23

The ms Macro Package

23.1 INTRODUCTION

We discuss the macro package ms in this chapter. This macro can be used in conjunction with nroff or troff to implement instructions that are not available through nroff or troff in the raw!

As mentioned in prior chapters, macros are collections of instructions which are grouped together and given a name. Hence, instructions from this macro can be included in the document that is to be formatted. In this way, a macro provides a *high-level* interface that simplifies the formatting of text.

Macro packages are collections of macros. The ms package is one of the easiest ones to use.

Before proceeding any further, let's review how a macro package is called from the command line:

```
$ nroff -ms file | lpr
```

This command calls the ms macro package. Keep in mind that the m is really the m from the -m option which is used to call macros. (Refer to Chapter 22 for complete details.) The s that follows is the name of the macro package, which exists in the directory /usr/lib/tmac.

23.2 THE MS MACRO PACKAGE

The ms package is perhaps the most widely available and easiest to use. Calls to ms commands are similar to `nroff` and `troff` instructions: they begin with a dot, are followed by one or more characters, and must be on a line by themselves. The main difference is that the instructions are uppercase, thereby being differentiated from lowercase `nroff` instructions. Current settings are usually stored inside specific number registers. (We referenced the page number register in the prior chapter.) Modifying these current settings results in variations in output. The following features of the ms package will be discussed:

- Page layout

- Paragraph styles

- Headings

- Titles

- Other miscellaneous features

The following source file will be used in subsequent examples:

```
$ cat source
```

When a child is born, he or she inherits certain characteristics
from the mother, and some from the father. With the passage of
time, this child develops traits which uniquely identify
him or her from the rest. This child is a combination of
characteristics inherited from the parents, and those
derived from the environment that he or she grows up in.
As we grow older, our outlook on life changes. Our dreams,
goals, and ambitions are derived from what we are taught,
and what we experience in the circle in which we grow up
and interact. And then, we pass on what we have learned
and achieved to those who are near and dear to us,
and give them the opportunity to build on what we built
ourselves.
$
```
```

23.3 PAGE LAYOUT

This section describes macros that do the following:

- Specify left/right margins

- Specify top/bottom margins

23.3.1 Left/Right Margins

First, the page layout has to be designed. This consists of specifying the left/right and top/bottom margins. We discuss the specification of the left and right margins in this section.

The default left margin in ms is zero inches; that is, output starts from the left edge of the page. The line length is 6 inches, so if the line starts at offset 0, the right margin is 2 1/2 inches (given a standard 8 1/2- by 11-inch page size).

The default margin settings can be changed by modifying the contents of the PO (page offset) and LL (line length) number registers. Number registers are always referenced via the .nr command, followed by the name of the register and a number specifying the value to be stored in it. Here's sample usage:

```
.nr PO 1.5i
.nr PO 2.5c
.nr PO 8n
.nr PO 8m
```

The above four commands set the page offset in different ways. The first command sets the page offset to 1.5 inches. The next one sets it to 2.5 centimeters. The third command sets the page offset to 8 "en" spaces (one en space equals the width of the n character). The last command sets the page offset to 8 "em" spaces (one em space equals the width of the m character).

And so you may wonder why we could not implement the same command simply via the .po command in nroff or troff. The .po command can be overridden anywhere in the document, and holds the same value only until the next instruction which changes it. The .nr PO command, on the other hand, is read at the start of each page as the document is being read. Hence, it is unaffected by any inadvertent instructions that may change it in the meantime.

The line length is set to 6 inches as follows:

```
.nr LL 6.0i
```

The PO instruction takes effect starting from the following page. Therefore, you should insert a regular .po to set your page offset for the first page.

23.3.2 Top/Bottom Margins

The default top and bottom margins in ms are 1 inch. The value of the top margin can be modified by setting the HM number register:

```
.nr HM 1.5i
```

The above command sets the top margin to 1.5 inches. The bottom margin can be specified by setting the FM register:

```
.nr FM 1.25i
```

The bottom margin is set to 1.25 inches.

23.3.3 ms Defaults

ms automatically displays page numbers at the top of each page except the first. The format of page numbers is −2− or −3−, etc. ms also automatically displays the current system date at the bottom of each page. The display of this date can be suppressed via the .ND command, which must be inserted at the beginning of the input text. The date can be changed via the .DA macro, as follows:

```
.DA May 2 1992
```

You can supply any format to the .DA macro, as long as it is a legal date. For example, the following format could have been used:

```
.DA 09/02/92
```

23.3.4 Sample Usage

Here's the source file with the relevant commands inserted:

```
.po 1.5"       \" Set page offset to 1.5"
.nr LL 6"      \" Set line length to 6"
.nr PO 1.5"  \" Set page offset via register to 1.5"
.nr HM 1.5"    \" Set top margin to 1.5"
.nr FM 1.5"       \" Set bottom margin to 1.5"
.ND          \" Suppress display of date
```
When a child is born, he or she inherits certain characteristics
from the mother, and some from the father. With the passage of
time, this child develops traits which uniquely identify
him or her from the rest. This child is a combination of
characteristics inherited from the parents, and those
derived from the environment that he or she grows up in.
As we grow older, our outlook on life changes. Our dreams,
goals, and ambitions are derived from what we are taught,
and what we experience in the circle in which we grow up
and interact. And then, we pass on what we have learned
and achieved to those who are near and dear to us,
and give them the opportunity to build on what we built
ourselves.

Here's what's typed at the command line:

```
$ troff -ms source | lpr
```

and here's the result:

When a child is born, he or she inherits certain characteristics
from the mother, and some from the father. With the passage of
time, this child develops traits which uniquely identify him or
her from the rest. This child is a combination of characteristics inherited from the parents, and those derived from the environment that he or she grows up in. As we grow older, our outlook on life changes. Our dreams, goals, and ambitions are
derived from what we are taught, and what we experience in the
circle in which we grow up and interact. And then, we pass on
what we have learned and achieved to those who are near and
dear to us, and give them the opportunity to build on what we
built ourselves.

In the interest of saving space, we do not display a number of blank lines that follow the last line in the source file. At the end of the page, following the blank lines, appears the page number:

-1-

23.4 PARAGRAPH STYLE

We now discuss paragraph styles. These can be:

- Blocked

- Indented first line

- Fully indented

- Hanging indents

- Nested

23.4.1 Blocked

Use the `.LP` macro to produce a blocked paragraph, where the left and right margins are flush. We do so now, and here's the result. You need to insert this at the beginning of each paragraph. The complete text is not shown, so you don't get tired of reading the same thing over and over.

```
.LP
```
When a child is born, he or she inherits certain characteristics
from the mother, and some from the father. With the passage of
time, this child develops traits which uniquely identify
him or her from the rest. This child is a combination of
characteristics inherited from the parents, and those
derived from the environment that he or she grows up in.
```
.LP
```
As we grow older, our outlook on life changes. Our dreams,

goals, and ambitions are derived from what we are taught,
and what we experience in the circle in which we grow up
and interact. And then, we pass on what we have learned
and achieved to those who are near and dear to us,
and give them the opportunity to build on what we built
ourselves.

---

and here's the result:

When a child is born, he or she inherits certain characteristics from the mother, and some from the father. With
the passage of time, this child develops traits which
uniquely identify him or her from the rest. This child is a
combination of characteristics inherited from the parents,
and those derived from the environment that he or she grows
up in.

As we grow older, our outlook on life changes. Our dreams,
goals and ambitions are derived from what we are taught, and
what we experience in the circle that we grow up and
interact. And then, we pass on what we have learned and
achieved to those who are near and dear to us, and give them
the opportunity to build on what we built ourselves.

Notice that ms automatically inserts a blank line between
paragraphs.

23.4.2 Indented First Line

An indented style can be created via the .PP command. It indents
5 spaces. We insert a .PP command after each .LP command
displayed in the source file in the prior example. Here's the new
output:

When a child is born, he or she inherits certain characteristics from the mother, and some from the father. With the passage of time, this child develops traits which uniquely identify him or her from the rest. This child is a combination of characteristics inherited from the parents, and those derived from the environment that he or she grows up in.

As we grow older, our outlook on life changes. Our dreams, goals, and ambitions are derived from what we are taught, and what we experience in the circle in which we grow up and interact. And then, we pass on what we have learned and achieved to those who are near and dear to us, and give them the opportunity to build on what we built ourselves.

Notice how two blank lines are inserted before the start of each paragraph. This is because the `.PP` command also inserts a blank line. We can remove the `.LP` commands inserted in the document previously, to alleviate this problem.

23.4.3 ms Defaults

`ms` automatically indents 5 n spaces for lines, if the `.PP` command is specified. The blank line is 1 vertical space for `nroff`, and .3 vertical spaces for `troff`. These values are stored inside the `PI` (paragraph indent) and `PD` (paragraph depth) registers, and can be changed as necessary. For example, you can change the values stored inside these registers as follows:

```
.nr PI 3m
.nr PD 3v
```

Then, each time you issue a `.LP` or `.PP`, the paragraph depth will be 3 vertical spaces instead of 1, and the line indent will be 3 em spaces instead of 5 n spaces.

23.4.4 Complete Indentation

The complete paragraph can be indented via the `.IP` macro (indent paragraph). The default setting of 5 spaces is used for the indentation. (You can change the value stored inside the `PI` register if this default is to be changed.) We replace the first instance of the `.PP` command with `.IP`, and let the `.PP` command just before the start of the second paragraph stay as it is. Selected portions of the new source file are now displayed, just so you know what we're talking about:

```
$ cat source
.po 1.5"
.nr LL 6"
.nr PO 1.5"
.nr HM 1.5"
.nr FM 1.5"
.ND
.IP
When a child is born, he or she inherits certain characteristics
.
.

.
derived from the environment that he or she grows up in.
.PP
As we grow older, our outlook on life changes.  Our dreams,
.
.

.
ourselves.
$
```

and here's the output:

    When a child is born, he or she inherits certain characteristics from the mother, and some from the father. With the passage of time, this child develops traits which uniquely identify him or her from the rest. This child is a combination of characteristics inherited from the parents, and those derived from the environment that he or she grows up in.

    As we grow older, our outlook on life changes. Our dreams, goals, and ambitions are derived from what we are taught, and what we experience in the circle in which we grow up and interact. And then, we pass on what we have learned and achieved to those who are near and dear to us, and give them the opportunity to build on what we built ourselves.

A paragraph can be indented from the left and the right via a call to the .QP macro (for quotation paragraph). We insert a call to .QP just before the first paragraph. Here's the output:

When a child is born, he or she inherits certain characteristics from the mother, and some from the father. With the passage of time, this child develops traits which uniquely identify him or her from the rest. This child is a combination of characteristics inherited from the parents, and those derived from the environment that he or she grows up in.

<Second paragraph starts from here and ends 3 character spaces beyond the previous paragraph>.

23.4.5 Hanging Indent

The .IP macro can be supplied an argument to produce a "hanging indent" style of paragraph. The argument supplied appears to the left of the remaining paragraph, which is completely indented. We insert the required argument at the beginning of the first paragraph, like this:

```
.IP 1-
```
When a child is born, he or she inherits certain characteristics

.

.

.

derived from the environment that he or she grows up in.

```
.IP 2-
```
As we grow older, our outlook on life changes. Our dreams,

.

.

.

ourselves.

---

which is formatted as follows:

1- When a child is born, he or she inherits certain characteristics from the mother, and some from the father. With
the passage of time, this child develops traits which uniquely identify him or her from the rest. This child is a
combination of characteristics inherited from the parents,
and those derived from the environment that he or she grows
up in.

2- As we grow older, our outlook on life changes. Our dreams,
goals, and ambitions are derived from what we are taught,
and what we experience in the circle in which we grow up and
interact. And then, we pass on what we have learned and
achieved to those who are near and dear to us, and give them
the opportunity to build on what we built ourselves.

As you can see, the characters 1- and 2- follow the .IP macro
in the source file. This results in these characters being displayed
to the left of the normal indentation of the paragraph, and the
remaining paragraph displaying in block format to the right. If you
wish to embed spaces in the argument that follows .IP, enclose the
string in double quotes, like so:

```
.IP "   (a)"
```

You can also specify the length in en spaces that you wish these
arguments to occupy.   This feature is useful if unequal length
arguments are to be placed to the left of the indented paragraph.
Consider the following example:

Sara - Sara is the redhead who comes late to work every day.
Maria - Maria is the brunette. She's the one with the attitude.
Elaine - Elaine is the dizzy blonde. She's OK, but that blue suit
she wore to work the other day has got to go!

Here's the source file:

```
.IP "Sara -"
Sara is the redhead who comes late to work every day.
.IP "Maria -"
Maria - Maria is the brunette.  She's the one with the attitude.
.IP "Elaine -"
Elaine is the dizzy blonde.  She's OK, but that blue suit she wore
to work the other day has got to go!
```

---

and the corresponding output:

Sara Sara is the redhead who comes late to work every day.
MariaMaria is the brunette. She's the one with the attitude.
ElainElaine is the dizzy blonde. She's OK, but that blue suit
    she wore to work the other day has got to go!

Notice how the dashes that follow the names are simply ignored,
and the paragraphs to the right of the alleged captions overlap
them. This is because not enough space has been allocated to the
captions. This problem can be solved by specifying the number of
en spaces the arguments are to occupy. Here's the modified source:

```
.IP "Sara -" 9
Sara is the redhead who comes late to work every day.
.IP "Maria -" 9
Maria is the brunette.  She's the one with the attitude.
.IP "Elaine -" 9
Elaine is the dizzy blonde.  She's OK, but that blue suit she wore
to work the other day has got to go!
```

---

and the corresponding output:

Sara -   Sara is the redhead who comes late to work every day.

Maria - Maria is the brunette. She's the one with the attitude.

Elaine - Elaine is the dizzy blonde. She's OK, but that blue
         suit she wore to work the other day has got to go!

23.4.6 Nested Lists

We add some text to the prior example to illustrate the need for
nested lists. Here's the modified source file:

Sara - Sara is the redhead who comes late to work every day. Her
assignments for the day include: 1) Prepare a report that describes
the sales history of Product_A. 2) Prepare a status report.
Maria - Maria is the brunette. She's the one with the attitude. Her
assignments for the day include: 1) Interview the new kid for the
entry level programming position. 2) Write a memo recommending

the candidate she considers fit for the job.
Elaine - Elaine is the dizzy blonde. She's OK, but that blue suit
she wore to work the other day has got to go! Her assignments
include: 1) Do a follow-up on our prospective clients.
This pretty much sums up the assignments for these three
women for today.

The numbered items are to appear as a list on their own. We can
achieve these results by using the `.RS` and `.RE` macros in
conjunction with the `.IP`.

The `.RS` (right shift) macro shifts all paragraphs following it to
the right. Once again, the shift length is determined by the value
stored inside the `PI` number register. The `.RE` macro cancels the
effect of the `.RS`. Here's the modified source file:

```
.IP "Sara -" 9
Sara is the redhead who comes late to work every day.  Her
assignments for the day include:
.RS
.IP 1)
Prepare a report that describes the sales history of Product_A.
.IP 2)
Prepare a status report.
.RE
.IP "Maria -" 9
Maria is the brunette.  She's the one with the attitude.  Her
assignments for the day include:
.RS
.IP 1)
Interview the new kid for the entry level programming position.
.IP 2)
Write a memo recommending the candidate she considers fit for the
job.
.RE
.IP "Elaine -" 9
Elaine is the dizzy blonde.  She's OK, but that blue suit she wore
to work the other day has got to go!  Her assignments include:
.RS
.IP 1)
Do a follow-up on our prospective clients.
.RE
```

```
. LP
```
This pretty much sums up the assignments for these three women for today.

Notice the .LP at the end of the source file. This instruction is required to produce a straight left margin for the text that follows. Here's the output:

Sara - Sara is the redhead who comes late to work every day. Her assignments for the day include:

1) Prepare a report that describes the sales history of Product_A.

2) Prepare a status report.

Maria - Maria is the brunette. She's the one with the attitude. Her assignments for the day include:

1) Interview the new kid for the entry level programming position.

2) Write a memo recommending the candidate she considers fit for the job.

Elaine - Elaine is the dizzy blonde. She's OK, but that blue suit she wore to work the other day has got to go! Her assignments include:

1) Do a follow-up on our prospective clients.

This pretty much sums up the assignments for these three women for today.

23.5 HEADINGS

Headings can be:

- Unnumbered

- Numbered

The next two sections describe these.

23.5.1 Unnumbered

Headings without numbers can be created via the .SH macro (section heading). They are underlined in nroff, and underlined and emboldened by troff. The text that follows the heading must begin with a .LP, .PP, or .IP; this is how the end of the heading is signaled to ms. If you omit one of these instructions, then ms will think that all subsequent text is a part of the heading. Let's add a heading to the prior example. Here's the source file:

```
.SH
Assignment List
.IP "Sara -" 9
```
Sara is the redhead who comes late to work every day. Her assignments for the day include:
```
.RS
.IP 1)
```
Prepare a report that describes the sales history of Product_A.
```
.IP 2)
```
Prepare a status report.
```
.RE
.IP "Maria -" 9
```
Maria is the brunette. She's the one with the attitude. Her assignments for the day include:
```
.RS
.IP 1)
```
Interview the new kid for the entry level programming position.
```
.IP 2)
```
Write a memo recommending the candidate she considers fit for the job.
```
.RE
.IP "Elaine -" 9
```
Elaine is the dizzy blonde. She's OK, but that blue suit she wore to work the other day has got to go! Her assignments include:

```
.RS
.IP 1)
Do a follow-up on our prospective clients.
.RE
.LP
This pretty much sums up the assignments for these three
women for today.
```

---

and here's the output:

Assignment List

Sara -   Sara is the redhead who comes late to work every day.
Her assignments for the day include:

    1)   Prepare a report that describes the sales history of Product_A.

    2)   Prepare a status report.

Maria - Maria is the brunette. She's the one with the attitude.
Her assignments for the day include:

    1)   Interview the new kid for the entry level programming position.

    2)   Write a memo recommending the candidate she considers fit for the job.

Elaine - Elaine is the dizzy blonde. She's OK, but that blue
suit she wore to work the other day has got to go!   Her
assignments include:

    1)   Do a follow-up on our prospective clients.

This pretty much sums up the assignments for these three women
for today.

23.5.2 Numbered

ms has the ability to automatically number up to five levels of headings. The required number is generated by supplying the level number with the .NH macro (numbered heading). Consider the following source file:

Table of Contents
Chapter 17 Commands for Manipulating Files
Comparing Files
diff
Options Available with diff
bdiff
Options Available with bdiff
sdiff
Options Available with sdiff
Splitting Files
split

The first five lines in the source file indicate five levels of headings in that order. The sixth line (bdiff) is a level four heading. The following line is once again a level five heading. Let's have ms number these headings accordingly. Here's the reedited source file:

.NH
Table of Contents
.NH 2
Chapter 17 Commands for Manipulating Files
.NH 3
Comparing Files
.NH 4
diff
.NH 5
Options Available with diff
.NH 4

```
bdiff
.NH  5
Options Available with bdiff
.NH  4
sdiff
.NH  5
Options Available with sdiff
.NH  3
Splitting Files
.NH  4
split
```

---

and here's the output:

---

1. Table of Contents

1.1 Chapter 17 Commands for Manipulating Files

1.1.1 Comparing Files

1.1.1.1 diff

1.1.1.1.1 Options Available with diff

1.1.1.2 bdiff

1.1.1.2.1 Options Available with bdiff

1.1.1.3 sdiff

1.1.1.3.1 Options Available with sdiff

1.1.2 Splitting Files

1.1.2.1 split

23.6 TITLES

Formatted documents can contain a title, the author or authors' names, a subtitle, and an abstract. `ms` provides macros that allow formatting of these items.

Titles are formatted via the `.TL` macro. Authors' names are formatted via `.AU`. Subtitles are created via the `.AI` macro. The abstract is created by placing text between the `.AB` and `.AE` macros. Although we reference titles, authors, subtitles, and abstracts, you can create any kind of cover sheet containing one or more of the above macros. The format will be as illustrated in the example that follows. Here's the source file:

```
.TL
Ranade's UNIX Primer
.AU
Jay Ranade and Saba Zamir
.AI
A Comprehensive Beginners' Guide to the
UNIX Operating System
.AB
This book is a primer intended for those who know nothing
whatsoever about the UNIX operating system.  It explains
features of UNIX via numerous examples and sample output.
It also describes differences in output, if any,  when
commands are run from the C, Bourne, and Korn shells, and
from the OSF/1 operating system environment.
.AE
```

Running this through `troff` will produce the following output:

Ranade's UNIX Primer

Jay Ranade and Saba Zamir

A Comprehensive Beginners' Guide to the
UNIX Operating System

This book is a primer intended for those who know
nothing whatsoever about the UNIX operating system.
It explains features of UNIX via numerous examples and
sample output. It also describes differences in output, if any, when commands are run from the C, Bourne,
and Korn shells, and from the OSF/1 operating system
environment.

There are some rules associated with the instructions for titles. These macros must always be the first input in the text. In addition to this, they must always appear in the order illustrated. Aside from this, we point out a few of the more obvious features. Any of the above macros can be repeated (but don't overlook their ordering!). Any of them can be left out. And each line in the title will display as is – what you type is what you get.

23.7 MISCELLANEOUS FEATURES

We describe a few more features in this section that are available in ms. These are:

- Footnotes

- Blocking of text that must appear together

- Displays

23.7.1 FOOTNOTES

You can use the `.FS` (footnote start) and `.FE` (footnote end) macros
to mark the start and end of a footnote. Here's the source file with
embedded instructions:

```
If you think of your life in a nutshell, you will realize just
how much has been derived from what you inherited from
your parents, what you learned from the social structure
that you grew up in, and what your own ambition drives
you to achieve. If features inherited from your parents could
be grouped together as one class, and features derived from
your social structure as another, then you are analogous
to a "derived" class; you have inherited features from your
base classes (your parents, education, and social
structure), and you have added a few unique characteristics
of your own (your ambitions, achievements, and more!).
.PP
Derived classes, as they exist in C++, are analogous
to the simple life story presented above.*
.FS
* From
.ul
C++ Primer for C Programmers by Ranade/Zamir.
.FE
.PP
We will now present some examples which illustrate the
use of derived classes.
```

Here's the output produced from `troff`. We present the output
in two parts, simply because there are a number of blank lines
between the two. Here's the first part:

If you think of your life in a nutshell, you will realize
just how much has been derived from what you inherited from your
parents, what you learned from the social structure that you grew
up in, and what your own ambition drives you to achieve. If

features inherited from your parents could be grouped together as one class, and features derived from your social structure as another, then you are analogous to a "derived" class; you have inherited features from your base classes (your parents, education, and social structure), and you have added a few unique characteristics of your own (your ambitions, achievements, and more!).

Derived classes, as they exist in C++, are analogous to the simple life story presented above.*

We will now present some examples which illustrate the use of derived classes.

This was the first half of the page. Notice that the footnote text does not appear here. At the bottom of the page, the footnote appears, it is formatted like this:

----
* From C++ Primer for C Programmers by Ranade/Zamir.

- 1 -

Notice that the footnote appears as is; what you type is what you get. Also, in `troff`, footnotes are printed in a smaller letter size. (`nroff` does not have this capability.) They are shorter in length than the current margin settings, and display underneath a dashed line.

23.7.2 Blocking Text to Be Kept Together

Sometimes it is necessary to keep text on the same page, so as not to lose the impact that it may carry. The `.KS` (keep start) and `.KE` (keep end) macros can be used to enclose this text. We continue with the last paragraph of the example just presented and insert the necessary instructions in it.

```
.KS
```
Derived classes, as they exist in C++, are analogous
to the simple life story presented above. A derived class
inherits characteristics from one or more base classes.
Then, it adds a few unique features of its own. This
class can then be used as a base class for some other
derived class, and so on. This is how a hierarchy of
classes is created. This is how one object is built from
another. This is what makes C++ the powerful language
that it is.
```
.KE
```

The above text will be displayed on the same page. If the text
does not fit on the same page, some blank lines will be left on the
current page and output will continue on the next page.

23.7.3 Displays

A display is a block of text that must appear exactly as it was typed
– no justification, adjusting, or whatever – and also be output on
the same page. The `.DS` (display start) and `.DE` (display end)
macros are used for this purpose. Here's the source file:

We would now like you to take a look at the dialogue from the play
titled "I Don't Know."
```
.sp
.DS
```
Mary: What do you want me to do about this?
John: I don't know.
Mary: But you have to tell me something. What am I going
       to do?
John: I don't know.
```
.DE
```

For reasons unknown, the author of the play above wishes to have the dialogue text display exactly as is. The author's request can be honored via the .DS and .DE macros. Here's how the output will look:

We would now like you to take a look at the dialogue from the play titled "I don't know."

Mary: What do you want me to do about this?
John: I don't know.
Mary: But you have to tell me something. What am I going
     to do?
John: I don't know.

Notice how the output of the first line is adjusted and filled, and the remaining lines appear as is.

Bourne Shell Implementation

The ms macro package will behave in the same way, regardless of the shell that it is called from.

Korn Shell Implementation

The ms macro package will behave in the same way, regardless of the shell that it is called from.

23.8 OSF/1 CONSIDERATIONS

The ms macro is also available in an OSF/1 operating system. All instructions will produce the same result as illustrated in this chapter.

23.9 REVIEW

We described features of the ms macro in this chapter. Table 23.1
summarizes the syntax and descriptions of the instructions
presented in this chapter.

Table 23.1 ms Macro Commands

Command	Syntax	Description
Specify page offset, left margin	.nr PO 1.5i	Specifies page offset of 1.5 inches.
Specify right margin	.nr LL 6.0i	Specifies line length of 6 inches. Right margin is determined by this setting and page offset.
Specify top margin	.nr HM 1.5i	Sets top margin to 1.5 inches.
Specify bottom margin	.nr FM 1.5i	Sets bottom margin to 1.5 inches.
Change default output of date	.DA May 2 1992	Sets date which displays at bottom of page to May 2, 1992.
Inhibit display of date	.ND	Inhibits automatic display of date at bottom of page.
Specify straight left margin	.LP	Text that follows has straight left margin.
Indent first line of block	.PP	Indents first line (5 spaces by default) of following paragraph.
Modify default indents	.nr PI 3m .nr PD 3v	Sets para indent to 3 ems and para depth to 3 vertical spaces.

Table 23.1 ms Macro Commands (Contd.)

Command	Syntax	Description
Indent entire paragraph	.IP .QP	Indents left margin of entire text of following paragraph. Indents left and right margins of paragraph.
Produce hanging indent	.IP - .IP - 6	Character(s) following .IP appear to the left of the remaining paragraph. Specifies number of "en" characters (6) that character following .IP is to occupy.
Produce nested lists	.RS <text> .RE	<text> indents to the right after .RS. .RE cancels .RS request.
Produce unnumbered heading	.SH <heading> .LP or .PP or .PI	Text following .SH is underlined until a .LP, .PP, or .PI is encountered. troff emboldens text.
Produce numbered headings	.NH <heading> .NH 2 .NH 3 .NH 4 .NH 5	<heading> is numbered based on the level number supplied with .NH. Up to five levels can be specified.

Table 23.1 ms Macro Commands (Contd.)

Command	Syntax	Description
Produce title, author's name, sub-title, and abstract	.TL <title> .AU <authors> .AI <subtitle> .AB .AE	Outputs headings as indicated, centered and underlined. Any of these macros may be omitted, but if they exist, they must appear in this order.
Produce footnote	.FS <footnote> .FE	<footnote> appears at bottom of page, exactly as typed, under a dashed line.
Keep text together	.KS <text> .KE	<text> is displayed on the same page. Blank lines are inserted in current page if <text> does not fit on it.
Keep "display"	.DS <display> .DE	Displays <display> on same page, exactly as typed. No filling or justification takes place.

Creating Tables
with tbl

24.1 INTRODUCTION

In this chapter we describe a utility called tbl that allows you to format text in rows and columns within a table. The tbl utility is designed to be used in conjunction with nroff or troff. tbl is a preprocessor. What that means is that the document which contains instructions for creating tables must be first be processed by tbl. The output produced by tbl is then piped to nroff or troff. All of our examples will pipe output to nroff. Keep in mind that most of these examples will produce similar output when piped to troff.

24.2 INVOKING TBL

Consider the following source file:

```
$ cat tbl_file
```
Honey, following is a list of the bills that are outstanding for the month of May:
Telephone $89.67
Gas and electric $134.56
Cable TV $18
Parking $75
Baby sitter $60
Honey, I have no more money, so don't expect any donations from me! This month's bills are on you....See you later.

We will be inserting commands inside the source file just listed to produce a table. `tbl` is invoked in conjunction with `nroff` or `troff` as follows:

`$ tbl tbl_file | nroff | lpr`

The output produced by `tbl` is piped to `nroff`, and the output produced by `nroff` is piped to the line printer. Now let's understand exactly how a table is created.

24.3 SPECIFYING TABLE FORMAT

A table is created via the `.TS` (table start) and `.TE` (table end) macros. Inside the `.TS` and `.TE` commands is text that can be broken up as follows:

- Specification of table layout

- Data for table

The following items must be taken into consideration in the specification of table layout:

- Position on the page

- Overall format (that is, how the rows and columns will be divided up, how they will display, etc.)

- Columnar format (that is, whether the data inside the columns will be centered, left or right adjusted, character or numeric data, etc.)

We will first describe the creation of the simplest form of a table using the sample source file. Then, a discussion will follow for each item just listed.

24.4 SAMPLE USAGE

As indicated previously, the start of a table is indicated by a `.TS` command. Following `.TS` is a line that specifies the options relating to the format of the table. Following this is a line that specifies the options relating to the columns within the table. Next appears the data that are to be formatted. The instruction which ends the table is `.TE`. Here's sample usage:

```
$ cat tbl_file
```
Honey, following is a list of the bills that are outstanding for
the month of May:
```
.sp                \" Insert blank line
.TS                \" Start table
tab ( );           \" Specifies field terminator is tab
1 1 .     \" Specifies two columns to be left aligned
\" Table data follow
Telephone          $89.67
Gas and electric   $134.56
Cable TV           $18
Parking            $75
Baby sitter        $60
.TE                \" End table
.sp                \" Insert blank line
```
Honey, I have no more money, so don't expect any donations
from me! This month's bills are on you....See you later.
```
$
```

Now, let's understand the embedded instructions, starting with
the second line in the source file.

```
tab ( );
```

This is the table options specification line. It instructs tbl that
the field separator is a tab. If each field in the table was separated
from the next by some other character, such as |, then this line
would have read like this:

```
tab (|);
```

and each field in each row in the table would have been separated
by a |, like so:

```
Telephone | $89.67
```

This line must be terminated by a semicolon (;).

Now take a look at the next line in the source file.

```
1 1 .
```

This is the column specification line. It indicates the number
and format of the columns. We specify two columns which are left
adjusted. Notice the period at the end of the line. This specifies
the end of the column formatting line or lines.

Following this line are the data that are to be formatted in the table. The end of the table is specified by the `.TE` command.

```
Telephone          $89.67
Gas and electric   $134.56
Cable TV           $18
Parking            $75
Baby sitter        $60
.TE                \" End table
```

The text that follows is to appear as a regular indented paragraph. Let's run this file through `tbl`, and pipe the output to `troff`:

$ tbl tbl_file | troff | lpr

This is the output:

Honey, following is a list of the bills that are outstanding for the month of May:

```
Telephone          $89.67
Gas and electric   $134.56
Cable TV           $18
Parking            $75
Baby sitter        $60
```

Honey, I have no more money, so don't expect any donations from me! This month's bills are on you....See you later.

We now discuss each item listed in Section 24.3 with reference to the specification of table layout.

24.5 POSITION ON PAGE

A table can be aligned with the left margin. This is the default; the prior example illustrated this type of format.

A table can also be centered on the page. This is specified in the table options specification line, as follows:

```
center tab (  );
```

Here's the modified source file:

```
$ cat tbl_file
Honey, following is a list of the bills that are outstanding for
the month of May:
.sp              \" Insert blank line
.TS              \" Start table
center tab ( );  \" Specifies field terminator is tab
1 1 .     \" Specifies two columns to be left aligned
\" Table data follows
Telephone        $89.67
Gas and electric $134.56
Cable TV         $18
Parking          $75
Baby sitter      $60
.TE              \" End table
.sp              \" Insert blank line
Honey, I have no more money, so don't expect any donations
from me!  This month's bills are on you....See you later.
$
```

And here's the resulting output:

Honey, following is a list of the bills that are outstanding for
the month of May:

Telephone	$89.67
Gas and electric	$134.56
Cable TV	$18
Parking	$75
Baby sitter	$60

Honey, I have no more money, so don't expect any donations from
me! This month's bills are on you....See you later.

24.6 OVERALL FORMAT OF TABLE

The following issues need to be addressed in order to determine the overall format of the table:

- Enclosing a table in a box

- Enclosing everything in a box

- Drawing lines between each row

  We briefly discuss each item.

24.6.1 Enclosing Table in a Box

You can enclose a table in a box by inserting box in the table options specification line:

```
center box tab ( );
```

Here's the modified source file. We have inserted blank lines within the text that is to appear in the table to enhance the appearance of the output, which follows on the next page.

```
$ cat tbl_file
Honey, following is a list of the bills that are outstanding for
the month of May:
.sp              \" Insert blank line
.TS              \" Start table
center box tab ( );  \" Specifies field term. is tab
l l .    \" Specifies two columns to be left aligned
\" Table data follow
Telephone        $89.67
.sp
Gas and electric  $134.56
.sp
Cable TV         $18
.sp
Parking          $75
.sp
Baby sitter      $60
.TE              \" End table
.sp              \" Insert blank line
Honey, I have no more money, so don't expect any donations
from me!  This month's bills are on you....See you later.
$
```

Honey, following is a list of the bills that are outstanding for the month of May:

Telephone	$89.67
Gas and electric	$134.56
Cable TV	$18
Parking	$75
Baby sitter	$60

Honey, I have no more money, so don't expect any donations from me! This month's bills are on you....See you later.

24.6.2 Enclosing Everything in a Box

The table and each item in that table can be enclosed in boxes by replacing box with allbox. The output immediately follows.

```
center allbox tab ( );
```

Honey, following is a list of the bills that are outstanding for the month of May:

Telephone	$89.67
Gas and electric	$134.56
Cable TV	$18
Parking	$75
Baby sitter	$60

Honey, I have no more money, so don't expect any donations from me! This month's bills are on you....See you later.

24.6.3 Drawing Lines between Rows

Lines can be inserted between one or more lines of text in the `tbl`
as follows:

```
$ cat tbl_file
```
Honey, following is a list of the bills that are outstanding for
the month of May:
```
.sp                     \" Insert blank line
.TS                     \" Start table
center box tab ( ); \" Specifies field term. is tab
l l .      \" Specifies two columns to be left aligned
\" Table data follows
```
Telephone $89.67
```
.sp
```

G̅as and electric $134.56
```
.sp
```

C̅able TV $18
```
.sp
```

P̅arking $75
```
.sp
```

B̅aby sitter $60
```
.TE                     \" End table
.sp                     \" Insert blank line
```
Honey, I have no more money, so don't expect any donations
from me! This month's bills are on you....See you later.
```
$
```

An underscore is inserted after each line in the table that
requires a line underneath it. The output is the same as the one
presented in the prior example for `allbox`, except for the absence
of the vertical rule. The horizontol lines appear because we
inserted an underscore between each row in the table. The
difference is significant when the underscore option is used to insert
lines between certain rows only.

So anyway, here's the output:

Honey, following is a list of the bills that are outstanding for the month of May:

Telephone	$89.67
Gas and electric	$134.56
Cable TV	$18
Parking	$75
Baby sitter	$60

Honey, I have no more money, so don't expect any donations from me! This month's bills are on you....See you later.

We now discuss features that relate to columnar format.

24.7 COLUMNAR FORMAT OF TABLE

The following issues need to be addressed in order to determine the columnar format of the table:

- Headings of columns

- Headings that span multiple columns

- Specification of numerical columns

- Specification of continuous text blocks in columns

  We now illustrate the specification of each item.

24.7.1 Headings of Columns

Headings of columns are specified as part of the data of the table itself. However, this line must precede the data that follow it. Also, another column specification line needs to be inserted to indicate the format of the headings. Take a look at the modified source file:

```
$ cat tbl_file1
Honey, following is a list of the bills that are outstanding for
the month of May:
.sp               \" Insert blank line
.TS               \" Start table
center box tab ( ); \" Specifies field term. is tab
cfI cfI        \" Heading format
1 1 .     \" Specifies two columns to be left aligned
\" Table data follow
Item Amount    \" Heading title
Telephone      $89.67
.sp

Gas and electric  $134.56
.sp

Cable TV          $18
.sp

Parking           $75
.sp

Baby sitter       $60
.TE               \" End table
.sp               \" Insert blank line
Honey, I have no more money, so don't expect any donations
from me! This month's bills are on you....See you later.
```

The first line that you should make a note of is:

```
cfI cfI     \" Heading format
```

This reads as c + f + I. This is the first column specification line, and so it applies to the first line of data in the table. The first line of data in our source code file is the heading line; hence, this applies to the format of the headings.

The c indicates that the two columns are to be centered. The fI indicates that they are to be italicized.

The second line of the column specification part of the document applies to the remaining columns of data in the table. The important thing to note here is that you can have one format line for each corresponding line of data. If there are fewer format lines than data lines, then the last format specification will apply to the remaining data lines. This is the case in our example.

The next line worthy of note is the heading title:

Item Amount \" Heading title

This line appears as a regular data line. tbl will ignore it, although it is embedded between the .TS and .TE instructions. Here's the output:

_____

Honey, following is a list of the bills that are outstanding for the month of May:

Item	Amount
Telephone	$89.67
Gas and electric	$134.56
Cable TV	$18
Parking	$75
Baby sitter	$60

Honey, I have no more money, so don't expect any donations from me! This month's bills are on you....See you later.

_____

24.7.2 Headings That Span Multiple Columns

Headings can be made to span multiple columns. You can think of this as the title of a table. We display the relevant portion of the source file to illustrate its usage.

```
$ cat tbl_file
Honey, following is a list of the bills that are outstanding for
the month of May:
.sp              \" Insert blank line
.TS              \" Start table
center box tab ( );  \" Specifies field term. is tab
cfI s            \" Indicates a spanned heading
cfI cfI          \" Heading format
1 1 .    \" Specifies 2 columns to be left aligned
\" Table data follow
```

```
Bills Owed
.sp
Item  Amount     \" Heading title
Telephone         $89.67
.sp
.

.
$
```

And here's the output:

Honey, following is a list of the bills that are outstanding for
the month of May:

Bills Owed	
Item	Amount
Telephone	$89.67
Gas and electric	$134.56
Cable TV	$18
Parking	$75
Baby sitter	$60

Honey, I have no more money, so don't expect any donations from
me! This month's bills are on you....See you later.

24.7.3 Specification of Numerical Columns

In case you haven't noticed, the numbers in the table in the sample
output are not aligned. We can specify proper alignment by
changing the format of the data that contain numbers, as follows:

```
l n .
```

The first column continues to be left justified. The second
column is specified to be numeric. Here's the resulting output:

Honey, following is a list of the bills that are outstanding for
the month of May:

Bills Owed	
Item	Amount
Telephone	$89.67
Gas and electric	$134.56
Cable TV	$18
Parking	$75
Baby sitter	$60

Honey, I have no more money, so don't expect any donations from
me! This month's bills are on you....See you later.

24.7.4 Specification of Continuous Text Blocks

Text can span multiple rows within the same cell, simply by typing
the entire field for the required number of rows, without inserting
a tab (or whatever field delimiter there is) in the text.   Here's
sample usage and its resulting output.

```
$ cat tbl_file
Honey, following is a list of the bills that are outstanding for
the month of May:
.sp              \" Insert blank line
.TS              \" Start table
center box tab ( ); \" Specifies field term. is tab
cfI s            \" Indicates a spanned heading
cfI cfI          \" Heading format
l n .            \" Specifies numeric column
\" Table data follow
Bills Owed
.sp
Item Amount      \" Heading title
Telephone        $89.67
.sp
```

—

```
Gas and electric;
this includes the
bill from last
month           $134.56
.sp

Cable TV         $18
.sp

Parking          $75
.sp

Baby sitter      $60
.TE                      \" End table
.sp                      \" Insert blank line
Honey, I have no more money, so don't expect any donations
from me!  This month's bills are on you....See you later.
$
```

Honey, following is a list of the bills that are outstanding for
the month of May:

Bills Owed	
Item	**Amount**
Telephone	$89.67
Gas and electric; this includes the bill from last month.	$134.56
Cable TV	$18
Parking	$75
Baby sitter	$60

Honey, I have no more money, so don't expect any donations from
me! This month's bills are on you....See you later.

24.8 MODIFYING TABLE FORMAT

The format of a table can be changed by inserting T&, followed by instructions and additional data for the modified table, in the necessary location. We modify the original source file and add a few more bills to the list:

```
$ cat tbl_file
```
Honey, following is a list of the bills that are outstanding for the month of May:
```
.sp               \" Insert blank line
.TS               \" Start table
center box tab ( ); \" Specifies field term. is tab
cfI s             \" Specifies spanned heading
cfI cfI           \" Heading format
l n .             \" Specifies numeric column
\" Table data follow
```
Bills Owed
```
.sp
```
Item Amount   \" Heading title
Telephone $89.67
```
.sp
```

Gas and electric;
this includes the
bill from last
month $134.56
```
.sp
```

Cable TV $18
```
.sp
```

Parking $75
```
.sp
```

Baby sitter $60
```
.T&
cfI s
cfI cfI
l n .
```
Some Additional Amounts
```
.sp 1
```
Item   Amount
```
.sp 1
```
Groceries $120.56
Gas/Tolls $32.00
```
.TE               \" End table
.sp               \" Insert blank line
```
Honey, I have no more money, so don't expect any donations

from me! This month's bills are on you....See you later.
$

And here's the resulting output:

Honey, following is a list of the bills that are outstanding for
the month of May:

Bills Owed	
Item	Amount
Telephone	$89.67
Gas and electric, this includes the bill from last month.	$134.56
Cable TV	$18
Parking	$75
Baby sitter	$60
Some Additional Amounts	
Item	Amount
Groceries	$120.56
Gas/Tolls	$32.00

Honey, I have no more money, so don't expect any donations from
me! This month's bills are on you....See you later.

Bourne Shell Implementation

The `tbl` utility behaves the same way, regardless of which shell it
is called from. All examples will produce the same result whether
`tbl` is invoked from the Bourne shell or the C shell.

Korn Shell Implementation

The tbl utility behaves the same way, regardless of which shell it is called from. All examples will produce the same result whether tbl is invoked from the Korn shell or the C shell.

24.9 OSF/1 CONSIDERATIONS

OSF/1 supports the tbl utility, and it produces the same results as in a UNIX environment. All examples will produce similar results when run from one of the available shells in an OSF/1 operating system.

24.10 REVIEW

This chapter described the commands used to output data in columnar format. Table 24.1 summarizes the syntax of the instructions, and provides brief descriptions as well.

Table 24.1 tbl Instructions

Command	Syntax	Description
Start table	.TS	Designates the start of the instructions that specify table format.
End table	.TE	Designates the end of the instructions that specify table format.
Specify field delimiter	tab ( );	Specifies field delimiter is a tab. This entry must end with a semicolon.
Specify table format	l l .	Specifies 2 columns, left aligned.
	r r .	Specifies 2 columns, right aligned.
	c c .	Specifies 2 columns, centered.

Table 24.1 tbl Instructions (Contd.)

Command	Syntax	Description
Enclose table in a box	center box tab( );	Encloses table data inside a box.
Enclose everything in a box	center allbox tab( );	Encloses table data inside a box, and draws lines under each row.
Draw lines between rows	_	Inserts underscore under row that requires a line underneath.
Insert heading	.cfl cfl head1 head2	Instructs tbl to display head1 and head2 as headings. c results in heading being centered. fl results in heading being italicized.
Insert heading spanning multiple columns	.cfl s Spanned heading	Instructs tbl to display Spanned heading over multiple columns.
Display numerical columns as numbers	l n .	Specifies 2 columns; first is left aligned, second is a numerical value.
Display text over multiple rows	- <text spanning multiple lines>	Displays text as typed, over multiple rows.
Modify table format	.T& cfl s Modified format .sp 1 .TE	.T& instructs tbl that all subsequent instructions are modifications to the original format of the table. .TE is the original statement that ends the specification of the table format.

Software Tools/
System Administration

Chapter

25

Software Development Tools

25.1 INTRODUCTION

This chapter covers those topics which are related to application development in a UNIX environment. The following topics will be discussed:

- The C compiler, as it relates to compiling single and multiple files

- Program maintenance using make

- Revision history maintenance using SCCS

It is beyond the scope of this book to cover the items listed in detail. We will give you enough information to get you going. We encourage you to refer to the relevant reference manuals if you require further details.

25.2 THE C COMPILER

Did you know that the UNIX operating system, and almost every tool supplied with this operating system, is written in the C language? That is why C is considered a systems software language. It is beyond the scope of this book to describe the language. We will describe the procedures required to create and compile a C program on the UNIX operating system. Then we will extend our discussion to describe how multiple files containing different parts of the source code for one program are compiled, linked, and executed.

25.2.1 The Compilation Process

There are three steps required to create and run a C program. First, a program must be created and named. A C program can be created via your favorite system editor; most programmers on the UNIX system use vi. Since indentation is so important in C programs, you may wish to set the autoindent shell variable to the number of columns of your choice. C programs must be suffixed with a .c in order for them to be recognized as such.

Once this is created, what you have is called the source code. The next step is to compile this source code. In the example below, the source code file is listed, and then compiled, via the cc option:

```
$ cat file1.c
#include <stdio.h>
main()
{
   printf ("This is file1 \n");
}
$ cc file1.c
$
```

The above command compiles a C program called file1.c. The complete process consists of many steps. A listing of these steps follows:

■ C source code is fed into the C *preprocessor*, which expands shorthand notations and macros contained in the program.

■ Expanded C source code is fed into the *compiler*, which produces assembly language code. C statements are translated into assembly language statements.

■ Assembly language code is passed to the system's *assembler*, which translates it into object code.

■ Object code is passed to the *linker*. The linker links the necessary source code segments and libraries to produce executable code.

■ Now the program can be run, by typing a.out at the system prompt. a.out is the default name for the executable code.

```
$ a.out
This is file1
$
```

If the program had not compiled properly, then the executable a.out would not have been produced. Error messages with reference to the compilation would have displayed, and a corresponding object file only would have been created. Object files are suffixed with a .o; an object file for file1.c would be called file1.o.

25.2.2 Compiling Multiple Source Files

Often C programmers divide their programs into several source files. Suppose one complete program resides in the following files:

```
$ ls file*.c
file1.c    file2.c    file3.c    file4.c
$
```

Then the complete program would be compiled and linked as follows:

```
$ cc file1.c file2.c file3.c file4.c
file1.c
file2.c
file3.c
file4.c
$
```

and it would be run, once again, by typing a.out. Notice that the name of each file is displayed as its compilation is completed.

Suppose file2.c did not compile properly. In that case, file2.c would have to be modified so that it can compile. The next time around, we can take a shortcut, and send the object files of the versions that did compile properly, along with the new version of the source code of the file2.c. Here's the command that would be typed:

```
$ cc file1.o file2.c file3.o file4.o
$
```

What this means for you as an applications developer is that only those segments of a program which have been modified have to be recompiled. All segments need not be recompiled each time.

25.2.3 Options Available With C Compiler

The following options will be described:

■ The −c option

■ The −o option

The −c option is used to produce object code only, and skips the subsequent steps that link and produce the executable file. For example, the following command:

```
$ cc −c file1.c
```

will produce the object code file file1.o:

```
$ ls file1.o
file1.o
$
```

but the executable a.out will not be produced.

The −o option is used to create an executable file with a specified name, instead of a.out. For example, the following command:

```
$ cc −o file1 file1.c
$
```

will result in the executable of file1.c being called file1, instead of a.out. Now typing file1 will result in its being executed. All that file1 does is output the line Hello. This is file1 to the terminal. Here's the command and its output:

```
$ file1
Hello. This is file1.
$
```

25.3 PROGRAM MAINTENANCE USING MAKE UTILITY

The make utility builds up-to-date versions of programs. In the prior section we touched briefly on how sometimes source code is divided across multiple files. This utility is designed to ensure that all components are up to date with one another. If they are not, then make takes appropriate steps.

The basic syntax of the make command looks like this:

```
make -f makefile
```

makefile is called the description file. This file will contain all of the information necessary for make to do its work. However, you can specify all relevant information right on the command line. We will use the -f option and insert all necessary information into a description file.

In addition to this, options, multiple target files, and macros can also be specified. Here's the complete syntax of the make command:

```
make -f makefile options targets macros
```

We will describe these features briefly later on in the chapter.

25.3.1 Basic Operation of the make Utility

The make utility works by comparing the creation date of the program that is to be built with the creation dates of the files that it is composed of. It looks at the time stamps on each file. The file that is to be built is called the *target* file. The files that it is composed of are called the *dependent* files. If the creation date of one or more of the dependent files is later than that of the target, then the files that are out of date are rebuilt. It should be obvious to you from what has just been said that in order for the make utility to work properly, the date and time of all files in the system should be synchronized.

If all files are up to date, then make simply issues a message stating this, and ends execution. There can be more than one target file, just as there can be more than one dependent. Only those targets whose dependents have a newer time stamp are re-created.

25.3.2 The Description File

The *description* file contains the following information:

- List of one or more target files

- List of one or more dependent files

- One or more macro definitions

- One or more commands that create the target files from dependents

The description file is usually called *makefile* or *Makefile*. We will continue our discussion by referencing makefile only. The command make is entered in the directory which contains the description file. If the description file is called makefile, then you do not have to use the −f option, make will automatically look for a file of this name. The −f option is necessary if the makefile is called something else.

The general format of a makefile follows the order listed. First comes the target name. The target name is followed by a colon, which is followed by a list of dependent file names. This is called the dependency line, and is followed by a list of one or more commands that are to be executed to bring the dependent files up to date with the target file. All commands must be indented by one tab character.

You also can (and should) insert comments in the makefile. Comments are inserted by using a number sign (#) followed by a comment. All comments must appear on lines by themselves.

25.3.3 Sample make Description File

Here's a sample makefile:

```
$ cat makefile
# Specify target and dependent files:
source1: file1.o file2.o file3.o
# Specify command to be peformed on them
    cc file*.o -o source1
# Specify next set of target and dependent files,
# and commands to be performed on them:
file1.o: file1.c
    cc -c file1.c
file2.o: file2.c
    cc -c file2.c
```

```
file3.o:  file3.c
   cc -c file3.c
$
```

This very simple make description file shows us that the program source1 depends on three files: file1.o, file2.o, and file3.o. Notice that the list consists of object files only. If any of the time stamps of file1.o, file2.o, or file3.o is more recent than that of source1, then the following command will be performed:

```
cc file*.o -o source1
```

The object files will be recompiled and the new executable will be called source1. Notice that the −o option is necessary in order to explicitly specify the name of the executable. If this option is not utilized, then the executable will be called a.out by default, and we would need to change the name of the target file to a.out instead of source1. Since every C program which is compiled without the −o option produces an a.out file, this make file would present quite a few problems for a.out files produced by other programs.

Notice the use of the asterisk. Metacharacters will be recognized inside make files, and can be used as necessary.

Let's continue with the make file:

```
.
file1.o:  file1.c
   cc -c file1.c
file2.o:  file2.c
   cc -c file2.c
file3.o:  file3.c
   cc -c file3.c
```

Each line will be scanned and executed, if necessary, in the order in which it appears. The target file file1.o is dependent on file1.c. If the time stamp for file1.c is more recent than the time stamp for file1.o, then file1.c will be recompiled. The remaining lines are to be read in the same way.

Now make can be executed to bring all files up to date as follows:

```
$ make
$
```

It was not necessary for us to specify the name of the makefile via the −f option, since it is called makefile. You can create separate makefiles for different projects; in those instances you will require the −f option, since you will need to give these description files different names.

Keep in mind that the make command must be executed from the same directory that the description files reside in.

25.3.4 Available Options with make Utility

We briefly describe two options available with make. Please refer to the appropriate man page for the make utility for other available options. (Type man make|lpr at the system prompt to get a hard copy of the manual pages for this utility.)

■ Do Not Echo option

make echoes back commands as it executes. This default condition can be inhibited by invoking make with the −s option, like this:

```
$ make −s
$
```

Specific commands within the description file can be marked so that make does not echo them as they are executed. Commands are marked by preceding them with an @ sign, like so:

```
@cc −c file1.c
```

If file1.c is recompiled, it will not be echoed at the terminal.

■ Do Not Stop Executing If Error option

The make utility stops executing if an error is encountered in one of the commands that it executes. For example, in the following set of commands:

```
file1.o:  file1.c
   cc −c file1.c
file2.o:  file2.c
   cc −c file2.c
file3.o:  file3.c
   cc −c file3.c
```

make will stop executing if it cannot find file1.c, and subsequent commands that compile file2.c and file3.c will not be executed. We can prevent make from stopping on errors via the −i option:

```
$ make -i
$
```

In addition to this, specific commands within the description file can also be marked so that make continues execution even if an error is encountered for them. Commands are marked by preceding them with a hyphen, like so:

```
-cc -c file1.c
```

25.3.5 Invoking Macros

Macros can be invoked from inside description files. A macro name is simply a shorthand reference to a longer string of characters. Macros will prove useful inside description files if the same set of instructions is to be implemented inside several different make files. A macro is defined as follows:

```
XYZ = file1.c file2.c file3.c file4.c
```

In the example above, XYZ is the name of the macro. The string of characters to the right of the equal sign (=) is what that macro represents.

Macros are invoked inside description files by preceding their name by a dollar sign. If the macro name is longer than one character, then the macro name only must be enclosed within curly brackets. Here's sample usage for the sample makefile created earlier in this chapter:

```
$ cat makefile
# Define macro
FILES = file1.o file2.o file3.o
# Specify target and dependent files using macro:
source1: ${FILES}
# Specify command to be peformed on them
   cc file*.o -o source1
# Specify next set of target and dependent files,
# and commands to be performed on them:
file1.o: file1.c
   cc -c file1.c
file2.o: file2.c
   cc -c file2.c
file3.o: file3.c
   cc -c file3.c
$
```

25.4 REVISION HISTORY MAINTENANCE USING SCCS

SCCS stands for *Source Code Control System*. This system allows you to perform the following tasks:

- Keep track of different versions of programs

- Disallow editing of files that are currently being edited by someone else

- Find out who was the last person who edited a file

- Reconstruct earlier versions of files

As you can see, SCCS is a very valuable utility. It is beyond the scope of this book to describe each feature available with SCCS. We will touch on the main topics, and encourage the reader to refer to the man pages or other documentation for further details.

25.4.1 SCCS Files

SCCS files usually reside on a directory called SCCS. Within this directory you can have the following types of files:

- The g files; these are the original source code files, and are prefixed with a g. For example, if the source file file1 is to be placed into an SCCS directory, it will be called g.file1.

- The s files; these are the modified versions of the files. Modifications can consist of deletions, insertions, or modifications to existing lines. In SCCS, deleted lines are marked, but not physically deleted. Changes are called deltas; all deltas contain text which describes the change made, the reason for it, and the person who made this change. The s file for file1 would be called s.file1. s files also contain the revision and version numbers of files, in that order. This is called an *SID*. For example, revision 1 version 2 of file1 would be identified by SID 1.2.

- The p files; these are the *lock* files. Each time a file is retrieved from SCCS, a lock is placed on it, so that it can be edited by only one person at a time. For example, if file1 is being edited by user1, and user2 tries to access it, then SCCS will inform user2 that the file is currently being edited, and will not deliver the specified copy of the file to him or her.

25.4.2 Information Stamps in SCCS Files

Relevant file identification information should be included in source files via the following syntax:

```
%x%
```

where % is the percent symbol and x is a single letter that has a special meaning for SCCS. Once this syntax is encountered, SCCS expands the keyword and replaces it with relevant information. Some ID keywords and their corresponding substitutions are:

%E%   Creation date of a change in the source file, in yy/mm/dd format

%F%   File name of the s file

%H%   Retrieval date of a source file, in mm/dd/yy format, using the `get` command

%I%   The highest SID number of a file

%M%   Current module name of file

%T%   Retrieval time of a g file, in hh:mm:ss format, using the `get` command

%U%   Creation time of a delta, in hh:mm:ss format

25.4.3 SCCS Commands

The SCCS system allows management of SCCS files via commands. Each command is preceded by the keyword `sccs`. The commands can be followed by one or more options. Following is a list of some commands and their functions, as they apply to `file1`.

Command	Description
`sccs admin file1`	Creates an s file for `file1`.
`sccs check file1`	Checks whether `file1` is being edited by someone else, and who is editing it.

`sccs create file1`	Creates an s file for `file1`, without removing the g file.
`sccs delta file1`	Places the edited g file of `file1` back into the SCCS directory, records changes, and removes the corresponding p file.
`sccs diffs file1`	Compares the latest edited version of the g file of `file1` with the last version.
`sccs edit file1`	Places the s file of `file1` in your directory, for you to edit, and creates a corresponding p file.
`sccs print file1`	Displays SID information for `file1`.
`sccs what file1`	Searches for SCCS ID pattern in `file1` and displays it.

25.4.4 Managing SCCS Files

The overall flow of managing an SCCS system consists of the following steps:

■ Creation of SCCS Directory

A directory needs to be created. By convention this directory is called SCCS. The ownership of this directory should be changed to the SCCS user ID. (This will be the group ID assigned to all users who are allowed to access the SCCS directory.) The permission set of this directory should be set so that non-SCCS users are unable to access it.

■ Placement of Files in SCCS Directory

The next step is to place files in that directory. The sccs create command can be used to create the s files and place them into the SCCS directory. Here's sample usage:

```
$ sccs create file1

file1
1.1
56 lines
$
```

SCCS displays the current revision and version number of the file, along with the total number of lines.

■ Retrieval of Files from SCCS Directory for Editing

Files can be retrieved for editing from SCCS via the `sccs edit` command. Here's sample usage:

```
$ sccs edit file1
1.1
new delta 1.2
56 lines
$
```

Notice the message `new delta 1.2`. This indicates that once `file1` is edited, it will be stored back into SCCS as revision 1, version 2.

■ Retrieval of Files from SCCS Directory, Not for Editing

Files can be retrieved for viewing or whatever, but not editing, via the `sccs get` command. Here's sample usage:

```
$ sccs get file1
1.1
56 lines
$
```

■ Placing Edited Files Back into SCCS

Once files have been edited, they can be placed back into SCCS via the `sccs delta` command. Here's sample usage:

```
$ sccs delta file1
Comments? Added code to check for device type "A".
1.2
15 inserted
3 deleted
53 unchanged
$
```

Notice how SCCS relates relevant statistics for the changes incurred.

Bourne Shell Implementation

All commands described in this chapter work in the same way, regardless of which shell they are invoked from. All examples will produce the same output if implemented from the Bourne shell.

Korn Shell Implementation

All examples will produce the same output if implemented from the Korn shell.

25.5 OSF/1 CONSIDERATIONS

All utilities described in this chapter are also supported by OSF/1. All examples will produce the same results when run from any of the supported shells running in an OSF/1 environment.

25.6 REVIEW

This chapter described support tools that are useful for software developers in a UNIX environment. The following tools were described:

- The C compiler.

The C compiler is invoked as follows:

```
$ cc file1.c
```

It can be invoked with the following options:

-c   This results in only object code being produced. Files are suffixed with a .o.

-o   This results in executable files being created of the specified name, as opposed to the default name (which is a.out on most UNIX systems).

■ The make utility.

The make utility is used to build up-to-date versions of programs. Commands that are to be executed are by convention stored inside a file called makefile.

This utility works by comparing the time stamp of the program that is to be built with the time stamps of the files that it is composed of. If there is a discrepancy, then the file is rebuilt via the instructions in makefile.

The description file is called the makefile. The target file is the file to be built. The dependent files are the files the target file is composed of. Target files are separated from dependent files by a colon (:). Commands inside makefile must be preceded by a tab.

make can be invoked with the following options:

−s   This results in commands not being echoed back to the terminal as they are executed.

−i   This results in make continuing to execute, even if it encounters an error.

Macros can be invoked inside makefile by defining a macro name equal to the dependent files, and inserting this name inside brackets.

■ SCCS utility.

The SCCS utility is used to maintain revision history. SCCS creates the following types of files:

g files   These files are the original source code files, and are prefixed with a g. Keep in mind that the dot at the end of the g is part of the prefix!

s files   These files are the modified versions of the source, and are prefixed with an s.

p files   These are the lock files, created if one of the sources is being edited by a user. They are prefixed by a p.

All SCCS source code files should contain SCCS ID keywords, which supply relevant information in the file. ID keywords are enclosed within % symbols.

The main steps involved in an SCCS system are:

- Creation of SCCS directory
- Placement of files in SCCS directory via `sccs create` command
- Retrieval of files for editing via `sccs edit` command
- Retrieval of files for review via `sccs get` command
- Placement of files back into SCCS via `sccs delta` command

- All utilities described in this chapter are also supported by the OSF/1 operating system. All examples presented will produce the same result in an OSF/1 operating system.

# Chapter 26

System Administration Basics

26.1 INTRODUCTION

System administration tasks consist of maintenance of the day-to-day running of the UNIX system. In this chapter we cover the fundamentals of system administration. The following topics will be discussed:

- Starting up the system

- Shutting down the system

- Managing the file system

- Adding users and groups to the system

- Removing users and groups from the system

The next chapter will cover the following topics, which are also related to system administration:

- Backing up the system

- Restoring the system

- Printer-related commands

- File integrity check commands

As you read this chapter, please note that the *superuser* is usually in charge of system administration tasks. The superuser logs in as su (root is sometimes used instead), and he/she has paramount permissions which supersede all others. Most of the commands that you will encounter in this chapter, therefore, will work only if you are logged in as the superuser.

In addition to this, keep in mind that many current UNIX systems provide menus and forms that implement the same tasks. You may never need to go through the sequence of events outlined in this chapter. Your specific menu should guide you each step of the way.

26.2 STARTING UP THE SYSTEM

Every installation comes with a manual that gives you step-by-step instructions on how to install the system. Since each vendor has its own method (although the set of instructions always follows the same lines), we cannot inform you exactly how to start up your system. But here are a few guidelines.

26.2.1 Media

The first thing that the manual will instruct you to do is insert the *media* into the appropriate slot. The media is what you use to install your system. Some examples of media would be tapes, floppy disks, etc. Therefore, if, for instance, your media is tape, make sure you understand the procedure for properly inserting, rewinding, and setting the tape on-line.

26.2.2 Boot-Up, Manual and Automatic

Once the software has been properly installed (it will inform you of this), you are now ready to *boot* it up. By *boot-up* is meant the set of tasks that are automatically initiated in order for the system to operate properly. The system can boot up automatically or manually. Automatic boot normally takes place if the system dies and recovers. At automatic boot, the system initiates the entire operation without any input from you, until it succeeds or fails. If it fails, in all likelihood, you have to perform a manual boot-up.

On manual boot-up, the system initiates a set of tasks, and expects input from the user before it continues with the boot.

26.2.3 Multiuser/Single-User Mode

The UNIX operating system can be booted up in *single-user* or *multiuser* mode. In single-user mode, with most installations, you get only a partial system. What this means is that you are able to derive only some of the capabilities of the UNIX operating system. Only the root file system is mounted (more on this later), and many essential programs are not started up. The reason for booting up in single-user mode would be to perform those tasks that should not be performed while there are other users logged on to the system.

In multiuser mode, the system automatically performs most of the functions for you: it starts up the necessary programs, configures, allocates resources, etc. It also reads a file which is usually located in the /etc directory. This file is called inittab. This file contains instructions that help it mount the necessary file systems, formulate links, set up the printer spooler and daemons (more on daemons later), and more.

You can also boot up in multiuser mode from single-user mode. Please refer to the appropriate documentation supplied with the system for further details.

26.2.4 Basic/Advanced Installation

In order for a boot operation to be successful, you must follow the instructions that appear on the screen explicitly. Sometimes an advanced installation (as opposed to the basic installation) may be required in order to load all of the utilities that are available with the system. Don't let the word *advanced* scare you away. Just follow the instructions, try to have the hardware specialists at your installation answer hardware-related questions (such as the name of slots in your machine, connected device names, etc.) that the system may ask you, and proceed with confidence. If worst comes to worst, all you have to do is restart, and this time call the vendor for support!

We recommend that you try to implement an advanced installation. It should take no more than a few hours, and you will probably be surprised at how easy it really is, as long as you know how to fill in some of the blanks (i.e., questions it asks along the way)!

26.2.5 Setting System Date

As you boot up, the system will ask you to enter the date and time. It is imperative that you answer the set of questions related to this function as accurately as possible, because a lot of procedures rely on computer time! The system may ask you questions such as what time zone you are located in (Eastern, Central, Mountain, Pacific), whether daylight saving time is in effect, and so on. If you do make a mistake, you can always run the date command to reset the time. Input to the date command is in this format:

    mmddhhmm.ssyy

where mm is the month, dd is the day, hh is the hour, mm is the minutes, . is the delimiter, ss is the seconds, and yy is the year.

Here's sample usage:

```
# date 05261530.0092
#
```

The above command sets the date and time to May 26, 15:30 hours, 00 seconds, 1992. Notice that the superuser system prompt (#) is displayed here.

26.3 SHUTTING DOWN THE SYSTEM

The system is usually shut down periodically for a number of reasons, such as upgrade of software, reconfiguration of disk partitions, examination of hardware-generated errors, file system corruption, etc. This section describes the general procedure to be followed in order to implement a controlled shutdown of the system.

26.3.1 Warn Users

Unless you know how to handle a group of very angry users, we suggest that you use one of the electronic mail utilities available with the UNIX system to inform users of the day, time, and possible duration of the shutdown of the system.

The shutdown command which is used to shut down the system can also be used to issue a warning. We discuss this program next.

26.3.2 The shutdown Program

The shutdown program performs a set of functions that results in an orderly closing down of all running system processes. The final task performed by this program is that it halts the processor, and what you have then is a machine without an operating system to run it. You have to reboot the system in order to restart it.

The shutdown program can be run with a variety of options. Its basic syntax is as follows:

```
shutdown options time message
```

The following options are available:

- -h   This option results in the system being shut down as indicated, and the processor being halted.

- -r   This option results in the system being shut down and then automatically rebooted.

The time field indicates the number of minutes from the current time that the shutdown will commence. The number must be preceded by a plus sign. Generally, 10 minutes is a fair number; it allows users to make last-minute changes and save any files that they may be editing. One minute sounds a little unfair; you can expect your unpopularity to soar a little bit!

message is a warning message that shutdown will issue to all users of the system at the time that you issue this command. Although users may not be doing much work at the time that you issue a shutdown command, you can expect a long string of complaints in response to your warning message; nobody likes system down time. We suggest that you be diplomatic about this situation, and issue a shutdown after or before hours.

In order to run the shutdown program, you have to log in as root and change to the root directory. Here's sample usage:

```
# cd \
# shutdown -h +10 System Shutting Down in 10 Minutes!!!
#
```

shutdown can also be run without the options. In this case, the system disables multiuser mode and places you in single-user mode. Here's sample usage:

```
# shutdown +10 System Shutting Down for Maintenance Reasons!
```

The system can be rebooted in multiuser mode after necessary maintenance tasks have been implemented.

26.3.3 Immediate Shutdown

A system can be shut down and processors halted immediately as follows:

```
# shutdown -h now
```

No warning messages are issued.

26.4 MANAGING THE FILE SYSTEM

In Chapter 3, "UNIX File Structure," we introduced you to the concept of file systems. In Chapter 6, "UNIX Directories and Metacharacters," we took you for a little tour of the UNIX directories and their contents. A *file system* is the structure in which directories and files are created and maintained in a system. It consists of directories on device partitions. Consider a structure to be a uniform pattern in which all files in a system are stored and maintained.

It is beyond the scope of this book to go into much detail with reference to the UNIX file system. Consider this section as a useful guide to topics that you may wish to explore in greater detail on your own. Refer to your system manual for further details.

26.4.1 UNIX File Systems

Most UNIX operating systems support the UNIX File System (UFS) and Network File System (NFS). Additional file systems can be and probably are supported. Each file system is differentiated from the next in its path, conventions, and limitations.

26.4.2 Basic Structure

File systems are universal in their structure. They contain:

■ Block 0, called the *boot* block. This is reserved for the initialization program.

■ Block 1, called the *superblock*. This contains quantitative and information statistics, such as its size, name, identification, and more.

■ A group of blocks following block 1, and are called *i-node* blocks. These blocks describe relevant information (such as owner, type, permission sets, etc.) about files in the file system. There is a correspondence between each file and its i-node block. The number of files in a file system is limited by the number of i-node blocks in it.

■ A count of the number of *links* or *references* to other files that this file forms.

As indicated in prior chapters, the UNIX file system is *hierarchical* in structure, like an upside down tree. All directories branch from root, which is at the *root* of it all. We refer you to Chapter 6 for an overview of the general contents of the directories within a UNIX operating system.

26.4.3 Special Files Used in Configuring File Systems

It is beyond the scope of this book to describe how to configure file systems. However, we describe some files that are used for configuration.

■ /etc/disktab

This file contains a list of names of disks and default partition sizes for the file system. A disk is composed of sectors, which are blocks that are capable of holding information. Sectors are grouped together to form partitions. This file is read by the newfs command, which is used to create file systems on disks.

■ /etc/fstab

This file contains device and disk partition information for the location of a file system, the mount point, the file system type, and more. It is read by the mount and umount commands, which are used to attach and remove file systems from existing directories. The order of the entries is important, since mounting and unmounting are performed in that order.

26.4.4 Special Commands Used to Manage File Systems

The following commands will be described briefly.

- `mount`

This command is used to mount file systems. Its syntax looks like this:

`mount options fs_name mount_point`

The following options can be used:

`-a`   Use of this option results in all file systems listed in `/etc/fstab` being mounted.

`-r`   This options mounts the file system as read only.

`-u`   This option changes the file system from read only to read/write.

`-l`   Use of this option results in the display of all file system options.

The `fs_name` is the name of the file system to be mounted.
The `mount_point` is the directory path on which the file system is to be mounted.
Refer to the `/etc/fstab` file at your installation for information corresponding to the options just described.

- `umount`

This command is used to unmount file systems. Its syntax looks like this:

`umount options mount_point`

The following option is one of many:

`-a`   Use of this option results in all currently mounted file systems being unmounted.

Please refer to the explanation for `mount_point` in the description of the `mount` command.

■ df

This command is used to check available disk space for all currently mounted file systems. Its syntax looks like this:

    df options file –names systems

The following options can be used:

–i   Use of this option results in a list of all available i-nodes.

–n   Use of this option results in previously obtained statistics for all mounted file systems being displayed.

    `file –names` are the names of files. Use of this option results in used disk space for the file name specified being displayed.

    `systems` are names of file systems. Use of this option results in available disk space for the file system specified being displayed.

26.5 ADDING USERS AND GROUPS TO THE SYSTEM

Entries have to be added to two files when a user or group is added to the system. These files are:

■ The `group` file

■ The `passwd` file

    We will first describe the contents of these files. Then we will describe how groups and users can be added manually and via the `adduser` program.

26.5.1 The group File

This file contains the names of the available groups that users can belong to. There are four fields for each line in this file, in this order:

■ The name of the group.

- The password of the user who belongs to that group. If an asterisk is placed in this field, this entry is ignored until a password has been assigned. This field is ignored as long as there is an asterisk in it.

- The ID number assigned to that group.

- The names of one or more users who belong to that group. If there are multiple users, then each name is separated from the next by a comma.

Each field in this file is separated by a colon, and each line ends in a carriage return. All four fields must exist in each line. If any user defined in this file has not ben assigned a password, then an asterisk will be placed in that field. Here's a sample group file:

```
# cat /etc/group
system:*:0:root,su,jackie
admin:*:4:root,ron,billy
acctg:*:10:sally,harry,gary,zamir
#
```

The first line of the group file just displayed indicates that the name of the group is system, the group ID is 0, and the users who belong to this group are root, su, and jackie. All subsequent lines of this file should be read accordingly.

26.5.2 The passwd File

The passwd file identifies pertinent information for each user of the system. This file contains seven entries for each line:

- The name of the user.

- The password assigned to this user. This field cannot be manually edited. It is automatically entered via the passwd command. However, you can enter an asterisk here, so as to prevent other users from accessing this account. Once a password has been assigned to a user, it will be entered here and encrypted; not even user root or the superuser can decrypt it. If this field is left blank, then all users will be able to log into that account!

- The ID number assigned to that user. This number must be unique for each user. ID number 0 is conventionally reserved for user name `root`.

- The group ID number assigned to that user. Group ID number 0 is conventionally reserved for group name `system`.

- The fifth field is free format. It can contain any kind of information about that user.

- The next field identifies the login directory that the user will be placed in automatically when he or she logs into the system.

- The last field shows the shell to be run when the user logs on.

As in the `group` file, each entry in `passwd` is also separated by a colon, and each line ends with a carriage return. Here's a sample `passwd` file:

```
# cat /etc/passwd
root:Ajl56Ui5670dD:0:0:ABSOLUTE SUPER USER:/:/bin/csh
zamir:*:2:10:ACCOUNTING USER:/usr/home/zamir:/bin/csh
#
```

We display only two lines in this file, but keep in mind that this file will contain one entry for each user of the system. The first entry shows a user called `root`, the next field is root's password encrypted, the user ID is 0, the group ID is 0, the next field is the free format field, the login directory is `root`, and the default shell is set to the C shell. The next line should be read in the same way. Make a note of the asterisk in the password field. This field will be automatically updated when a password is added for this user via the `passwd` command.

26.5.3 Adding Groups to the System Manually

You should be familiar with the concept of a *group*. It identifies the grouping of users. Groups are important, since varying permissions can be given to different groups, and thereby system security can be enhanced as necessary. For example, the group called `admin` can contain entries for a group of users who can perform system administration tasks, while the group called `acctg` could be a group of users who are allowed to access accounting-specific applications that may reside on only one directory. These users are not allowed to access the system directories.

In order to add a group to the system, an entry has to be added to the `group` file in the specified format. Keep in mind that you have to be logged in as `root` in order to modify this file. The `group` file can be edited using `vi`. Once an entry has been added in the `group` file for specific users, the `passwd` file has to be edited to add that group ID to the corresponding user accounts.

26.5.4 Adding Users to the System Manually

In order to add or update information for a user, the `passwd` file has to be edited. Keep in mind that you have to be logged in as `root` if you want to modify this file. The `vipw` command is used to edit this file, and it invokes the `vi` editor by default. Using this command in place of `vi` has the advantage of locking this file while it is being edited. An entry has to be added to this file in order to add a user, and existing entries should be modified to include any additional information, such as new groups, etc. Once an entry has been added, the `passwd` command should be run for this user.

26.5.5 Running the passwd Command

Run the `passwd` command for a user who requires one. Here's sample usage:

```
# passwd zamir
Changing passwd for zamir.
New password: xxxxxx
Retype new password: xxxxxx
#
```

Various systems have different rules for passwords. Some may require that there be at least one uppercase letter in it. The password typed will not be echoed back on the terminal. Most installations require that it be at least six characters long. The responses to `New password` and `Retype new password` must be identical, in order for the system to accept the input. Once this command has been run successfully, take a look at the `passwd` file again. Notice that there is a encrypted password in the location that used to contain an asterisk.

Once the `passwd` command has been run, all that is required is the creation of the home directory for the user just added to the system.

26.5.6 Creation of Home Directory

The *home* directory is the default directory that is specified in the passwd file (the sixth field). Different installations have varying rules for the path of the user directories. We assume that all user directories are to be created on /usr/home.

Create a home directory for the user added to the system as follows:

- Change to the specified path:

  # cd /usr

- Change the ownership of the user's group directory to the group that the user belongs to, so that all users in that group have access to it. Ownership of a group is changed via the chgrp command:

  # chgrp acctg_dir acctg

  Please note that you must be in the parent directory of the directory being operated on in order for this and subsequent commands listed to execute.

- Change the permissions of the directory as required. For example, if you wish to give read, write, and execute permission to the group, and read permission only to all other users, this is what you would do:

  # chmod 744 acctg_dir

- Create the user directory. By convention, this directory has the same name as the user:

  # mkdir zamir
  #

- Change the group of this directory to the required group for this user:

  # chgrp acctg zamir

- Change the ownership of this directory to the user name. The chown command is used to change ownership. Here's sample usage:

```
# chown zamir zamir
```

- And last but not least, change the permissions of the directory just created as necessary. We prefer to have read, write and execute permission for the user, and read and execute permission only for the group and all other users:

```
# chmod 755 zamir
```

26.5.7 Adding Groups and Users Automatically via adduser

The adduser utility can be used to automatically perform most of the tasks just outlined. Specifically, it adds an entry for the user to the passwd file, updates the group file for that user, sets up the home directory with the corresponding startup files (.login and .cshrc for the C shell; .profile for the Bourne and Korn shells), and also sets up a mail file directory (/var/spool/mail), which is used to store mail messages in (read the appendix for further details on the mail facilities available with UNIX). All of this information is derived from the responses that are entered to the questions asked when this utility is run. Here's sample usage:

```
# adduser
New login name: zamir
User full name: Saba Zamir
User login group ? acctg
Another group that 'zamir' should be a member of. <CR for none>
Base directory for 'zamir' : /usr/home
User zamir added.
#
```

26.6 REMOVING GROUPS AND USERS FROM THE SYSTEM

In order to remove a group, delete the required entry from /etc/group using vi. Then, use vipw to edit out the corresponding group IDs from /etc/passwd.

In order to remove a user, delete the required entry from the /etc/passwd file using vipw. Then, use the rmdir commands to remove the corresponding directory. Or, use the rm -r command to recursively remove all files and subdirectories that may exist in that directory. Here's sample usage:

```
# rm -r /usr/home/zamir
```

Also, use the same command to remove the corresponding mail file directory:

```
# rm -r /var/spool/mail/zamir
```

Bourne Shell Implmentation

All commands described in this chapter will work the same way when implemented from the Bourne shell environment.

Korn Shell Implementation

All commands described in this chapter will work the same way when implemented from the Korn shell environment.

26.7 OSF/1 CONSIDERATIONS

All procedures and utilities described in this chapter are supported by OSF/1. All commands described will work the same way and produce the same output.

26.8 REVIEW

In this chapter we described some commands that implement basic system administration tasks. The following topics were discussed:

- A system can be booted up manually or automatically by following documented instructions.

- A UNIX system can be booted up in single-user or multiuser mode.

- A basic or an advanced installation can be implemented.

- A system can be shut down via the shutdown program. shutdown can be used with the following options:

-h   This option results in the processor being halted.

-r   This option results in the system being rebooted
       automatically after shutdown.

- The `/etc/disktab` file contains a list of system disks and
  default partition sizes.

- The `/etc/fstab` file contains device and disk partition
  information.

- The `mount` command is used to mount file systems.

- The `umount` command is used to dismount file systems.

- Groups can be added to the system by modifying the
  `/etc/group` file.

- Users can be added to the system by editing the `/etc/passwd`
  file.

- The `adduser` utility can be used to add groups and users
  automatically.

- Groups and users can be removed from the system by deleting
  their corresponding entries from the `group` and `passwd` files.

System Administration
Maintenance Tasks

27.1 INTRODUCTION

The following topics will be discussed in this chapter:

- Backup commands

- `restore` commands

- Printer-related commands

- File integrity check commands

27.2 BACKUP COMMANDS

All directories and files in a system should be backed up periodically, in case of inadvertent file loss, system crashes, etc. System files (that is, those files which are responsible for the smooth operation of the operating system) are generally static; their contents do not change. These files can be backed up only once. User data files are dynamic, and these should be backed up on a regular basis. If daily backups are made, then they should be maintained for at least a month. End of the month backups should be maintained for the course of a year.

Directories should be set up in such a way that the static files are grouped together on file systems that are backed up occasionally and dynamic files are on file systems that are backed up regularly.

Full backups can be implemented, in addition to incremental backups. Full backups are those in which all files in the system are saved. Incremental backups are those in which only those files which have been modified since the last backup are saved . The schedule set up for backups should be adhered to.

The following commands can be used to implement backups:

- `dump`

- `tar`

A discussion follows of each command.

27.2.1 The dump Command

The `dump` command can be used to implement full and partial backups. Backups are stored on the default device. This device varies with each installation. You will need to check the system documentation or with your system administrator for the default setting at your installation. Here's the syntax of this command:

`dump options file_system`

Only one `file_system` path can be specified. In order to back up three file systems or directory paths, `dump` will need to be run three times. For this reason, it is common for `dump` commands to be written to shell script files, which are then executed as per the predefined backup schedule.

The following options can be used.

- An integer number from 0 to 9

The number 0 is used to implement a full dump of the specified directory path. Here's sample usage:

`# dump 0 /usr/home`

The command above performs a full backup of /usr/home.

All subsequent numbers perform incremental backups. Each level performs an incremental backup relative to the prior level. For example, a level 2 backup will be implemented for all files that have changed since the last level 1 backup. Here's sample usage:

```
# dump 1 /usr/home
```

The command above performs an incremental backup of /usr/home for all files that have changed since the last level 0 backup.

- The −f option, followed by the name of a file

This writes the dump to the device specified by dump_file, instead of the default device. Here's sample usage:

```
# dump −0f /etc /dev/f01
```

The command above dumps the entire /etc directory to the device /dev/f01. Notice how the 0 option is combined with −f.

- The −u option

The use of this option results in the /etc/dumpdates file being updated to record the time and dump level of the current dump. This file is referenced each time an incremental backup is requested, to determine the last level dump implemented. It can be edited manually, if necessary, using any of the UNIX system editors. Here's sample usage:

```
# dump −0u /bin
```

The above command performs a full backup of /bin directory, and records in /etc/dumpdates that a level 0 backup of /bin has been implemented, along with the current system time.

Bourne Shell Implementation

The dump command works in the same way, regardless of which shell it is invoked from. Hence, all examples presented in this chapter will produce the same results when run from the Bourne shell.

Korn Shell Implementation

The dump command works in the same way when invoked from the Korn shell as from the C and Bourne shells. All examples will produce the same result.

27.2.2 The tar Command

The name `tar` is an abbreviation of tape archive. This command is used to perform backups in specified formats. It also writes informative headers to the device which is used for the backup, and performs *checksums* (checks the integrity of the data copied). Here's the syntax:

```
tar options files
```

As you can see, the `tar` command is not restricted to just one file system or directory path. Multiple individual files can be specified as arguments to it. `tar` is usually not used for backup purposes. It is better suited for copying a directory from one system and installing it on another. `tar` is also often used to install new software on a system. The following options can be used.

- The c option

This informs `tar` that the current backup is a new archive. Here's sample usage:

 # tar c /dev/f01

The command above performs a backup of the `root` directory to the device /dev/f01.

- The f option

This specifies that the argument name or names that follow it belong to a file. Here's sample usage:

 # tar f /dev/f01 *.doc

`tar` is instructed to back up all files that end with .doc and start with zero or more characters to the device /dev/f01.

- The t option

This is used to list the table of contents of the files archived previously. Here's sample usage:

```
# tar tf /dev/f01
product_a.doc
product_b.doc
```

```
.
<Other files>
.
#
```

As you can see, the complete list of files on the device /dev/f01 is displayed.

■   **The v option**

This instructs tar to be verbose in its execution. Normally, tar outputs no messages as it executes.

■   **The x option**

Files stored on devices (for example, tapes) can be extracted via the x option. Here's sample usage:

```
# tar xf /dev/f01 *.doc
```

The above command extracts all files that start with zero or more characters and end with .doc to the directory from which the command is run.

The directory name (and path, if necessary) can also be specified explicitly:

```
# tar xf /dev/f01 *.doc zamir
```

tar is instructed to extract all files on /dev/f01 that end with .doc and restore them to zamir directory.

If the path is specified explicitly, then tar stores it in the archive in exactly the same way. For example, the following command:

```
# tar f /dev/f01 /usr/zamir/*.doc
```

will result in all files that end in .doc in /usr/zamir being stored on /dev/f01, with the path name /usr/zamir preceding the name. Now if you need to retrieve, say, product_a.doc, the complete path has to be specified, because this is how it was archived. This is how the tar command would be specified:

```
# tar xf /dev/f01 /usr/zamir/product_a.doc
```

The above command will result in usr/zamir/product_a.doc being restored to the directory that tar is run from.

Bourne Shell Implementation

The tar command works in the same way, regardless of which shell it is invoked from. Hence, all examples presented in this chapter will produce the same results when run from the Bourne shell.

Korn Shell Implementation

The tar command works in the same way when invoked from the Korn shell as from the C and Bourne shells. All examples will produce the same result.

27.3 THE RESTORE COMMAND

The restore command is used to restore file systems or files stored via the dump utility. Following is its syntax.

```
restore options
```

The following options can be used.

■ The −r option

This option is used to restore the entire contents of the file system stored to a device via the dump command. First, you must change to the directory that the file system is to be restored to via the cd command. Then, issue this command. Here's sample usage:

```
# cd /bin
# restore −r
```

The above command restores the entire contents of the file system stored to the /bin directory.

■ The −x option

This option is followed by the names of one or more files and/or directories that are to be restored. If files are specified, then they must be preceded by a dot and forward slash (./). Here's usage:

```
# restore -x ./file1
# restore -x ./dir_1
```

The first command restores `file1` from the default device, and the second command restores the directory `dir_1`. If `dir_1` contains subdirectories, then they will all be recursively restored.

■ The `-f` option

This option is followed by the name of a device and is used to specify that the dump is to be restored from this device name, instead of from the default. Here's sample usage:

```
# restore -f /dev/f12
```

The above command restores all files from the device `/dev/f12`, instead of from the default device. As noted previously, the default device name is installation-specific. Refer to your system documentation or talk to your system administrator for further information.

■ The `-t` option

This option is used to list a table of contents of the files stored to tape via the `dump` command. Once issued, it can be used to ascertain exactly which files or file systems are to be restored. Here's sample usage:

```
# restore -t
```

The system responds with a complete listing of files stored. You can also follow the `-t` option with the names of specific files or directories, in order to see if they are stored on that tape. Here's sample usage:

```
# restore -t /usr/zamir/if_script
# restore -t /usr/zamir
```

The first command will list `if_script` if it exists on the tape. The second command will list the entire contents of `/usr/zamir` only. There may or may not be other directories stored on this tape.

- The −i option

This option is used to interactively restore contents stored to tape via the dump command. restore invokes an interactive interface with you, allowing you to specify the specific files that you would like to be restored. Here's sample usage:

```
# restore -i /usr/zamir
```

The system will respond with the name of each file contained in /usr/zamir directory, and expects a response of y from the user before a file is restored.

Bourne Shell Implementation

The restore command works in the same way, regardless of which shell it is invoked from. Hence, all examples presented in this chapter will produce the same results when run from the Bourne shell.

Korn Shell Implementation

The restore command works in the same way when invoked from the Korn shell as from the C and Bourne shells. All examples will produce the same result.

27.4 PRINTER-RELATED COMMANDS

You have encountered use of the lpr command throughout this book. In this section we will describe some of the facilities associated with printing. The following topics will be discussed:

- The /etc/printcap file

- The printer spooling directories

- Examination of print jobs in printer queue

- Removal of print jobs in printer queue

27.4.1 The /etc/printcap File

This file contains entries for each printer in the UNIX system.

27.4.2 The Printer Spooling Directories

Each printer must have its own directory that will contain the files that are sent to it for printing. This directory must have the same name as the printer. These directories are usually created under /usr/spool/lpd.

In each of these directories are two files that control the printing of a file: the *status* file and the *lock* file. The status file contains information with reference to the current printer status. The lock file contains information about the current file that is being printed.

27.4.3 Examination of Printer Jobs in Printer Queue

The lpq command is used to examine existing jobs scheduled in the printer queue. Its syntax is like this:

```
lpq options
```

Use of the lpq command without the options results in the contents of the default printer's spooling queue being displayed. Here's sample usage:

```
# lpq
Rank       Owner       Job       Files           Total Size
active     zamir       10        acctg1.doc      12450 bytes
1st        sirvent     11        letter.rvw      15678 bytes
#
```

An explanation of the title at the top of each column follows.

```
Rank
```

This column lists the order in which files sent to the printer queue will be printed. The word *active* implies that this file is currently being printed.

```
Owner
```

This column lists the owner of the print request, or the user who issued the request.

```
Job
```

This is the job identification number assigned to the print request.

```
Files
```

This is the name of the file that is being printed.

```
Total Size
```

This is the size of the file in bytes.

Now a description of the options that can be used with the `lpq` command is presented.

- The -P option

This option is followed by a printer name, and is used to obtain information about the specified printer instead of the default printer. Here's sample usage:

```
# lpq -Paccounting
Rank    Owner     Job  Files          Total Size
active  ranade    12   acctg3.doc     750 bytes
1st     raphael   13   review.doc     678 bytes
#
```

The above command is used to display the printer queue status information for the printer named `accounting`. (Maybe this printer is designated for the accounting department.)

- Job ID

This option can be used to request information about a specified print request by the job identification number assigned to it. Here's sample usage:

```
# lpq 12
Rank    Owner     Job     Files         Total Size
active  ranade    12      acctg3.doc    750 bytes
#
```

■ User name

Print status requests can also be issued via the name of the user
issuing them. Here's sample usage:

```
# lpq ranade
Rank     Owner      Job   Files        Total Size
active   ranade     12    acctg3.doc   750 bytes
1st      ranade     15    acctg4.doc    756 bytes
#
```

   Apparently, user name `ranade` has issued two print requests
to the default printer.

Bourne Shell Implementation

The `lpq` command works in the same way, regardless of which shell
it is invoked from. Hence, all examples presented in this chapter
will produce the same results when run from the Bourne shell.

Korn Shell Implementation

The `lpq` command works in the same way when invoked from the
Korn shell as from the C and Bourne shells. All examples will
produce the same result.

27.4.4 Removal of Print Jobs from the Printer Queue

The `lprm` command is used to remove print jobs from the spooling
queue. There could be several reasons for the use of this command:
maybe the wrong file name was supplied as an argument to the `lpr`
command, maybe the file being printed is too long, maybe it is a
nonprintable file (an executable binary file), and so on.
   Only the user who issued the print request can remove it from
the queue. However, there is an exception to this rule. The
superuser can remove any print job, regardless of the user issuing
the request. In the examples that follow we will assume that the
user who issued the print request is also the one issuing the `lprm`
command.
   The syntax of `lprm` is as follows:

```
lprm options
```

Use of the `lprm` command without any options results in the currently active print job issued by the user to the default printer being removed from the print queue.

The following options can be used:

■ The -P option

This option is followed by the printer name, and results in print jobs being removed from the printer queue for the printer name specified instead of the default printer. Here's sample usage:

\# **lprm -Paccounting**

The command above results in all print requests to the printer called `accounting` being removed.

■ The - option

This option is used to remove all print jobs invoked by the user issuing this command.

\# **whoami**
zamir
\# **lpr file1 file2**
\# **lprm -**

The above command will result in the print requests for `file1` and `file2` issued by the user `zamir` being removed from the default printer queue.

■ Job ID

The job ID can be specified to remove specific jobs from the printer queue. Keep in mind that you must be the user who issued these print requests in the first place. Here's sample usage:

\# **lprm 12**

The above command will result in the print request which was assigned job identification number 12 being removed from the printer queue.

■ User name

Print requests can also be cancelled by user name. Here's sample usage:

```
# lprm zamir
#
```

The above command will result in all print requests issued by zamir being cancelled from the printer queue.

Bourne Shell Implementation

The lprm command works in the same way, regardless of which shell it is invoked from. Hence, all examples presented in this chapter will produce the same results when run from the Bourne shell.

Korn Shell Implementation

The lprm command works in the same way when invoked from the Korn shell as from the C and Bourne shells. All examples will produce the same result.

27.5 FILE INTEGRITY CHECK COMMANDS

This section describes commands that are used to check the integrity of file systems, files, and the group and passwd files. The following commands will be described:

- File system integrity check command: fsck

- The group file check command: grpck

- The passwd file check command: pwck

We now take time out to review the structure of the file system, described in Chapter 26. File systems contain:

- Block 0, which is called the *boot* block.

- Block 1, which is called the *super* block and contains statistical and quantitative information for that file system.

- *I-node* blocks, which follow block 1. An i-node block contains information about the owner, type, permissions, etc. of a file in the file system. Each i-node block corresponds to a file in that file system.

- A count of the number of *links* or *references* to other files that this file has.

Based on the description of the file system just listed, the following discrepancies can occur:

- Block 0 or 1 can be missing from the system.

- More than one i-node block could reference the same file.

- A file can exist as a stand-alone.

The `fsck` and `icheck` commands are designed to check the integrity of the file system based on the items just listed.

In addition to this, as also described in Chapter 26, the superuser has the capability to edit the `group` and `passwd` commands. The `grpck` and `pwck` commands verify the accuracy of the entries in these files.

We now describe the usage of each of these commands.

27.5.1 The fsck Command

The `fsck` command performs a file system check. This command is often inserted in a shell script that is executed on boot-up of the system. It is beyond the scope of this book to give complete details of the working of this command. We refer you to the appropriate system administrator's manual for further information. We will, however, give you enough guidance so that you understand what is going on.

`fsck` performs its work in several phases. Here's sample usage:

```
# /etc/fsck
* * Phase 1 - Check Blocks and Sizes
* * Phase 2 - Check Path Names
* * Phase 3 - Check Connectivity
* * Phase 4 - Check Reference Counts
* * Phase 5 - Check Free List
#
```

A brief description of each phase follows.

- Phase 1 – The consistency of the i-nodes is checked in this phase.

- Phase 2 – If any i-nodes are found to be in error, then this phase checks for the directories which are pointed to by the i-nodes which were found to be in error.

- Phase 3 – This phase checks undetermined directories.

- Phase 4 – The number of link counts is checked in this phase.

- Phase 5 – Duplicate, corrupt, and unused blocks in the list of unused blocks are checked in the final phase of the `fsck` command.

The sample usage of the `fsck` command illustrated a clean run. If any discrepancies are found, then informative messages are displayed on the terminal, and `fsck` makes an effort to clear the system of any discrepancies. For example, if it finds duplicate i-nodes, it will remove one of them. However, before it removes the duplicate, `fsck` will ask the user if it is OK to remove it. A response of y to the questions it asks will result in the appropriate discrepancies being removed.

Bourne Shell Implementation

The `fsck` command works in the same way, regardless of which shell it is invoked from.

Korn Shell Implementation

The `fsck` command works in the same way, regardless of which shell it is invoked from.

27.5.2 The grpck Command

The `grpck` command is used to verify that the information in the `group` file is consistent with the information that exists in the `passwd` file. Recall that the `group` file contains names of users, whose names should also exist in the `passwd` file. Here's sample usage:

```
# grpck
acctg:*:10:sally,harry,gary,zamir
zamir - Logname not found in password file
#
```

If there is a discrepancy, an informative message stating this will be displayed. It will be your responsibility to make the necessary modifications to either one or both files, to bring them into sync.

Bourne Shell Implementation

The grpck command works in the same way, regardless of which shell it is invoked from.

Korn Shell Implementation

The grpck command works in the same way, regardless of which shell it is invoked from.

27.5.3 The pwck Command

The pwck command is used to check for inconsistencies in the passwd file. The number of fields, login name, user and group IDs, and existence of login directory are verified. Here's sample usage:

```
# pwck
zamir:*:2:1056667:ACCOUNTING USER:/usr/home/zamir:/bin/csh
    Invalid group ID
#
```

The message informs us that the group number 1056667 does not exist in the system. Once again, it is your responsibility to bring the group and passwd files into sync.

Bourne Shell Implementation

The pwck command works in the same way, regardless of which shell it is invoked from.

Korn Shell Implementation

The `pwck` command works in the same way, regardless of which shell it is invoked from.

27.6 OSF/1 CONSIDERATIONS

All commands described in this chapter are also supported by OSF/1, and will produce the same results.

27.7 REVIEW

In this chapter we described a few more tasks related to system administration. The following topics were described:

- The `dump` utility, which is used to implement full and partial backups. An integer number of 0 supplied as an argument results in a full backup. All subsequent numbers result in incremental backups.

- The `tar` utility, which is also used to perform backups in specified formats.

- The `restore` command, which is used to restore file systems backed up via the `dump` command.

- The `/etc/printcap` file, which contains printer information for the system.

- The `lpq` command, which is used to examine the status of jobs scheduled in the printer queue.

- The `lprm` command, which is used to remove print requests from the printer queue.

- The `fsck` command, which is used to check the integrity of file systems.

- The `grpck` command, which is used to check the validity of the entries in the `group` file.

- The `pwck` command, which is used to check the validity of the entries in the `passwd` file.

UNIX Editors

Appendix A lists some of the most commonly used commands in the following UNIX editors:

- The vi screen editor

- The ed line editor

- The sed stream editor

Table 1 vi Commands

Command	Syntax	Description
Create file	vi file1	Creates file1.
Exit vi	:wq	Writes file and quits.
	:q! :x ZZ	Exits without saving.
Input information	o	Opens line for input below current cursor position.
	a	Appends text to the right of current cursor position.
	i	Inserts text to the left of current cursor position.
	O	Opens line above current cursor position.
	A	Appends text at end of line.
	I	Appends text at beginning of line.
Position on lines	Left, right, up, down arrow keys	Moves cursor one position to the left, right, above, or below current position.
	Press h, j, k, or l key	Moves cursor one position to the left, below, above, or to the right of current position.
		Either one of the above commands can be preceded by a number to move the cursor that number of times.
	:n	Moves to line n, where n is a number.
	:$	Moves to last line in file.
	.	Implies current line.
	w	Moves to next word in current line.

Table 1 vi Commands (Contd.)

Command	Syntax	Description
Save current file to another	:w anotherfile	Writes current file to anotherfile, given that anotherfile does not exist.
	:w! newfile2	Overwrites current file to newfile2.
	:m,n w newfile3	Writes lines m through n of current file to newfile3.
Deleting characters	x	Deletes character to right of cursor position.
	nx	Deletes n - 1 characters.
	X	Deletes character to left of cursor position.
Deleting lines	dd	Deletes line at current cursor position.
	dn	Deletes n - 1 lines at current cursor position (includes current line).
Undoing commands	u	Undoes the last command issued.
Replacing text	R<new text>ESC	Replaces text starting from R, and continuing until ESC is hit.
	rc	Replaces only one character at current cursor position (c is character replaced).
Searching for patterns	/pattern	Positions cursor at the next occurrence of pattern.
Substituting patterns	s/old/new	Substitutes old pattern for new at current line.
	m,n s/old/new	Substitutes all occurrences of old pattern with new from line m to n.

Table 1 vi Commands (Contd.)

Command	Syntax	Description
Copy text	:m,n co y	Copies lines m through n to after line y.
Move text	:m,n mo y	Moves lines m through n to after line y.
Implement system command from within vi	:!command	Implements UNIX or user-specified command from within the vi session.

Table 2 ed Commands

Command	Syntax	Description
Create file	ed file1	Creates file1.
Exit ed	wq	Writes and exits.
	q	Exits without saving; warning will be issued.
Input information	a	Appends, before line.
	i	Inserts, after line.
Position on lines	p	Displays current line.
	.=	Displays current line number.
	$=	Displays last line number.
	2	Positions on line 2.
	<Return>, +	Positions on next line.
	-	Positions on previous line.
	.+2	Moves forward 2 lines.
	.-2	Moves back 2 lines.
View buffer	1,$p	Views entire buffer.
	1,5p	Views lines 1 through 5.
	5p	Views line 5.
Edit lines	s/old/new/	Substitutes, for old, new.
	1s/old/new/	Substitutes, for old, new on line 1.
	2,5s/old/new	Substitutes for old, new for lines 2 through 5.

Table 2 ed Commands (Contd.)

Command	Syntax	Description
Undo commands	u	Undoes the last command issued.
Change globally	1,$s/old/new/g	Changes all occurrences of old to new.
Delete	s/string//	Deletes string.
	d	Deletes current line.
	2d	Deletes line 2.
	2,5d	Deletes lines 2 through 5.
Load files into current buffer	r filename	Loads filename into current location.
	e filename	Loads filename into current location; deletes current buffer.
Save current file to another	w anotherfile	Writes current file to anotherfile.
	2,5w anotherfile	Writes lines 2 through 5 of current file to anotherfile.
Search for patterns	/pattern/	Searches forward for pattern.
	?pattern?	Searches backward for pattern.
	//	Searches prior pattern.
	??	Searches prior pattern.

Table 2 ed Commands (Contd.)

Command	Syntax	Description
Change text	2,5c <new text> .	Deletes lines 2 through 5; inserts new text in that location until dot is encountered.
	2c <new text> .	Deletes line 2; inserts new text in that location until dot is encountered.
Copy text	2,5t8	Copies lines 2 through 5 and inserts them after line 8.
	2,5t0	Copies lines 2 through 5 and inserts them at top of buffer.
	2,5t$	Copies lines 2 through 5 and inserts them at bottom of buffer.
Move text	2,5m8	Moves lines 2 through 5 and inserts them after line 8.
	2,5m0	Moves lines 2 through 5 and inserts at top of buffer.
	2,5m$	Moves lines 2 through 5 and inserts them at bottom of buffer.
Implement system commands from ed	!command	Implements UNIX or user-specified command without leaving ed session.

Table 3 Some Common sed Commands

Command	Syntax	Description
Add strings to end of file	$a\ string1\ string2	$ indicates end of line. a appends to right of text. \ must follow a. Strings must be on lines by themselves, and followed by \.
Add strings to beginning of file	^i\ string1\ string2	^ indicates start of line. i inserts to left of text. All rules listed for a also apply to i.
Substitute for all occurrences of pattern1, pattern2	/pat1/s/pat1/pat2/g	The first /pat1/ finds the pattern. s substitutes. /pat1/ and /pat2/ must be enclosed by slashes. g performs a global change on all occurrences of pat1.
Write all occurrences of pattern1 to another file	/pat1/w file	w writes to file.

Table 3 Some Common sed Commands (Contd.)

Command	Syntax	Description
Change all instances of digits to asterisks	/[0-9]/s/[0-9]/*/	[0-9] specifies the range for the pattern. The backslash precedes the * because the * is a special character. \ takes away its special meaning. All special characters must be preceded by \ to take away their special meaning.
Print lines 1 through 5	1,5p	Line number ranges are specified by inserting a comma in between. p prints the line.
Print lines between the strings pat1 and pat2	/pat1/,/pat2/p	Strings specified as ranges must be enclosed between slashes.

Table 3 Some Common sed Commands (Contd.)

Command	Syntax	Description
Remove all blank lines from a file	/^[ ]*$/d	^ specifies beginning of line. [ ] specifies match on space. * specifies match on zero or more spaces. d deletes the line that matches the criterion.
Remove all tabs from a file	/[^I]/s/[^I]//g	^I indicates tab character. All other rules are the same as for the removal of blank lines.

The UNIX Shell

Appendix B contains the following tables, which relate to the C, Bourne, and Korn shells:

- Overview of common shell commands.

- The test command

- Shell control structures

- The shell environment

- Shell built-in variables

- Some common shell commands and settings

- Additional built-in variables in OSF/1

- Programming constructs for each shell

- Other features of the shell

Table 1 Overview of Common Shell Commands

Command	C Shell	Bourne Shell	Korn Shell
Determine your shell	echo $SHELL	echo $SHELL	echo $SHELL
Change shell	/bin/csh	bin/sh	/bin/ksh
Store values in variables	set variable=10	variable=10	variable=10
Pass arguments	Use $1, $2, etc., in shell script	Use $1, $2, etc., in shell script	Use $1, $2 in shell script
Count total arguments	echo $#	echo $#	echo $#
Reference arguments	echo $*	echo $*	echo $*
Execute multiple commands	Use semicolon(;), logical and (&&), logical or (||)	Use semicolon(;), logical and (&&), logical or (||)	Use semicolon(;), logical and (&&), logical or (||)
Create pipes and filters	Use | to join commands to create pipes and filters	Use | to join commands to create pipes and filters	Use | to join commands to create pipes and filters
Take away meaning of one special character	Use backslash followed by character	Use backslash followed by character	Use backslash followed by character
Take away meaning of all special characters	Enclose group of characters in single quotes	Enclose group of characters in single quotes	Enclose group of characters in single quotes
Take away meaning of all special characters except $, \, and '	Enclose group of characters in double quotes	Enclose group of characters in double quotes	Enclose group of characters in double quotes

Table 2 The test Command

Syntax	Explanation
test *expression* returns zero for *strings,* where *expression* is:	
string1 = string2	If string1 is identical to string2
string1 != string2	If string1 is not identical to string2
string	If string is not null
-n string	If string is not null
-z string	If string is null
test *expression* returns zero for *integers,* where *expression* is:	
int1 -eq int2	If int1 is equal to int2
int1 -lt int2	If int1 is less than int2
int1 -gt int2	If int1 is greater than int2
int1 -ne int2	If int1 is not equal to int2
int1 -le int2	If int1 is less than or equal to int2
int1 -ge int2	If int1 is greater than or equal to int2
test *expression* returns zero for *files,* where *expression* is:	
-d file	If file is a directory
-f file	If file is not a directory
-s file	If file has nonzero length
-r file	If file is readable
-w file	If file is writable
-x file	If file is executable

Table 3 Shell Control Structures

Construct	Description/Features
The *if - else* construct:	

if this command executes
then
   execute this command
else
   execute this command
fi
	If command following if is successful, then commands between then and else are executed.
	
	Otherwise, commands between else and fi are executed.

The *elif* construct:	

if this command executes
then
   execute this command
elif this command executes
then
   execute this command
else
   execute this command
fi
	If command following if is successful, then commands between then and elif are executed.
	
	If not, then command following elif is executed.
	
	If this is successful, then commands between then and else are executed.
	
	Otherwise, commands between else and fi are executed.

The *case* construct	
case argument in pattern 1) execute this;; pattern 2) execute this;; esac	Argument is a single value or integer or string. Match patterns are specified in pattern. They must be delimited by a brace. If pattern matches argument, then one or more commands following the match pattern are executed, up to the next double semicolon.

Table 3 Shell Control Structures (Contd.)

Construct	Description/Features
The *for* loop	
for var in value1, value2 do this command done	for loop executes for number of times that value is listed. value1 is substituted into var the first time. value2 is substituted into var the second time. Block of commands within do and done is executed for value1, value2, and so on.
The *while* command	

while this command executes
do
  this command
  and this command
done
	Command following while is executed.
	
	Block of commands between do and done is executed for as long as command following while executes successfully.

The *until* command	

until this command fails
do
  this command
  and this command
done
	Command following until is executed.
	
	Block of commands between do and done is executed for as long as command following until does *not* execute successfully.

Table 4 The Shell Environment

C Shell Implementation	Bourne Shell Implementation	Korn Shell Implementation
Execute system login scripts (path names follow)		
Not applicable	/etc/profile	/etc/profile
Execute local login scripts (file names follow)		
.cshrc; .login	.profile	.profile
Set environment variables (syntax follows)		
setenv var=value	var=value export var	var=value export var
Set shell or local variables (syntax follows)		
set var=value	var=value export var	var=value export var
Make variables set in session permanent (method follows)		
Insert in .cshrc $source .cshrc	Insert in .profile Cannot run source	Insert in .profile Cannot run source
Display global environment settings (syntax follows)		
setenv	env	env
Display local environment settings (syntax follows)		
set	set	set
Reset environment variables (syntax follows)		
unsetenv	unset	unset
Reset local variables (syntax follows)		
unsetenv	unset	unset
Specify aliases (syntax follows)		
alias name cmd	Not applicable	alias name cmd
Execute logout script (method and file names follow)		
Insert $HOME/.logout	Insert in .profile Use trap command	Insert in .profile Use trap command

Table 5 Shell Built-in Variables

Variable Name	Description	Applicable Shell
HOME	Default login directory	C, Bourne, Korn
HOST	Name of computer	C, Bourne, Korn
LOGNAME	Login name	C, Bourne, Korn
PATH	Collection of search paths	C, Bourne, Korn
SHELL	Default shell	C, Bourne, Korn
TERM	Terminal type	C, Bourne, Korn
PROMPT	System prompt	C, Bourne, Korn
EDITOR	Default editor	C, Bourne, Korn
PS1	Command line prompt	Bourne, Korn
PS2	Command continuation prompt	Bourne, Korn
HISTSIZE	Specify size of history buffer	Korn
MAILCHECK	Frequency of mail check	Bourne, Korn

Table 6 Some Common Shell Commands and Settings

Command	Description	Syntax
clear; all shells	Clear the screen.	clear
trap; Bourne, Korn	Execute commands based on signals received.	trap command signal; signal can be 0 (logout), 2 (interrupt), 15 (software termination), or others
history; C, Korn	Create history buffer for specified number of commands.	set history=n, where n is number of commands in buffer
savehist; C, Korn	Save commands in buffer for next session.	set savehist=n, where n is number of commands in buffer
noclobber; all shells	Do not overwrite pre-existing files via redirection.	set noclobber
notify; all shells	Notify user on completion of process.	set notify
umask; all shells	Specify permission set of all new files and directories.	umask nnn, where nnn is an octal number
alias; C, Korn	An alternative name for a command.	alias name command where name is the alias.

Table 7 Additional Built-In Variables In OSF/1

Variable	Description
LANG	Defines system locale, comprising language, territory, and character codeset.
LC_COLLATE	Defines collating sequence.
LC_TYPE	Defines classification rules for character sets.
LC_MESSAGES	Defines language of system messages.
LC_MONETARY	Defines monetary format.
LC_NUMERIC	Defines numeric format.
LC_TIME	Defines date and time format.

Table 8 Programming Constructs for Each Shell

C Shell	Bourne Shell	Korn Shell

if command
then
   command
fi
	if command
	then
	   command
	fi
		if command
		then
		   command
		fi

if command
then
   command
else
   command
fi
	if command
	then
	   command
	else
	   command
	fi
		if command
		then
		   command
		else
		   command
		fi

if command
then
   command
elif command
then
   command
else
   command
fi
	if command
	then
	   command
	elif command
	then
	   command
	else
	   command
	fi
		if command
		then
		   command
		elif command
		then
		   command
		else
		   command
		fi

case argument in
pattern 1)
   command;;
pattern 2)
   command;;
esac
	case argument in
	pattern 1)
	   command;;
	pattern 2)
	   command;;
	esac
		case argument in
		pattern 1)
		   command;;
		pattern 2)
		   command;;
		esac

for
var in val_1, val_2
do
   command
done
	for
	var in val_1, val_2
	do
	   command
	done
		for
		var in val_1,val_2
		do
		   command
		done

while command
successful
do
   command
done
	while command
	successful
	do
	   command
	done
		while command
		successful
		do
		   command
		done

until command
unsuccessful
do
   command
done
	until command
	unsuccessful
	do
	   command
	done
		until command
		unsuccessful
		do
		   command
		done

Table 9 Other Features of the Shell

C Shell	Bourne Shell	Korn Shell
Feature: Aliases		
Description: Abbreviates or renames long commands.		
alias name cmnd	Not supported	alias name cmnd
unalias alias	Not supported	unalias alias
Feature: Command history		
Description: Stores commands in history buffer, and reexecutes.		
set history=n	Not supported	history=n
set savehist=n	Not supported	savehist=n
Feature: Automatic file name completion		
Description: System automatically completes partial file name entered at the command line.		
set filec ls name<ESC> ls name<Cntrl> D	Not supported	EDITOR=vi ls name<ESC>= Append name
Feature: Restricted shell		
Description: Shell that provides restricted capabilities.		
Not supported	/bin/rsh	Not supported
Feature: Edit commands in history buffer		
Description: Edits and reexecutes commands in history buffer.		
Not supported	Not supported	fc [-e editor] [-nlr] [range1] [range2] fc -e - [old=new] [match string]
Feature: Signal trapping via trap command		
trap cmnd signal	trap cmnd signal	trap cmnd signal

File/Text Manipulation Tools

Appendix C contains tables which describe the following:

- The `sort` command

- Syntax for output of the `diff` command

- Miscellaneous file manipulation commands

- `grep` commands

- `awk` commands, basic syntax and command specification

- Control structures recognized by `awk`

- Functions recognized by `awk`

- Predefined statements in `awk`

- The `find` command

- The `whereis` and `wc` commands

- The `cut` command

- The `paste` command

Table 1 The sort Command

Command	Syntax	Description
Sort alphabetically	sort file1	Sorts file1 in alphabetical order.
Sort by specific field	sort +1 file1	Skips field 1, and starts sort at field 2.
Inhibit sort at specific field	sort -2 file1	Stops sorting after field 2; restarts sorting at field 1.
Sort on numeric value	sort -n file1	Sorts field as numeric, not ASCII characters.
Remove leading blanks	sort -b file1	Removes leading blanks from field before sorting.
Redirect output	sort -o ofile file1	Redirects sorted output to ofile.
Redirect output	sort file1 > ofile	Redirects sorted output to ofile via redirection.
Sort multiple files	sort file1 file2	Sorts file1 and file2, and produces 1 output file.
Sort presorted files	sort -m file1 file2	Sorts file1 and file2. Assumes they are presorted.
Remove duplicate lines	sort -u file1 file2	Removes duplicate lines from the output.

Table 2 Syntax of Output of the diff Command

Syntax	Description
d	Line has been deleted.
a	Line has been added.
c	Line has been changed.
< text	Old version of text.
> text	New version of text.
----	Delineates old and new versions of changed text.

Table 3 Miscellaneous File Manipulation Commands

Syntax	Description
The cmp command:	
cmp file1 file2	Compares file1 with file2 on a byte-by-byte basis. Stops execution after pointing out the first difference.
cmp -l file1 file2	Displays all differences in hexadecimal between the two files.
The comm command:	
comm file1 file2	Displays similarities between two files in columnar format: Col. 1: Lines in file1, not in file2. Col. 2: Lines in file2, not in file1. Col. 3: Lines in both files.
The split command:	
split bigfile	Splits bigfile into 1000-line chunks. Each subfile is named x followed by the sequence of alphabetic characters aa, ab, and so on.
split -100 bigfile	Splits bigfile into 100-line chunks.
The lpr command:	
lpr file1	Queues request to print file1 to the spooler. Prints file1.
lpr file1 file2 file3	Prints multiple files in specified sequence.
lpr -n4 file1	Prints 4 copies of file1.
lpr -m file1	Mails message to user after printout.

Table 3 Miscellaneous File Manipulation Commands (Contd.)

Syntax	Description
The pr command:	
pr file1	Outputs headers, footers, etc., and writes to file1.
pr -h "FILE1" file1	Writes header "FILE1" on each page of file1.
pr -n file1	Writes line number for each line in file1.
pr -t file1	Suppresses header and trailers in file1.
pr -l 24 file1	Adjusts default page length of 66 to 24.
pr -o5 file1	Explicitly sets left margin to 5 columns.
pr file1 | lpr	Pipes output produced by pr to line printer.

Table 4 grep Commands

Command	Syntax	Description
Find pattern in file	grep pattern file1	Finds match on pattern in file1.
	grep "pattern" file1	Finds match on pattern in file1. $, \, and ' retain their special meaning.
	grep 'pattern' file1	Finds match on pattern in file1. All special characters lose their special meaning.
Find pattern in multiple files	grep pattern file1, file2, ... ,filen	Finds match on pattern in file1, file2, up to filen.
Use meta-characters in file names	grep pattern file*	Finds match on pattern in all files that start with file and end in zero or more characters.
	grep pattern [a-z]file	Finds match on pattern in all files that start with any letter between lowercase a through z, and end with file.

Table 4 grep Commands (Contd.)

Command	Syntax	Description
Use meta-characters in regular expressions	grep '^pattern' file1	Matches on pattern if it is found at beginning of line.
	grep 'pattern$' file1	Matches on pattern if it is found at end of line.
	grep '^pattern$' file1	Matches on pattern if it is the only string found in a line.
	grep '.' file1	Matches on any single character in location specified.
	grep 'pattern*' file1	Matches on zero or more characters in location of asterisk.
	grep '[a-z]pattern' file1	Matches on range specified within square brackets in location specified.
	grep '[^pattern]' file1	Matches on anything except pattern.
	grep '[^A-B]pattern' file1	Matches on anything except range specified in brackets. pattern must be part of the match as is.

Table 4 grep Commands (Contd.)

Command	Syntax	Description
Using options with grep	grep -h 'pattern' file1	Omits file header that displays when a match is found.
	grep -c 'pattern' file1	Displays count of matching lines, instead of lines themselves with match.
	grep -i 'pattern' file1	Ignores case while finding a match.
	grep -n 'pattern' file1	Displays line number of match.
	grep -v 'pattern' file1	Finds match on everything except pattern.
	grep -l 'pattern' file1	Lists names of files with match instead of lines which contain the match.

Table 5 awk Commands
Basic Syntax and Pattern Specification

Syntax	Description
Basic syntax of awk	
awk /pattern/ {action}	awk performs action on records that contain pattern.
awk -f cmd_file source	awk performs commands contained in cmd_file on file called source.
awk /pattern/	awk finds records matching pattern, and prints them. No action is performed on these lines.
awk {action}	awk performs action on all records.
awk /pattern/ cmd_file source1 source2 source3	awk performs action on records with pattern in multiple files.
Pattern specification	
awk /fixed string/	fixed string must be enclosed within slashes.
awk /33/	Numbers can be specified within pattern.
awk /$1/	The number of the field referenced must be preceded by a dollar sign.
awk /$var1/	Locally or globally assigned variables can also be specified as pattern.

Table 5 awk Commands
Basic Syntax and Pattern Specification (Contd.)

Syntax	Description
Pattern specification (continued)	
awk /awk_builtin/	awk_builtins are variables recognized by awk; they are referenced as follows:
$n	$n references field, where n is field number.
$0	$0 references current record.
FILENAME	FILENAME references current file being processed.
NR	NR references number of record being processed.
NF	NF references total number of fields in current record.
FS	FS references field separator.
RS	RS references record separator.
OFS	OFS references output field separator.
ORS	ORS references output record separator.
awk /regular expresson/	regular expression can be any expression which utilizes metacharacters.
awk /pat1/ && /pat2/	pat1 and pat2 can be any valid patterns recognized by awk. Two (or more) patterns can be combined via && to specify that both patterns must hold true for a valid match.

Table 5 awk Commands
Basic Syntax and Pattern Specification (Contd.)

Syntax	Description
Pattern specification (continued)	
awk /pat1/ || /pat2/	pat1 and pat2 can be any valid patterns recognized by awk. Two (or more) patterns can be combined via || to specify that one or the other pattern must hold true for a valid match.
awk !/pattern/	A ! before pattern instructs awk to match on anything but the pattern specified.
Pattern specification using relational operators (expr1 and expr2 can be any pattern recognized by awk)	
expr1 == expr2	expr1 is equal to expr2.
expr1 != expr2	expr1 is not equal to expr2.
expr1 < expr2	expr1 is less than expr2.
expr1 > expr2	expr1 is greater than expr2.
expr1 <= expr2	expr1 is less than or equal to expr2.
expr1 >= expr2	expr1 is greater than or equal to expr2.
expr1 ~ expr2	expr1 matches regular expression expr2.
expr1 !~ expr2	expr1 does not match regular expression expr2.

Table 5 awk Commands
Basic Syntax and Pattern Specification (Contd.)

Syntax	Description
Pattern specification using math operators expr1 and expr2 can be numbers, fields, and variables that contain numeric values.	
expr1 + expr2	expr1 is added to expr2.
expr1 - expr2	expr2 is subtracted from expr1.
expr1 * expr2	expr1 is multiplied by expr2.
expr1 / expr2	expr1 is divided by expr2.
expr1 % expr2	expr1 is divided by expr2 to obtain remainder.
expr1++	expr1 is incremented by 1 after expr1 is evaluated.
++expr1	expr1 is incremented by 1 before expr1 is evaluated.
expr1--	expr1 is decremented by 1 after expr1 is evaluated.
--expr1	expr1 is decremented by 1 before expr1 is evaluated.
expr1 += expr2	expr1 = expr1 + expr2.
expr1 -= expr2	expr1 = expr1 - expr2.
expr1 *= expr2	expr1 = expr1 * expr2.
expr1 /= expr2	expr1 = expr1 / expr2.
expr1 %= expr2	expr1 = expr1 % expr2.

Table 6 Control Structures Recognized by awk

Construct	Description
The if construct	

if (expression is true)
  {
    do this
    and this
  }
	This is the simplest form of conditional execution.
	Braces are optional if there is only one enclosed statement.

The else construct	

if (expression is true)
  {
    do this
    and this
  }
else
  {
    do this
    and this
  }
	This is a derivative of the if construct.
	Braces are optional if there is only one enclosed statement.

The while loop	

while (condition is true)
  {
    do this
    and this
  }
	There should be some statement within the loop that will change the status of the condition; otherwise the loop will execute forever.

The for loop	

for (initialize; test;
    reevaluate)
  {
    do this
    and this
  }
	The for loop is a more concise derivative of the while loop. Initialization, testing, and reevaluation are all contained within one statement.

Table 7 Functions Recognized by awk

Function	Description
index (string1, string2)	Returns character postion of string2 in string1. Returns 0 if string2 does not exist in string1.
substr(string1, pos, n)	Returns substring of string1, starting at position pos. n characters are returned.
length(string)	Returns length of argument string.
print string1 string2 ...	Prints each argument specified. Concatenates arguments if they are not separated by commas. Uses value stored in OFS (output field separator) as field delineator if commas exist between arguments.
printf "format", string1, string2 ...	Formats arguments string1, string2, ... as specified in format.

Table 8 Predefined Statements in awk

Statement	Description
next	Discards current record being processed and picks up the next one. Processing starts from the first command, instead of the next command after next.
break	Immediately exits from enclosing for or while loop, regardless of number of iterations still required within the loop.
continue	Performs next iteration of the loop, without implementing any subsequent statements that may appear.
exit	Immediately unconditionally exits from the program.
#comment	Recognizes the text that follows to be a comment.

Table 9 The find Command

Command	Syntax	Description
find	find path options file(s) action	Searches recursively for file(s) specified in path, applies options, and performs action.
Options available with find:		
By user name: find path -user user1 -print		Finds all files in path that are owned by user user1 and displays to standard output.
By group name: find path -group group1 -print		Finds all files in path that are owned by group group1 and displays to standard output.
By size in blocks: find path -size num -print		Finds all files in path that are num (a number) blocks long (1 block is 512 bytes), and displays.
By time last accessed: find path -atime num -print		Finds all files in path that were accessed in the last num (a number) days, and displays.
By time last modified: find path -mtime num -print		Finds all files in path that were modified in the last num (a number) days, and displays.
Issuing system commands on files found: find . -name file -exec cmd {} \; find . -name file -exec -ok cmd {} \;		Implements command (cmd) on each file found. Asks for reaffirmation with ok option.

Table 10 whereis and wc Commands

Command	Syntax	Description
whereis	whereis cmd	Locates source, binary, and manual pages of system command cmd.
Options available with whereis:		
Binary file: whereis -b cmd		Locates binary file only.
Manual pages: whereis -m cmd		Locates manual pages only.
wc	wc file	Gives count of total number of lines, words, and characters in file.
Options available with wc:		
Lines only: wc -l file		Counts lines only.
Words only: wc -w file		Counts words only.
Characters only: wc -c file		Counts characters only.

Table 11 The cut Command

Command	Syntax	Description
cut	cut -cnum file cut -fnum file	Extracts specified characters or fields from each line of file.
Options available with cut		
Specifying characters: cut -cnum file		Extracts character number num from file.
cut -cm-n file		Extracts characters from range m through n.
cut -c-n file		Extracts characters 1 through n.
cut -cm- file		Extracts characters from range m through the end of the line.
cut -cnum,m-n file		Extracts character number num, and range m through n.
Specifying fields: cut -fnum file		Extracts field number num from file.
cut -fm-n file		Extracts fields from range m through n.
cut -f-n file		Extracts fields 1 through n.
cut -fm- file		Extracts fields from range m through the end of the line.
cut -fnum,m-n file		Extracts field number num, and range m through n .

Table 12 The paste and tr Commands

Command	Syntax	Description
paste	paste file1 file2	Joins corresponding lines in file1 with file2 and writes to standard outputs
Options available with paste		
Specifying join field: paste -dfield file1 file2		Specifies field as join field, instead of the default space.
Pasting from one file only: paste -s file1		Joins all lines of file1 together.
tr	tr cr1 cr2	Translates character(s) cr1 to character(s) cr2. cr1 and cr2 can be character ranges.
Options available with tr		
Deleting multiple occurrences of characters: tr -s cr1 cr2		Translates character(s) cr1 to character(s) cr2, and deletes multiple subsequent occurrences of them in the process.
Deleting any occurrence of character(s): tr -d cr1		Deletes all occurrences of character(s) cr1.

Document Formatting Utilities

Appendix D contains tables that describe the following:

- `nroff` commands

- More `nroff` commands

- Options supplied to `nroff`

- `troff` commands (different from `nroff`)

- `ms` macro commands

- `tbl` commands

Table 1 nroff Commands

Command	Syntax	Description
Set page offset or left margin	.po num	Sets page offset to num columns from left edge of page. + or - before num sets offset relative to current position.
Set right margin	.po num1 .ll num2	Sets page offset in conjunction with line length to num1 and num2.
Set indent	.in num	Sets indent to num. + or - sets indent relative to current setting.
Insert blank line	.sp num	Inserts num blank lines.
Add comments	\"	nroff ignores remainder of line.
Set off right justification	.na	nroff automatically right justifies. This command turns this feature off.
Set off line filling, turn it back on	.nf	nroff automatically fills lines. This command turns this feature off.
	.fi	Turns filling back on.
Set hyphenation off and on	.nh	nroff automatically hyphenates. This command turns this feature off.
	.hy	Turns hyphenation back on.

Table 1 nroff Commands (Contd.)

Command	Syntax	Description
Flush left, ragged right	.ad l	Adjusts justification as indicated.
Ragged left, flush right	.ad r	Adjusts justification as indicated.
Center lines	.ad c .ce num	Adjusts lines as indicated. Centers num lines.
Set line spacing	.ls num	Sets line spacing to num.
Indent single lines	.ti num	Indents following line by num columns.
Insert blank lines	.sp num Carriage return	Inserts num blank lines. Inserts blank line.
Keep blocks on same page	.ne num	Keeps next num lines on same page.
Specify page breaks	.bp	Inserts page break in that location.
Center text	.ce num	Centers the next num lines.
Underline text	.ul num .cu num	Underlines each word of the next num lines. Underlines the complete line.
Define macro	.de XY <instruc- tions> ..	Defines macro called XY, which contains a group of nroff instructions. The ".." ends the definition.
Reference macros	.XY	Executes a group of instructions contained in macro XY.
Define trap	.wh +num XY .wh -num XY	Executes macro XY at num lines from top of each page in document. Executes macro XY at num lines from bottom of each page in document.

Table 2 nroff Commands and Options

Command	Syntax	Description
Specify titles	.tl 'l'c'r'	Specifies left (l), center (c), and right (r) titles on top of page. Any one of these fields can be blank; quotes must exist.
Specify page #s in title	.tl 'Page %'''	Substitutes page number in % field, displays at left edge of page.
Specify title length	.lt 60	Specifies title length of 60. Overrides margin settings.
Underlines characters in words	.ul M\c ain	Underlines the M in text Main only.
Embed nroff commands in text	\&.ce	Use zero width character \& to take away special meaning of nroff command.
Keep blocks of words together	Main\ Menu\ Options	Use backslash followed by a space ("\ "), the unpaddable space character, to keep groups of words together.
Switching to input from another file	.so otherfile	Input is read from otherfile and then nroff returns to current file.
Switching to standard input	.rd .rd address:	System beeps and waits for you to input something at the terminal. Terminate input by 2 carriage returns. System displays prompt "address:" instead of beeping.
Specify dimensional arguments	.po 1.3i .po 2.5c	Page offset is set to 1.3 inches. Page offset is set to 2.5 centimeters.

Table 3 Options Supplied to nroff

Option	Syntax	Description
Print specific pages	nroff -o4 file|lpr nroff -o2-4 file|lpr nroff -o-3 file|lpr nroff -o5- file|lpr	Prints page 4. Prints pages 2 through 4. Prints pages 1 through 3. Prints pages 5 through end.
Stop at specific page	nroff -s5 file|lpr	Stops at page 5 of each document.
Specify start page #	nroff -n23 file|lpr	First page number starts at 23.
Produce equal space words	nroff -e file|lpr	All words are equally spaced.
Use macro packages	nroff -mname file|lpr	Uses macro package "name" with nroff.

Table 4 troff Commands (different From nroff).

Command	Syntax	Description
Italicize text	.ul	Italicizes text, instead of underlining it like nroff.
Specify dimension arguments	.in 5m .in 5n	Indents by 5 m characters. Indents by 5 n characters.
Specify point size	.ps 14	Sets point size to 14.
Specify font	.ft R	Sets font to Times Roman.
Specify vertical space	.vs 0.5c	Sets height of row to .5 centimeter.

Table 4 ms Macro Commands

Command	Syntax	Description
Specify page offset, left margin	.nr PO 1.5i	Specifies page offset of 1.5 inches.
Specify right margin	.nr LL 6.0i	Specifies line length of 6 inches. Right margin is determined by this setting and page offset.
Specify top margin	.nr HM 1.5i	Sets top margin to 1.5 inches.
Specify bottom margin	.nr FM 1.5i	Sets bottom margin to 1.5 inches.
Change default output of date	.DA May 2 1992	Sets date which displays at bottom of page to May 2, 1992.
Inhibit display of date	.ND	Inhibits automatic display of date at bottom of page.
Specify straight left margin	.LP	Text that follows has straight left margin.
Indent first line of block	.PP	Indents first line (5 spaces by default) of following paragraph.
Modify default indents	.nr PI 3m .nr PD 3v	Sets para indent to 3 ems and para depth to 3 vertical spaces.

Table 4 ms Macro Commands (Contd.)

Command	Syntax	Description
Indent entire paragraph	.IP	Indents left margin of entire text of following paragraph.
	.QP	Indents left and right margins of paragraph.
Produce hanging indent	.IP -	Character(s) following .IP appear to the left of the remaining paragraph.
	.IP - 6	Specifies number of en characters (6) that character following .IP is to occupy.
Produce nested lists	.RS <text> .RE	<text> indents to the right after .RS. .RE cancels .RS request.
Produce unnumbered heading	.SH <heading> .LP or .PP or .PI	Text following .SH is underlined until a .LP, .PP, or .PI is encountered. troff emboldens text.
Produce numbered headings	.NH <heading> .NH 2 .NH 3 .NH 4 .NH 5	<heading> is numbered based on the level number supplied with .NH. Up to five levels can be specified.

Table 4 ms Macro Commands (Contd.)

Command	Syntax	Description
Produce title, author's name, sub-title, and abstract	.TL <title> .AU <authors> .AI <subtitle> .AB .AE	Outputs headings as indicated, centered and underlined. Any of these macros may be omitted, but if they exist, they must appear in this order.
Produce footnote	.FS <footnote> .FE	<footnote> appears at bottom of page, exactly as typed, under a dashed line.
Keep text together	.KS <text> .KE	<text> is displayed on the same page. Blank lines are inserted in current page if <text> does not fit on it.
Keep "display"	.DS <display> .DE	Displays <display> on same page, exactly as typed. No filling or justification takes place.

Table 5 tbl Instructions

Command	Syntax	Description
Start table	.TS	Designates the start of the instructions that specify table format.
End table	.TE	Designates the end of the instructions that specify table format.
Specify field delimiter	tab ( );	Specifies field delimiter is a tab. This entry must end with a semicolon.
Specify table format	l l .	Specifies 2 columns, left aligned.
	r r .	Specifies 2 columns, right aligned.
	c c .	Specifies 2 columns, centered.
Enclose table in a box	center box tab( );	Encloses table data inside a box.
Enclose everything in a box	center allbox tab( );	Encloses table data inside a box, and draws lines under each row.
Draw lines between rows	_	Inserts underscore under row that requires a line underneath.

Table 5 tbl Instructions (Contd.)

Command	Syntax	Description
Insert heading	.cfl cfl head1 head2	Instructs tbl to display head1 and head2 as headings. c results in heading being centered. fl results in heading being italicized.
Insert heading spanning multiple columns	.cfl s Spanned heading	Instructs tbl to display Spanned heading over multiple columns.
Display numerical columns as numbers	l n .	Specifies 2 columns; first is left aligned, second is a numerical value.
Display text over multiple rows	- <text spanning multiple lines>	Displays text as typed, over multiple rows.
Modify table format	.T& cfl s Modified format .sp 1 .TE	.T& instructs tbl that all subsequent instructions are modifications to the original format of the table. .TE is the original statement that ends the specification of the table format.

Index